The Constitutional and Legal Development of the Chinese Presidency

The Constitutional and Legal Development of the Chinese Presidency

The Emperors' New Clothes?

Zhang Runhua

LEXINGTON BOOKS
Lanham • Boulder • New York • London

Published by Lexington Books
An imprint of The Rowman & Littlefield Publishing Group, Inc.
4501 Forbes Boulevard, Suite 200, Lanham, Maryland 20706
www.rowman.com

Unit A, Whitacre Mews, 26-34 Stannary Street, London SE11 4AB, United Kingdomm

British Library Cataloguing in Publication Information Available

Library of Congress Cataloging-in-Publication Data

Zhang, Runhua, 1973- author.
The constitutional and legal development of the Chinese presidency : the emperors' new clothes? / Zhang Runhua.
pages cm.
Based on author's thesis (doctoral - Chinese University of Hong Kong, 2010) issued under title: The dynamic presidency and the evolution of constitutional law in China.
Includes bibliographical references and index.
ISBN 978-0-7391-8989-4 (cloth : alk. paper) -- ISBN 978-0-7391-8990-0 (electronic)
1. Presidents--Legal status, laws, etc.--China. 2. Constitutional law--China. 3. China--Politics and government--1949- I. Title.
KNQ2540.Z48 2015
342.51'062--dc23
2014021894

∞™ The paper used in this publication meets the minimum requirements of American National Standard for Information Sciences Permanence of Paper for Printed Library Materials, ANSI/NISO Z39.48-1992.

Printed in the United States of America

In memory of my mother, Wang Xiabing

Contents

Foreword

President Xi Jinping is arguably the most powerful Chinese leader since the Ming Emperor Zhu Yuanzhang (1368–1644), though Zhu abolished the office of prime minister, which he saw as a unnecessary fetter on his power while Xi's China retains that office (premier). To understand what is happening and what may happen in the future to the governance of China, Zhang Runhua's book is a must.

An independent judiciary, like a referee in a game of sport, is not an option if chaos and violence are to be avoided in the long term. An independent judiciary is a key element of constitutionalism and an objectively defined Rule of Law. In China the constitution and law have been evolving rapidly but have not yet embraced an independent judiciary. The difficulty is the judiciary's role vis-à-vis the preeminent position of the Communist Party.

This book is not directly about the judiciary but it is about the Chinese constitution and specifically the evolving office of president in an increasingly legal context. Lessons learned here are a vital clue to the evolution of the constitution in general and specifically the all-important judiciary. The book studies the evolution of the presidency of the People's Republic of China since its establishment in 1954, to its abolition in 1975, and its restoration in 1982, and examines how law has developed in China regarding the presidency. It will be seen that the Chinese presidency has evolved from a traditional Chinese personal title into a political position, and then to a state institution that has the constitutional facade of a Western-style presidency. Mao Zedong ruled China without an institutional title for many years. To cope, Western commentators coined the description "paramount leader," a description gelling with traditional Confucian concepts of the "Charismatic Leader," and describes a leader deriving power from his person, not an office within an institution. However, politically the presidency has functioned in a Stalinist party-state with Chinese characteristics, whose candidate has so far been produced according to the Communist Party of China's (CCP) step-by-step succession rules designated by former paramount leaders of China. Real political decision-making power has not only been limited by these succession rules, but also defined by the candidate's role and status within the CCP's supreme collective decision-making body. Underlying such decades of constitutional evolution and political dynamics has been changing foreign influences and local demands on China. As China becomes more global and its traditions of "rule of man" gradually die out, law and politics surrounding this office has become more compatible, thus giving rise to a nascent Rule of Law.

In contrast to other works on Chinese politics or Chinese law, this book pioneers an all-around investigation on the legal and political development of the Chinese presidency from both normative and positivist perspectives, weaves both themes together, and incorporates findings from multiple disciplines. It explores not only the political implications of those constitutional provisions and amendments regarding this office, but also the constitutional significance of the CCP's major political practices, such as Mao Zedong's "power of last say," his idea of "two fronts," his controversial abolition of the chairmanship, Deng Xiaoping's idea of "the core of leadership," and "diplomacy of the head of state" by Chinese presidents, thus illuminating how law has been given birth in those unpredictable political environments and how politics has been shaped by law.

The office of president has not been the subject of much attention from scholars in the past, and this book helps fill the breach. With regard to the development of law in China, the book adopts an institutional perspective, different from research conducted either on an all-round scale or into certain legal fields and sheds new light on continuing academic discussions.

I recommend this book to anyone with an interest in the political and legal history and future of China.

Michael D. Pendleton

Emeritus Professor of Law,Murdoch University, Australia;
Formerly Professor, Chinese University of Hong Kong and
University of Hong Kong; Adjunct Professor, School of Law,
University of Canterbury, New Zealand

Preface

This book has its genesis in a PhD thesis accepted by the Chinese University of Hong Kong in 2010. Born in China, I grew up amid Deng Xiaoping's reforms, which allowed me to enjoy more freedom and opportunities than my parents, such as to study for my master and doctoral degrees and to travel abroad. During my years in the United Kingdom and Hong Kong, I acquired personal life experience of so-called capitalist societies and was impressed by their respect for individuals. I have also witnessed the dramatic transformation that China has undergone, and suffered, as well as benefited, from those old and new traditions and tricks that still exert tremendous impact on the daily life of every Chinese. It compels me to think about a more fundamental question: how we have come to this "best of times, worst of times"?[1]

In my quest for answers, it occurred to me that among all Chinese constitutional topics the presidency has been the most ambiguous and receives the least scholarly discussion. As I pondered further I realized that this issue provided a huge insight. The presidency exemplifies how the Chinese system of government operates in determining people's lives. I feel compelled to make available my findings to the general public for the sake of a better China and world.

Many people have pleasantly involved themselves in the formation of this book, and I want to express my heartfelt gratitude to them. Among all, I owe a lot to my supervisor, Professor Michael Pendleton, who has always been so kind, experienced, and supportive. I am also grateful to Professor Chen Hongyi at the University of Hong Kong; Professors Mike McConville, Stephen Hall, Eva Pils, Scully-Hill Anne, Zhao Yuhong, Xi Chao, and Hie Hok Fung, Faculty of Law of the Chinese University of Hong Kong; Professor Yu Xingzhong at Cornell University; Professor Ling Bing, the University of Sydney; Professors Liu Xianquan, Wang Junmin, Chen Yi, Wu Yunfeng, and

Huang Changgen at the East China University of Political Science and Law; Professor Wang Jiangyu of National University of Singpore; Professor Wang Chengguang, Tsinghua University; Professor Cai Dingjian, China University of Politics and Law; Professor Huang Xingtao, Renmin University; Professor Zou Pingxue, Shenzhen University; Wang Huanan; Yang Qianer; Huang Daixing; and Hu Shuangquan. They have inspired and helped me with their brilliant ideas, good advices, and various assistances when I wrote my doctoral thesis. During the publishing process, I received assistance from Luo Yi, Wang Qiang, Dai Axing, Qiu Ling, Tian Jianchao, and Wu Jianhua, without which it would be more difficult for me to focus on my work. I also want to thank Brian Hill and Kathleen Bromelow at Lexington Books for their appreciation and wonderful work in making the publication available. I of course take full responsibility for what is in the book. In particular, all Chinese sources are my own translation unless otherwise noted.

Last, but most importantly, I am indebted to my family members for their love and support. This book is specifically written in memory of my mother, to whom I owe the most. As an old Chinese saying goes, it is the saddest that parents have gone when the children want to honor them ("Zi yu yang, er qin bu dai").

NOTE

1. Charles Dickens, *A Tale of Two Cities*, 1859.

List of Abbreviations and Acronyms

CCP	Chinese Communist Party
CCPCC	Central Committee of the Chinese Communist Party
CEC	Central Executive Committee
CMC	Central Military Commission
CND	Council of National Defense
Comintern	Communist International
CPGC	Central People's Government Council
CPPCC	Chinese People's Political Consultative Conference
CSR	China Soviet Republic
CWIPB	Cold War International Project Bulletin
GAC	Government Administration Council
GS	General Secretary
KMT	Chinese Nationalist Party
NPC	National People's Congress of the People's Republic of China
NPCSC	Standing Committee of the NPC
PCC	Political Consultative Conference
PRC	People's Republic of China
PSC	Standing Committee of the Political Bureau of the CCP
ROC	Republic of China
SSC	Supreme State Conference

USA	United States of America
USSR	Union of Soviet Socialist Republic

Chapter One

Introduction to the Chinese Presidency

As China continues to rise above the global horizon, its new president, Xi Jinping, has attracted growing attention around the world, so as to be ranked fifty-ninth among the top one hundred influential leaders on earth by *Time* magazine in 2013.[1] On the other hand, observers have been keenly watching the development of constitutionalism and rule of law in China. While understanding that the Chinese president and its constitution should not be simply seen as the same as their Western counterparts,[2] observers could still be puzzled at the dramatic relationship between Chinese presidents and constitutions, if with a brief knowledge of modern history of China.

PRC CHAIRMAN AND PRESIDENTS

In 1949, the People's Republic of China (PRC) was founded. According to the Organic Law of the Central People's Government of the PRC, the Central People's Government Council (CPGC) consisted of a chairman (hereafter refer to Chinese "Zhuxi") and six vice-chairmen. Mao Zedong, chairman of the Chinese Communist Party (CCP), was elected by the first Plenary Session of the Chinese People's Political Consultative Conference (CPPCC) as that chairman.

Five years later, the PRC convened its first National People's Congress (NPC) and adopted its first constitution (hereafter referred to as "the 1954 constitution"), which provided an office of the chairman of the PRC with a term of four years. Again Mao Zedong was elected to take such an office. However, after officially assuming that office in 1954, Mao Zedong could not wait for the end of his term to declare that he did not want to take that office any more. In the end, he did not take a second term and Liu Shaoqi was elected in 1959 as the second chairman of the PRC.

In 1965, Liu Shaoqi was elected by the third NPC to take a second term, but was purged out of office in 1966 soon after the Cultural Revolution started. Unconstitutionally, he was declared to be removed from the chairmanship by the CCP in 1968. Nor could the constitution protect him from brutally violence.

Ever since then the office of chairman had been vacant and it was not until 1972 that Vice-Chairman Dong Biwu started to exercise the chairmanship's power and function in the capacity of "Deputy Chairman." When a new constitution was made in 1975 (hereafter referred to as "the 1975 constitution"), the office of chairman was abolished at the order of Mao Zedong. After that, another short-lived constitution made in 1978 (hereafter referred to as "the 1978 constitution") followed suit.

The office of chairman was not re-installed until a fourth constitution was made (hereafter referred to as "the 1982 constitution") in 1982. But this time, the Chinese chairman was officially translated into "president" in English, not its equivalent "chairman" as had been done in previous constitutional documents, despite that its Chinese name remained as "Zhuxi." Up till now, this change of English translation has been followed, and the presidency has been taken successively by Li Xiannian from 1982 to 1988, Yang Shangkun to 1993, Jiang Zemin to 2003, and Hu Jintao to 2013 before Xi Jinping took it in March of that year.

In 2004, the 1982 constitution was amended to provide, among others, the president with a new function to "engage in activities involving state affairs."[3] This is the first time that functions and powers of the presidency have ever been revised since the promulgation of the 1982 constitution.

OVERVIEW OF THE BOOK

As outlined in the above, PRC presidency has been consistently named as "Zhuxi" in Chinese ("chairman," in English), not "Zongtong" ("president," in English), which may suggest that they can be different from the Western presidency in spite of the recent change of its English translation. If so, a question would easily arise: What makes the PRC "presidency" different from its Western counterpart? More importantly, after the abolishment and reinstallation, has the Chinese presidency finally been well "defined" by its constitution? To answer them, this book adopts historical and comparative methods, examines legal and political development of the Chinese presidency within the framework of the party-state by incorporating knowledge and findings from multiple disciplines, explores not only constitutional implications of the CCP's political practices of decision making such as Mao Zedong's "power of last say," his idea of "two fronts," his controversial abolition of the chairmanship, Deng Xiaoping's idea of "the core of leadership," but also political significance of those relevant constitutional provisions and amendment, like "diplomacy of the head of state," and analyzes how the constitutions and political practices have been intertwined with each other to determine the evolution of this office, all of which will be elaborated in the following eleven chapters.

As the start, the second chapter goes back the origin of modern China when the ancient dynastic empire was ended under foreign influence and domestic forces, which gave the "old bottle" of Chinese chairman new content. Then it studies the chairman of the China Soviet Republic, including its constitutional making history, comparison with chairman of the USSR, difficulties when performing his power and function, and its significance to the CCP and PRC.

The fourth chapter will examine the chairman of the Central People's Government as provided by the 1949 Common Program of PRC. It will first discuss how Mao Zedong had become the chairman of the CCP and what decision-making power he had enjoyed as the chairman within the CCP. Then it will investigate how the chairman of PRC was designed in the constitutional documents and analyze similarities and differences between this office and its predecessor as well as the Russian models. In the end, it will evaluate the true situation of this office by examining how Mao Zedong had been elected into office and performed his constitutional duties at home and abroad.

The chairmanship of the 1954 constitution is the focus of the next three chapters. Based on the constitutional making of this office in 1954, it will compare this office with its previous and foreign counterparts and analyze the influence on it by the former Soviet Union and Mao Zedong's ideas about it during the making process. Then it will study the election of Mao Zedong and Liu Shaoqi into this office and their performances, ended with discussion on the constitutional implication of Liu Shaoqi's removal from the office and its later abolishment.

Chapters 8 through 11 will concentrate on the presidency provided by the 1982 constitution. The political situation in 1982 will be introduced first, followed by a brief account of the constitutional-making history of this office. Deng Xiaoping's ideas and influence on it will also be explored. After summarizing the performance of the first two presidents, the book will continue to discuss why Jiang Zemin had been able to take all offices as the "core of leadership" and analyze his diplomacy during his terms of office. Hu Jintao's succession to the presidency and the 2004 constitutional amendment will be further studied.

NOTES

1. http://time100.time.com/2013/04/18/time-100/slide/rand-paul/#/2013/04/18/time-100/slide/xi-jinping/?&_suid=137005541208703915355829156439.

2. The making of American and Chinese president has been compared in a brief video. See https://www.scmp.com/news/china/article/1390031/communist-party-launches-international-charm-offensive-show-and-tell.

3. See Zhonghua Renmin Gongheguo Xianfa Xiuzheng An [Amendment to the Constitution of the People's Republic of China] (adopted at the second session of the Tenth National People's Congress on March 14, 2004, and published for enforcement by the announcement of the National People's Congress of the People's Republic of China on March 14, 2004), art. 28.

Chapter Two

Chinese President and Chairman before 1949

INTRODUCTION OF AMERICAN PRESIDENCY AFTER QING DYNASTY

When the constitution of the United States was drafted by the constitutional convention, the term "president" was first used by the drafting committee to refer to the head of the executive branch of the government. It was familiar and reassuring to people who had feared that delegates to the convention might create a monarchical or tyrannical office because it had been known as a title referring to the presiding person of congress or other legislative bodies. This proposal was accepted by the convention without debate.[1] Since then, the American presidency had been followed in various forms throughout the world.

By the 1800s, China had been almost completely isolated from the outside world by the Qing emperors, except for a small territory outside the southern city of Canton (now Guangzhou) that was designated specifically by the government for foreign trade with Westerners. Chinese there had started to learn about Western countries through business transactions, including the American presidency. For example, the United States president was described as the "head" ("Tou Ren" in Chinese) elected to serve a term of four years by a local Chinese official in his report written to the emperor in 1817. As more and more cities were forced to open to foreigners after the Opium War, Chinese learned more about Western ideas of presidency. By the 1890s, the English word "president" had been generally translated into Chinese as "Zong Tong."[2]

When some southern provinces started to fight against the decayed Qing dynasty in 1912, Chinese had the chance to put their knowledge of Western notions of presidency into practice and announced to establish the Republic of China (ROC), headed by a provisional president.[3] Modeled after the United States,[4] such a presidency was first taken by the famous revolutionary Sun Zhongshan (Sun Yat-sen), and then by the conservative northern General Yuan Shikai in exchange for the peaceful abdication of the Qing emperor and unification of China.

Thus the thousands-years dynastic ruling ended and the emperorship was replaced by the presidency, which was regarded as a constitutional head of state exercising his power and function based on the constitution, such as the power to call the congress, to appoint and remove governmental officials, to submit or veto the legislative bill, to promulgate the law, to declare war, to enter treaties, to lead the army, to pardon, and so on.[5]

Since then, this newly introduced presidency began its tortuous localization on Chinese soil, with powers and functions fluctuating from the American model to a figurehead of state in the cabinet system,[6] then back to the emperorship,[7] and to an office in between,[8] subject to political deceit, bribery, and ultimately military muscle at the time. In the end, the ROC presidency was reduced to either "Provisional Governor" ("Linshi Zhizheng" in Chinese)[9] or "Grand Marshel."[10]

MOSCOW'S INFLUENCE ON THE CHINESE CHAIRMAN

Chairman: "Old Bottle with New Wine"

Originated in China, the term "chairman" ("Zhuxi" in Chinese) had been used by ancient people to refer to the seat of a table at which the host sat when holding a banquet or receiving guests.[11] Especially in a banquet, it also referred to the person in charge of that banquet.[12] According to Chinese tradition, such a seat should be taken by the host, normally the head of the family, or someone senior in those occasions. "If five people gather together, *a specific seat should be designated for the elder*."[13] Therefore, the ancient Chinese chairman had been generally related to the family head and his seat. By 1868, such traditional usages were still in common and known to Western missionaries visiting China.[14]

But as foreign knowledge poured in, traditions were transformed and the chairman had been given a third meaning, referring to the person who chaired a board or committee, similar to the term "president" before being used by the American constitutional makers. These usages were recorded by Herbert A. Giles in his English and Chinese dictionary in 1890, which defined the Chinese "Zhuxi" as either "the host at dinner" or "chairman of a board."[15]

Later on, the chairman had been frequently used in the latter sense by Chinese in their writings and social activities. For example, during the constitutional-making process for the ROC, a chairman was elected for the drafting committee in its preparatory meeting held on July 10, 1913.[16] In this new usage, the chairman had been understood as being only responsible for presiding over meetings and maintaining good order of meetings[17] when the committee convened. At the beginning of the meeting, a chairman would be produced out of the participants either by election or by mutual agreement. During the meeting, the chairman participated in the decisions equally with other attendants and enjoyed no privileges over others. Once the meeting completed, the chairman would then be absolved. Therefore, the chairman had mainly been a temporary presiding body of the meeting, with a term of function depending on the life of that meeting. By no means was the chairman a permanent office with distinctive decision making power.

The Nationalist Chairman

Witnessing the misfortune suffered by the presidency of ROC in Beijing, the first, yet provisional, President Sun Zhongshan had stood up against those Beijing warlords time and again, but had made little achievement. Failing to build a constitutional order for the split China, he gradually developed an interest in the former Soviet Union. At first, Sun Zhongshan refused to accept the Russian model. In the joint declaration he made with the Russian agent, the Soviet-style government was claimed not to fit China.[18] But his refusal was reversed when they joined hands, and the Soviet-style party-state started to make its way to China. Assisted by Mikhail Markovich Borodin, who was deployed by Moscow, Sun Zhongshan not only entered into alliance with the Communist Party of China (CCP), another Chinese political party coached by Moscow, reorganized his Chinese Nationalist Party (KMT), established his own army, but he also decided to form a government led by the KMT.

The KMT's party constitution was almost a duplicate of its Russian model.[19] Based on the Russian principle of democratic centralism, the KMT was organized by the congress of delegates and the executive committee elected by the former at each level, with the National Congress and Central Executive Committee (CEC) at the top to take the lead. When both the National Congress and CEC were convened, a chairman was designated respectively for them.

But when it came to the function of the chairman, a departure was made from the Russian model. According to the constitution, the head of the KMT was titled as the "premier" ("Zongli" in Chinese), who concurrently served as the chairman of the National Congress and CEC and enjoyed a "power of last say" overruling decisions made by the National Congress and CEC. In this way, Sun Zhongshan could personally overturn the collective voting. As a matter of fact, it was specially made in recognition of Sun Zhongshan as the

KMT paramount leader.[20] Sun Zhongshan also wanted it. He demanded all had to show their loyalty to him by stamping their fingerprints if to become a KMT member.

But what if he died? Then there would no individual leader within the KMT who could take his place.[21] As such, the collegiate committee was formed for the government established by the KMT in Canton on July 1, 1925.[22] In this party-government committee, a chairman was designated to preside over meetings.[23] Although it was still referred to as "chairman" in Chinese, it was translated into "president" in English.[24] Hence, the term chairman took the place of president and became a title for the head of government. When the KMT government came close to its end in mainland China, it promulgated a constitution in 1946, in which the head of the government was not titled as the chairman any more. Instead, it was named in Chinese as "Zongtong," that is, president in English.[25]

THE CCP CHAIRMAN

"General Secretary" of the CCP

While China was splitting, newly revolutionized Russia joined the game of power in China, trying to find partners and have a friendly Far-Eastern neighbor to protect its interest after the 1917 revolution.[26] After meeting Chen Duxiu, Verkinsky, the Russian agent, proposed and assisted to organize a communist group in Shanghai in 1920,[27] thus establishing the CCP. Chen Duxiu was the head of this Shanghai group, being titled as the secretary ("Shuji," in Chinese).[28]

In the next year, the CCP convened the First National Congress secretly and passed a brief party program, which provided that all CCP members would be organized into committees, the national level would have a National Congress which would then produce a Central Executive Committee (CEC), and the organization of the CEC would be stipulated by other party rules.[29] As the CCP only had dozens of members by then,[30] the CEC was actually not produced; instead, a provisional committee of three members was elected, including a secretary and two other members respectively responsible for workers and propaganda affairs.[31] Although Chen Duxiu was absent from the congress, he was unanimously elected as that secretary by the congress.[32]

In spite of the secret ballot being casted,[33] the election had been previously arranged by Zhang Guotao, the congress chairman, and Henker Slievlied Maring,[34] Moscow's new agent in China in place of Verkinsky at that time. While Maring porposed[35] and financed[36] the convening of the congress, and monitored the congress behind Zhang Guotao,[37] Zhang Guotao had negotiated with participants on the election.[38] Therefore, the choice of Chen Duxiu could be the desire of Moscow.

Why would Moscow have favored Chen Duxiu? Because he was not only one of the earlier founders of the CCP, but he also enjoyed a high social status.[39] By that time, Chen Duxiu had already been considered by the congress participants as their leader.[40] As Chen Duxiu recalled later, Lenin thought that the infant CCP needed a prestigious and magnetic leader and this idea was passed to Maring by the Communist International (Comintern).[41]

The title of secretary had been used in ancient China to refer to the copyist,[42] the lowest rank in the government hierarchy,[43] whose main function had been recording and documentation.[44] To a Chinese, someone in charge of workers or propaganda affairs would be more powerful than the unimportant secretary. Then why did Chen Duxiu take it instead of the other two positions? It could have originated from Russia,[45] but it could also be favored by Chen Duxiu personally. Regarding the organization of the CCP, he opposed the personal leadership of Western style and preferred the Russian way of collective leadership by a committee. According to him, the Russian style of committee in which a secretary was responsible for communication, and other members took charge of organizational and propaganda affairs, was suitable for China because it was more democratic and had been proved by the success of Russia; to promote democracy within the CCP and prevent personal dictatorship and bureaucratic abuses, the power and function of the committee secretary should be limited by using more votes in decision making.[46] His ideas were accepted by the First National Congress to organize the CCP.[47] Besides, participants of the congress were opposed to becoming government officials with substantial powers.[48] Such an aversion could also make the secretary more acceptable.

The barely provided three-member provisional committee was improved by a party constitution adopted by the Second CCP National Congress held in 1922. While the National Congress was the highest organ of the CCP, a larger size CEC of five members was formally installed as the highest when the congress closed,[49] which could be gathered any time by its "Committee Head" ("Weiyuanzhang," in Chinese)[50] to execute decisions made by the National Congress, deliberate the party's policies and all means to enforce them,[51] and convene the National Congress once a year.[52] Thus the CEC was a standing committee of the National Congress, or a presidium to make and execute policies.

The CCP gained an accelerated development, especially after the Third National Congress approved the controversial policy of allying with the Nationalist Party, another Chinese political party led by Sun Zhongshan, which made the CCP go on the national stage. As members[53] and works[54] increased, its central organization underwent further institutionalization. The

Third National Congress not only revised the old party constitution, but also made an organic law for the CEC. According to these new party rules, the CEC was expanded to nine members and divided. While four of them were dispatched to various local committees, the remaining five members formed a Central Bureau,[55] performing functions in the name of the CEC[56] by weekly meeting between two CEC meetings, which were held every four months.[57] In other words, the Central Bureau was a standing committee of the CEC right on its top. As a result, the CCP central organization became a three-level hierarchy, that is, the National Congress, the CEC, and the Central Bureau, which was followed later by the Fourth National Congress convened in early 1925.

Literally, the lower level in such a hierarchical organization should prevail its upper body in decision making, with the National Congress as the most powerful at the base and the other two organs should be subject to it. But the size and meeting frequency of a committee were crucial to its operation. On one hand, the more participants a committee had, the more difficult to convene it and reach consensus. On the other hand, the less frequent the committee convened, the less it became effective in performing its function. As the biggest and least convened committee, the yearly National Congress practically became the least decisive leading organ in spite of claiming supremacy. As a result, it had to delegate most of the decision making and execution to smaller organs that convened more frequently in the year. For example, as the First National Congress was convened secretly and did not have sufficient time, it had to authorize the provisional committee to decide on unfinished works.[58] The Second National Congress also made delegation to its CEC to decide on the relationship with the KMT.[59] To make matters worse, the GS Chen Duxiu was said to regard congress resolutions as mere scraps of official paper and was unwilling to put into execution,[60] and the CEC decision could be delayed in exectution.[61] Ultimately, it was the Central Bureau that managed the CCP at most times, as it was the most stable leading organ at the central level. As the party constitution also required that all local party committees had to follow directions of the National Congress, the Central Bureau could virtually command the CCP during the absence of the other two organs. As a CCP member observed then, during two and a half years between the Fourth and Fifth National Congresses, the CEC only convened two or three times, and it was essentially the Central Bureau who managed the CCP.[62]

Along with the institutionalization, a head also emerged within the CEC, which was initially titled as the "Committee Head" by the Second and Third National Congress,[63] then the "General Secretary" (GS, "Zong Shuji," in Chinese) by the fourth one,[64] suggesting a move closer to Moscow as the term "general secretary" had been used for Stalin in 1922. While standing out from his peers, the head's function also became prominent. As the Committee Head or the GS, he was to convene the CEC any time[65] and take overall charge of the party affairs,[66] which had been boasted as nationwide by the Fourth National Congress,[67] whereas other CEC members should assist him by managing specific duties such as political, labor, youth, women, and so on.[68] Therefore, the CEC was divided into the GS and eight other members, with party duties also being divided among them and four of them being deployed to local organizations.

How would the division of party duties be made among them? The party constitutions did not provide, but the CEC organic law once required that the CEC should divide the duties among its members at its first meeting,[69] which it did in the first plenary of the Third CEC.[70] Although neither party constitutions nor the organic law stipulated clearly how the CEC should divide party duties at the first meeting, they all required that decisions in party meetings had to be made based on majority opinions of participants and followed by dissenting members,[71] which could mean that the CEC could perform its function by way of meeting and dividing party duties by majority opinion of attendants. Since no stipulation was written on how majority opinions should be solicited in the meeting, it could also suggest that both voting, secret or by hand, and consultation would be acceptable so long as a consensus was reached. Hence, the CEC could divide the party duties at its first meeting either by voting or consultation.

According to the same organic law, the first meeting should also decide which four CEC members be deployed locally. As a result, it would be the Central Bureau composed by the GS and other four members that stayed at the central organization, which should be supposed to function similarly in the same way, that is, making decisions based on majority opinions in its weekly meeting. As no provision was made regarding how the CCP be managed in the other days of the week when the Central Bureau did not meet, it should be up to the individual member to take charge of their specified duties based on the division of party duties.

If compared with a Western government, each of the CEC members would be both policy makers and executors. When the Central Bureau convened, it acted like a legislative committee, in which each member was a "legislator" and participated in the policy making; while it was closed, each member should carry out the collective decision making with respect to his own divided work, thus becoming a government minister. Among all members, the GS surely had more weight. According to the party constitutions, the Committee Head or GS should take charge of the CCP party affairs on the whole. Textually speaking, the "party affairs" under his overall charge could mean either administrative affairs of the CCP central organization, or the CCP's decision making. Since the Third National Congress had specifically provided a secretary and an accountant in the Central Bureau, it could mean that the Committee Head had been relieved of these administrative chores, and what fell under his overall charge was the CCP's decision making.[72] Besides, he could also possibly have some divided work under his jurisdiction. Hence, he was more than a minister: he was the head minister who was implicated to take accountablity for the CCP.

Apart from these executory functions, the GS had other functions. According to the same organic law, the five-person Central Bureau should be composed of the Committee Head, a secretary, an accountant, and other two CEC members, in which the Committee Head could preside over all meetings of the CEC and Central Bureau.[73] Jointly with the secretary, he could also call to order and set the agenda for the meeting of the CEC, and sign party documents.[74] If these rules were applicable afterwards, the GS should also have these functions, which were similar to those of the committee chairman in Western legislature. In other words, he acted like a legislative chairman. Therefore, the GS was both the president and the legislative chairman.

Then a fundamental question would arise concerning such a decision-making arrangement. What if the majority opinion reached in the Central Bureau's weekly meetings disagreed with an individual member's daily decision made on his assigned work? In particular, could the GS intervene or even overturn decisions made by other member, or the committee's majority opinion by asserting his overall responsibility? Theoretically, it should be the majority that prevailed; but in practice, the answer was far more complex.

The GS Became "the Family Head"

Being successively elected as the Committee Head and GS by the Second, Third, and Fourth National Congresses, Chen Duxiu's role in the CCP's decision making had not been straight-forward, suffering from challenges of opposing factions, mostly resulting from "policy controversies which were inevitably rooted in different social background of members."[75] As early as the CCP was in its founding period, some participants had disagreed with Chen Duxiu's idea of following the Russian way of organization during the founding period and left the CCP.[76] After the First National Congress, the provisional committee was divided over the relationship with the Comintern and its agent Maring. Like most of his colleagues, Chen Duxiu had insisted on being independent and rejecting the finance and direction of the Comintern,[77] whereas Zhang Guotao, the chairman of the First National Congress and then a member of the provisional committee in charge of labor work, had been much more supportive of Maring.[78] Complaining that Chen Duxiu's way of organizing the CCP was too loose,[79] Zhang Guotao had been more radical and seemed to have been interested in replacing Chen Duxiu after the First National Congress when Chen Duxiu had not taken office in Shanghai.[80] Disappointed, Maring had suggested Zhang Guotao take the place of the uncooperative secretary.[81]

Compromise had not been made until Maring spent much effort on rescuing Chen Duxiu out of a police arrest.[82] In return, Chen Duxiu conceded and convinced his colleagues to accept the Comintern,[83] whereas Maring agreed not to interfere with the CCP internal affairs by indicating his respect for the independence of the CCP and only maintaining regular contacts with its head to discuss policy issues.[84] Such a "guardianship" was further endorsed by the Second National Congress, thus officially making the CCP the Comintern's Chinese branch.

While gaining externally, Chen Duxiu could have almost been toppled by Zhang Guotao, who refused Maring's suggestion[85] but forged an opposing force based on his personal connections with those having the same education background in Beijing University as him and those relating to his divided work.[86] When the Second National Congress was completed, he and his men successfully took four of the five seats in the CEC,[87] with Chen Duxiu being the committee head. Having known Zhang Guotao's ambition,[88] Chen Duxiu chose to resign.[89]

It was Maring who had Chen Duxiu back in position.[90] When Maring returned China with Moscow's demand on the CCP to ally with the KMT after the Second National Congress, he met with unanimous opposition from the CCP.[91] The factional wrestling within the CCP gave him the excuse for a CEC meeting, in which he not only successfully restored Chen Duxiu, but also suppressed Zhang Guotao with a unsigned resolution and obtained an unwritten commitment to Moscow's policy from the CCP by imposing the Comintern's superiority,[92] after defeating an amendment submitted by Zhang Guotao with the decisive vote from Chen Duxiu who had cast it out of "respect for the Comintern."[93] The controversial allying policy barely survived the Third National Congress, with only several affirming votes more than for the negative.[94] Insistently opposing Moscow's allying policy,[95] Zhang Guotao was further excluded from the CEC in the Third National Congress,[96] only winning six favorable votes out of forty votes,[97] which was not difficult for Maring to achieve as Maring had been dominant in the congress who not only proposed the roster of candidates,[98] but also made lobbying[99] before the hand votes.[100]

Since then, Chen Duxiu's influence began to ascend within the CCP.[101] Although Maring was replaced by Verkinsky as Russia's new agent for the CCP after the Third National Congress,[102] the latter had been more modest and supportive to Chen Duxiu.[103] When it came to the Fourth National Congress held in early 1925, the size of the CCP had been remarkably expanded, and Chen Duxiu started to reach his peak of power.

As the GS, he individually took charge of the Central Secretariat and Organizational Department, the former of which handled the CCP's central administration, including paperwork and budget funded by the Comintern, and the latter managed party work concerning personnel appointment. Thus he controlled the monetary and personnel matters effectively.[104]

Besides, Chen Duxiu had been delegated a "power of last say" occasionally. The First National Congress had intended to issue a declaration, but it did not reach consensus on it. So he was authorized by the congress to make a final decision on this issue, which he decided negatively.[105] In February 1926, he was also given a new delegation to make the final decision on the residing place of the CCP's central organs.[106]

While Chen Duxiu was on the rise, the collective decision making required by the party rules had not been effectively practiced. As a secret party, working places of the CCP's central organs had been unstable,[107] and central leaders had to hide most of the time, which made them difficult to meet and hold talks.[108] Even if a meeting was held, not all members could attend because some of them had always been away to handle other affairs.[109] Even if most members were present in the meeting, some of them could be "free riders," because sometimes certain members would rather focus on their own business and were unwilling to participate in the decision making.[110] Even when meetings were held, voting was not always been adopted as no results had been gained due to different opinions among members in many meetings,[111] suggesting no votes had been cast. In the end, it could easily lead to dictatorship, as admitted by Chen Duxiu.[112]

By then, Chen Duxiu had his own followers within the CCP. As more and more people returned from overseas, mostly by way of Moscow, they became an important new force within the CCP.[113] These "returned students" who had been familiar with the leadership worship taking place in Moscow also regarded Chen Duxiu as their leaders and gathered together under his umbrella.[114]

Being the party chief, Chen Duxiu also had informational advantage. Compared with his CCP colleagues, Chen Duxiu was closest to those Russian agents and could access more Russian information, despite those who kept their information hidden from the CCP.[115] A CCP member once criticized that the central leaders had implemented a "policy of obscurantism" and not publicized the Comintern resolutions.[116]

Personally, Chen Duxiu was in a superior position. Among the vast illiterate populace and the few people introducing Marxism to Chinese, he was better educated than his colleagues who only knew Marxism after joining the CCP.[117] As others were either his students, consultants, or translators, he was older and senior to them, which put him in a better position when debating with others[118] at a time when the old tradition of seniority did not vanish. He had a strong personality with his own will,[119] easy-to-lose temper,[120] often scolded his opponents in debates,[121] and always acted like a family head.[122]

Because of these traits, Chen Duxiu became dominant in the CCP. When the CCP's central organization had been settled down in Shanghai after the Fourth National Congress, the Central Bureau had two different types of meeting every week, one of which were held within the CCP, without attendance of Verkinsky, but not limited to the Central Bureau members. Mainly concerned with daily works, it was more like a central working conference.[123] In these meetings, Chen Duxiu played such a decisive role that no arguments occured.[124] As a result, Chen Duxiu was nicknamed "the old man,"[125] and was criticized by his opponents of acting like "the family head."[126]

Resignation of the GS

But Chen Duxiu had to restrain himself when dealing with the Russians. In Shanghai, the Central Bureau also held weekly meeting with Verkinsky, mostly discussing policy issues. As a precursor to the CCP Politburo later produced by the Fifth National Congress, this type of meeting was said to be well organized and conducted quite democratically. Although Chen Duxiu acted as the chairman and set topics for discussion for each meeting, participants were free to speak and majority opinions were fairly respected.[127]

More problematic was his relation with Bordin,[128] Stalin's man in China. Different from Verkinsky, Bordin was thought to be insincere and was not trusted by the CCP.[129] More fundamentally, they were divided over the alliance policy.[130] Under direct command of Stalin,[131] Bordin acted on his own "diplomatic ways"[132] and directed CCP Guangzhou Committee disregarding Chen Duxiu,[133] whereas Chen Duxiu repeatedly proposed to withdraw from the KMT.[134] In vain, Chen Duxiu not only lost control over the local CCP Guangzhou Committees,[135] but also made Moscow contemplate removing the reluctant GS. Around the end of 1926, a delegation was sent by Moscow to China to investigate, wishing to find someone who was both loyal to its policies and close to the KMT.[136]

To make things worse, the internal oppositions gradually came to the extreme within the CCP. Apart from Zhang Guotao, another opposition could have been created by Chen Duxiu himself partially, which was Qu Qiubai, a Central Bureau member of the Third National Congress. Unsatisfied with what Qu QiuBbai and Borodin had done in Guangzhou, Chen Duxiu and Cai Hesen summoned Qu Qiubai back to Shanghai in the name of CEC[137] and suspended his function in the Central Bureau for a period of time.[138] Qu Qiubai carried a grudge from that point on.[139] While Chen Duxiu objected to the KMT's North Expedition plan and had a big quarrel with Zhang Guotao over it, Qu Qiubai first chose to look on, and then quit his function by pleading illness, choosing to be an opposition behind the scenes.[140] Eventually these two joined hands with the excuse of opposing excessive centralization of power in the hands of Chen Duxiu.[141]

As the KMT's force successfully pushed forward to Wuhan in the North Expedition, Chen Duxiu's objection seemed to be wrong and Bordin's ideas took upper wind, turning the oppositions to surface.[142] Chen Duxiu's authority started to decline. Bordin was given greater say over Verkinsky by Moscow.[143] Three insurgents, that is, Zhang Guotao, Qu Qiubai, and Tan Pingshan, formed another CCP Central in Wuhan, regarding their general secretary who had lagged in Shanghai.[144] When Chen Duxiu joined them in April 1927, he became the minority and was manipulated, even scolded, in the meetings by them.[145] The National Congress was requested to convene to remove him[146] and adopt the collective leadership.[147]

Whether Chen Duxiu could continue to take the lead became a major concern in the Fifth National Congress amid the bloody massacre of the CCP by the KMT forces controlled by General Jiang Jieshi.[148] Earlier investigation by the Russian delegation found that Chen Duxiu still enjoyed unparalleled authority within the CCP.[149] Among those Russian agents in China, Verkinsky was still in favor of him.[150] Therefore, Moscow still had to have him elected as the GS, but isolated him by removing his followers from the leadership.[151]

The CCP central organization was also restructured to "let some fresh air in."[152] The Central Committee, renamed from the CEC, was expanded.[153] With a larger base, more level of standing organs had to be built up, and a fourth organ was produced out of the Central Bureau, which was now also renamed as the Political Bureau (Politburo), that is, the Politburo Standing Committee (PSC), to handle daily business of the CCP.[154] As a result, a four-tier leading organization was formulated at the central level of the CCP,[155] with each upper one serving as a standing body when the lower organ closed, with the PSC on the top as the most permanent body.

Furthermore, Chen Duxiu was reduced to a nominal head despite that he continued to act as the GS of the Central Committee, because the GS's function of "taking as overall responsibility" was deleted from the newly revised party constitution, which suggested that he enjoyed no prominence and had to participate in the CCP's decision making as an equal member.

Facing the coming split of the KMT, Stalin continued to press for the CCP to stay allied with the KMT, which was "considered impossible to enforce by everyone."[156] Chen Duxiu was in an awkward situation. As the head, even being nominal, he had to take accountability for the loss of colleagues and deteriorating situations in China, which made him very depressed.[157] On the other hand, he had to follow Moscow's directions as the Chinese branch of Comintern. These two sides did not always agree with each other.[158] Such a dilemma of accountability set Chen Duxiu gradually apart from Moscow. He acted passively,[159] echoed Bordin's ideas,[160] who became dominant in the CCP,[161] and refused Moscow's directions.[162] Finally when the Russians intended to remove him[163] by summoning him to Moscow,[164] he resigned.[165] In his letter to the CCP, he said he was unable to work and asked to be relieved of his duty,[166] saying he had no way out because the Comintern had wanted him to perform his own policy, but was not allowed to withdraw from the alliance with the KMT.[167] He became the scapegoat of Moscow[168] and the CCP Politburo[169] for their failure in China.

Replacing GS with Chairman

Gone with the strong hold of Chen Duxiu, Moscow tightened its grip on the CCP, first reorganizing the CCP's central organs. Being summoned back home, Borodin executed Moscow's order and replaced the old PSC with a new one before leaving.[170] Upon arrival in China, the new Russian agent Lominadze reshuffled the CCP once again.[171] As personnel changes were not enough, new policies had to be formulated by a new National Congress, which was the sixth one and had to be convened in Moscow.[172]

While endorsing the four-tier central leading organizations, that is, the National Congress, Central Committee, Politburo, and PSC,[173] neither the new party constitution said neither about the decision-making rules of majority opinions and the division of work in the Politburo and PSC, nor provide the title of GS because Moscow still wanted Chen Duxiu back to the CCP,[174] but someone had to be produced to be called to preside over the PSC meeting.[175]

All of these was solved by practice. When the CEC held its first meeting, Moscow named seven people as the Politburo members and decided their division of works, among them Xiang Zhongfa was made the Politburo chairman.[176] To reduce conflicts within the CCP, leaders of party factions, that is, Zhang Guotao and Qu Qiubai, were held out by Moscow.[177]

Previously, the CCP had adopted the term chairman to refer to a temporary meeting convener in its party constitutions, which had provided that "when this special committee convenes, one member of this executive committee should be the chairman."[178] Now under influence of Moscow, it replaced the GS as the CCP's head. But Chairman Xiang Zhongfa was only a nominal chief.[179] During his term of service until he died in the KMT's prison, decision making of the CCP had actually been dominated successively by various members,[180] such as Cai Hesen,[181] Zhou Enlai,[182] Li Lisan,[183] Qu Qiubai,[184] Wang Ming,[185] Zhang Guotao,[186] and lastly Bo Gu,[187] all of whom were subject to the will of Moscow.

To summarize, the American presidency was first introduced to modernize the shattered China at the end of the Qing dynasty, but failed to take root and was replaced by the chairman, a traditional Chinese phrase which not only had been related to the family head, but also been transformed into a political title and position for the committee member who chaired that committee and presided at its meetings, when Moscow intensified its influence on China.

The experience of Chen Duxiu suggested that the authority of the CCP chairman was not only decided by the written rules, which were flexibly revised to suit the changing situation of the time, but also more by his personal capacity, policies, and struggles of party factions, all of which were ultimately subject to the interest of Moscow.

NOTES

1. Sidney M. Milkis and Michael Nelson, *The American Presidency: Origins and Developments, 1776-2002* (CQ Press, 2003), 4th ed., 49.

2. For Chinese, evolving ideas about the president of the United States and various Chinese translations of the English word "president," see Xiong Yuezhi, "Wanqing Jige Zhengzhi Cihui De Fanyi He Shiying" [Translations and Usages of Several Political Vocabularies in Late Qing Dynasty], Shilin, no. 1 (1999); *Zhongguo Jindai Minzhu Sixiang Shi* [The History of Democratic Thoughts in Modern China] (Shanghai: Shehui Kexue Chubanshe, 2002), 138-149; "Wanqing Zhongguo Dui Meiguo Zongtongzhi De Jiedu" [Chinese Interpretation of American Presidency in Later Qing Dynasty], Shilin, no. 1 (2007).

3. Organic Law of the Provisional Government of the Republic of China (October 13, 1911).

4. Jin Zhiren, *Zhongguo Lixian Shi* [Constitutional History of China] (Taiwan: Lianjing Chuban Shiye Gongsi, 1984), 220.

5. In a book written in 1903, the head of state was defined to include the emperor, constitutional monarch, or the president; for a constitutional head of state, it had power and function such as the power to call the congress, to appoint and remove government officials, to submit and veto the legislative bill and promulgate the law, to declare war, to enter treaties, to lead the army, to pardon, and so on; see Wang Rongbao and Ye Lan (eds.), *Xin Er'ya* (Taiwan: Wenhai Chuban Youxian Gongsi, 1977), 18-19. The author had studied in Japan and they wrote this book to promote modern political and social ideas to Chinese, to whom these ideas were new at that time.

6. Provisional Law of the Republic of China (March 8, 1912).

7. Constitution of the Republic of China (May 1, 1914).

8. Constitution of the Republic of China (October 10, 1924).

9. Regulation on the Provisional Government of the Republic of China (November 24, 1924). It was revised on December 24, 1925.

10. Order on the Organization of the Military Government (June 17, 1927).

11. See Zhongwen Dacidian Bianzuan Weiyuanhui (ed.), *Zhongwen Da Cidian* [The Chinese Dictionary] (Taiwan: Zhonghua Wenhua Yanjiusuo, 1962), vol. 1, 460; Zhongguo Dacidian Bianzuanchu (ed.), *Guoyu Cidian* [Chinese Dictionary] (Taiwan: Shangwu Yinshuguan, 1971), 2710; Luo Zufeng (ed.), *Hanyu Da Cidian* [Chinese Dictionary] (Hong Kong: Sanlian Shudian, 1987), 701.

12. Luo Zufeng (ed.), *Hanyu Da Cidian* [Chinese Dictionary] (Hong Kong: Sanlian Shudian, 1987), 701; Feng Jinrong et al. (ed.), *Jinxiandai Hanyu Xinci Ciyuan Cidian* [Dictionary of the Origins of New Vocabularies in Modern China] (Beijing: Hanyu Da Cidian Chubanshe, 2004), 351.

13. Qu Li, *Book of Rites*.

14. Yong John Allen, *The Church News* (Taiwan: Huawen Shuju), no. 1 (1868): 6.

15. Herbert A. Giles, *A Chinese-English Dictionary* (Taibei: Cheng-Won Publishing House, 1912), 315.

16. Li Guilian (ed.), *Minguo Beijing Zhengfu Zhixian Shiliao* [Constitutional-Making Materials of Beijing Government of the Republic of China] (Beijing: Xianzhuang Shuju, 2007), vol. 1, 5.

17. Zhongwen Dacidian Bianzuan Weiyuanhui (ed.), *Zhongwen Da Cidian* [The Chinese Dictionary] (Taiwan: Zhonghua Wenhua Yanjiusuo, 1962), vol. 1, 460; Luo Zufeng (ed.), *Hanyu Da Cidian* [Chinese Dictionary] (Hong Kong: Sanlian Shudian, 1987), 701; Zhongguo Dacidian Bianzuanchu (ed.), *Guoyu Cidian* [Chinese Dictionary] (Taiwan: Shangwu Yinshuguan, 1971), 2710; Feng Jinrong et al. (ed.), *Jinxiandai Hanyu Xinci Ciyuan Cidian* [Dictionary of the Origins of New Vocabularies in Modern China] (Beijing: Hanyu Da Cidian Chubanshe, 2004), 351.

18. "Joint Declaration by Su Zhongshan and Adolf Abramovich Joffe," in Huang Yang (ed.), *Sun Wen Xuanji* [Collection of Sun Wen] (Guangzhou: Guangdong Renmin Chubanshe, 2006), vol. 2, 211-213.

19. For a comparison between these two party constitutions, see Wang Qisheng, *Dangyuan Dangquan Yu Dangzheng* [Party member, power and struggle] (Beijing: Huawen Chubanshe, 2010), revised, 13-14.

20. Zhonghua Minguo Shishi Jiyao Bianji Weiyuanhui, *Zhonghua Minguo Shishi Jiyao Chugao* [Summary of history of the Republic of China (first draft)] (Taibei: Zhonghua Minguo Shiliao Yanjiu Zhongxin, 1974), 239.

21. Guangdongsheng Shehui Kexueyuan Lishi Yanjiusuo, et al., *Sunzhongshan Quanji* [Collection of Sunzhongshan] (Beijing: Zhonghua Shuju, 1986), vol. 9, 136-137.

22. Li Yunhan, *Cong Ronggong Dao Qingdang* (Taiwan: Zhongguo Xueshu Zhuzuo Jiangzhu Weiyuanhui, 1966), 372-375.

23. Zhonghua Minguo Guomi Zhengfu Zuzhi Fa [Organic Law of the National Government of the Republic of China].

24. For example, "Economic Commission of the Presidents' Field Headquarter," "Presidents' Headquarters at Chungking." See Sun Xiufu, *Jindai Zhongguo Huayang Jigou Yiming Shouce* [A Handbook for the Translation of the Chinese and Foreign Institutions in Modern China] (Beijing: Tuanjie Chubanshe, 1992), 117, 261.

25. See Zhonghua Minguo Xianfa [Constitution of the Republic of China] (1946).

26. Li Yuzhen, "Sunwen Yuefei Huitan De Muhou Taiqian" [The Meeting of Sunwen and Yuefei] *Guangdong Shehui Kexue* 1 (2011): 111, 118.

27. Zhonggong Zhongyang Dangshi Yanjiushi Diyi Yanjiubu (ed.), *Gongchan Guoji Liangongbu Yu Zhongguo Geming Wenxian Ziliao Xuanji: 1926-1927* [Selected Documents concerning the Incomtern, the Soviets of the Communist Party (Bolsheviks) and Chinese Revolution 1926-1927] (Beijing: Beijing Tushuguan, 1998), vol. 6, 546-547; Zhongguo Shehui Jexueyuan Xiandaishi Yanjiushi, Zhongguo Geming Bowuguan Dangshi Yanjiushi (eds.), *Yi Da Qian Hou-Zhongguo Gongchandang Diyici Daibiao Dahui Qianhou Ziliao Xuanbina* [Before and After the First National Congress: Elected Documents Before and After the First National Congress of the Communist Party of China], vol. 2 (Beijing: Renmin Chubanshe, 1980), 34-35, 372-373.

28. Zhongguo Shehui Jexueyuan Xiandaishi Yanjiushi, Zhongguo Geming Bowuguan Dangshi Yanjiushi (eds.), *Yi Da Qian Hou-Zhongguo Gongchandang Diyici Daibiao Dahui Qianhou Ziliao Xuanbina* [Before and After the First National Congress: Elected Documents Before and After the First National Congress of the Communist Party of China] (Beijing: Renmin Chubanshe, 1980), vol. 2, 8, 20; Bao Huiseng, *Bao Huiseng Huiyi Lu* [Memoirs of Bao Huiseng] (Beijing: Renmin Chubanshe, 1983), 18.

29. Art. 7, 9, 13, 15, the program of the CCP, adopted by the First National Congress in 1921.

30. Zhongguo Shehui Jexueyuan Xiandaishi Yanjiushi, Zhongguo Geming Bowuguan Dangshi Yanjiushi (eds.), *Yi Da Qian Hou-Zhongguo Gongchandang Diyici Daibiao Dahui Qianhou Ziliao Xuanbina* [Before and After the First National Congress: Elected Documents Before and After the First National Congress of the Communist Party of China] (Beijing: Renmin Chubanshe, 1980), vol. 2, 53, 289.

31. Zhang Guotao, *Wo De Huiyi* [My Memory] (Beijing: Dongfang Chubanshe, 2004), vol. 1, 137.

32. Zhongguo Shehui Jexueyuan Xiandaishi Yanjiushi, Zhongguo Geming Bowuguan Dangshi Yanjiushi (eds.), *Yi Da Qian Hou-Zhongguo Gongchandang Diyici Daibiao Dahui Qianhou Ziliao Xuanbina* [Before and After the First National Congress: Elected Documents Before and After the First National Congress of the Communist Party of China] (Beijing: Renmin Chubanshe, 1980), vol. 2, 182.

33. Zhongguo Shehui Jexueyuan Xiandaishi Yanjiushi, Zhongguo Geming Bowuguan Dangshi Yanjiushi (eds.), *Yi Da Qian Hou-Zhongguo Gongchandang Diyici Daibiao Dahui Qianhou Ziliao Xuanbina* [Before and After the First National Congress: Elected Documents Before and After the First National Congress of the Communist Party of China] (Beijing: Renmin Chubanshe, 1980), vol. 2, 214.

34. Zhonggong Zhongyang Dangshi Yanjiushi Diyi Yanjiubu (ed.), *Gongchan Guoji Liangongbu Yu Zhongguo Geming Wenxian Ziliao Xuanji: 1917-1925* [Selected documents concerning the Incomtern, the Soviets of the Communist Party (Bolsheviks) and Chinese Revolution 1917-1925] (Beijing: Beijing Tushuguan, 1997), 262.

35. Zhongguo Shehui Jexueyuan Xiandaishi Yanjiushi, Zhongguo Geming Bowuguan Dangshi Yanjiushi (eds.), *Yi Da Qian Hou-Zhongguo Gongchandang Diyici Daibiao Dahui Qianhou Ziliao Xuanbina* [Before and After the First National Congress: Elected Documents Before and After the First National Congress of the Communist Party of China] (Beijing: Renmin Chubanshe, 1980), vol. 2, 10.

36. Zhongguo Shehui Jexueyuan Xiandaishi Yanjiushi, Zhongguo Geming Bowuguan Dangshi Yanjiushi (eds.), *Yi Da Qian Hou-Zhongguo Gongchandang Diyici Daibiao Dahui Qianhou Ziliao Xuanbina* [Before and After the First National Congress: Elected Documents Before and After the First National Congress of the Communist Party of China] (Beijing: Renmin Chubanshe, 1980), vol. 2, 377.

37. Zhongguo Shehui Jexueyuan Xiandaishi Yanjiushi, Zhongguo Geming Bowuguan Dangshi Yanjiushi (eds.), *Yi Da Qian Hou-Zhongguo Gongchandang Diyici Daibiao Dahui Qianhou Ziliao Xuanbina* [Before and After the First National Congress: Elected Documents Before and After the First National Congress of the Communist Party of China] (Beijing: Renmin Chubanshe, 1980), vol. 2, 377.

38. Zhongguo Shehui Jexueyuan Xiandaishi Yanjiushi, Zhongguo Geming Bowuguan Dangshi Yanjiushi (eds.), *Yi Da Qian Hou-Zhongguo Gongchandang Diyici Daibiao Dahui Qianhou Ziliao Xuanbina* [Before and After the First National Congress: Elected Documents Before and After the First National Congress of the Communist Party of China] (Beijing: Renmin Chubanshe, 1980), vol. 2, 117, 214, 321.

39. Zhongguo Shehui Jexueyuan Xiandaishi Yanjiushi, Zhongguo Geming Bowuguan Dangshi Yanjiushi (eds.), *Yi Da Qian Hou-Zhongguo Gongchandang Diyici Daibiao Dahui Qianhou Ziliao Xuanbina* [Before and After the First National Congress: Elected Documents Before and After the First National Congress of the Communist Party of China] (Beijing: Renmin Chubanshe, 1980), vol. 2, 131.

40. Zhongguo Shehui Jexueyuan Xiandaishi Yanjiushi, Zhongguo Geming Bowuguan Dangshi Yanjiushi (eds.), *Yi Da Qian Hou-Zhongguo Gongchandang Diyici Daibiao Dahui Qianhou Ziliao Xuanbina* [Before and After the First National Congress: Elected Documents Before and After the First National Congress of the Communist Party of China] (Beijing: Renmin Chubanshe, 1980), vol. 2, 11.

41. Zhongguo Shehui Jexueyuan Xiandaishi Yanjiushi, Zhongguo Geming Bowuguan Dangshi Yanjiushi (eds.), *Yi Da Qian Hou-Zhongguo Gongchandang Diyici Daibiao Dahui Qianhou Ziliao Xuanbina* [Before and After the First National Congress: Elected Documents Before and After the First National Congress of the Communist Party of China] (Beijing: Renmin Chubanshe, 1980), vol. 2, 136.

42. Zhongguo Shehui Jexueyuan Xiandaishi Yanjiushi, Zhongguo Geming Bowuguan Dangshi Yanjiushi (eds.), *Yi Da Qian Hou-Zhongguo Gongchandang Diyici Daibiao Dahui Qianhou Ziliao Xuanbina* [Before and After the First National Congress: Elected Documents Before and After the First National Congress of the Communist Party of China] (Beijing: Renmin Chubanshe, 1980), vol. 2, 23.

43. Zhang Yue, "Zhonggong Jigou Bianqian Shi: Zuigao Lingdao Weihe Cheng Zong Shuji" [Evolution of the Organization of the Communist Party: Why Was the Supreme Leader Called as the General Secretary], *Nanfang Weekly*, October 10, 2007.

44. Zhang Jingru (ed.), *Zhongguo Gongchandang Quanguo Daibiao Dahui Congshu* [Series on the National Congress of the CCP] (Shengyang: Wangjuan Chuban Gongsi, 2012), vol. 2, 145.

45. Zhongguo Shehui Jexueyuan Xiandaishi Yanjiushi, Zhongguo Geming Bowuguan Dangshi Yanjiushi (eds.), *Yi Da Qian Hou-Zhongguo Gongchandang Diyici Daibiao Dahui Qianhou Ziliao Xuanbina* [Before and After the First National Congress: Elected Documents Before and After the First National Congress of the Communist Party of China] (Beijing: Renmin Chubanshe, 1980), vol. 2, 23.

46. Zhongguo Shehui Jexueyuan Xiandaishi Yanjiushi, Zhongguo Geming Bowuguan Dangshi Yanjiushi (eds.), *Yi Da Qian Hou-Zhongguo Gongchandang Diyici Daibiao Dahui Qianhou Ziliao Xuanbina* [Before and after the First National Congress: Elected Documents Before and After the First National Congress of the Communist Party of China] (Beijing: Renmin Chubanshe, 1980), vol. 2, 137.

47. Zhongguo Shehui Jexueyuan Xiandaishi Yanjiushi, Zhongguo Geming Bowuguan Dangshi Yanjiushi (eds.), *Yi Da Qian Hou-Zhongguo Gongchandang Diyici Daibiao Dahui Qianhou Ziliao Xuanbina* [Before and After the First National Congress: Elected Documents Before and After the First National Congress of the Communist Party of China] (Beijing: Renmin Chubanshe, 1980), vol. 2, 137.

48. *Zhongguo Dangan Guan Bian: Zhongguo Gongchan Dang Diyici Daibiao Dahui Dangan Ziliao* [Documents of the First National Congress of the Communist Party of China] (Revised and Enlarged) (Beijing: Renmin Chubanshe, 1983), 12-13.

49. Art. 17, the Constitution of the CCP, adopted by the Second National Congress in 1922.

50. Art. 16, the Constitution of the CCP, adopted by the Second National Congress in 1922; Art. 17, the Constitution of the CCP, adopted by the Third National Congress in 1923; Art. 17, the Constitution of the CCP, adopted by the Fourth National Congress in 1925.

51. Art. 9, the Constitution of the CCP, adopted by the Second National Congress in 1922.

52. Art. 11, the Constitution of the CCP, adopted by the Second National Congress in 1922.

53. *Wang jianying: Zhonggong Zhongyang Jiguan Lishi Yanbina Kaoshi* [Study on the Historical Evolution of the Central Organs of the Communist Party of China] (Beijing: Zhonggong Dangshi Chubanshe, 2005), 591.

54. http://news.cntv.cn/2012/11/03/ARTI1351936662607202.shtml.

55. Art. 2, the Organic Law of the Central Executive Committee of the CCP, adopted by the Third National Congress in 1923.

56. Art. 3, the Organic Law of the Central Executive Committee of the CCP, adopted by the Third National Congress in 1923.

57. Art. 4, the Organic Law of the Central Executive Committee of the CCP, adopted by the Third National Congress in 1923.

58. Zhongguo Shehui Jexueyuan Xiandaishi Yanjiushi, Zhongguo Geming Bowuguan Dangshi Yanjiushi (eds.), *Yi Da Qian Hou-Zhongguo Gongchandang Diyici Daibiao Dahui Qianhou Ziliao Xuanbina* [Before and After the First National Congress: Elected Documents Before and After the First National Congress of the Communist Party of China] (Beijing: Renmin Chubanshe, 1980), vol. 2, 182; Zhang Guotao, *Wo De Huiyi* [My Memory] (Beijing: Dongfang Chubanshe, 2004), vol. 1, 137.

59. Zhonggong Zhongyang Dangshi Yanjiushi Diyi Yanjiubu (ed.), *Gongchan Guoji Liangongbu Yu Zhongguo Geming Wenxian Ziliao Xuanji: 1917-1925* [Selected Documents concerning the Incomtern, the Soviets of the Communist Party (Bolsheviks) and Chinese Revolution 1917-1925] (Beijing: Beijing Tushuguan, 1997), 341.

60. Zhonggong Zhongyang Dangshi Yanjiushi Diyi Yanjiubu (ed.), *Gongchan Guoji Liangongbu Yu Zhongguo Geming Wenxian Ziliao Xuanji: 1926-1927* [Selected Documents concerning the Incomtern, the Soviets of the Communist Party (Bolsheviks) and Chinese Revolution 1926-1927] (Beijing: Beijing Tushuguan, 1998), vol. 2, 546-547.

61. Zhang Zhidan, *Shui Zhu Chengfu Zhongguo Gongchandang Disici Quanguo Daibiao Dhui* [Who Decided: The Fourth National Congress of the CCP] (Shijiazhuang: Hebei Renmin Chubanshe, 2012), 21.

62. Zheng Chaoling, *Zheng Chaoling Huiyi Lu* [Memoire of Zheng Chaoling] (Beijing: Dongfang Chubanshe, 2004), vol. 2, 216.

63. Art. 9, the Constitution of the CCP, adopted by the Second National Congress in 1922; Art. 10, the Constitution of the CCP, adopted by the Third National Congress in 1923.

64. Art. 10, the Constitution of the CCP, adopted by the Fourth National Congress in 1925.

65. Art. 16, the Constitution of the CCP, adopted by the Second National Congress in 1922; Art. 17, the Constitution of the CCP, adopted by the Third National Congress in 1923; Art. 17, the Constitution of the CCP, adopted by the Fourth National Congress in 1925.

66. Art. 9, the Constitution of the CCP, adopted by the Second National Congress in 1922; Art. 10, the Constitution of the CCP, adopted by the Third National Congress in 1923; Art. 10, the Constitution of the CCP, adopted by the Fourth National Congress in 1925.

67. Zhang Zhidan, *Shui Zhu Chengfu Zhongguo Gongchandang Disici Quanguo Daibiao Dhui* [Who Decided: The Fourth National Congress of the CCP] (Shijiazhuang: Hebei Renmin Chubanshe, 2012), 98.

68. Art. 9, the Constitution of the CCP, adopted by the Second National Congress in 1922; Art. 10, the Constitution of the CCP, adopted by the Third National Congress in 1923; Art. 10, the Constitution of the CCP, adopted by the Fourth National Congress in 1925.

69. Art. 2, the Organic Law of the Central Executive Committee of the CCP, adopted by the Third National Congress in 1923.

70. Luo Zhanglong, *Chunyuan Zaiji* [Tecord in Chunyuan] (Shanghai: Shenghuo Dushu Xinzhi Sanlian Shudian, 1984), 277.

71. Art. 24, the Constitution of the CCP, adopted by the Second National Congress in 1922; Art. 11, the Constitution of the CCP, adopted by the Third National Congress in 1923; Art. 24, the Constitution of the CCP, adopted by the Fourth National Congress in 1925; Art. 67, the Constitution of the CCP, adopted by the Politburo of the CCP in 1927.

72. Zhang Jingru (ed.), *Zhongguo Gongchandang Quanguo Daibiao Dahui Congshu* [Series on the National Congress of the CCP] (Shengyang: Wangjuan Chuban Gongsi, 2012), vol. 1, 232-233.

73. Art. 3, the Organic Law of the Central Executive Committee of the CCP, adopted by the Third National Congress in 1923.

74. Arts. 3 and 5, the Organic Law of the Central Executive Committee of the CCP, adopted by the Third National Congress in 1923.

75. Shi Guang, et al. (ed.), *Erda He Sanda: Zhongguo Guochandang Dier Sanci Daibiao Dahui Ziliao Xuanbian* [Selected Documents concerning the Second and Third National Congress of the CCP] (Beijing: Zhongguo Shehui Kexue Chubanshe, 1985), 491.

76. *Zhongguo Dangan Guan Bian: Zhongguo Gongchan Dang Diyici Daibiao Dahui Dangan Ziliao* [Documents of the First National Congress of the Communist Party of China] (Revised and Enlarged) (Beijing: Renmin Chubanshe, 1983), 64-70.

77. Bao Huiseng, *Bao Huiseng Huiyi Lu* [Memoirs of Bao Huiseng] (Beijing: Renmin Chubanshe, 1983), 367, 369-370; Zhongguo Shehui Jexueyuan Xiandaishi Yanjiushi, Zhongguo Geming Bowuguan Dangshi Yanjiushi (eds.), *Yi Da Qian Hou-Zhongguo Gongchandang Diyici Daibiao Dahui Qianhou Ziliao Xuanbina* [Before and After the First National Congress: Elected Documents Before and After the First National Congress of the Communist Party of China] (Beijing: Renmin Chubanshe, 1980), vol. 2, 384, 387-388.

78. Zhang Guotao, *Wo De Huiyi* [My Memory] (Beijing: Dongfang Chubanshe, 2004), vol. 1, 150-151.

79. Zhongguo Shehui Jexueyuan Xiandaishi Yanjiushi, Zhongguo Geming Bowuguan Dangshi Yanjiushi (eds.), *Yi Da Qian Hou-Zhongguo Gongchandang Diyici Daibiao Dahui Qianhou Ziliao Xuanbina* [Before and After the First National Congress: Elected Documents Before and After the First National Congress of the Communist Party of China] (Beijing: Renmin Chubanshe, 1980), vol. 2, 377.

80. Bao Huiseng, *Bao Huiseng Huiyi Lu* [Memoirs of Bao Huiseng] (Beijing: Renmin Chubanshe, 1983), 369.

81. Zhang Guotao, *Wo De Huiyi* [My Memory] (Beijing: Dongfang Chubanshe, 2004), vol. 2, 150-151.

82. Zhongguo Shehui Jexueyuan Xiandaishi Yanjiushi, Zhongguo Geming Bowuguan Dangshi Yanjiushi (eds.), *Yi Da Qian Hou-Zhongguo Gongchandang Diyici Daibiao Dahui Qianhou Ziliao Xuanbina* [Before and After the First National Congress: Elected Documents Before and After the First National Congress of the Communist Party of China] (Beijing: Renmin Chubanshe, 1980), vol. 2, 391.

83. Yao Jinguo, *Chen Duxiu Yu Mosike De Enen Yuanyuan* [Grudges between Chen Duxiu and Moscow] (Fuzhou: Fujian Renmin Chubanshe, 2010), 21.

84. Zhang Guotao, *Wo De Huiyi* [My Memory] (Beijing: Dongfang Chubanshe, 2004), vol. 1, 156-157.

85. Zhang Guotao, *Wo De Huiyi* [My Memory] (Beijing: Dongfang Chubanshe, 2004), vol. 1, 151.

86. Zheng Chaoling, *Zheng Chaoling Huiyi Lu* [Memoire of Zheng Chaoling] (Beijing: Dongfang Chubanshe, 2004), vol. 2, 471-472; Bao Huiseng, *Bao Huiseng Huiyi Lu* [Memoirs of Bao Huiseng] (Beijing: Renmin Chubanshe, 1983), 9; Zhongguo Shehui Jexueyuan Xiandaishi Yanjiushi, Zhongguo Geming Bowuguan Dangshi Yanjiushi (eds.), *Yi Da Qian Hou-Zhongguo Gongchandang Diyici Daibiao Dahui Qianhou Ziliao Xuanbina* [Before and After the First National Congress: Elected Documents Before and After the First National Congress of the Communist Party of China] (Beijing: Renmin Chubanshe, 1980), vol. 2, 216.

87. Zhonggong Zhongyang Dangshi Yanjiushi Diyi Yanjiubu (ed.), *Gongchan Guoji Liangongbu Yu Zhongguo Geming Wenxian Ziliao Xuanji: 1917-1925* [Selected Documents concerning the Incomtern, the Soviets of the Communist Party (Bolsheviks) and Chinese Revolution 1917-1925] (Beijing: Beijing Tushuguan, 1998), 477.

88. Zhang Guotao, *Wo De Huiyi* [My Memory] (Beijing: Dongfang Chubanshe, 2004), vol. 1, 154.

89. Zhongguo Shehui Jexueyuan Xiandaishi Yanjiushi, Zhongguo Geming Bowuguan Dangshi Yanjiushi (eds.), *Yi Da Qian Hou-Zhongguo Gongchandang Diyici Daibiao Dahui Qianhou Ziliao Xuanbina* [Before and After the First National Congress: Elected Documents Before and After the First National Congress of the Communist Party of China] (Beijing: Renmin Chubanshe, 1980), vol. 3, 100-101; Zhongyang Danganguan (ed.), *Zhongguo Gongchandang Diyici Daibiao Dahui Dangan Ziliao* (Zengding Ben) [Documents of the First National Congress of the CCP (revised)] (Beijing: Renmin Chubanshe, 1984), 79.

90. Zhonggong Zhongyang Dangshi Yanjiushi Diyi Yanjiubu, (ed.), *Gongchan Guoji Liangongbu Yu Zhongguo Geming Wenxian Ziliao Xuanji: 1917-1925* [Selected Documents concerning the Incomtern, the Soviets of the Communist Party (Bolsheviks) and Chinese Revolution 1917-1925] (Beijing: Beijing Tushuguan, 1998), 477.

91. Zhang Guotao, *Wo De Huiyi* [My Memory] (Beijing: Dongfang Chubanshe, 2004), vol. 1, 223.

92. Zhang Guotao, *Wo De Huiyi* [My Memory] (Beijing: Dongfang Chubanshe, 2004), vol. 1, 225-227.

93. Zhang Guotao, *Wo De Huiyi* [My Memory] (Beijing: Dongfang Chubanshe, 2004), vol. 1, 274-279.

94. Zhonggong Zhongyang Dangshi Yanjiushi Diyi Yanjiubu (ed.), *Gongchan Guoji Liangongbu Yu Zhongguo Geming Wenxian Ziliao Xuanji: 1917-1925* [Selected Documents concerning the Incomtern, the Soviets of the Communist Party (Bolsheviks) and Chinese Revolution 1917-1925] (Beijing: Beijing Tushuguan, 1998), 481-482; Zhang Jingru (ed.), *Zhongguo Gongchandang Quanguo Daibiao Dahui Congshu* [Series on the National Congress of the CCP] (Shengyang: Wangjuan Chuban Gongsi, 2012), vol. 1, 228.

95. Zhongguo Shehui Jexueyuan Xiandaishi Yanjiushi, Zhongguo Geming Bowuguan Dangshi Yanjiushi (eds.), *Yi Da Qian Hou-Zhongguo Gongchandang Diyici Daibiao Dahui Qianhou Ziliao Xuanbina* [Before and After the First National Congress: Elected Documents Before and After the First National Congress of the Communist Party of China] (Beijing: Renmin Chubanshe, 1980), vol. 3, 100-103; Zhang Guotao, *Wo De Huiyi* [My Memory] (Beijing: Dongfang Chubanshe, 2004), vol. 1, 267-279; Shi Guang et al. (ed.), *Erda He Sanda: Zhongguo Guochandang Dier Sanci Daibiao Dahui Ziliao Xuanbian* [Selected Documents

concerning the Second and Third National Congress of the CCP] (Beijing: Zhongguo Shehui Kexue Chubanshe, 1985), 675-678.

96. Shi Guang et al. (ed.), *Erda He Sanda: Zhongguo Guochandang Dier Sanci Daibiao Dahui Ziliao Xuanbian* [Selected Documents concerning the Second and Third National Congress of the CCP] (Beijing: Zhongguo Shehui Kexue Chubanshe, 1985), 682.

97. Zhu hong, *Chen Duxiu Yu Disan Guoji Renwu Lun* [Study on Chen Duxiu and People from the Comintern] (Beijing: Zhongguo Danan Chubanshe, 2003), 105.

98. Luo Zhanglong, *Chunyuan Zaiji* [Tecord in Chunyuan] (Shanghai: Shenghuo Dushu Xinzhi Sanlian Shudian, 1984), 275.

99. Luo Zhanglong, *Chunyuan Zaiji* [Tecord in Chunyuan] (Shanghai: Shenghuo Dushu Xinzhi Sanlian Shudian, 1984), 270-271

100. Shi Guang et al. (ed.), *Erda He Sanda: Zhongguo Guochandang Dier Sanci Daibiao Dahui Ziliao Xuanbian* [Selected Documents concerning the Second and Third National Congress of the CCP] (Beijing: Zhongguo Shehui Kexue Chubanshe, 1985), 678.

101. Zhang Guotao, *Wo De Huiyi* [My Memory] (Beijing: Dongfang Chubanshe, 2004), vol. 1, 303.

102. Zhang Guotao, *Wo De Huiyi* [My Memory] (Beijing: Dongfang Chubanshe, 2004), vol. 1, 285.

103. Zhang Guotao, *Wo De Huiyi* [My Memory] (Beijing: Dongfang Chubanshe, 2004), vol. 1, 368.

104. Zhang Guotao, *Wo De Huiyi* [My Memory] (Beijing: Dongfang Chubanshe, 2004), vol. 1, 368-369.

105. Zhongguo Shehui Jexueyuan Xiandaishi Yanjiushi, Zhongguo Geming Bowuguan Dangshi Yanjiushi (eds.), *Yi Da Qian Hou-Zhongguo Gongchandang Diyici Daibiao Dahui Qianhou Ziliao Xuanbina* [Before and After the First National Congress: Elected Documents Before and After the First National Congress of the Communist Party of China] (Beijing: Renmin Chubanshe, 1980), vol. 2, 421, 426.

106. Ren Jianshu, *Chen Duxiu Dazhuan* [Biography of Chen Duxiu] (Shanghai: Shanghai Renmin Chubanshe, 2012), 278-279.

107. Shi Guang, et al. (ed.), *Erda He Sanda: Zhongguo Guochandang Dier Sanci Daibiao Dahui Ziliao Xuanbian* [Selected Documents concerning the Second and Third National Congress of the CCP] (Beijing: Zhongguo Shehui Kexue Chubanshe, 1985), 168, 172,

108. Zhang Guotao, *Wo De Huiyi* [My Memory] (Beijing: Dongfang Chubanshe, 2004), vol. 1, 263-265.

109. Zhongguo Shehui Jexueyuan Xiandaishi Yanjiushi, Zhongguo Geming Bowuguan Dangshi Yanjiushi (eds.), *Yi Da Qian Hou-Zhongguo Gongchandang Diyici Daibiao Dahui Qianhou Ziliao Xuanbina* [Before and After the First National Congress: Elected Documents Before and After the First National Congress of the Communist Party of China] (Beijing: Renmin Chubanshe, 1980), vol. 2, 2-3; Zhonggong Zhongyang Dangshi Yanjiushi Diyi Yanjiubu (ed.), *Gongchan Guoji Liangongbu Yu Zhongguo Geming Wenxian Ziliao Xuanji: 1926-1927* [Selected documents concerning the Incomtern, the Soviets of the Communist Party (Bolsheviks) and Chinese Revolution 1926-1927] (Beijing: Beijing Tushuguan, 1998), vol. 1, 338-364; Zheng Chaoling, *Zheng Chaoling Huiyi Lu* [Memoire of Zheng Chaoling] (Beijing: Dongfang Chubanshe, 2004), vol. 2, 85-86, 477.

110. Zhang Guotao, *Wo De Huiyi* [My Memory] (Beijing: Dongfang Chubanshe, 2004), vol. 1, 303-304.

111. Zhongguo Shehui Jexueyuan Xiandaishi Yanjiushi, Zhongguo Geming Bowuguan Dangshi Yanjiushi (eds.), *Yi Da Qian Hou-Zhongguo Gongchandang Diyici Daibiao Dahui Qianhou Ziliao Xuanbina* [Before and After the First National Congress: Elected Documents Before and After the First National Congress of the Communist Party of China] (Beijing: Renmin Chubanshe, 1980), vol. 2, 76.

112. Zhonggong Zhongyang Dangshi Yanjiushi Diyi Yanjiubu (ed.), *Gongchan Guoji Liangongbu Yu Zhongguo Geming Wenxian Ziliao Xuanji: 1926-1927* [Selected Documents concerning the Incomtern, the Soviets of the Communist Party (Bolsheviks) and Chinese Revolution 1926-1927] (Beijing: Beijing Tushuguan, 1998), vol. 1, 338-364.

113. Zheng Chaoling, *Zheng Chaoling Huiyi Lu* [Memoire of Zheng Chaoling] (Beijing: Dongfang Chubanshe, 2004), vol. 2, 218.

114. Zheng Chaoling, *Zheng Chaoling Huiyi Lu* [Memoire of Zheng Chaoling] (Beijing: Dongfang Chubanshe, 2004), vol. 1, 475-477.

115. Zhang Guotao, *Wo De Huiyi* [My Memory] (Beijing: Dongfang Chubanshe, 2004), vol. 1, 234-236.

116. Li lisan, "Dangshi Baogao" [Report about the Party's History], in Zhongyang Dangan Guan ed., *Zhonggong Dangshi Baogao Xuanbian* (Beijing: Zhonggong Zhongyang Dangxiao Chubanshe, 1982), 249.

117. Bao Huiseng, *Bao Huiseng Huiyi Lu* [Memoirs of Bao Huiseng] (Beijing: Renmin Chubanshe, 1983), 18.

118. Tang Baolin and Chen Tie jian, *Chen Duxiu Yu Qu Qiubai* [Chen Duxiu and Qu Qiubai] (Beijing:Tuanjie Chubanshe, 2008), 95.

119. Zhongguo Shehui Jexueyuan Xiandaishi Yanjiushi, Zhongguo Geming Bowuguan Dangshi Yanjiushi (eds.), *Yi Da Qian Hou-Zhongguo Gongchandang Diyici Daibiao Dahui Qianhou Ziliao Xuanbina* [Before and After the First National Congress: Elected Documents Before and After the First National Congress of the Communist Party of China] (Beijing: Renmin Chubanshe, 1980), vol. 2, 133-134.

120. Shi Guang et al. (ed.), *Erda He Sanda: Zhongguo Guochandang Dier Sanci Daibiao Dahui Ziliao Xuanbian* [Selected Documents concerning the Second and Third National Congress of the CCP] (Beijing: Zhongguo Shehui Kexue Chubanshe, 1985), 172, 586.

121. Zheng Chaoling, *Zheng Chaoling Huiyi Lu* [Memoire of Zheng Chaoling] (Beijing: Dongfang Chubanshe, 2004), vol. 1, 17; vol. 2, 246; Zhongguo Shehui Jexueyuan Xiandaishi Yanjiushi, Zhongguo Geming Bowuguan Dangshi Yanjiushi (eds.), *Yi Da Qian Hou-Zhongguo Gongchandang Diyici Daibiao Dahui Qianhou Ziliao Xuanbina* [Before and After the First National Congress: Elected Documents Before and After the First National Congress of the Communist Party of China] (Beijing: Renmin Chubanshe, 1980), vol. 2, 78; Bao Huiseng, *Bao Huiseng Huiyi Lu* [Memoirs of Bao Huiseng] (Beijing: Renmin Chubanshe, 1983), 15.

122. Zhang Guotao, *Wo De Huiyi* [My Memory] (Beijing: Dongfang Chubanshe, 2004), vol. 1, 222; Bao Huiseng, *Bao Huiseng Huiyi Lu* [Memoirs of Bao Huiseng] (Beijing: Renmin Chubanshe, 1983), 369; Zhongguo Shehui Jexueyuan Xiandaishi Yanjiushi, Zhongguo Geming Bowuguan Dangshi Yanjiushi (eds.), *Yi Da Qian Hou-Zhongguo Gongchandang Diyici Daibiao Dahui Qianhou Ziliao Xuanbina* [Before and After the First National Congress: Elected Documents Before and After the First National Congress of the Communist Party of China] (Beijing: Renmin Chubanshe, 1980), vol. 2, 76.

123. Zhang Guotao, *Wo De Huiyi* [My Memory] (Beijing: Dongfang Chubanshe, 2004), vol. 1, 328-329.

124. Zheng Chaoling, Zheng Chaoling Huiyi Lu [Memoire of Zheng Chaoling] (Beijing: Dongfang Chubanshe, 2004), vol. 1, at 217.

125. Zhongguo Shehui Jexueyuan Xiandaishi Yanjiushi, Zhongguo Geming Bowuguan Dangshi Yanjiushi (eds.), *Yi Da Qian Hou-Zhongguo Gongchandang Diyici Daibiao Dahui Qianhou Ziliao Xuanbina* [Before and After the First National Congress: Elected Documents Before and After the First National Congress of the Communist Party of China] (Beijing: Renmin Chubanshe, 1980), vol. 2, 54.

126. Zhang Guotao, *Wo De Huiyi* [My Memory] (Beijing: Dongfang Chubanshe, 2004), vol. 1, 303-304, 371.

127. Zhang Guotao, *Wo De Huiyi* [My Memory] (Beijing: Dongfang Chubanshe, 2004), vol. 1, 328-329.

128. Zhonggong Zhongyang Dangshi Yanjiushi Diyi Yanjiubu (trans.), *Liangongbu Gongchan Guoji Yu Zhongguo Guomin Geming Yundong: 1920-1925* [The Soviets of the Communist Party (Bolsheviks), the Incomtern and Chinese National Revolution Movement 1920-1925] (Beijing: Beijing Tushuguan, 1997), 549; Zhonggong Zhongyang Dangshi Yanjiushi Diyi Yanjiubu (ed.), *Gongchan Guoji Liangongbu Yu Zhongguo Geming Wenxian Ziliao Xuanji: 1926-1927* [Selected documents concerning the Incomtern, the Soviets of the Communist Party (Bolsheviks) and Chinese Revolution 1926-1927] (Beijing: Beijing Tushuguan, 1998), vol. 2, 437.

129. Zhonggong Zhongyang Dangshi Yanjiushi Diyi Yanjiubu (trans.), *Liangongbu Gongchan Guoji Yu Zhongguo Guomin Geming Yundong: 1920-1925* [The Soviets of the Communist Party (Bolsheviks), the Incomtern and Chinese National Revolution Movement 1920-1925] (Beijing: Beijing Tushuguan, 1997), 612.

130. Zhonggong Zhongyang Dangshi Yanjiushi Diyi Yanjiubu (trans.), *Liangongbu Gongchan Guoji Yu Zhongguo Guomin Geming Yundong: 1920-1925* [The Soviets of the Communist Party (Bolsheviks), the Incomtern and Chinese National Revolution Movement 1920-1925] (Beijing: Beijing Tushuguan, 1997), 549.

131. Zhang Guotao, *Wo De Huiyi* [My Memory] (Beijing: Dongfang Chubanshe, 2004), vol. 1, 411.

132. Zhonggong Zhongyang Dangshi Yanjiushi Diyi Yanjiubu (trans.), *Liangongbu Gongchan Guoji Yu Zhongguo Guomin Geming Yundong: 1920-1925* [The Soviets of the Communist Party (Bolsheviks), the Incomtern and Chinese National Revolution Movement 1920-1925] (Beijing: Beijing Tushuguan, 1997), 612.

133. Ren Jianshu, *Chen Duxiu Dazhuan* [Biography of Chen Duxiu] (Shanghai: Shanghai Renmin Chubanshe, 2012), 261; Zhang Guotao, *Wo De Huiyi* [My Memory] (Beijing: Dongfang Chubanshe, 2004), vol. 1, 368.

134. Zhonggong Zhongyang Dangshi Yanjiushi Diyi Yanjiubu (ed.), *Gongchan Guoji Liangongbu Yu Zhongguo Geming Wenxian Ziliao Xuanji: 1926-1927* [Selected documents concerning the Incomtern, the Soviets of the Communist Party (Bolsheviks) and Chinese Revolution 1926-1927] (Beijing: Beijing Tushuguan, 1998), vol. 2, 564, 566.

135. Zhang Guotao, *Wo De Huiyi* [My Memory] (Beijing: Dongfang Chubanshe, 2004), vol. 12, 368, 415.

136. Zheng Chaoling, *Zheng Chaoling Huiyi Lu* [Memoire of Zheng Chaoling] (Beijing: Dongfang Chubanshe, 2004), vol. 2, 248.

137. Zhang Zhidan, *Shui Zhu Chengfu Zhongguo Gongchandang Disici Quanguo Daibiao Dhui* [Who Decided: The Fourth National Congress of the CCP] (Shijiazhuang: Hebei Renmin Chubanshe, 2012), 130-131.

138. Tang Baolin and Chen Tie jian, *Chen Duxiu Yu Qu Qiubai* [Chen Duxiu and Qu Qiubai] (Beijing:Tuanjie Chubanshe, 2008), 11-12.

139. Zheng Chaoling, Zheng Chaoling Huiyi Lu [Memoire of Zheng Chaoling] (Beijing: Dongfang Chubanshe, 2004), vol. 2, at 15-16.

140. Zheng Chaoling, *Zheng Chaoling Huiyi Lu* [Memoire of Zheng Chaoling] (Beijing: Dongfang Chubanshe, 2004), vol. 1, 18, 480; vol. 2, 428.

141. Zhang Guotao, *Wo De Huiyi* [My Memory] (Beijing: Dongfang Chubanshe, 2004), vol. 1, 371-372.

142. Zheng Chaoling, *Zheng Chaoling Huiyi Lu* [Memoire of Zheng Chaoling] (Beijing: Dongfang Chubanshe, 2004), vol. 1, 243-247.

143. Zhonggong Zhongyang Dangshi Yanjiushi Diyi Yanjiubu (trans.), *Liangongbu Gongchan Guoji Yu Zhongguo Guomin Geming Yundong: 1926-1927* [The Soviets of the Communist Party (Bolsheviks), the Incomtern and Chinese National Revolution Movement 1926-1927] (Beijing: Beijing Tushuguan, 1998), vol. 1, 564, 623-624.

144. Zheng Chaoling, *Zheng Chaoling Huiyi Lu* [Memoire of Zheng Chaoling] (Beijing: Dongfang Chubanshe, 2004), vol. 2, 19, 249-250, 481.

145. Zheng Chaoling, *Zheng Chaoling Huiyi Lu* [Memoire of Zheng Chaoling] (Beijing: Dongfang Chubanshe, 2004), vol. 2, 19, 249-250, 481.

146. Zhonggong Zhongyang Dangshi Yanjiushi Diyi Yanjiubu (ed.), *Gongchan Guoji Liangongbu Yu Zhongguo Geming Wenxian Ziliao Xuanji: 1926-1927* [Selected documents concerning the Incomtern, the Soviets of the Communist Party (Bolsheviks) and Chinese Revolution 1926-1927] (Beijing: Beijing Tushuguan, 1998), vol. 1, 421.

147. Zhonggong Zhongyang Dangshi Yanjiushi Diyi Yanjiubu (trans.), *Liangongbu Gongchan Guoji Yu Zhongguo Guomin Geming Yundong: 1926-1927* [The Soviets of the Communist Party (Bolsheviks), the Incomtern and Chinese National Revolution Movement 1926-1927] (Beijing: Beijing Tushuguan, 1998), vol. 2, 209.

148. Zheng Chaoling, *Zheng Chaoling Huiyi Lu* [Memoire of Zheng Chaoling] (Beijing: Dongfang Chubanshe, 2004), vol. 2, 253; Zhang Guotao, *Wo De Huiyi* [My Memory] (Beijing: Dongfang Chubanshe, 2004), vol. 1, 571.

149. Zheng Chaoling, *Zheng Chaoling Huiyi Lu* [Memoire of Zheng Chaoling] (Beijing: Dongfang Chubanshe, 2004), vol. 2, 89, 481-482.

150. Zhonggong Zhongyang Dangshi Yanjiushi Diyi Yanjiubu (trans.), *Liangongbu Gongchan Guoji Yu Zhongguo Guomin Geming Yundong: 1926-1927* [The Soviets of the Communist Party (Bolsheviks), the Incomtern and Chinese National Revolution Movement 1926-1927] (Beijing: Beijing Tushuguan, 1998), vol. 2, 271, 418; Zhonggong Zhongyang Dangshi Yanjiushi Diyi Yanjiubu (ed.), *Gongchan Guoji Liangongbu Yu Zhongguo Geming Wenxian Ziliao Xuanji: 1926-1927* [Selected documents concerning the Incomtern, the Soviets of the Communist Party (Bolsheviks) and Chinese Revolution 1926-1927] (Beijing: Beijing Tushuguan, 1998), vol. 2, 478.

151. Zheng Chaoling, *Zheng Chaoling Huiyi Lu* [Memoire of Zheng Chaoling] (Beijing: Dongfang Chubanshe, 2004), vol. 1, 253, 377; vol. 2, 482.

152. Tang Baolin and Chen Tie Jian, *Chen Duxiu Yu Qu Qiubai* [Chen Duxiu and Qu Qiubai] (Beijing:Tuanjie Chubanshe, 2008), 12-13.

153. Art. 22, the Constitution of the CCP, adopted by the CCP Politburo in 1927.

154. Art. 22, the Constitution of the CCP, adopted by the CCP Politburo in 1927.

155. Also see Wang Jianying, *Zhonggong Zhongy Jiguan Lishi Yanbian Kaoshi* [An Examination on the Evolution of the Central Institutions of the CCP] (Beijing: Zhonggong Dangshi Chubanshe, 2005), 1-7.

156. Zhonggong Zhongyang Dangshi Yanjiushi Diyi Yanjiubu (ed.), *Gongchan Guoji Liangongbu Yu Zhongguo Geming Wenxian Ziliao Xuanji: 1926-1927* [Selected documents concerning the Incomtern, the Soviets of the Communist Party (Bolsheviks) and Chinese Revolution 1926-1927] (Beijing: Beijing Tushuguan, 1998), vol. 2, 582.

157. Zhang Guotao, *Wo De Huiyi* [My Memory] (Beijing: Dongfang Chubanshe, 2004), vol. 1, 569.

158. For analysis on Moscow's inconsistent policies and impact on the CCP, see Li Ying, *Chen Duxiu Yu Gongchan Guoji* [Chen Duxiu and the Comintern] (Hunan: Renmin Chubanshe, 2005), 305-316.

159. Zhonggong Zhongyang Dangshi Yanjiushi Diyi Yanjiubu (ed.), *Gongchan Guoji Liangongbu Yu Zhongguo Geming Wenxian Ziliao Xuanji: 1926-1927* [Selected documents concerning the Incomtern, the Soviets of the Communist Party (Bolsheviks) and Chinese Revolution 1926-1927] (Beijing: Beijing Tushuguan, 1998), vol. 2, 564, 570; Zhang Guotao, *Wo De Huiyi* [My Memory] (Beijing: Dongfang Chubanshe, 2004), vol. 1, 570.

160. Zhang Guotao, *Wo De Huiyi* [My Memory] (Beijing: Dongfang Chubanshe, 2004), vol. 1, 572-573.

161. Zhonggong Zhongyang Dangshi Yanjiushi Diyi Yanjiubu (trans.), *Liangongbu Gongchan Guoji Yu Zhongguo Guomin Geming Yundong: 1926-1927* [The Soviets of the Communist Party (Bolsheviks), the Incomtern and Chinese National Revolution Movement 1926-1927] (Beijing: Beijing Tushuguan, 1998), vol. 2, 292, 301-302.

162. Zhonggong Zhongyang Dangshi Yanjiushi Diyi Yanjiubu (trans.), *Liangongbu Gongchan Guoji Yu Zhongguo Guomin Geming Yundong: 1926-1927* [The Soviets of the Communist Party (Bolsheviks), the Incomtern and Chinese National Revolution Movement 1926-1927] (Beijing: Beijing Tushuguan, 1998), vol. 2, 361.

163. Zhonggong Zhongyang Dangshi Yanjiushi Diyi Yanjiubu (trans.), *Liangongbu Gongchan Guoji Yu Zhongguo Guomin Geming Yundong: 1926-1927* [The Soviets of the Communist Party (Bolsheviks), the Incomtern and Chinese National Revolution Movement 1926-1927] (Beijing: Beijing Tushuguan, 1998), vol. 2, 322-323.

164. Zhonggong Zhongyang Dangshi Yanjiushi Diyi Yanjiubu (trans.), *Liangongbu Gongchan Guoji Yu Zhongguo Guomin Geming Yundong: 1926-1927* [The Soviets of the Communist Party (Bolsheviks), the Incomtern and Chinese National Revolution Movement 1926-1927] (Beijing: Beijing Tushuguan, 1998), vol. 2, 153, 302-303, 317.

165. Zheng Chaoling, *Zheng Chaoling Huiyi Lu* [Memoire of Zheng Chaoling] (Beijing: Dongfang Chubanshe, 2004), vol. 1, 483; Zhonggong Zhongyang Dangshi Yanjiushi Diyi

Yanjiubu (trans.), *Gongchan Guoji Liangongbu Yu Zhongguo Geming Wenxian Ziliao Xuanji: 1926-1927* [Selected documents concerning the Incomtern, the Soviets of the Communist Party (Bolsheviks) and Chinese Revolution 1926-1927] (Beijing: Beijing Tushuguan, 1998), vol. 1, 546.

166. Zhang Guotao, *Wo De Huiyi* [My Memory] (Beijing: Dongfang Chubanshe, 2004), vol. 1, 600.

167. Zhonggong Zhongyang Dangshi Yanjiushi Diyi Yanjiubu (ed.), *Gongchan Guoji Liangongbu Yu Zhongguo Geming Wenxian Ziliao Xuanji: 1926-1927* [Selected documents concerning the Incomtern, the Soviets of the Communist Party (Bolsheviks) and Chinese Revolution 1926-1927] (Beijing: Beijing Tushuguan, 1998), vol. 2, 354.

168. Ren Jianshu, *Chen Duxiu Dazhuan* [Biography of Chen Duxiu] (Shanghai: Shanghai Renmin Chubanshe, 2012), 349.

169. Zhang Guotao, *Wo De Huiyi* [My Memory] (Beijing: Dongfang Chubanshe, 2004), vol. 1, 607.

170. Li Weihan, *Huiyi Yu Yanjiu* [Memory and Study] (Beijing: Zhonggong Dangshi Ziliao Chubanshe, 1986), vol. 1, 158-159.

171. Li Weihan, *Huiyi Yu Yanjiu* [Memory and Study] (Beijing: Zhonggong Dangshi Ziliao Chubanshe, 1986), vol. 1, 165.

172. Wang Jianying, *Minzhu Geming Shiqi Zhonggong Lijie Zhongyang Lingdao Jiti Shuping* [Study on the Successive Central Leading Group of the CCP during the Period of Democratic Revolution] (Beijing: zhonggong dangshi chubanshe, 2007), vol. 1, 201.

173. Art. 40, the Constitution of the CCP, adopted by the CCP in 1928.

174. Li Ying, *Chen Duxiu Yu Gongchan Guoji* [Chen Duxiu and the Comintern] (Hunan: Renmin Chubanshe, 2005), 304.

175. Wang Jianying, *Minzhu Geming Shiqi Zhonggong Lijie Zhongyang Lingdao Jiti Shuping* [Study on the Successive Central Leading Group of the CCP during the Period of Democratic Revolution] (Beijing: zhonggong dangshi chubanshe, 2007), vol. 1, 235.

176. Zhang Guotao, *Wo De Huiyi* [My Memory] (Hongkong: Mingbao Yuekan Chubanshe, 1973), vol. 2, 792.

177. Zheng Chaoling, *Zheng Chaoling Huiyi Lu* [Memoire of Zheng Chaoling] (Beijing: Dongfang Chubanshe, 2004), vol. 1, 174.

178. Art. 10, the CPC's constitution adopted by its Second National Congress.

179. Zheng Chaoling, Zheng Chaoling Huiyi Lu [Memoire of Zheng Chaoling] (Beijing: Dongfang Chubanshe, 2004), vol. 1, at 489.

180. For a brief summarization, see Feng Jianhui, *Cong Chen Duxiu Dao Mao Zedong* [From Chen Duxiu to Mao Zedong] (Beijing: Zhongyang Wenxian Chubanshe, 1998), 79-80.

181. Zheng Chaoling, *Zheng Chaoling Huiyi Lu* [Memoire of Zheng Chaoling] (Beijing: Dongfang Chubanshe, 2004), vol. 1, 380, 489; vol. 2, 93.

182. Li Weihan, *Huiyi Yu Yanjiu* [Memory and Study] (Beijing: Zhonggong Dangshi Ziliao Chubanshe, 1986), vol. 1, 303-304.

183. Zheng Chaoling, *Zheng Chaoling Huiyi Lu* [Memoire of Zheng Chaoling] (Beijing: Dongfang Chubanshe, 2004), vol. 2, 293-294.

184. Wang Jianying, *Minzhu Geming Shiqi Zhonggong Lijie Zhongyang Lingdao Jiti Shuping* [Study on the Successive Central Leading Group of the CCP during the Period of Democratic Revolution] (Beijing: zhonggong dangshi chubanshe, 2007), vol. 1, 309-310.

185. Feng Jianhui, *Cong Chen Duxiu Dao Mao Zedong* [From Chen Duxiu to Mao Zedong] (Beijing: Zhongyang Wenxian Chubanshe, 1998), 74.

186. Zhang Guotao, *Wo De Huiyi* [My Memory] (Beijing: Dongfang Chubanshe, 2004), vol. 2, 328-329.

187. Wang Jianying, *Minzhu Geming Shiqi Zhonggong Lijie Zhongyang Lingdao Jiti Shuping* [Study on the Successive Central Leading Group of the CCP during the Period of Democratic Revolution] (Beijing: zhonggong dangshi chubanshe, 2007), vol. 1, 411-412.

Chapter Three

Chairman Mao of the China Soviet Republic

THE SOVIET-STYLE GOVERNMENT

When allying with the KMT, the CCP had not sought to set up the Soviet government in China.[1] But when their alliance broke, and facing the brutal killing by the KMT forces, the CCP gradually changed its policy and strove to establish a Soviet government.[2] Meanwhile, Moscow also changed its opposition and supported the CCP's new goal.[3] Thus, under the direction of Moscow,[4] the CCP took chances that the KMT was tied in wars with other Chinese warlords, and managed to set up a dozen Soviet areas by arms.[5] Then in May of 1930, the CCP initiated a "Conference of Delegates from the Various Soviet Areas of All China" in Shanghai, announcing to convene the First Soviet Congress and establish the Provisional Central Government of the China Soviet Republic (CRS).[6]

As the CCP failed to establish this government in big cities, like Wuhan, Changsha, or Nanchang,[7] the famous Soviet area set up by Mao Zedong and Zhu De in Jiangxi province was finally chosen as the place where the congress was held,[8] and designated as the Central Soviet Area. To take charge of the preparatory works, the CCP also set up a Central Bureau[9] and named Mao Zedong as the deputy secretary. On December 7, 1931, the long-delayed First Soviet Congress was convened there,[10] and the CRS Provisional Government was finally established.[11]

How was such a government organized? Before the commencement of the First Soviet Congress, Moscow and the CCP had written several law drafts for this new Provisional Government, including two different constitutional drafts, that is, "the Fundamental Law (Constitution) Draft of the China Soviet Republic" (Zhonghua Suweiai Gongheguo Guojia Genbenfa [Xianfa]

Caoan) and "the Constitutional Draft of the China Soviet Republic" (Zhonghua Suweiai Gongheguo Xianfa Caoan),[12] but somehow they had not been adopted by the First Soviet Congress.[13] Instead, a "seventeen constitutional principles" was telegrammed to the Congress by the Politburo of the CCP and Eastern Department of the Comintern from Shanghai,[14] and the congress set up a constitutional committee, which included a member who had studied and practiced law in the former Soviet Union,[15] referred to as the Russian constitution, and drafted a "Basic Constitutional Program."[16]

According to the Basic Constitutional Program passed by the congress:[17]

> Supreme power in the Chinese Soviet Republic shall belong to the all-Chinese Congress of Soviets of Workers', Peasants', and Soldiers' Deputies; in the interval between congresses the highest organ of power shall be the all-Chinese Central Executive Committee of soviets; attached to the Central Executive Committee shall be organized the Council of People's Commissars, which shall conduct all current administrative affairs and issue laws, decrets, and decrees.[18]

This means that the CSR government had a three-level structure, in which the Congress was at the top, the CEC in the middle and the Council of People's Commissars at the bottom. Not only these names were translated from Russian, but also their functions were the same as those in the Russian constitution. Clearly it was a Russian duplicate.

CHAIRMAN MAO OF THE CHINA SOVIET REPUBLIC

Moscow's Interest in Mao Zedong

Regarding how the CEC and Council of People's Commissars organized, neither the Basic Constitutional Program provided, nor the First Soviet Congress made, any relevant laws. But the absence of law could not delay the government's formation. Sixty-three people were proposed by the presidium of the First Soviet Congress and elected by the congress by hand voting as the CEC members.[19] After the congress, the CEC held the first meeting on the 27th, which not only formed the Council of People's Commissars, but also elected Mao Zedong as the chairman and Xiang Ying and Zhang Guotao as vice-chairmen for both the CEC and the Council of People's Commissar.[20] In addition, the CEC had also decided that a Central Revolutionary Military Commission set up under the Council of People's Commissars and Zhu De act as the chairman two days before the first meeting.[21]

Why was it Mao Zedong, not the CCP chairman Xiang Zhongfa, that was chosen as the CRS chairman? As matter of fact, prior to the First Soviet Congress, Moscow and the CCP had already decided not only those CEC members,[22] but also Mao Zedong to be the chairman. On February 20, 1931, the CCP Politburo held a meeting in Shanghai to discuss the CRS organization and candidates for government positions. Different people had been proposed for the CRS chairman, and two selection standards had set, requiring the candidate should have a national fame and work in the Soviet areas. In the end, Mao Zedong was considered to meet these two criteria as the candidate for the CEC chairman. This choice was further approved by Moscow,[23] who had already noticed Mao Zedong's military success in the Central Soviet Area and thought highly of him.[24] Later, Mao Zedong was further nominated by the CCP as the chairman of the Council of People's Commissars.[25]

Chairman Mao in Command

Before the First Soviet Congress, Mao Zedong had been given various titles according to his positions within the CCP, such as "Mao Weiyuan" (Commissioner Mao), or "Mao Shizhang" (Divisional Commander Mao).[26] Now as the double chairmen, Mao Zedong became known as "Chairman Mao,"[27] despite that he had been criticized for commanding like the head of a family.[28]

What power and function did he have as the double chairmen? According to the Constitutional Draft that had been written based on the constitution of the USSR made in 1924, the CEC should elect a presidium with a chairman. In that case, the chairman was supposed to work within this presidium as one of its members. But while the Constitutional Draft had not been adopted by the First Soviet Congress, neither the Basic Constitutional Program made provisions to the CEC presidium or to its chairman, nor organic law was made for the Central Provisional Government. Then the CEC chairman could be understood as an individual office operating independently on behalf of the CEC when the latter did not convene. Besides, as Mao Zedong concurrently took the chairmanship of the Council of People's Commissars, he could be a head of government with real power in policy making and executing of both civil and military affairs.

In fact, such a personal chairman was not exceptional in the CRS government. It can also be found at the most basic level of the CRS government, that is, the town Soviet. According to the Organic Law on Local Soviet Government promulgated by the CEC, local governments did not have the Council of People's Commissars. Instead, a chairman should be elected by each of the various levels of soviets, including the town, city, district, county, and province.[29] Whereas other local levels of chairmen were supposed to work within a presidium formed by the chairman and one or two vice-chairmen,[30] the town chairman worked alone when the town Soviet closed, because neither executive committee nor the presidium had been provided for the town Soviet by the organic law[31] and the town Soviet could only elect a chairman who had to work independently to call the meeting of the town Soviet once in ten days, to supervise the execution of decisions made by the town Soviet, and to handle daily business.[32] If the town was large in size, the town Soviet was permitted to have a vice-chairman,[33] and the chairman had to work together with the vice-chairman who had to co-sign the governmental documents together with the chairman.[34] But the vice-chairman could not take the place of the chairman when the latter was absent. Instead, a deputy chairman had to be elected to exercise the power and function on behalf of the chairman.[35]

"Chinese Kalinin"

However, Chairman Mao did not take much administration after election. Instead, he spent most of his time on the most crucial military affairs, leading the Red Army to defend against attacks from the KMT troops, until Zhou Enlai arrived at the Central Soviet Area about two months after the First Soviet Congress. Meeting opposition from Mao Zedong as the deputy secretary, the CCP appointed Zhou Enlai as the secretary of the Central Bureau to strengthen the implementation of its policy in the Central Soviet Area to protect the former Soviet Union by attacking major Chinese cities. Being replaced by Zhou Enlai, Mao Zedong started to lose control of the Central Bureau and the military. Mao Zedong was forced to leave in the name of sickness. Although he was invited back to command in the capacity of the CSR chairman when the Red Army was defeated, his military command did not last long as the CCPCC tightened its control over the Central Bureau. Mao Zedong's military command in the capacity of the CSR chairman was deprived and he had to retain his military leadership as the political commissar of the Red Army. In the end, he was stripped of his command over the Red Army completely in the Ningdu meeting held in October 1932.[36] He had to take sick leave once again.[37]

His retirement was not ended until after the CCPCC retreated from Shanghai and arrived at the Central Soviet Area in January 1933. As he had still been the dual government chairmen,[38] he was deployed by the CCPCC to deal with the governmental work,[39] which had previously been completed by Xiang Ying,[40] one of the two vice-chairmen during his absence. The other vice-chairman, Zhang Guotao, never came to the Central Soviet Area[41] in spite that his name continued to appear in the official documents as a co-signer together with his other two colleagues.

Once in control, the CCPCC also took actions of sovietization. The CRS governmental organization was further restructured toward Moscow, starting at the local levels. In December 1933, a new Organic Law on Local Soviet

Government was promulgated, which not only eliminated the exception by requiring the presidium elected for all the town soviets,[42] either large or small in size, but also made the stipulation on the number of members of presidiums at all local soviets,[43] minimally from five people at the town level up to thirteen people at the province, which had not been clearly provided by the previous Organic Law.

Two months later, the Second Soviet Congress convened in January 1934. An Organic Law was adopted for the Central Government, in which a presidium with no more than twenty-five members including one chairman and two to four vice-chairmen[44] was installed for the CEC to serve as the supreme organ when the CEC was not in session.[45] It was also a duplicate of its Russian model in 1930s based on the 1924 constitution.[46] So far, the presidium was set at all levels of the government as a standing organ when relevant executive committees were not in session. As a result, the chairmen at various levels were confined to a presidium member.

Although Mao Zedong was decided to serve as the CEC chairman for a second term by the Second Soviet Congress, he also became a member of the newly introduced CEC presidium at the same time. Being limited by the presidium, he enjoyed no more independence at the policy making. For the worse, well before the Second Soviet Congress, the CCP had replaced him with Zhang Wentian as the chairman of the Council of People's Commissars, to which the Second Soviet Congress only gave the postmortem official endorsement. With the new chairman in charge, the Council of People's Commissars soon changed Mao Zedong's policies that had been against the will of the CCPCC.

As a result, after being stripped of leading positions in the CCP, military, and the government one by one, Mao Zedong was only left with the CEC chairman and regarded as the Chinese counterpart of Mikhail Kalinin[47] who served as the figurehead of state of the USSR in the capacity of the chairman of the CEC presidium. Even so, the CCPCC had intended to send him and Zhou Enlai to Moscow to retire on sick leave.[48] He was so ignored that he could have not been allowed by the CCPCC to join the Long March when the CCPCC decided to retreat from the Central Soviet Area, if not for his nominal title of the chairman of the China Soviet Republic.[49]

MAO ZEDONG'S SUCCESSION TO THE CCP CHAIRMAN

Succession Rivals to Mao Zedong

During the Long March, survival was critical, and successful military actions became the first priority for the CCP. Again Mao Zedong's unrivalled and romantic military capacity was recognized, for which he gradually revived in spite of all those unpleasant ups and downs he endured.[50] Well after the Long

March started, he entered an alliance with Zhang Wentian and Wang Jiaxiang.[51] After consulting Mao Zedong, Wang Jiaxiang proposed to convene the Politburo and gained support of Zhang Wentian, Zhou Enlai, and Zhu De.[52] To be prepared, Mao Zedong specially discussed with the other two and wrote a draft. Actions were also taken to exclude Otto Braun, the German consultant deployed by the Comintern, from military direction the night before the meeting.[53] In the enlarged Politburo meeting held in January 1935, now widely heralded as "Zunyi Meeting," this three-member group fired long-time attacks on the military direction of the official three members, that is, Bo Gu, the nominal leader of the CCP, Otto Braun, and Zhou Enlai, mainly targeting Bo Gu. Mao Zedong's speech won most attendants. Zhou Enlai had to strongly recommend him to lead the military.[54]

It became clear that the leadership had to change. The Politburo promoted Mao Zedong to the PSC, ordered the PSC to make a new division of work among its members, absolved the command of those three people, and designated Zhou Enlai as the one to make the final decision on military affairs on behalf of the CCP.[55] After this round of reorganization, the military command within the PSC was transferred from Bo Gu, then the nominal leader of the CCP, to Zhou Enlai.[56]

The division of work within the PSC was not realized until about half a month later. In the Zunyi meeting, most participants intended Zhang Wentian to replace Bo Gu as the one taking overall responsibility for the CCP, but Zhang Wentian refused.[57] As a result, Bo Gu formally remained as the nominal head, but could not command and convene the PSC. Absence of leadership caused a delay in military action and the PSC had to be convened on February 5.[58] Zhang Wentian proposed Mao Zedong, but Mao Zedong smartly rejected and insisted Zhang Wentian to take the place.[59] Then Mao Zedong was specified to assist Zhou Enlai in military work.[60] About two months later, Mao Zedong further proposed, and was accepted, that the military direction should be concentrated into the hands of three people, namely, Zhou Enlai, Wang Jiaxiang, and himself.[61] Thus for the first time, the CCP's supreme leadership peacefully changed hands without involving Moscow, in which Mao Zedong entered the CCP's highest leading clique and regained his control over the military.

The delegation to Zhou Enlai indicated that the military affairs demanded a more specialized and efficient direction by a capable person than the collective leadership in a critical time of life or death like the Long March. But it also had a risk that this individual could destroy the collective leadership if he abused his military power, which soon became a reality.

Under direction of Mao Zedong, the CCP successfully got rid of KMT troops and joined with another Red Army led by Zhang Guotao, then a Politburo member. Competition started from the moment of the ceremonial handshake between the two military commanders. As his army had more soldiers, was better equipped, and hence was more powerful than that led by the PSC,[62] Zhang Guotao requested the position of the CCP's military chairman and full delegation of military execution by the Politburo by mouth of his man.[63] Surely it was a challenge to Mao Zedong. For the first time, the military was involved in the CCP's highest succession. Zhang Wentian intended to vacate his nominal GS to Zhang Guotao, but was prevented by Mao Zedong.[64] As a compromise, the PSC decided that Zhang Guotao should take the place of Zhou Enlai as the army's General Political Commissar and the final decision maker.[65] But this did not end the competition as Mao Zedong remained his control on the military as the CCP's military chairman. Zhang Guotao was unable to take command.[66] A choice had to be made between them.

On one hand, Zhang Guotao requested to enlarge the central organization by including more people.[67] Obviously he wanted to dilute Mao Zedong's influence by sending more of his men to the central organization, and at best, have himself elevated to the PSC. But his attempt failed. The PSC meeting held on August 19 not only made the decision in favor of Mao Zedong as the military commander, but also adopted Mao Zedong's suggestion that the PSC should hold meetings once a week so as to exert its function fully.[68] By meeting more frequently, the PSC, and eventually Mao Zedong, could take a firmer grip on the army. Unsatisfied, Zhang Guotao ordered his men to "launch inner-party struggle."[69]

Inner-party struggle was nothing new to Mao Zedong. When Chen Duxiu took charge, it had been mild, as the most severe punishment to dissenters was expulsion. But with more and more members returning from Moscow and the worsening situation, bloody purge was also introduced to the CCP. Luckily, Mao Zedong was alerted in advance[70] and persuaded other CCP leaders to run away with him.[71] As a counter-measure, Zhang Guotao established his own "Central Committee" and made himself the chairman.[72] The split did not end until Moscow intervened.[73] Mao Zedong survived the first challenge.

But another challenge came soon after the CCP settled down in Yanan, which was from Wang Ming. After the death of CCP Chairman Xiang Zhongfa, Wang Ming had controlled the CCP in Shanghai for a short period of time, and relieved the leadership to Bo Gu when he went to Moscow. Now Moscow wanted the increasingly independent CCP to ally with the KMT for its own interest. To press the CCP to better comply with this policy, Moscow sent Wang Ming back to China in December 1935.[74] Although pre-warned by Moscow to show respect to Mao Zedong and not to compete for the GS,[75] Wang Ming took the strategy of Zhang Guotao, requesting to enlarge the Politburo and showing an interest in replacing Zhang Wentian.[76]

Concession was made. On one hand, the PSC was expanded to nine members to include Wang Ming and two other people who also returned from Moscow. On the other hand, the principle of collective decision making was further enforced. Zhang Wentian was no longer the GS,[77] and a Central Secretariat of five members was produced out of the PSC to serve as the GS.[78] Thus the CCP's central organs were divided into five levels from up down, that is, the Central Secretariat, PSC, Politburo, Central Committee, and National Congress.[79] As the rivalry continued, the flattened PSC soon split into two power centers, Yan'an, headed by Mao Zedong as the one, whereas the other being Wuhan, where Wang Ming resided.[80]

Ren Bishi was sent to Moscow for arbitration.[81] Again Moscow settled for Mao Zedong, whose message was conveyed by Wang Jiangxiang[82] in the sixth plenary meeting of the CCP's sixth Central Committee in September 1938:

> Zhu De and Mao Zedong led the army and executed the new policy. The Comintern thinks the CCP's political policy is correct. The CCP has truly applied the Marxism and Leninism to complicated and difficult situations. Problems should be solved within the leading organ headed by Mao Zedong.[83]

In the same meeting Mao Zedong delivered the political report on behalf of the CCP, suggesting that he had finally won the majority support within the CCP.[84]

Mao Zedong Became the CCP Chairman

When the anti-Japanese war came to the most difficult time in 1942, Mao Zedong took the chance to consolidate his position within the center of power. The principle of "centralized leadership" ("Yiyuanhua Lingdao," in Chinese) was implemented, which not only required the concentration of decision-making powers on all affairs, including party, military, and civil affairs into the hands of the CCP's party committees at local levels,[85] but also streamlined the organization of local party committees to "a leading core" ("Lingdao hexin," in Chinese) of three people" according to Stalin's indoctrination.[86] Among these three people, the one who was more capable should be the center of such a leading core.[87]

The centralization reached its climax several months later. The Politburo decided in March 1943 that all local affairs be under the charge of five Politburo members who were in turn accountable to the Central Secretariat,[88] and all working organs at the central level be restructured into the propaganda and organization committees which were also led by the Central Secretariat.[89] As a result, the Central Secretariat commanded all daily work from local to central.

As for the Central Secretariat, it was provided with the power to decide all daily issues according to policies set by the Politburo when the Politburo did not convene.[90] Over the years, the role of the Central Secretariat had been in gradual rise so as to outlive the PSC in the sixth plenary meeting in 1938.[91] But at that time, it had been regarded more as an execution arm of the Central Committee and the Politburo and lacked full autonomy in daily work as it could not "make new decisions" unless "important emergency occurred and the Politburo could not convene," which were subject to ex post approval of such "new decisions" by the Politburo,[92] and when it convened, the Politburo members staying at the same place should attend.[93] When Liu Shaoqi arrived at Yan'an at the request of Mao Zedong in early 1943, he proposed that the Secretariat should be given the power to take charge of daily issues.[94] He was suggesting more decision-making power for the Secretariat and had good reason. As the Politburo members scattered in different places, it was difficult for them to gather together and convene meetings, especially in a critical time of war and when the CCP was developing rapidly as a legal political party. His proposal was accepted by the Politburo, and the Secretariat was finally elevated to a standing committee.

Regarding the organization of the Secretariat, the Politburo also decided that:

> the Secretariat be formed by Mao Zedong, Liu Shaoqi and Ren Bishi; Mao Zedong is the chairman of the Secretariat, who can convene the meeting of the secretariat at any time and have the power of 'last say' ("Zuihuo jueding quan," in Chinese) over issues discussed in the meeting.[95]

This means that the Central Secretariat was under the sole command of Mao Zedong. As the Central Secretariat also set the agenda for the Politburo and Mao Zedong was "agreed ("Tuiding," in Chinese) by the Politburo as its chairman,"[96] Mao Zedong could also exert great influence on the Politburo. Thus with the power of last say, Mao Zedong effectively became the paramount leader of the CCP to whom the power was ultimately centralized.[97]

The power of last say was nothing new to the CCP. Its major opponent the KMT had done this before. For the sake of its paramount leader Sun Zhongshan, "the father of the ROC," the KMT constitution had specially made provisions in this regard. In other words, while the Soviet-style party-government replaced the American model, the Russian model had once been modified by both the KMT and the CCP for their paramount leaders by giving them the power of last say.

"The Power of Last Say"

But clearly such a provision of the power of last say had violated the Russian principle of democratic centralism.[98] Counter measures had to be taken. In the seventh plenary meeting of the sixth CCPCC convened a year later, the Politburo decision was changed. A presidium was set up in place of both the Politburo and the Central Secretariat as the new leading organ of the CCP.

The presidium was larger, with five people, including not only the old three people of the Secretariat, that is, Mao Zedong, Liu Shaoqi, and Ren Bishi, but also two new members, that is, Zhou Enlai and Zhu De. Although Mao Zedong was decided as not only the chairman of this presidium, but also the chairman of the Central Committee,[99] the power of last say was not mentioned any more.

These changes were further endorsed in the new party constitution adopted by the CCP's Seventh National Congress in 1945, which provided that the Politburo, the Central Secretariat, and a chairman shall be elected by the Central Committee in plenary session, and the chairman would concurrently serve as the chairman of the Central Committee, the Politburo, and the Central Secretariat to "guide and supervise" ("Zhidao Jiandu," in Chinese) all working organs set up by the Central Committee at the central level.[100] Although the CCP's Sixth National Congress convened in Moscow in 1928 had produced a chairman, the chairman had not been mentioned in the party constitution. Now for the first time the chairman was written in the party constitution in the CCP's history. Undoubtedly, the chairman could be no one other than Mao Zedong.

Compared with the 1943 Politburo decision, the newly made party constitution followed the suit of the seventh plenary meeting of the sixth CCPCC and did not mention the power of last say. It would be embarrassing to put it down in the party constitution for a party claiming collective leadership. This literally meant that Mao Zedong's power of last say had only lasted for about fourteen months,[101] and he could not dictate the Central Secretariat any more. Besides, as the new Central Secretariat was formed by those same five people of the presidium, Mao Zedong could weigh less in its decision making. Thus seemingly Mao Zedong's paramount leadership could have been curtailed in the Seventh National Congress.

However, words should not be taken for granted. Although losing command of the Central Secretariat, Mao Zedong did not lose control of daily operation of the CCP because he was provided by the party constitution to guide and supervise the central working organs with equal status to the Central Committee and Central Secretariat. In spite that "to guide and supervise" does not equal to "the power of last say" by words, the chairman did not have to deal with the working organs through the Central Secretariat. Instead, he could give guidance and supervision directly on his own.

Theoretically, any personal guidance and supervision made by Mao Zedong on daily work should be subject to decisions of the Central Committee, the Politburo, and the Central Secretariat. But like previous party documents, the new party constitution provided neither on the relationship of the chairman to those three organs, nor how often the Politburo and Central Secretariat should convene to perform their leading functions in the half year between two Central Committee meetings. Without rigid requirements, the scattered CCP decision makers could meet less frequently, which could in turn allow Mao Zedong more room to exert his discretion when guiding and supervising those working organs.

More importantly, Mao Zedong gained more authority implied in the party constitution, except being more prominent in daily operations. After the Rectification Movement, his thoughts had become "the only correct application of Marxism and Leninism in China" and had been endorsed by the new party constitution as the guidance for all work,[102] which gave him an ideological advantage over his colleagues. By such an ideological supremacy, he was not only made equal with Stalin in China, but also given a weapon that could be used against any policy dissenters by branding them as "ideologically wrong." He became the final judge of any policy disputes.

Besides, as the 1943 Politburo decision had accorded Mao Zedong with the power of last say by way of "agreement" among its members, there would be no reason why such a way of informal compromise not be followed by the new Politburo and Central Secretariat under such a circumstance in which people at Yan'an seemed to lose their backbone when Chairman Mao was away and could not feel reassured until he returned.[103] As long as Mao Zedong continued to prove himself as "the correct application of Marxism and Leninism in China," why should his leadership not be followed?

As matter of fact, the idea of "the power of last say" was not exceptional even after the Japanese were defeated. During the civil war between the CCP and KMT, such a power had been practiced by some governments set up in areas taken by the CCP troops from the KMT. To achieve efficiency, chairmen of those governments were given the power of last say.[104] For example, in the government of Shang-Gan-Ning Border Area, the chairman of the Administrative Council had the power of last say over issues discussed in the council.[105] In the Provisional Government of Central Area, the Administrative Council chairman also had the power.[106]

Therefore, Mao Zedong's power of last say could have been partially incorporated into the party constitution and partially implied by unspoken political compromise among the CCP senior leaders. Mao Zedong personally liked such a dominant, yet undefined chairmanship. As long as his absolute authority had been effectively established,[107] he would not have to be troubled with the formality. After all, this was only the first step forward in his "Long March" toward the People's Republic of China. As his interpreter recalled:

> Once when we chat, he (Chairman Mao) told me: 'they call me as Chairman Mao. But do they call me as the chairman of the Central Military Committee, or the chairman of the CCPCC? Nevertheless, my chairmanship of the Central Military Committee has been decided.' it was before the seventh party congress that he told me this when he had been designated as the chairman of the

> central military committee, but the party had not installed the chairman. He showed his preference to the title of chairman. He explained: 'the chairman is the main figure, the host ("Zhurengong," in Chinese).' The seventh party congress decided that he was the party chairman.[108]

To summarize, the experience of Chairman Mao in the China Soviet Republic suggests that the CEC chairmanship was legally provided as an independent government office taken by an individual, but completely subject to the CCP and ultimately to Moscow from afar, not only in terms of his policies, but also of his official functions and performances, which could be practically reduced to a title of a figurehead if without a firm leading position within the CCP and over the administration as well as the army. Law was bypassed by politics.

NOTES

1. Wang Yongxiang, *Zhongguo Xiandai Xianzheng Yundong Shi* [History of Constitutional Movement in Modern China] (Beijing: Renmin Chubanshe, 1996), 187; Jiang Boying and Guo Ruoping, *Zhongsu Suqu Zhengquan Jianshe Shi* [The History of Government Construction of the Central Soviet Region] (Fujian: Xiamen Daxue Chubanshe, 1999), 16; Zeng Weidong and Zeng Wencai (eds.), *Zhonghua Suweiai Gongheguo Shenpan Shi* [History of Adjudication of the China Soviet Republic] (Beijing: Renmin Fayuan Chubanshe, 2004), 2-3; Xie Yibiao, *Zhonghua Suweiai Gongheguo Xianzheng Yanjiu* [Study on the Constitutionalism of the China Soviet Republic] (Beijing: Zhongyang Wenxian Chubanshe, 2002), 5, 9.
2. See Han Damei, *Xin Minzhu Zhuyi Xianzheng Yanjiu* [Study on Constitutionalism of New Decmocracy] (Beijing: Renmin Chubanshe, 2005), 29-44; Wang Yongxiang, *Zhongguo Xiandai Xianzheng Yundong Shi* [History of Constitutional Movement in Modern China] (Beijing: Renmin Chubanshe, 1996), 187-190; Jiang Boying and Guo Ruoping, *Zhongsu Suqu Zhengquan Jianshe Shi* [The History of Government Construction of the Central Soviet Region] (Fujian: Xiamen Daxue Chubanshe, 1999), 15-22; Xie Yibiao, *Zhonghua Suweiai Gongheguo Xianzheng Yanjiu* [Study on the Constitutionalism of the China Soviet Republic] (Beijing: Zhongyang Wenxian Chubanshe, 2002), 26.
3. For the change of Moscow's policy in this regard, see Jiang Boying and Guo Ruoping, *Zhongsu Suqu Zhengquan Jianshe Shi* [The History of Government Construction of the Central Soviet Region] (Fujian: Xiamen Daxue Chubanshe, 1999), 11-15.
4. For Moscow's support to the CCP's effort to establish the Soviet government, see Zeng Weidong and Zeng Wencai (eds.), *Zhonghua Suweiai Gongheguo Shenpan Shi* [History of Adjudication of the China Soviet Republic] (Beijing: Renmin Fayuan Chubanshe, 2004), 10-12.
5. For the establishment of various Soviet areas by the CCP, see Shu Long and Ling Buji (eds.), *Zhonghua Suweiai Gongheguo Shi* [History of the China Soviet Republic] (Jiangsu: Jiangsu Renmin Chubanshe, 1999), 17-47.
6. For the CCP's effort to establishment this national Soviet government, see Jiang Boying and Guo Ruoping, *Zhongsu Suqu Zhengquan Jianshe Shi* [The History of Government Construction of the Central Soviet Region] (Fujian: Xiamen Daxue Chubanshe, 1999), 170-177; Zeng Weidong and Zeng Wencai (eds.), *Zhonghua Suweiai Gongheguo Shenpan Shi* [History of Adjudication of the China Soviet Republic] (Beijing: Renmin Fayuan Chubanshe, 2004), 12-16; Shu Long and Ling Buji (eds.), *Zhonghua Suweiai Gongheguo Shi* [History of the China Soviet Republic] (Jiangsu: Jiangsu Renmin Chubanshe, 1999), 48-76.
7. See Shu Long and Ling Buji (eds.), *Zhonghua Suweiai Gongheguo Shi* [History of the China Soviet Republic] (Jiangsu: Jiangsu Renmin Chubanshe, 1999), 56-63.

8. See Shu Long and Ling Buji (eds.), *Zhonghua Suweiai Gongheguo Shi* [History of the China Soviet Republic] (Jiangsu: Jiangsu Renmin Chubanshe, 1999), 65.

9. See Shu Long and Ling Buji (eds.), *Zhonghua Suweiai Gongheguo Shi* [History of the China Soviet Republic] (Jiangsu: Jiangsu Renmin Chubanshe, 1999), 66.

10. For a brief account of the progress of the First Soviet Congress, see Jiang Boying and Guo Ruoping, *Zhongsu Suqu Zhengquan Jianshe Shi* [The History of Government Construction of the Central Soviet Region] (Fujian: Xiamen Daxue Chubanshe, 1999), 177-180; Shu Long and Ling Buji (eds.), *Zhonghua Suweiai Gongheguo Shi* [History of the China Soviet Republic] (Jiangsu: Jiangsu Renmin Chubanshe, 1999), 83-88; Zeng Weidong and Zeng Wencai (eds.), *Zhonghua Suweiai Gongheguo Shenpan Shi* [History of Adjudication of the China Soviet Republic] (Beijing: Renmin Fayuan Chubanshe, 2004), 12-16.

11. Zhonghua Suweiai Gongheguo Linshi Zhengfu Duiwai Xuanyan [Declaration of the Provisional Government of the China Soviet Republic (November 7, 1931)], in Zhongyang Dang'an Guan (ed.), *Zhonggong Zhongyang Wenjian Xuan* [Selection of the CCPCC Documents] (Beijing: Zhonggong Zhongyang Dangxiao Chubanshe, 1991), vol. 7, 802-803.

12. However, there is an opinion suggesting that a third constitutional draft had been made; see Xie Yibiao, *Zhonghua Suweiai Gongheguo Xianzheng Yanjiu* [Study on the Constitutionalism of the China Soviet Republic] (Beijing: Zhongyang Wenxian Chubanshe, 2002), 49; Yu Boliu and Ling Buji, *Zhongy Suqu Shi* [History of the Central Soviet Region] (Jiangxi: Jiangxi Renmin Chubanshe, 2001), 873-877. But such a draft has not appeared as yet.

13. There are three different opinions to explain why they had not been adopted by the First Soviet Congress. One opinion suggested that the constitutional draft of the China Soviet Republic had not been submitted to the First Soviet Congress; see Zhang Xipo and Han Yanlong (eds.), *Zhongguo Geming Fazhishi* [History of Chinese Revolutionary Legal Systems] (Beijing: Zhongguo Shehui Kexue Chubanshe, 2007), 28. The second idea held that it had been submitted, but not been accepted by the First Soviet Congress; see Zhang Jinfan (ed.), *Zhongguo Fazhi Shi* [Legal History of China] (Beijing: Gaodeng Jiaoyu Chubanshe, 2003), 367-368; Xie Yibiao, *Zhonghua Suweiai Gongheguo Xianzheng Yanjiu* [Study on the Constitutionalism of the China Soviet Republic] (Beijing: Zhongyang Wenxian Chubanshe, 2002), 47-49. The latter work also made a brief summarization on earlier accounts of these two opposing opinions; see Xie Yibiao, *Zhonghua Suweiai Gongheguo Xianzheng Yanjiu* [Study on the Constitutionalism of the China Soviet Republic] (Beijing: Zhongyang Wenxian Chubanshe, 2002), 46-47. However, a third opinion held that the constitutional drafts had not arrived at the central Soviet successfully at all; see Zhonggong Jiangxi Shengwei Dangshi Yanjiushi (ed.), *Renbishi Zai Jiangxi* [Ren Bishi in Jiangxi] (Jiangxi: Jiangxi Renmin Chubanshe, 2004), 43; Yu Boliu and Ling Buji, *Zhongyang Suqu Shi* [History of the Central Soviet Region] (Jiangxi: Jiangxi Renmin Chubanshe, 2001), 351-352.

14. See Xie Yibiao, *Zhonghua Suweiai Gongheguo Xianzheng Yanjiu* [Study on the Constitutionalism of the China Soviet Republic] (Beijing: Zhongyang Wenxian Chubanshe, 2002), 60-63.

15. Zhonggong Zhejiang Xinchang Xianwei Dangshi Bangongshi, *Liang Baitai* (Beijing: Dangdai Zhongguo Chubanshe, 1994), 14-18, 149-155; Yang Musheng, *Zhongyang Suqu Fazhi Jianshe* [Legal Construction of Central Soviet Region] (Beijing: Zhonggong Dangshi Chubanshe, 2000), 242-249.

16. Yu Boliu and Ling Buji, *Zhongyang Suqu Shi* [History of the Central Soviet Region] (Jiangxi: Jiangxi Renmin Chubanshe, 2001), 351-352.

17. For the Chinese version of the Basic Constitutional Program of the China Soviet Republic, see Han Yanlong and Chang Zhaoru (eds.), *Zhongguo Xin Minzhu Zhuyi Geming Shiqi Genjudi Fazhi Wenxian Xuanbian* [Selection of Legal Documents of the Revolutionary Bases During the Period of New Democratic Revolution of China] (Beijing: Zhongguo Shehui Kexue Chubanshe, 1981), vol. 1, 9. For its English translation, see W. E. Butler (ed.), *The Legal System of the Chinese Soviet Republic 1931-1934* (New York: Transnational Publishers, Inc., 1983), 123-125.

18. Zhonghua Suweiai Gongheguo Xianfa Dagang [The Basic Constitutional Program of the China Soviet Republic], Art. 3, in Han Yanlong and Chang Zhaoru (eds.), *Zhongguo Xin Minzhu Zhuyi Geming Shiqi Genjudi Fazhi Wenxian Xuanbian* [Selection of Legal Documents

of the Revolutionary Bases During the Period of New Democratic Revolution of China] (Beijing: Zhongguo Shehui Kexue Chubanshe, 1981), vol. 1, 9.

19. See Yu Boliu and Ling Buji, *Zhongyang Suqu Shi* [History of the Central Soviet Region] (Jiangxi: Jiangxi Renmin Chubanshe, 2001), 362.

20. See Zhonghua Suweiai Gongheguo Zhongyang Zhixing Weiyuanhui Bugao Diyihao [Notice of the Central Executive Committee of the China Soviet Republic (No. 1)], in Xiamen Daxue Falvxi and Fujian Sheng Dang'an Guan (eds.), *Zhonghua Suweiai Gongheguo Falv Wenjian Xuanbian* [Selection of Legal Documents of the China Soviet Republic] (Nanchang: Jiangxi Renmin Chubanshe, 1984), 201-202.

21. Yu Boliu and Ling Buji, *Zhongyang Suqu Shi* [History of the Central Soviet Region] (Jiangxi: Jiangxi Renmin Chubanshe, 2001), 295-298, 365-366. But this was not recorded in the first notice issued by the Central Executive Committee of the China Soviet Republic.

22. See Shu Long and Ling Buji (eds.), *Zhonghua Suweiai Gongheguo Shi* [History of the China Soviet Republic] (Jiangsu: Jiangsu Renmin Chubanshe, 1999), 74; Yu Boliu and Ling Buji, *Zhongyang Suqu Shi* [History of the Central Soviet Region] (Jiangxi: Jiangxi Renmin Chubanshe, 2001), 332.

23. See Yu Boliu and Ling Buji, *Zhongy Suqu Shi* [History of the Central Soviet Region] (Jiangxi: Jiangxi Renmin Chubanshe, 2001), 348; Zhonggong Jiangxi Shengwei Dangshi Yanjiushi (ed.), *Renbishi Zai Jiangxi* [Ren Bishi in Jiangxi] (Jiangxi: Jiangxi Renmin Chubanshe, 2004), 41.

24. About Moscow's appreciation of Mao Zedong, see Yang Kuisong, *Mao Zedong Yu Mosike De En En Yuan Yuan* [The Scores between Mao Zedong and Moscow] (Jiangxi: Jiangxi Renmin Chubanshe 2003), 19-20.

25. See Yu Boliu and Ling Buji, *Zhongy Suqu Shi* [History of the Central Soviet Region] (Jiangxi: Jiangxi Renmin Chubanshe, 2001), 348-349.

26. See Lu Lin and Chen Dejin (eds.), *Hongse Jiyi: Zhongguo Gongchandang Lishi Koushu Shilu (1921-1949)* [Red Memory: Oral History of the CCP (1921-1949)] (Shandong: Jinan Chubanshe, 2002), 91.

27. See Yu Boliu and Ling Buji, *Zhongy Suqu Shi* [History of the Central Soviet Region] (Jiangxi: Jiangxi Renmin Chubanshe, 2001), 363; Chen Yushu and Chen Lihua, *Kaiguo Qianye: Maozedong Zai Xibaipo De Fengyun Suiyue* [The Eve before the Founding of the Republic: Mao Zedong's Days and Nights at Xibaipo] (Beijing: Zhonggong Dangshi Chubanshe, 2003), 238; Huang Yunsheng, *Maozedong San Qi San Luo, Kaipi Zhongguo Geming Daolu De Jiannan Yu Quzhe* [Three Times Rise and Fall of Mao Zedong: Hardship and Tortuous to Explore the Road of Chinese Revolution] (Beijing: Zhongyang Wenxian Chubanshe, 2006), 232.

28. Gao Hua, *Hong Taiyang Shi Zenyang Shengqi De* [How did the Red Sun Rise Up] (Hong Kong: Chinese University Press, 2000), 7-9.

29. Suweiai Difang Zhengfu De Zanxing Zuzhi Tiaoli [Provisional Regulation on the Organization of Soviet Local Governments] (promulgated by the first meeting of the Central Executive Committee of the China Soviet Republic in November 1931), Art. 6, 19, 34.

30. Suweiai Difang Zhengfu De Zanxing Zuzhi Tiaoli [Provisional Regulation on the Organization of Soviet Local Governments] (promulgated by the first meeting of the Central Executive Committee of the China Soviet Republic in November 1931), Art. 19, 34. However, the Organic Law did not provide how many members a presidium should consist of. Besides, according to these two stipulations, the city Soviet had no executive committee, as provided for the district, county, and province soviets.

31. Suweiai Difang Zhengfu De Zanxing Zuzhi Tiaoli [Provisional Regulation on the Organization of Soviet Local Governments] (promulgated by the first meeting of the Central Executive Committee of the China Soviet Republic in November 1931), Art. 6.

32. Suweiai Difang Zhengfu De Zanxing Zuzhi Tiaoli [Provisional Regulation on the Organization of Soviet Local Governments] (promulgated by the first meeting of the Central Executive Committee of the China Soviet Republic in November 1931), Art. 16.

33. Suweiai Difang Zhengfu De Zanxing Zuzhi Tiaoli [Provisional Regulation on the Organization of Soviet Local Governments] (promulgated by the first meeting of the Central Executive Committee of the China Soviet Republic in November 1931), Art. 6.

34. Suweiai Difang Zhengfu De Zanxing Zuzhi Tiaoli [Provisional Regulation on the Organization of Soviet Local Governments] (promulgated by the first meeting of the Central Executive Committee of the China Soviet Republic in November 1931), Art. 69.

35. Suweiai Difang Zhengfu De Zanxing Zuzhi Tiaoli [Provisional Regulation on the Organization of Soviet Local Governments] (promulgated by the first meeting of the Central Executive Committee of the China Soviet Republic in November 1931), Art. 6.

36. See Yu Boliu and Ling Buji, *Zhongy Suqu Shi* [History of the Central Soviet Region] (Jiangxi: Jiangxi Renmin Chubanshe, 2001), 450-454.

37. For this part of history, see Jin Chongji, *Mao Zedong Zhuan: Shui Zhu Chengfu (1893-1937)* [Biography of Mao Zedong: Who Commanded the Rise and Fall (1893-1937)] (Hong Kong: Mingliu Chubanshe, 1997), 374-401.

38. See Li Weihan, *Huiyi Yu Yanjiu* [Memory and Study] (Beijing: Zhongyang Dangshi Ziliao Chubanshe, 1986), vol. 1, 338.

39. For Mao Zedong's performance of his administrative affairs, see Jin Chongji, *Mao Zedong Zhuan: Shui Zhu Chengfu (1893-1937)* [Biography of Mao Zedong: Who Commanded the Rise and Fall (1893-1937)] (Hong Kong: Mingliu Chubanshe, 1997), 401-429

40. See Yang Musheng, *Zhongyang Suqu Fazhi Jianshe* [Legal Construction of the Central Soviet Region] (Beijing: Zhonggong Dangshi Chubanshe, 2000), 228; Wang Fuyi, *Xiang Ying Zhuan* [Biography of Xiang Ying] (Beijing: Zhongong Dangshi Chubanshe, 2008), 124.

41. See Wang Fuyi, *Xiang Ying Zhuan* [Biography of Xiang Ying] (Beijing: Zhongong Dangshi Chubanshe, 2008), 124.

42. Zhonghua Suweiai Gongheguo Defang Suweiai Zanxing Zuzhi Fa (Caoan) [Provisional Organic Law on Local Soviet of the China Soviet Republic (Draft)] (made by the China Soviet Republic on December 12, 1933), Art. 34.

43. Zhonghua Suweiai Gongheguo Defang Suweiai Zanxing Zuzhi Fa (Caoan) [Provisional Organic Law on Local Soviet of the China Soviet Republic (Draft)] (made by the China Soviet Republic on December 12, 1933), Art. 11, 34, 60, 72, 85.

44. Zhonghua Suweiai Gongheguo Zhongyang Suweiai Zuzhi Fa [Organic Law on Central Soviet of the China Soviet Republic] (promulgated by the China Soviet Republic on February 17, 1934), Art. 15.

45. Zhonghua Suweiai Gongheguo Zhongyang Suweiai Zuzhi Fa [Organic Law on Central Soviet of the China Soviet Republic] (promulgated by the China Soviet Republic on February 17, 1934), Art. 17.

46. W. E. Butler (ed.), *The Legal System of the Chinese Soviet Republic 1931-1934* (New York: Transnational Publishers, Inc., 1983), 48, 50.

47. See Shu Long and Ling Buji (eds.), *Zhonghua Suweiai Gongheguo Shi* [History of the China Soviet Republic] (Jiangsu: Jiangsu Renmin Chubanshe, 1999), 128; Huang Yunsheng, *Maozedong San Qi San Luo, Kaipi Zhongguo Geming Daolu De Jiannan Yu Quzhe* [Three Times Rise and Fall of Mao Zedong: Hardship and Tortuous to Explore the Road of Chinese Revolution] (Beijing: Zhongyang Wenxian Chubanshe, 2006), 274; Li Weihan, *Huiyi Yu Yanjiu* [Memory and Study] (Beijing: Zhongyang Dangshi Ziliao Chubanshe, 1986), vol. 1, 338-339, 353.

48. Wu Liangping, "Wei Zhengli er Douzheng" [Fight for the Truth], in Huiyi Zhang Wentian Bianji Zu (ed.), *Huiyi Zhang Wentian* [Recall Zhang Wentian] (Hunan: Hunan Renmin Chubanshe, 1985), 55.

49. See Wu Xiuquan, "Wu Xiuquan Tongzhi Huiyilu" [Memoirs of Comrade Wu Xiuquan], *Zhonggong Dangshi Ziliao*, no. 1 (1982): 176.

50. Huang Yunsheng, *Maozedon San Qi San Luo, Kaipi Zhongguo Geming Daolu De Jiannan Yu Quzhe* [Three Times Rise and Fall of Mao Zedong: Hardship and Tortuous to Explore the Road of Chinese Revolution] (Beijing: Zhongyang Wenxian Chubanshe, 2006), 197.

51. Liu Ying, *Zai Lishi De Jiliu Zhong: Liu Ying Huiyilu* [In the Torrent of History: The Memoire of Liu Ying] (Beijing: Zhonggong Dangshi Chubanshe, 1992), 59.

52. Jin Chongji (ed.), *Zhou Enlai Zhuan* [Biography of Zhou Enlai] (Beijing: Zhongyang Wenxian Chubanshe, 1998), vol. 1, 461.

53. Zhou Enlai, "Dang De Lishi Jiaoxun" [Historical Lesson of the Party], in Zhonggong Zhongyang Wenxian Zhengji Weiyuan Hui (ed.), *Zunyi Huiyi Wenxian* [Documents Concerning Zunyi Meeting] (Beijing: renmin chubanshe, 1985), 66.

54. Jin Chongji (ed.), *Zhou Enlai Zhuan* [Biography of Zhou Enlai] (Beijing: Zhongyang Wenxian Chubanshe, 1998), vol. 1, 462.

55. See Wang Jianying, *Zhonggong Zhongy Jiguan Lishi Yanbian Kaoshi* [An Examination on the Evolution of the Central Institutions of the CCP] (Beijing: Zhonggong Dangshi Chubanshe, 2005), 296.

56. See Wang Jianying, *Zhonggong Zhongy Jiguan Lishi Yanbian Kaoshi* [An Examination on the Evolution of the Central Institutions of the CCP] (Beijing: Zhonggong Dangshi Chubanshe, 2005), 297.

57. Cheng Zhongyuan, *Zhang Wentian Zhuan* [Biography of Zhang Wentian] (Beijing: Dangdai Zhongguo Chubanshe, 2000), rev., 249-250.

58. Cheng Zhongyuan, *Zhang Wentian Zhuan* [Biography of Zhang Wentian] (Beijing: Dangdai Zhongguo Chubanshe, 2000), rev., 250-252.

59. Zhou Enlai, "Dang De Lishi Jiaoxun" [Historical Lesson of the Party], in Zhonggong Zhongyang Wenxian Zhengji Weiyuan Hui (ed.), *Zunyi Huiyi Wenxian* [Documents Concerning Zunyi Meeting] (Beijing: renmin chubanshe, 1985), 72.

60. Wang Jianying, *Zhonggong Zhongy Jiguan Lishi Yanbian Kaoshi* [An Examination on the Evolution of the Central Institutions of the CCP] (Beijing: Zhonggong Dangshi Chubanshe, 2005), 296.

61. Pang Xianzhi (ed.), *Mao Zedong Nianpu 1893-1949* [The Chronicle of Mao Zedong 1893-1949] (Beijing: Zhongyang Wenxian Chubanshe, 2002), vol. 1, 490.

62. Pang Xianzhi and Jin chongji (eds.), *Mao Zedong Zhuan* [Biography of Mao Zedong] (Beijing: Zhongyang Wenxian Chubanshe, 2011), 2nd ed., 361.

63. Pang Xianzhi (ed.), *Mao Zedong Nianpu 1893-1949* [The Chronicle of Mao Zedong 1893-1949] (Beijing: Zhongyang Wenxian Chubanshe, 2002), vol. 1, 501.

64. Feng Jianhui, *Cong Chen Duxiu Dao Mao Zedong* [From Chen Duxiu to Mao Zedong] (Beijing: Zhongyang Wenxian Chubanshe, 1998), 433-434.

65. Pang Xianzhi (ed.), *Mao Zedong Nianpu 1893-1949* [Chronicle of Mao Zedong 1893-1949] (Beijing: Zhongyang Wenxian Chubanshe, 2002), vol. 1, 502.

66. Zhang Guotao, *Wo De Huiyi* [My Memory] (Beijing: Dongfang Chubanshe, 2004), vol. 2, 402-405.

67. Zhang Guotao, *Wo De Huiyi* [My Memory] (Beijing: Dongfang Chubanshe, 2004), vol. 1, 408-411.

68. Pang Xianzhi (ed.), *Mao Zedong Nianpu 1893-1949* [Chronicle of Mao Zedong 1893-1949] (Beijing: Zhongyang Wenxian Chubanshe, 2002), vol. 1, 506-507.

69. Pang Xianzhi and Jin chongji (eds.), *Mao Zedong Zhuan* [Biography of Mao Zedong] (Beijing: Zhongyang Wenxian Chubanshe, 2011), 2nd ed., 366.

70. Pang Xianzhi (ed.), *Mao Zedong Nianpu 1893-1949* [The Chronicle of Mao Zedong 1893-1949] (Beijing: Zhongyang Wenxian Chubanshe, 2002), vol. 1, 511.

71. Yang Kuisong, *Tanwang Yuejin: Zhonggong Dangshi Fangtan Lu* [Discussing the Past and Today: An Interview Record on the History of the CCP] (Beijing: Jiuzhou Chubanshe, 2012), 124-125.

72. Lu Haijiang, *Zhang Guotao Zhuanji He Nianpu* [Biography and Chronicle of Zhang Guotao] (Beijing: Zhonggong Dangshi Chubanshe, 2003), 61.

73. Pang Xianzhi and Jin chongji (eds.), *Mao Zedong Zhuan* [Biography of Mao Zedong] (Beijing: Zhongyang Wenxian Chubanshe, 2011), 2nd ed., 396-397.

74. Pang Xianzhi and Jin chongji (eds.), *Mao Zedong Zhuan* [Biography of Mao Zedong] (Beijing: Zhongyang Wenxian Chubanshe, 2011), 2nd ed., 509-510.

75. Yang Kuisong, *Tanwang Yuejin: Zhonggong Dangshi Fangtan Lu* [Discussing the Past and Today: An Interview Record on the History of the CCP] (Beijing: Jiuzhou Chubanshe, 2012), 122.

76. Zhang Guotao, *Wo De Huiyi* [My Memory] (Beijing: Dongfang Chubanshe, 2004), vol. 2, 559-560.

77. Yang Kuisong, *Tanwang Yuejin: Zhonggong Dangshi Fangtan Lu* [Discussing the Past and Today: An Interview Record on the History of the CCP] (Beijing: Jiuzhou Chubanshe, 2012), 62.

78. Ding Xiaoping, *Wangming Zhongdu Shijian Diaocha* [Investigation of Wangming's Poisoning] (Beijing: Zhongguo Qingnian Chubanshe, 2012), 48.

79. Wang Jianying, *Zhonggong Zhongy Jiguan Lishi Yanbian Kaoshi* [An Examination on the Evolution of the Central Institutions of the CCP] (Beijing: Zhonggong Dangshi Chubanshe, 2005), 267-268, 592.

80. Yang Kuisong, *Tanwang Yuejin: Zhonggong Dangshi Fangtan Lu* [Discussing the Past and Today: An Interview Record on the History of the CCP] (Beijing: Jiuzhou Chubanshe, 2012), 62.

81. Ding Xiaoping, *Wangming Zhongdu Shijian Diaocha* [Investigation of Wangming's Poisoning] (Beijing: Zhongguo Qingnian Chubanshe, 2012), 57.

82. Mao Zedong, "Guanyu Wang Jiaxiang De Pingjia" [Comments on Wang Jiaxiang], in Zhonggong Zhongyang Wenxian Yanjiushi (ed.), *Wenxian He Yanjiu* [Documents and Research] (Beijing: Renmin Chubanshe, 1988), 71

83. Wang Jiaxiang, "Guoji Zhishi Baogao" [Report on the Incomtern's Direction], in Zhonggong Zhongyang Wenxian Yanjiushi (ed.), *Wenxian He Yanjiu* [Documents and Research] (Beijing: Renmin Chubanshe, 1988), 68-71.

84. Jin Chongji (ed.), *Mao Zedong Zhuan* [Biography of Mao Zedong] (Beijing: Zhongyang Wenxian Chubanshe, 1996), 600.

85. Zhongyang Danganguan (ed.), *Zhonggong Zhongyang Wenjian Xuanji* [Collection of the CCPCC Documents] (Beijing: Zhonggong Zhongyang Dangxiao Chubanshe, 1991), vol. 13, 426-436; Yang Kuisong, *Mao Zedong Yu Mosike De Enen Yuanyuan* [The Scores between Mao Zedong and Moscow] (Jiangxi: Jiangxi Renmin Chubanshe 2003), 143-144; Chen Lifeng, *Zhongguo Gongchan Dang Lingdao Tizhi De Lishi Kaocha 1921-2006* [A Historical Study on the Leading System of the CCP 1921-2006] (Shanghai: Renmin Chubanshe, 2008), 144-147.

86. Zhongyang Danganguan (ed.), *Zhonggong Zhongyang Wenjian Xuanji* [Collection of the CCPCC Documents] (Beijing: Zhonggong Zhongyang Dangxiao Chubanshe, 1991), vol. 13, 465, 467.

87. Zhongyang Danganguan (ed.), *Zhonggong Zhongyang Wenjian Xuanji* [Collection of the CCPCC Documents] (Beijing: Zhonggong Zhongyang Dangxiao Chubanshe, 1991), vol. 13, 465, 467.

88. Zhongguo Renmin Jiefang Jun Guofang Daxue Dangshi Dangjian Zhenggong Jiaoyan Shi (ed.), *Zhonggong Dangshi Jiaoxue Cankao Ziliao* [Reference Document for Teaching of the CCP History] (Beijing: Guofang Daxue Chubanshe, 1986), vol. 12, 345-346.

89. Zhongguo Renmin Jiefang Jun Guofang Daxue Dangshi Dangjian Zhenggong Jiaoyan Shi (ed.), *Zhonggong Dangshi Jiaoxue Cankao Ziliao* [Reference Document for Teaching of the CCP History] (Beijing: Guofang Daxue Chubanshe, 1986), vol. 12, 345-346.

90. Zhongguo Renmin Jiefang Jun Guofang Daxue Dangshi Dangjian Zhenggong Jiaoyan Shi (ed.), *Zhonggong Dangshi Jiaoxue Cankao Ziliao* [Reference Document for Teaching of the CCP History] (Beijing: Guofang Daxue Chubanshe, 1986), vol. 12, 345-346.

91. The document adopted by that meeting provided working rules for the Central Committee and the Secretariat, but did not mention the Standing Committee. It is said that the Politburo Standing Committee was replaced by the Secrtariat; see Li Lin, "Zhonggong Zhongyang shuji Chu Zuzhi Yange Yu Gongneng Bianqian" [Organizational and Functional Evolution of the Central Secretatriat of the CCPCC], *Zhonggong Dangshi Yanjiu* 3 (2007): 14. Another opinion suggests that both of them were megerd together; see Wang Jianying, *Zhonggong Zhongy Jiguan Lishi Yanbian Kaoshi* [An Examination on the Evolution of the Central Institutions of the CCP] (Beijing: Zhonggong Dangshi Chubanshe, 2005), 592-593. It should be noted that the PSC was first installed in the CCP constitution revised in 1925, which had been translated as "Secretariat." Therefore, these two could be the same thing. For the revised party constitution, see Benshu Bianxie Zu, *Zhongguo Gongchan Dang Zhangcheng Huibian* [Colletion of the CCP Constitutions] (Beijing: Zhonggong Dangshi Chuban She, 2007), 24.

92. "Zhonggong Kuoda De Liuzhong Quanhui Guanyu Zhongyang Weiyuanhui Gongzui Guize Yu Jilv De Jueding" [Decision of the Enlarged Sixth Plenary of the CCP Regarding Rule

and Discipline of the Central Committee], in Zhongyang Dangan Guan (ed.), *Zhonggong Zhongyang Wenjian Xuanji* [Selection of Documents of the CCPCC] (Beijing: Zhogngong Zhongyang Dangxiao Chubanshe, 1991), 760-765.

93. "Zhonggong Kuoda De Liuzhong Quanhui Guanyu Zhongyang Weiyuanhui Gongzui Guize Yu Jilv De Jueding" [Decision of the Enlarged Sixth Plenary of the CCP Regarding Rule and Discipline of the Central Committee], in Zhongyang Dangan Guan (ed.), *Zhonggong Zhongyang Wenjian Xuanji* [Selection of Documents of the CCPCC] (Beijing: Zhogngong Zhongyang Dangxiao Chubanshe, 1991), 760-765.

94. Zhongyang Wenxina Yanjiu Shi (ed.), *Ren Bishi Nianpu* [The Chronicle of Ren Bishi] (Beijing: Zhongyang Wenxian Chubanshe, 2004), 438.

95. Zhongguo Renmin Jiefang Jun Guofang Daxue Dangshi Dangjian Zhenggong Jiaoyan Shi (ed.), *Zhonggong Dangshi Jiaoxue Cankao Ziliao* [Reference Document for Teaching of the CCP History] (Beijing: Guofang Daxue Chubanshe, 1986), vol. 12, 345-346.

96. Zhongguo Renmin Jiefang Jun Guofang Daxue Dangshi Dangjian Zhenggong Jiaoyan Shi (ed.), *Zhonggong Dangshi Jiaoxue Cankao Ziliao* [Reference Document for Teaching of the CCP History] (Beijing: Guofang Daxue Chubanshe, 1986), vol. 12, 345-346.

97. Yang Kuisong, *Mao Zedong Yu Mosike De Enen Yuanyuan* [The Scores between Mao Zedong and Moscow] (Jiangxi: Jiangxi Renmin Chubanshe, 2003), 145-146.

98. Li Donglang, "Mao Zedong Zuihou Jueding Quan Wenti Pingxi" [Analysis on the Issue of Mao Zedong's Power of Last Say], *Zhonggong Dangshi Yanjiu* 2 (2007): 69.

99. Zhongyang Wenxina Yanjiu Shi (ed.), *Ren Bishi Nianpu* [The Chronicle of Ren Bishi] (Beijing: Zhongyang Wenxian Chubanshe, 2004), 463.

100. Art. 34, the Constitution of the CCP, adopted by the Seventh National Congress in 1945.

101. Chen Lifeng, *Zhongguo Gongchan Dang Lingdao Tizhi De Lishi Kaocha 1921-2006* [A Historical Study on the Leading System of the CCP 1921-2006] (Shanghai: Renmin Chubanshe, 2008), 123.

102. Liu Shaoqi, "Lun Dang" [On the Party], in Zhonggong Zhongyang Wenxian Bianji Weiyuanhui (ed.), *Liu Shaoqi Xuanji* [Selected Works of Liu Shaoqi] (Beijing: Renmin Chubanshe, 2004), 331-334.

103. Shi Zhe, *Wo De Yisheng* [My Life] (Beijing: Renmin Chubanshe, 2001), 224.

104. Zhang Xipo (ed.), *Geming Genju Di Fazhi Shi* [Legal History of Revolutionary Bases] (Beijing: Falv Chubanshe, 1994), 612-613.

105. Art. 24, "Provisional Organic Regulation on the Shangganning Border Area," in Han Yanlong and Chang Zhaoru (eds.), *Zhongguo Xin Minzhu Zhuyi Geming Shiqi Genjudi Fazhi Wenxian Xuanbian* [Selection of Legal Documents of the Revolutionary Bases During the Period of New Democratic Revolution of China] (Beijing: Zhongguo Shehui Kexue Chubanshe, 1981), vol. 1, 9.

106. Art. 12, "The Organic Program of Central Area Provisoinal Government," in Han Yanlong and Chang Zhaoru (eds.), *Zhongguo Xin Minzhu Zhuyi Geming Shiqi Genjudi Fazhi Wenxian Xuanbian* [Selection of Legal Documents of the Revolutionary Bases During the Period of New Democratic Revolution of China] (Beijing: Zhongguo Shehui Kexue Chubanshe, 1981), vol. 2, 476-477.

107. Yang Kuisong, *Mao Zedong Yu Mosike De Enen Yuanyuan* [The Scores between Mao Zedong and Moscow] (Jiangxi: Jiangxi Renmin Chubanshe 2003), 157.

108. See Shi Zhe, *Mao Zedong De Fanyi Shi Zhe Yanzhong De Gaoceng Renwu* [High-Level Characters in the Eyes of Mao Zedong's Interpreter Shi Zhe] (Beijing: Renmin Chubanshe, 2005), 36-37.

Chapter Four

Chairman Mao of the People's Republic of China from 1949 to 1954

CHAIRMAN MAO'S BID WITH MOSCOW FOR A NEW CHINA

Mao Zedong's Idea of a United Government

Having retreated from the Central Soviet Area, the CCP and Red Army finally settled down in Shangxi province, and gradually revived. With the Japanese force being driven out of China, war between the CCP and KMT government broke out. As the PLA started to fight back from its first withdrawals, Mao Zedong also began to think about the establishment of a new Chinese government. It seemed that he had envisioned a united government as early as March 1948. In his cable exchange with Stalin, he suggested the creation of a central government including liberal bourgeoisie and gained Stalin's support.[1] To have a better idea about how such a coalition government could operate, Mao Zedong attempted to pay a visit to Moscow and the Eastern European countries,[2] but was declined by the hesitant Moscow.[3]

After the CCP initiated a call for a Political Consultative Conference (PCC) and the PLA had won several major battles against the KMT army, Mao Zedong became more eager for such a visit. In his cable to Stalin on July 28, Mao Zedong not only stressed to go to Moscow as soon as possible,[4] but also wrote about seven issues he intended to discuss in Moscow, including relations with small democratic parties and groups (and democratic figures), the convocation of a PCC, industrial restoration and construction in China, a silver loan of US$30 million, foreign relations, and so on.

Obviously, Mao Zedong had become more optimistic about his success and his consideration of the new government had gone beyond the organization of that united government to its specific works and policies.[5] But he could have known that by then Stalin had given up on the idea of united governments and imposed one-party system in those Eastern European countries after splitting with Yugoslavia, he may be uncertain whether Moscow still supported his idea of a united government in China, let alone those works and policies. Therefore, Mao Zedong ended the cable by emphasizing the need to reach an agreement with the USSR.[6]

While the trip to Moscow had been delayed time and again,[7] the situation in China changed so fast that Mao Zedong could not wait any more to organize the central government. He first raised the issue in a CCP Politburo meeting held in September 1948, by asking: "should our government adopt the parliamentary system, or the democratic centralism?"[8] To answer this question, he drew attention to their past experience of the China Soviet Republic during the 1930s, saying:

> In the past we called the system 'soviet representative congress.' But as 'soviet' meant 'congress,' we also called it 'soviet,' then the 'soviet representative congress' becomes 'congress of congress.' This is a rigid transplantation of foreign vocabulary. Now we can use the name 'people's congress' and adopt the democratic centralism.[9]

Thus he gave the Soviet system a Chinese name, that is, People's Congress. He also compared the democratic centralism with parliamentary system from both domestic and international considerations:

> Parliamentary system had been practiced by Yuan Shikan and Cao Kun and been disliked by the people. It is very appropriate for China to adopt the democratic centralism. If we propose to convene the people's congress, the Nationalists cannot oppose because they have been repeating Sun Zhongshan's will to convene the national congress.[10]

> Internationally, neither the capitalist countries nor socialist ones could oppose, because Jiang Jieshi convened the national congress twice and those capitalist countries did not oppose him; the Democratic Germany and North Korea also did similarly.[11]

Therefore, he concluded that:

> I think we can decide so and it is unnecessary to adopt the capitalists' parliamentary system and the separation of three powers.[12]

He further conceived a two-step plan. As the first step, the PCC could be prepared from then and hold a meeting in late 1948 or the first half of 1949, then in the fourth year of the civil war, that is, 1950, a provisional central government would be established.[13]

As Mao Zedong decided to set up a united government by adapting the model of the China Soviet Republic to the new Chinese situation, the chairman could be a possible organ in the new central government. As a matter of fact, this had already been under consideration. In a CCP internal draft revised by Zhou Enlai in November 1948, it was provided that "the new Political Consultative Conference shall elect the chairman, vice-chairmen and people's commissars of the provisional central government so as to form the council of people's government to handle state affairs at home."[14] Then who could be that chairman?

Stalin Lagged Behind

By the end of 1948, Mao Zedong's plan seemed to be realized. He told Stalin in a cable on December 30, 1948, that conditions had been met and a political consultative meeting of the representatives of various democratic parties, groups, and people's organizations could be convened to create a democratic united government around the summer of 1949.[15] In reply on January 6, 1949, Stalin agreed that the creation of the coalition government was a question on one hand,[16] and on the other hand urged the CCP to establish the government immediately after the liberation of Beijing, not in the summer as planned by the CCP.[17] While admitting Stalin's time frame was feasible, Mao Zedong insisted on conducting his long-delayed visit to the USSR before the creation of the government on January 10.[18]

Seemingly, Stalin and Mao Zedong were thinking about different things. Whereas Stalin paid his attention to the timing of the formation of this united government, Mao Zedong was more concerned with how such a united government could be organized in the Soviet way and its future policies. For him, the formation of this government could have not been a problem anymore. At that time, his army was ready to cross the Yangtze River to deliver the final defeat to the KMT government, and the negotiation for a PCC to produce that united government were right under way. During the negotiation, the CCP was bidding hard to obtain a leadership over those democratic parties and people so as to exert a leading role in the PCC and that united government. With the support from Moscow, his position would be better strengthened in that competition.

But Moscow was still uncertain about such an outlook for China. Rather, Stalin had a different picture. On January 14, 1949, he advised Mao Zedong:

> To create the central united government organs in such a way that approximately three fifths of seats in the consultative council and two thirds of the posts in the government would be retained by the communists, and the other seats and posts would be distributed between other democratic parties and the KMT. Second, it is necessary that the posts of the prime minister, commander in chief, and *if possible, that of the president,* be occupied by communist.[19]

By using the term "president," Stalin obviously did not mean the Soviet model. By saying "possible," he also cast his doubt about the victory of the CCP and in particular the leading role of Mao Zedong in China. In his mind, Mao Zedong was not a possible candidate for the presidency of this new united government. He could suggest that Jiang Jieshi, then nominal Chinese leader and Mao Zedong's chief opponent, could be a better occupant of the presidency. If so, Moscow's interest in China could be more secure because Jiang Jieshi had already joined a friendship agreement with Moscow. Besides, Jiang Jieshi was more popular than Mao Zedong among the capitalist countries. On the contrary, Mao Zedong had long been suspected by Moscow as being too national and militant. If he took the lead, he could pursue new policies for which not only Moscow would have to renegotiate with him to maintain its interest in the far East, as Mao Zedong revealed in their previous communications, but also Moscow's deal with other great powers in Yalta could be challenged.

To narrow their differences, Mao Zedong agreed to Stalin's suggestion of sending someone to pay a visit to the CCP.[20] From January 26 to February 7, 1949, Anastas Mikoyan made a secret journey to China.[21] During his secret visit to Xibaipo, the final transit before Mao Zedong settled in Beijing, Mikoyan was informed by Mao Zedong that:

> Now we are facing some problems. The first one is the establishment of the new government, including its nature, form, composition and name, etc., which has been on our schedule because we have thought about it . . . the second question is the composition and members of the government. We think it should be a united government, but the leadership of the new government should remain in the hands of the CCP. . . . In one word, the future government will be organized in this way, in which the CCP is the core and the main stray.[22]

He continued to introduce the composition of the united government as follows:

> We do not intend to use the parliamentary form . . . . in the future government communists and leftist democrats will take probably 2/3 of all seats. . . . The structure of the central government is similar to the government of the U.S.S.R. It is headed by *a presidium with a chairman*, the premier has not been confirmed yet but probably, it will be Zhou Enlai.[23]

Then who would be that chairman? Mao Zedong said Song Qingling, Sun Zhongshan's widow, would be the chairman of the presidium, and he would join the government as a member of the presidium in the capacity of the CCP chairman.[24]

However, both Ren Bishi and Zhou Enlai, the other two CCP members who were present at their talk, did not agree with Mao:

> It is better for Mao Zedong to be the chairman of the presidium; . . . if Mao does not take the post of the chairman of the presidium, this will not be understood by the people. In any case, if Sun's widow becomes the chairman of the presidium, Mao should take the premier's post.[25]

After hearing their objections, Mao Zedong continued to propose three other CCP senior members as candidates, including Zhu De, Dong Biwu, and Liu Bocheng.[26] Zhu De had led the Red Army together with Mao Zedong and been ranked only after Mao Zedong in the Politburo. Dong Biwu was one of the founding members of the CCP and older in age than Mao Zedong. He had acted as the chairman of the government of the area where the CCP had occupied after it had evacuated from the China Soviet Republic and entered into the anti-Japanese united front with the KMT. Both of them had enjoyed a high reputation within the CCP and could act as a figurehead similar to Song Qingling. Being a military general, Liu Bocheng was less famous than his two colleagues so it could be less possible for him to take that position as he had never had a similar experience before.[27]

Their conversation revealed that Mao Zedong had conceived two different arrangements. One was to have a nominal head of government other than Mao Zedong, which was similar to Stalin's advice, but he rejected Stalin's suggestion of Jiang Jieshi. The other one was to let Mao Zedong be the chairman, which was preferred by the CCP, but new to Stalin. These two arrangements were not new to Mao Zedong because he had experienced both of them in the China Soviet Republic. As Mikoyan had claimed at the very beginning of their talks that he could only hear on behalf of Stalin and not been supposed to give any opinion during his visit, Moscow's attitude remained unclear. Therefore, Mao Zedong concluded at the end of their talk that the question of the chairman had to be solved after taking into account the internal and international situations.[28]

He could have had to acknowledge this. On one hand, Stalin seemed still not ready to accept the new plan by then because Mikoyan once praised Zhou Enlai as the best choice of the premier for the new government in his private conversation with Mao Zedong's Russian interpreter, but did not mention Mao Zedong in this regard.[29] On the other hand, Chinese democratic parties and figures participating in negotiation for the PCC were still hesitate to accept the leadership of the CCP in the united government. On January 22, 1949, well in the middle of Mikoyan's visit, fifty-five representatives of democratic parties and figures announced to accept the leadership of the CCP "in the course of people's liberation war," without mentioning the CCP's leading role in the new united government.[30] In other words, the CCP still had to strive for their final support.

Soon a decision was made. From March 3-15, 1949, the CCP held the second Plenary Session of its Seventh Central Committee. This meeting not only approved the plan to establish the new united government based on the Soviet model rather than on the parliamentary system adopted by the capitalist countries,[31] but it also confirmed that Mao Zedong and Zhou Enlai would join that government, in which Mao Zedong would be the chairman of the presidium and Zhou Enlai would be the premier; such an arrangement was supposed to ensure the leadership of the CCP over the new government.[32]

Stalin's Question on the Chairman

As the CCP expanded its military success at battlefields by taking Nanjing and Shanghai in the following April, Moscow also changed its uncertain attitude toward the CCP. It not only redeployed its ambassador lingering in Guangzhou, but also discussed with Mao Zedong about his request of a loan of US$300 million and invited Liu Shaoqi to pay a secret visit to Moscow.[33]

On June 21, 1949, Liu Shaoqi started his pioneering visit to Moscow.[34] After his arrival, Liu Shaoqi submitted a report to Stalin on July 4, which had been drafted by him and revised by Mao Zedong.[35] In this report, he introduced the CCP's preparation for the new government as follows:

> We have decided to convene in August a new political consultative conference and set up a united government . . . a preparatory committee on PCC convocation has already been set up. It comprises 134 members, among them 43 communists, 48 progressive figures who will certainly support us, 43 centrists, with 12 centrists with rightist leanings among them. The progressive include 15 undercover communists. The leadership of the preparatory committee is securely with the communist party. A standing presidium of 21 has been set up within the preparatory committee. Leadership in this presidium has likewise been secured for the communist party . . . all told, 45 organizations will be represented in the PCC by 510 delegates. The communists will make up a majority.[36]

The composition of the united government was further described as follows:

> We have decided to convene a new political consultative conference and establish a united government. . . . The organization of this new central government has not been decided as yet. Except for the military council, the new central government will set up finance and economy committee, culture and education committee, and political and legal committee under the cabinet of ministers. Besides, various ministries will also be established, which will include ministry of railroad, agriculture, forestry, commerce, metallurgy, textile, fuels, transportation and post and communication, etc. *Comrade Mao Zedong will be*

> *the chairman* of the central government and Comrade Zhou Enlai will be the premier of the cabinet.[37]

When reading that Mao Zedong would be the chairman, Stalin underlined it and marked a question beside: "*Is this in fact the president*?"[38]

Stalin had good reasons to cast his doubt. When drafting the Russian constitution in 1936, which was later branded as "Stalin constitution," he had claimed that:

> The Supreme Soviet presidium is the collective president of the U.S.S.R. One of the characteristics in the state organization of the U.S.S.R is being completely democratic, i.e., there is no individual head of state. In the U.S.S.R, *there should not have an individual president* elected by the people in contrast to the Supreme Soviet which is also elected by the people. Rather, in the U.S.S.R, *the president is collective*, which is the presidium of the Supreme Soviet, including the chairman. Such a presidium is elected by and should report to the Supreme Soviet . . . such a way is the most democratic.[39]

Hence, according to his theory, if Mao Zedong was an individual president, then such a united government would not be the one "close to the regime of soviets," as claimed by Liu Shaoqi and endorsed by Stalin in Liu's report. Liu Shaoqi had said in his report that "the people's democratic dictatorship . . . comes closer to the regime of soviets." Stalin endorsed this point by marking "Yes." But if Mao Zedong was an individual president, such a united government would not be the one close to the regime of soviets, according to Stalin's above statement.[40] On the contrary, it could be something the least democratic that had only been adopted by the capitalist states.

More importantly, Stalin could be doubtful for other practical reasons. He could have known that, during the first meeting of the preparatory committee of the new political consultative conference convened from June 15 to 19, well just before Liu Shaoqi started his Moscow's trip, Mao Zedong had debated with his democratic partners about the foreign policy that the new Chinese government would adopt. While Mao Zedong insisted on his orientation toward Moscow, the democratic parties suggested that China should put emphasis both on the USA and the Soviet Union. A non-CCP person even proposed Mao Zedong to follow the example of Yugoslavia and be a "Chinese Tito."[41] Although Mao Zedong ended this debate by declaring the "lean-on-one-side" policy publicly on 30,[42] Stalin surely could have had that in his mind when he read Liu Shaoqi's report. Being skeptical of Mao Zedong being likely as another Tito, Stalin would have preferred a more Soviet-style chairman limited by the presidium than the capitalist individual president.

Therefore, when meeting Liu Shaoqi again to discuss his report together with the Russian Politburo members and generals in the night of July 10,

Stalin raised his question again and asked Liu Shaoqi whether the chairman was the same as the president and what the nature of the relations between the chairman and premier was. Liu Shaoqi replied that the presidium was a collective president, while the cabinet shall comply with the presidium and was the executive body of the central government. On hearing this, Stalin said that such a system would be appropriate for China at this stage.[43] He may imply that it was not acceptable in the future. In other words, Stalin was still reserved about the Chinese chairman.

Stalin's Other Advice to the CCP

Then Stalin further suggested to his CCP guests that they could use the Common Program for the time being, but should adopt a constitution in 1954.[44] In their last meeting in August, Stalin asked Liu Shaoqi when the CCP was going to announce the founding of the central government because the KMT government had been paralyzed while the CCP had been ready to take its place. Liu Shaoqi replied that it would be in January 1950, and possibly on January 1. Stalin then suggested that the enemies could interfere by taking advantage of that situation and the CCP should be cautious.[45]

His advice had merit. In the CCP's previous negotiation with John Leighton Stuart, then American ambassador to China, the US government also claimed that it could not give up recognition of the KMT government because no other government had been set up to replace the Nationalist government.[46] During this trip, the Russians also informed the Chinese that an Islamic Republic was plotted to set up in areas around China's Xinjiang province under the support of the United States, whose recognition would be given immediately upon its establishment.[47] Hence, Stalin's advice was sent back home and accepted soon by the CCP.[48] When Liu Shaoqi arrived in Shenyang, China, in late August, they learned that the new government would be established on October 1.[49]

THE MIXED CHAIRMAN OF THE CENTRAL PEOPLE'S GOVERNMENT

Constitutional Making of the CPPCC

Before Liu Shaoqi started his trip to Moscow, the Preparatory Committee of the New Political Consultative Conference[50] held its first meeting in Beijing from June 15-20, 1949. The meeting attendees decided to set up a Standing Committee headed by Mao Zedong and six working groups responsible for drafting relevant documents, among which the third group, led by Zhou Enlai, was assigned to draft the Common Program of the Chinese People Political Consultative Conference (the Common Program), and the fourth group, led by Dong Biwu, was to draft the Organizing Law of the Central People's Government (the Organic Law).

On June 18, the third group held its first meeting and decided the CCP members should write the first draft. About two months later, Zhou Enlai completed a draft titled "the New Democratic Common Program."[51] On August 22, Mao Zedong personally revised it five times.[52] While the CCP continued the revision, the drafts were also submitted by the CCP formally on September 6[53] and underwent seven meetings' deliberation, including three meetings of the third working group, two meetings of representatives of the PCC, and two meetings of the preparatory committee.[54]

Also on June 18, the fourth working group held its first meeting to discuss the Organic Law. Dong Biwu not only made a keynote speech on principles to be laid down in this draft,[55] but also wrote the first draft.[56] His draft was further discussed by the fourth working group, the Standing Committee and the Preparatory Committee successively.[57] On September 17, the Preparatory Committee held its second meeting and the 126 members passed both law drafts by standing votes.[58] Then when the First Congress of Chinese People's Political Consultative Conference (CPPCC) convened its first session from September 21, these two drafts were reported to the session on the second day[59] and passed unanimously on September 27 by hand votes[60] with a few minor changes.[61]

It seems that the practice of the China Soviet Republic was inherited to divide policy issues and governmental organization into two separate laws. The common program made policy statements, whereas governmental organization was stipulated in the organic law. Similarly, the China Soviet Republic of the 1930s not only had a constitutional program which had primarily been concerned with policy issues, but also had two organic laws, one for the central government and the other about the local government.

The Common Program had a preamble and seven chapters. Apart from the first chapter about the general principle and the second chapter about organs of state power, the remaining five chapters were all policy statements in terms of military, economic, cultural and educational, foreign affairs as well as nationalities. With respect to state organs, the second chapter did not make a full account. Instead, it only provided that the state power belongs to the people,[62] who were to exercise through state organs organized by two different procedures, pending on the convocation of the All-China People's Congress. Before the convocation of the All-China People's Congress, the Plenary Session of the Chinese People's Political Consultative Conference would take the place of the All-China People's Congress, enact the Organic Law of the Central People's Government, elect the Central People's Government Council (CPGC) and vest it with the authority to exercise state power;[63] after that, the All-China People's Congress shall be the supreme organ of state power and when it was not in session, the Central People's Government shall exercise the state power as the supreme organ.[64] The democratic centralism should be practiced by all organs of state power.[65] To know more about the governmental structure at the central level, the organic law of the central government had to be referred to.

A Four-layer Central Government

As the supreme state organ, the CPGC consisted of sixty-three members elected by the CPPCC, including a chairman, six vice-chairmen, a secretary general, and fifty-five other members,[66] and was provided to represent the PRC in international relations and assume the leadership of the state apparatus at home.[67] Under it, there were four more parallel organs, that is, the Government Administration Council (GAC) as the highest executive body, the People's Revolutionary Military Council as the commander of armed forces, the Supreme People's Court (SPC) as the highest judicial body, and the People's Procurator-General's Office as the highest supervisory organ.[68] Headed by the premier,[69] the GAC had the premier, vice premiers, secretary general, and a number of members, all of whom were to be appointed by the CPGC.[70] Under the GAC, there were three committees to direct the work of about thirty ministries, commissions, and so on.[71] Therefore, the Central People's Government of the PRC would be a four-level bureaucracy from top to bottom.

Compared with the Central Government of the China Soviet Republic, these two had some similarities. For example, the CPGC was almost the same size as the first CEC, and both had no presidium within them; the GAC can be seen as another Council of People's Commissars. In particular, similar to the CRS, the armed forces of PRC has been separated from the administrative body responsible to an independent committee, that is, the People's Revolutionary Military Council, which also consisted of a chairman, several vice-chairmen, and other members.[72] But differences could also be discerned easily. Whereas the CEC was subject to the All-Chinese Congress of Soviets, the CPGC was the highest state organ, since the All-China People's Congress was yet to be established in 1954. Besides, the GAC had more levels of subordinates and was more sophisticated than the flat structure of the Council of People's Commissars.

The Central People's Government Council

As the authority to exercise state power,[73] the CPGC was vested with ten items of powers, including: making and interpreting law, deciding administrative policies, correcting the Government Administration Council's decisions and orders, ratifying foreign treaties, handling issues concerning war and peace, approving state budget, granting amnesty and pardon, giving honorary awards, appointing and removing senior officials, and preparing and convening the National People's Congress.[74] In his report on the drafting process to the first Plenary Session of the CCPCC, Dong Biwu remarked as follows: "The powers and functions of the Central People's Government Council are often provided by other countries' constitutions as those of the heads of state."[75] Thus the CPGC was intended to be the head of state of the PRC, and it was a collective one because of its sizable membership. By the "collective theory," he may have implied that the chairman of the Central People's Government the Council was not.

Taking into consideration the provision of the Organic Law stipulating that the CPGC represented the PRC in international relations and assumed the leadership of the state apparatus at home,[76] this could be true. Compared with the China Soviet Republic, this is a progress, because the latter had not mentioned this point at all, either in its laws or by its law makers, possibly because it was not an effective government at that time. This is also an agreement with Stalin's theory of collective head of state. Stalin should be relaxed at this point.

Then if examined in detail, these powers were of different natures according to Western theories. In Western countries, some of these powers belonged to parliaments, such as law making and interpreting, approval of government budget and correcting the administration; some were owned by the administration independently or jointly with the parliament, like determining administrative policies, dealing with wars and peace, and promulgating general amnesty; and some were performed by the head of state, with or without the prior decisions of the parliament, such as appointment of government officials and issuing pardons. Besides, the power to interpret law fell to the jurisdiction of the court in some Western countries.[77] Therefore, to be more accurate, the CPGC was a Soviet style of head of state, that is, a collective head of state with mixing legislative, administrative, and judicial powers.

However, the capacity of the CPGC to exercise power was constrained by time because it was provided to convene a meeting in every two months,[78] suggesting it could perform its power and function when it gathered and take accountability from the GAC, etc.[79] In these meetings, three different procedures were provided for the CPGC to make laws. It could either legislate on bills submitted by the GAC,[80] or accept resolutions submitted by the Plenary Session of the CPPCC prior to the convocation of the All-China People's Congress.[81] It could also consider proposals from the National Committee of the CPPCC.[82]

In particular, even if the CPGC could be regarded as the supreme administrative organ,[83] its involvement with the administrative affairs was constrained. According to the legal provisions, the CPGC was supposed to focus mainly on major administrative policy setting,[84] rather than specific implementation, which should be carried out by the GAC, legally "the highest executive body for state administration."[85] Besides, at the top of the four levels of bureaucracies, the CPGC would find it difficult to control the ministries' working.

The Chairman of the Central People's Government

Based on the Organic Law, the CPGC chairman had several powers, first of which was to convene and preside over the CPGC meetings.[86] It was mandatory that the chairman should convene such a meeting once every two months, but he could decide to meet earlier or later when conditions demanded.[87] In other words, the chairman had full discretion to choose when the council should meet as long as the requirement of once in two months was satisfied. His second power was to "direct" ("Lingdao" in Chinese) the work of the CPGC,[88] thus being distinguished from his peers in the CPGC. He was the "director" and the rest members were to be directed by him. In other words, the CPGC members were not equal and the chairman was a senior member among them.

Compared with the chairman of the China Soviet Republic, the power to direct is unique because no chairmen had been accorded legally with such an advantageous power in the China Soviet Republic. The First Soviet Congress had only elected one chairman and two vice-chairmen. Since they had not formed a presidium and their relationship had not been defined, the chairman could be regarded independent from his vice-chairmen. On the other hand, the Second Soviet Congress had followed the example of the former Soviet Union and formed a presidium and the title of chairman had carried no substance for the person who held it. In other words, the chairman of the presidium had been no more than an equal member within the presidium, enjoying no privileges by law.

This could be a necessary device to ensure the CCP's leadership over the government. As it was a united government with those democratic parties and figures who had different ideas from the CCP, it was crucial for the CCP to maintain a leading role in the CPGC to ensure the ideological direction. By "directing" the CPGC, the chairman could help to achieve this goal at large.

However, the Organic Law did not elaborate on the substance and procedure of such a power of direction. Although it did require that a regulation on the organization of the CPGC be made,[89] such a regulation had never been made ever since. Therefore, how the chairman performs his "direction" in the CPGC remains unclear. For example, although it could be expected that the chairman's direction should be within the limits of powers and functions of the CPGC as he was also its member, what if his direction contradicts with the Common Program and Organic Law? More fundamentally, since the CPGC should work by meeting once every two months with attendance of more than one half of its sixty-three members, and to decide any resolution upon the concurrence of over one half of the members present at that particular meeting,[90] what if the chairman's direction conflicts with the voting of the CPGC?

Since the CPGC only convened once every two months, a standing body had to be set up to oversee the daily operation of the government when the CPGC absolved, such as the execution of the GAC.[91] In the USSR, this was fulfilled by the Presidium of the Supreme Soviets, which had been defined by Stalin as the collective head of state, whereas the chairman of the Russian Presidium was no more than an equal member to the rest, taking no individual responsibility for the administration. The Russian model had been followed by the Second Soviet Congress of the China Soviet Republic. Since the CPGC was composed of the chairman and six vice-chairmen, a presidium could also be a feasible choice.

But the Organic Law did not provide so, and the CPGC had no presidium. Instead, both the vice-chairmen and the secretary general were required to "assist the chairman in the discharge of his duty."[92] Why was the Soviet model not followed? It was explained as follows:

> The Soviet Union adopts federal system and has sixteen states. Each of these has a vice-chairman in its central government, thus forming its presidium. We are not a federal one in fact and should not imitate such a system. As for the daily business, the Central People's Government Council can elect a Secretary-General among its members and lead the Secretariat of the council to take charge.[93]

It was true that the unitary system had been adopted by the Common Program and local government did not have the same elevated status as those of the former Soviet Union, therefore the Soviet-style presidium may not suit the case of China. But neither the secretary general nor the Secretariat should be expected as the appropriate bodies to oversee the execution of the GAC. Instead, they should be supposed to deal with the internal administration of the CPGC, and seek final decision from the chairman when the Central People's Government Council adjourned, as the chairman was provided to "direct" the work of the CPGC. In other words, it could only be the chairman of the CPG to serve as a standby body. After all, it was also provided that when the CPGC adjourned, the GAC should be responsible and accountable to the chairman.[94] Therefore, implicitly the chairman could act as the presidium.

Then it was inevitable for the chairman to get involved with the administration. Although no law was made concerning how the GAC should be accountable to the chairman, the role of the chairman was intended to be supervisory and concentrated on policy issues and overall operation rather than detailed affairs.[95] On one hand, since the GAC was legally the highest executor of state administration,[96] the chairman was not supposed to take the place of the GAC in the execution of state administration. On the other hand, there were two more administrative levels, that is, the committees and ministries under the GAC,[97] suggesting the chairman was designed to maintain the necessary supervision without direct contact with the specific administration of state affairs.[98]

Therefore, while conforming to Stalin's theory of collective head of state, the new Chinese government had not followed the Russian model completely in terms of the chairman of the CPGC. For the PRC, the CPG chairman is more like the chairman of the CEC of the First Soviet Congress in the China Soviet Republic, working in a committee with same size and same organization. But distinctively, the PRC chairman was more secure and significant legally than his predecessor. By law, he was not only an internal "director" of the collective head of state, that is, the CPGC, but also externally could be regarded as a personal presidium, supervising the daily operation of the multi-level state apparatus. With such a legal seniority, the chairman could virtually function as an individual head of state. Mao Zedong might just have thought so when he was elected to take this post.

CHAIRMAN MAO ZEDONG IN OFFICE

Diplomacy of Chairman Mao

On September 27, 1949, the Plenary Session of the CPPCC decided that the CPGC should consist of six vice-chairmen and fifty-six members, and their candidates be produced by the presidium based on negotiations among the participating units of the plenary session.[99] The decision did not mention the chairman of the CPGC, possibly because it could have been acknowledged that there would be only one chairman and he would be Mao Zedong. Three days later, the Plenary Session elected the sixty-three CPGC members, with Mao Zedong as the chairman.[100] On the morning of October 1, these members sworn into office and held the first CPGC meeting, naming Zhou Enlai as the premier of the GAC and the foreign minister, and Mao Zedong as the chairman of the People's Revolutionary Military Council.[101]

On the second day of the founding of PRC, the former Soviet Union declared its recognition of this new government. On October 16, 1949, Mao Zedong received the Russian ambassador to China and accepted his letter of credence.[102] Such a duty was normally undertaken by the head of state. Although the CPGC was construed as the head of state, it could be impractical for such a big group of people to act. Considering the senior role of the chairman, it would be understandable for the chairman to perform as the head of state on behalf of the council, which was also a Russian practice. Since then, Chairman Mao continued to receive innumerous foreign visitors, including ambassadors and diplomats from other countries.

At the end of 1949, Mao Zedong started his long-planned visit to Moscow to carry out his "lean-on-one-side" foreign policy. Throughout his entire life, Mao Zedong had only been abroad two times, both of which had been to Moscow. This was the first time of his two overseas visits. The main goal of this state visit was to conclude a new friendship treaty with the former Soviet Union.[103] On the first day of his arrival, he raised this issue to Stalin and asked whether Zhou Enlai, the premier and foreign minister, should come to Moscow, implying that if a new treaty be signed, Zhou Enlai would have to come.[104] Stalin rejected at first, but conceded later on January 2, 1950.[105] Having gained this consensus, Mao Zedong soon informed his CCP colleagues in Beijing of this "breakthrough" and instructed them about the basic purpose and main content to prepare for the forthcoming negotiations.[106]

After his arrival in Moscow on January 20, 1950, Zhou Enlai joined Mao Zedong in the negotiations with their Russian partners. After Mao Zedong settled the general principles and major issues with Stalin, Zhou Enlai took charge of the rest of their negotiations, including preparing document drafts, deliberating details with his Russian counterparts.[107] On February 14, 1950, in the presence of Mao Zedong and Stalin, Zhou Enlai signed the new treaties on behalf of the Chinese government with the Russia foreign minister.

Why had Mao Zedong insisted on Zhou Enlai coming to Moscow? It was suggested as a matter of international formality. During their talks, Stalin could have thought that as the real leader of both countries, Mao Zedong and he could jointly negotiate and sign the treaties, without the involvement of Zhou Enlai.[108] But Mao Zedong could have thought otherwise. He could have thought that they were not equal, either because he was the head of state of China, while Stalin was the chairman of the People's Commissars, a position similar to Chinese Premier,[109] or because he surpassed Stalin and did not want to have any connection with Stalin by joint signature.[110] Also, it could be "more than a question of protocol," rather it was to "signal the Chinese leadership's intense interest in concluding a new treaty."[111] In addition, Mao Zedong could have intended to "avoid signing the potentially damaging document" and not to "take full responsibility for the pact,"[112] so he put Zhou Enlai out front while controlling from behind.[113]

Whereas all these ideas could have relevance, there could be other reasons. Zhou Enlai was called for possibly because Mao Zedong needed the assistance of Zhou Enlai as he was more capable and experienced than Mao Zedong in foreign affairs. Mao Zedong had been known as a strategist, and Zhou Enlai had been more popular for his diplomacy. As evidenced in this Moscow round of negotiation, a clear division of labor could be found between Mao Zedong and Zhou Enlai, that is, Mao Zedong set the major policies and general principles, and Zhou Enlai executed them. Mao Zedong was the ultimate decision maker, and Zhou Enlai was more specialized in execution. Such a way of cooperation between them could be traced back to the "Chongqing negotiation" in 1945 when the CCP and KMT tried to negotiate a possible peace agreement after defeating the Japanese. At that time, Mao Zedong reached accord with the KMT leader Jiang Jieshi, whereas Zhou Enlai hammered out the details of their agreements.

More importantly, by law, Mao Zedong was not delegated to sign any international treaty. As the CPG chairman, he could direct the council to ratify treaties, and supervise the work of the GAC, including the Foreign Minister's negotiations. But neither the Common Program nor the Organic Law provided him with the power to conclude any treaty with other countries. On the contrary, Zhou Enlai was the foreign minister and had sufficient legal authority to negotiate and sign any treaty with foreign states, even if such treaty had to be approved by the CPGC.

As a result, despite that neither the Common Program nor Organic Law did explicitly or implicitly authorized either the CPGC or its chairman with functions concerning receiving foreign guests and conducting diplomatic negotiations, Chairman Mao's practices added new items to the legal power and function of the chairman to serve in China's foreign affairs, not only fulfilling the formality required for the head of state, but also participating in negotiations of international treaties jointly with the GAC and the foreign minister.

Chairman Mao as the Supreme Leader at Home

After returning from Moscow, Mao Zedong led the government to launch a series of movements to restore social order and consolidate governance. Generally he followed the procedures laid down by the Common Program and Organic Law, that is, he imitated policy, which was then accepted by the CCPCC and submitted to the CPPCC or the GAC, who in turn proposed it to the CPGC.[114] For example, in a letter written by Liu Shaoqi about a legal draft on January 28, 1951, he replied that:

> Comrade Liu Shaoqi, Zhou Enlai, Chen Yun and Peng Zhen: The draft is concerned with the jurisdiction of the military and court. Therefore it should be passed by the meeting of the CPGC, and promulgated by the chairman. Before this, members of the Standing Committee of the CPPCC, the CPGC, the court, judicial department and procuratorate should be convened for their consensus in this regard. Besides, in the CPGC meeting, some officials should report on the recent situation about the Anti-Revolutionaries activities.[115]

According to his opinion, the CPGC held the eleventh meeting on February 20, 1951. In this meeting, five local officials from several Administrative

Regions reported about their work in these areas and the Ordinance on the Punishment of Anti-Revolutionaries was adopted by the CPGC.[116]

Since the founding of the PRC on October 1, 1949, to September 9, 1954, when the first constitution was adopted, the CPGC had convened thirty-four meetings altogether.[117] However, if examined by year, that legal requirement of meeting once every two months had not been followed strictly. It met four times in 1949, six times in 1950, three times in 1951, six times in 1952, ten times in 1953, and five times in 1954. Compared with the other three years, meetings in 1951 were much less, and those in 1953 were far more than the legal requirement. This could suggest that while conforming to the legal requirement generally, the chairman had also quite often exercised his discretion given by law.

For example, on January 18, 1950, Mao Zedong telegrammed Liu Shaoqi that Wang Jiaxiang, then the Chinese ambassador to the USSR, be nominated as the head of Chinese delegation to the UN. It was also decided that:

> The procedure of his appointment to be completed by the Central People's Government Council can be made in its sixth meeting *to be held in the future.* If you think it is necessary, you can invite the vice-chairmen of the Central People's Government Council and leaders of those democratic parties to have a discussion about this.[118]

When sending this telegram, Mao Zedong was in Moscow for his first state visit. Before his departure, the CCP Politburo had decided that Liu Shaoqi convened the CPGC on behalf of Mao Zedong during his absence.[119] By this telegram, Mao Zedong could suggest that Liu Shaoqi did not have to convene the sixth meeting and it could be held after he returned from his Moscow trip. This was true. The sixth meeting was not held until April 11, 1950, when Mao Zedong had been back in Beijing, about three months later after this telegram.

In addition to the irregularity of certain meetings, participants to the CPGC meetings also varied. Although the CPGC had sixty-three members, about a dozen of those members could not attend each meeting before 1953 because they had taken positions in local government and been dispersed throughout the country.[120] As a result, mostly, the attendance was around forty,[121] and even as little as thirty-three in the fifth meeting held on January 8, 1950.[122] But even after these local officials were moved to Beijing successively in 1953, the attendance seemed to remain approximately the same. Besides, from the second meeting, the CPGC had invited other people to sit in, but their numbers had also been varying, ranging from one person in the second meeting to around two hundred people[123] at most in the thirtieth meeting.[124]

In these meetings, the CPGC made laws and decisions, approved personnel appointments, and heard reports by the executive, military, and judicial organs. It appears that Mao Zedong had played a very comprehensive role in these meetings, not only by nominating key government officials in advance, as indicated by the above telegram, but also by deciding who could speak in the council meeting. For instance, when reading Zhou Enlai's report about the Sino-USSR treaty to be delivered to the sixth CPGC meeting, he directed that:

> In this meeting, in addition to Zhou Enlai, Chen Yun, Lin Biao and Deng Xiaoping who would speak, it seems to be better if other six people, i.e., Zhang Zhizhong, Cheng Qian, Zhang Lan, Li Jisheng, Huang Yanpei and Guo Moruo, also be given the opportunities to speak. Zhou Enlai please considers it and informs them to be prepared. Beside, to explain the marriage law, Wang Ming would better to make some introduction to it.[125]

Sometimes, his direction was so detailed as to require that Zhou Enlai's report should be printed and dispersed to council members who would attend that meeting.[126]

Although no legal stipulations had been made regarding how the GAC should be accountable to the CPG chairman when the CPGC did not meet, it seems that a procedure of "report and approval" had been adopted as a way of accountability, in which the premier filed a report on certain issue to the chairman and promulgated a piece of administrative order after the chairman approved his report. Such a practice was firstly found on June 7, 1951, when an administrative order was issued by the GAC to protect the state secrecies, declaring that this had been given prior approval by the chairman.[127] Following this case, two more similar instances were recorded on August 16, 1951,[128] and August 9, 1952,[129] respectively.

Tightening Control of the CCP Chairman over the Government

However, apart from such an occasional formal practice of "report and approval," there was one more active and constant way for the chairman to control the government. This was the "order and report" mechanism of the CCP, by which the CCPCC issued orders to its party subordinates at various levels and received reports from them as a feedback. Such a mechanism had first been adopted by Mao Zedong within the CCP after he became its chairman and was well established by Mao Zedong during the civil war.

Soon after the founding of the PRC, the CCP formed its party groups within the government apparatus. At the central level, there were two party groups, one being in the CPGC led by Mao Zedong, and the other in the

GAC, led by Zhou Enlai.[130] Similar party organs were also established within the local government at each level, which also were led by Zhou Enlai.

By issuing internal directives to and receiving reports from these party groups in the government from top to the bottom, Mao Zedong obtained a second way of control over the government in the capacity of the CCP chairman. For example, in the "Three-anti Movement" taking place from 1951 to 1952, more than two hundred directives had been issued from the CCPCC and its subdivisions in the six Administrative Regions, whereas laws and regulations issued by the central government numbered less than ten pieces.[131] While sending out directives, Mao Zedong also demanded reports about the government affairs from various local party organs, sometimes so far down the line as to the county level. For example, in an internal directive, Mao Zedong demanded that the county committee of the CCP should file a report about the work of investigating and punishing those who engage in bribery directly to the CCPCC.[132] In these directives, Mao Zedong provided detailed instructions on state affairs; from local reports, he checked and oversaw the governmental implementation of his directives. Hence, by this vertical "order and report" mechanism, he had also exerted a comprehensive involvement into the administration far more than he could achieve through the formal government apparatus. Therefore, Chairman Mao's influence on the administration had been far greater than "supervisory" by combining both the authority of the CCP's chairman and CPG chairman.

When it came to the middle of 1952, the consolidation of the new government was about to be completed, and the economic development became the top priority. The CCP started to draft the first five-year plan. As the economy was to be concentrated, the decision-making power had to be further centralized. This meant the loose multi-level government organization was no longer adequate and had to be restructured. In August 1952, Mao Zedong proposed the first adjustment on the CCP and government apparatus, in which the direction over local government and economic affairs was changed from the GAC to the CPGC. As a result, the vertical government body was flattened and the chairman's control was extended accordingly.[133]

According to Mao Zedong's idea, the Chinese revolution had to go through stages. The first step was to establish a "new democratic nation,"[134] and the second step was to build a socialist one. The second step was based on the first step and would not be initiated until the new democratic nation had achieved fully development. Mao had estimated that it would have to take at least two or three decades after its founding before China was ready to take the second step.[135]

However, in three years since its founding to 1952, the new republic soon recovered from the war, and the government had been fairly consolidated. As such, Mao Zedong changed his mind and suggested that China could start the second step from that time rather than several decades later. In other words, he would give up his "new democratic policies" and accelerate his speed toward the Stalinist socialism. This change was a fundamental one and completely new to his colleagues, who were still inclined to follow their new democratic policies.

To win Moscow's support for his new idea, Mao Zedong asked Liu Shaoqi to take advice from Stalin during his visit to the former Soviet Union while attending the nineteenth congress of the CPSU in October 1952,[136] during which Stalin not only endorsed China's new plan, but also repeated his suggestions that the Chinese make a constitution and form the one-party government, which had been made earlier in 1949 and 1950, respectivly, when Liu Shaoqi and Mao Zedong paid their visits to Moscow.[137] Then Mao Zedong decided that China should begin its "transition to a socialist state" since then, not a dozen years later as he had envisioned before. This new policy meant that the Stalinist one-party state would then be the final goal of the CCP for China, in which the CCP would be the focus of the final decision making of the state affairs.

But the old double way of governance could not meet the requirements of the new situation and new policy. If the Stalinist state was to be established in China, the government would be more predominantly controlled by the CCP. In other words, the CCP's leadership over the government had to be further tightened. On the other hand, the focus of government work had to change. According to the new policy, those democratic people would no longer be the allied partners of the CCP. Instead, they would become the new target that the CCP was going to lead the government to fight against, and had to be further limited. With the changing focus, the government also had to weigh more toward the CCP.

Besides, there had also been practical problems existing between the double systems of governance. As the government chairman, Mao Zedong was constrained by the vertical bureaucratic structures and his direction over the execution should mainly be supervising the overall operation of the GAC, only covering the level of the premier. But as the CCP's chairman, he was the final authority of decision making and demanded a more substantive control over the state affairs. Thus the limited government chairman could not match perfectly with the requirement of the CCP chairman for a more direct and regular control over the governmental affairs.[138]

Since the establishment of the Central People's Government, several cases had occurred that the government departments had failed to seek his prior approval on some government issues.[139] Between the party's command and the formal government bureaucracy, Mao Zedong had been different from Zhou Enlai and Dong, Biwu had always preferred the former,[140] emphasizing the control of major policy issues[141] and key governmental affairs, for example, the security department,[142] by the CCP. These cases were considered by him a risk of the government being invaded from the leadership of the CCP.[143]

For all these reasons, more adjustment to the government became inevitable. On March 10, 1953, an internal directive was issued from Chairman Mao, which not only demanded that all major actions by the government should seek the permission of the CCPCC before being implemented, thus changing the leadership of the CCP over the government from ex post approval to prior permission, but also specified fourteen senior party cadres holding positions in the government to be directly responsible to the CCPCC for their assigned works.[144]

After these adjustments, the double command systems became substantially opted toward the side of the party, and the decision-making power was further concentrated in the CCPCC:

> The abolishment of the party group in the GAC had a great impact on its daily work, resulting in a 'vacuum' in the agenda of the GAC meeting. Before that, a lot of working summaries and policy reports had been sent to the GAC from its various subordinates, from which the GAC had discretion to decide to list in its agenda. Now, since all these documents had to be examined and approved by the CCPCC in advance before submitting to the GAC, the GAC had no item to list in its agenda before the approval of the CCPCC. The GAC official who was responsible for setting the agenda was very worried and discussed with us. I had by chance a report from the People's Bank about the management of gold and silver. To avoid the cancellation of the GAC meeting, I thought it was a minor issue and could be added to the agenda, while being examined by the CCPCC in the meantime. At that time, Mao Zedong was not in Beijing. Zhou Enlai sent my suggestion to Liu Shaoqi for approval, who decided it could be better to submit to the GAC after the CCPCC examined it. As a result, the GAC meeting had to delay for once.[145]

In such a shift of decision-making focus, Mao Zedong stood out from his colleagues in the Central Secretariat by his final approval on behalf of the CCPCC: "Any documents and telegram that were sent out in the name of the Central Committee should be reviewed by me beforehand. Otherwise they should be invalid."[146] Therefore, the decision-making power ultimately fell in the hands of Mao Zedong.[147]

In summary, although the new Chinese government was modeled after the former Soviet Union, the CPG chairman was an exception, which was more akin to, and also more distinct than, that of the First Soviet Congress of the China Soviet Republic. The CPG chairman seemed to be a combination of both chairmen of the CSR, working in the Central People's Government Council on one hand, but exerting a superior role and functioning permanently on the other hand. As a leading member of the Council, he directed the Council's works, such as policy making, and assumed final responsibility for all government works, including military, civil administration, and judicial affairs. According to the drafters' explanation, Stalin's theory of collective head of state had been followed and the chairman could be regarded as a member of the collective head of state. However, neither the chairman of the Presidium in the former Soviet Union nor any modern Western presidency had ever enjoyed such a dominant authority.

As the CCP was far more organized and effective than the government apparatus, there could be a risk that the government chairmanship be overshadowed and even overturned by the CCP chairmanship, if without a clear harness on the operation of both authorities. By occupying the majority in the government and loose legal constraints on one hand, and enjoying the supreme authority in the CCP on the other hand, Mao Zedong successfully overcome the formal limits on his governmental chairmanship by way of the CCP's leadership during the process of "learning from the big brother." As a result, the decision-making power was further concentrated into the hand of the CCP's chairman Mao Zedong. The legally provided governance headed by the CPG chairman had been overshadowed and become obsolete since then, and a new office was needed to take its place.

NOTES

1. Cold War International Project Bulletin (CWIPB), issue 16, 114-115. The relevant information about the communication between Moscow and the CCP will be from this bulletin. However, as it is made clear in this bulletin, information in that regard has been incomplete as it was translated from the Russian source, which had been omitted and tampered. See CWIPB, issue 16, 105.
2. Sergei N. Goncharov, John W. Lewis, and Xue Litai, *Uncertain Partners: Stalin, Mao, and the Korean War* (Stanford: Stanford University Press, 1993), 299-300.
3. For a brief introduction and analysis about Mao Zedong's repeated requests to visit the USSR, see CWIPB, issue 16, 106.
4. CWIPB, issue 16, 119.
5. CWIPB, issue 16, 120.
6. CWIPB, issue 16, 120.
7. CWIPB, issue 16, 106-107.
8. Mao Zedong, "Zai Zhonggong Zhongyang Zhengzhiju Huiyi Shang De Baogao" [Report at the Meeting of the CCPCC Politburo], in Mao Zedong Wenji (ed.), *Zhonggong Zhongyang Wenxian Yanjiushi* [Collection of Mao Zedong's Writings] (Beijing: Renmin Chubanshe, 1996), vol. 5, 136-137.
9. Mao Zedong, "Zai Zhonggong Zhongyang Zhengzhiju Huiyi Shang De Baogao" [Report at the Meeting of the CCPCC Politburo], in Mao Zedong Wenji (ed.), *Zhonggong Zhongyang Wenxian Yanjiushi* [Collection of Mao Zedong's Writings] (Beijing: Renmin Chubanshe, 1996), vol. 5, 136-137.
10. Mao Zedong, "Zai Zhonggong Zhongyang Zhengzhiju Huiyi Shang De Baogao" [Report at the Meeting of the CCPCC Politburo], in Mao Zedong Wenji (ed.), *Zhonggong Zhongyang Wenxian Yanjiushi* [Collection of Mao Zedong's Writings] (Beijing: Renmin Chubanshe, 1996), vol. 5, 136-137.
11. Mao Zedong, "Zai Zhonggong Zhongyang Zhengzhiju Huiyi Shang De Baogao" [Report at the Meeting of the CCPCC Politburo], in Mao Zedong Wenji (ed.), *Zhonggong Zhongyang Wenxian Yanjiushi* [Collection of Mao Zedong's Writings] (Beijing: Renmin Chubanshe, 1996), vol. 5, 136-137.

12. Mao Zedong, "Zai Zhonggong Zhongyang Zhengzhiju Huiyi Shang De Baogao" [Report at the Meeting of the CCPCC Politburo], in Mao Zedong Wenji (ed.), *Zhonggong Zhongyang Wenxian Yanjiushi* [Collection of Mao Zedong's Writings] (Beijing: Renmin Chubanshe, 1996), vol. 5, 136-137.

13. Mao Zedong, "Zai Zhonggong Zhongyang Zhengzhiju Huiyi Shang De Baogao" [Report at the Meeting of the CCPCC Politburo], in Mao Zedong Wenji (ed.), *Zhonggong Zhongyang Wenxian Yanjiushi* [Collection of Mao Zedong's Writings] (Beijing: Renmin Chubanshe, 1996), vol. 5, 136-137.

14. Nanshan, "Gongheguo Linshi Xianfa Chutai Shimo" [The Making of Provisional Constitution of the Republic], *Dangshi Bolan*, no. 7 (2003): 6; Liu Wushang, *Zhou Enlai Zai Jianshe Niandai* [Zhou Enlai in the Construction Era] (Beijing: Renmin Chubanshe, 2008), 17.

15. CWIPB, issue 16, 124.

16. CWIPB, issue 16, 125.

17. CWIPB, issue 16, 125.

18. CWIPB, issue 16, 125.

19. CWIPB, issue 6-7, 29.

20. CWIPB, issue 16, 129.

21. For study on Anastas Mikoyan's visit to China, see Dieter Heinzig, *The Soviet Union and Commuist China, 1945-1950: The Arduous Road to the Alliance* (Armonk, NY: M.E. Sharpe, 2004), 135-156; Sergi N. Goncharov, John W. Lewis, and Xue Litai, *Uncertain Partners: Stalin, Mao, and the Korean War* (Stanford: Stanford University Press, 1993), 38-51; Sergey Radchenko and David Wolff, "To the Summit via Proxy-Summits: New Evidence from Soviet and Chinese Archives on Mao's Long March to Moscow, 1949," CWIPB, issue 16, 107-109. And also see Shi Zhe, *Zai Lishi Juren Shenbian: Shi Zhe Huiyilu* [Beside the Historical Giant: Memoire of Shi Zhe] (Beijing: Zhongyang Wenxian Chubanshe, 1995), 372-388; *Wo De Yisheng* [My Life] (Beijing: Renmin Chubanshe, 2001), 273-284; Shi Zhe, *Mao Zedong De Fanyi Shi Zhe Yanzhong De Gaoceng Renwu* [High-Level Characters in the Eyes of Mao Zedong's Interpreter Shi Zhe] (Beijing: Renmin Chubanshe, 2005), 63.

22. Shi Zhe, *Wo De Yisheng* [My Life] (Beijing: Renmin Chubanshe, 2001), 273-274; *Mao Zedong De Fanyi Shi Zhe Yanzhong De Gaoceng Renwu* [High-Level Characters in the Eyes of Mao Zedong's Interpreter Shi Zhe] (Beijing: Renmin Chubanshe, 2005), 63-65.

23. CWIPB, issue 16, 156.

24. CWIPB, issue 16, 156.

25. CWIPB, issue 16, 156.

26. CWIPB, issue 16, 156.

27. Later on, he became the mayor of Nanjing city, the former capital of the Nationalist government.

28. CWIPB, issue 16, 156.

29. Shi Zhe, *Mao Zedong De Fanyi Shi Zhe Yanzhong De Gaoceng Renwu*[High-Level Characters in the Eyes of Mao Zedong's Interpreter Shi Zhe] (Beijing: Renmin Chubanshe, 2005), 164-165; *Wo De Yisheng* [My Life] (Beijing: Renmin Chubanshe, 2001), 283-284.

30. "Daoda Jiefangqu De Minzhu Renshi Li Jishen Deng Wushiwu Ren Fabiao Dui Shiju Yijian" [Opinions to the Current Situation Made by Fifty-five People Who Includes Li Jishen and Have Arrived at the Liberated Areas], in Yang Jiangxin, Shi Guangshu, and Yuan Tinghua (eds.), *Wuxing Hongqi Cong Zheli Shengqi-Zhonghua Renmin Zhengzhi Xieshanghuiyi Dansheng Jishi Ji Ziliao Xuanbian* [Five-Star Red Flag Rises From Here: The Birth of the Chinese People's Political Consultative Conference and Selection of Relevant Documents] (Wenshi Ziliao Chubanshe, 1984), 216.

31. Mao Zedong, "Zai Zhonggong Qijie Erzhong Quanhui Shang De Zongjie" [Summary at the Second Plenary of the Seventh CCPCC], in Zhonggong Zhongyang Wenxian Yanjiushi (ed.), *Mao Zedong Wenji* [Collection of Mao Zedong's Writings] (Beijing: Renmin Chubanshe, 1996), vol. 5, 265.

32. Zhang Xuexin (ed.), *Ren Bishi Zhuan* [Biography of Ren Bishi] (Beijing: Zhongyang Wenxian Chubanshe, 1994), 713; Bian Yingji (ed.), *Yidai Weiren: Mao Zedong Shihua* [The Great Man: History of Mao Zedong] (Xinjiang: Xinjiang Renmin Chubanshe, 2002), vol. 2,

114; Bo Yibo, *Ruogan Zhongda Juece Yu Shijian De Huigu* [Review of Some Important Decision-Makings and Matters] (Beijing: Renmin Chubanshe, 1997), 30.

33. Chen Dunde, *Kaiguo Waijiao Shiji* [Diplomacy in the Founding Year] (Beijing: Jiefangjun Wenyi Chubanshe 2007), 159. According to the CWIPB, Mao Zedong requested three hundred million dollars on February 6, 1949, ten times of his original figure of 30 million dollars suggested in July 1948. See CWIPB, issue 16, 109. It is also said that the CCP requested four hundred million dollars, but Moscow only agreed to a loan of three hundred million dollars. See Wu Lengxi, *Shinian Lunzhan Yijiu Wuliu Yijiu Liuliu Zhongsu Guanxi Huiyilu* [Ten Years of Debates: Memory of Sino-USSR Relations between 1956 and 1966] (Beijing: Zhongyang Wenxian Dhubanshe, 2000), 324.

34. For discussion about Liu Shaoqi's visit to Moscow in 1949, see Dieter Heinzig, *The Soviet Union and Commuist China, 1945-1950: The Arduous Road to the Alliance* (Armonk, NY: M.E. Sharpe, 2004), 174-231; Sergi N. Goncharov, John W. Lewis, and Xue Litai, *Uncertain Partners: Stalin, Mao, and the Korean War* (Stanford: Stanford University Press, 1993), 61-75; Sergey Radchenko and David Wolff, "To the Summit via Proxy-Summits: New Evidence from Soviet and Chinese Archives on Mao's Long March to Moscow, 1949," CWIPB, issue 16, 110-111. And Shi Zhe, *Zai Lishi Juren Shenbian: Shi Zhe Huiyilu* [Beside the Historical Giant: Memoire of Shi Zhe] (Beijing: Zhongyang Wenxian Chubanshe, 1995), 395-426; *Wo De Yisheng* [My Life] (Beijing: Renmin Chubanshe, 2001), 273; Shi Zhe, *Mao Zedong De Fanyi Shi Zhe Yanzhong De Gaoceng Renwu* [High-Level Characters in the Eyes of Mao Zedong's Interpreter Shi Zhe] (Beijing: Renmin Chubanshe, 2005), 63.

35. Odd Arne Westad (ed.), *Brothers in Arms: The Rise and Fall of the Sino-Soviet Alliance, 1945-1963* (Washington, DC: Woodrow Wilson Center Press; Stanford: Stanford University Press, 1998), 301. For the English version of this report translated from the Russian publication and amended according to its original document, see Odd Arne Westad (ed.), *Brothers in Arms: The Rise and Fall of the Sino-Soviet Alliance, 1945-1963* (Washington, DC: Woodrow Wilson Center Press; Stanford: Stanford University Press, 1998), 301-313. For its Chinese text, see Zhonggong Zhongyang Wenxian Yanjiushi (ed.), *Jianguo Yilai Liu Shaoqi Wengao* [Liu Shaoqi's Writings since the Founding of the People's Republic of China] (Beijing:Zhongyang Wenxian Chubanshe, 1998) vol. 1, 1-28. For Chinese translation from Russian writing, see Chen Dhunhua and Liu Cunkun (trans.), *Si Dalin Yu Zhongguo* [Stalin and China] (Beijing: Xinhua Chubanshe, 2001), 102-115. For a recording on this report by the Chinese interpreter participating Liu Shaoqi's visit to Moscow, see Shi Zhe, *Wo De Yisheng* [My Life] (Beijing: Renmin Chubanshe, 2001), 299-300; *Mao Zedong De Fanyi Shi Zhe Yanzhong De Gaoceng Renwu* [High-Level Characters in the Eyes of Mao Zedong's Interpreter Shi Zhe] (Beijing: Renmin Chubanshe, 2005), 220-221.

36. Odd Arne Westad (ed.), *Brothers in Arms: The Rise and Fall of the Sino-Soviet Alliance, 1945-1963* (Washington, DC: Woodrow Wilson Center Press; Stanford: Stanford University Press, 1998), 303-304.

37. See Zhonggong Zhongyang Wenxian Yanjiushi (ed.), *Jianguo Yilai Liu Shaoqi Wengao* [Liu Shaoqi's Writings since the Founding of the People's Republic of China] (Beijing:Zhongyang Wenxian Chubanshe, 1998), vol. 1, 5. It is translated by the author based on the Chinese text. There are no differences among those various Chinese versions on this point, but the English version in "Brothers in Arms" has some discrepancies in meaning from those Chinese texts, which translates it as: "Comrade Mao Zedong *has been nominated* chairman of the central government, and Comrade Zhou Enlai prime minister." See Odd Arne Westad (ed.), *Brothers in Arms: The Rise and Fall of the Sino-Soviet Alliance, 1945-1963* (Washington, DC: Woodrow Wilson Center Press; Stanford: Stanford University Press, 1998), 304.

38. It is translated by the author based on the Chinese text. There is no substantive difference between this translation with that in "Brothers in Arms," which is "what's that: president in fact?" See Odd Arne Westad (ed.), *Brothers in Arms: The Rise and Fall of the Sino-Soviet Alliance, 1945-1963* (Washington, DC: Woodrow Wilson Center Press; Stanford: Stanford University Press, 1998), 304.

39. Liang Da et al. (trans.), *Sulian Xianfa Jiaocheng* [Textbook of the Soviet Constitution] (Beijing: Wushi Niandai Chubanshe, 1950), 170.

40. See Odd Arne Westad (ed.), *Brothers in Arms: The Rise and Fall of the Sino-Soviet Alliance, 1945-1963* (Washington, DC: Woodrow Wilson Center Press; Stanford: Stanford University Press, 1998), 305.

41. Chen Dunde, *Kaiguo Waijiao Shiji* [Diplomacy in the Founding Year] (Beijing: Jiefangjun Wenyi Chubanshe 2007), 112.

42. Mao Zedong, "Lun Renmin Minzhu Zhuanzheng" [On People's Democratic Dictatorship], in *Mao Zedong Xuanji* [Selections of Mao Zedong] (Beijing: Renmin Chubanshe, 1960), 1362.

43. Zhonggong Zhongyang Wenxian Yanjiushi (ed.), *Jianguo Yilai Liu Shaoqi Wengao* [Liu Shaoqi's Writings since the Founding of the People's Republic of China] (Beijing:Zhongyang Wenxian Chubanshe, 1998), vol. 1, 22, 24. No Russian record on this point has been found until now. The Chinese interpreter who witnessed this meeting only recalled that Stalin confirmed CCP's designation of the new government and its foreign policy summarized in Liu Shaoqi's report and did not mentioned whether Stalin had ever raised such a question. See Shi Zhe, *Wo De Yisheng* [My Life] (Beijing: Renmin Chubanshe, 2001), 299-300; *Mao Zedong De Fanyi Shi Zhe Yanzhong De Gaoceng Renwu* [High-Level Characters in the Eyes of Mao Zedong's Interpreter Shi Zhe] (Beijing: Renmin Chubanshe, 2005), 220-221.

44. Shi Zhe, *Wo De Yisheng* [My Life] (Beijing: Renmin Chubanshe, 2001), 299-300; *Mao Zedong De Fanyi Shi Zhe Yanzhong De Gaoceng Renwu* [High-Level Characters in the Eyes of Mao Zedong's Interpreter Shi Zhe] (Beijing: Renmin Chubanshe, 2005), 220-221.

45. Shi Zhe, *Wo De Yisheng* [My Life] (Beijing: Renmin Chubanshe, 2001), 316-317; *Mao Zedong De Fanyi Shi Zhe Yanzhong De Gaoceng Renwu* [High-Level Characters in the Eyes of Mao Zedong's Interpreter Shi Zhe] (Beijing: Renmin Chubanshe, 2005), 237.

46. Huang Hua, "Situ Leideng Lihua Zhenxiang" [The Truth of John Leighton Stuart's leaving China], in *Yanda Wenshi Ziliao* (Beijing: Beijing University Press, 1995), no. 9, 76.

47. Li Ge, "Mao Zedong Choujian Zhongyang Renmin Zhengfu De Jihua He Jiben Yuanze" [Mao Zedong's Plan and Basic Principal for the Establishment of the Central People's Government], *Dang De Wenxian*, no. 6 (2007): 54.

48. In a telegram dated on August 6, from Zhou Enlai to his wife, Deng Yingchao, Zhou Enlai informed her that the New Political Consultative Conference would meet in September. See Ma Yongshun, *Zhou Enlai He Renmin Zhengxie* [Zhou Enlai and the People's Consultative Conference] (Beijing: Zhongguo Wenshi Chubanshe, 2004), 9. Therefore, Stalin's suggestion must have played a major role in CCP's changing its plan. But there is also other viewpoint among Chinese scholars that the CCP made its decision independently. See Chen Dunde, *Kaiguo Waijiao Shiji* [Diplomacy in the Founding Year] (Beijing: Jiefangjun Wenyi Chubanshe 2007), 167.

49. Shi Zhe, *Wo De Yisheng* [My Life] (Beijing: Renmin Chubanshe, 2001), 316-317; *Mao Zedong De Fanyi Shi Zhe Yanzhong De Gaoceng Renwu* [High-Level Characters in the Eyes of Mao Zedong's Interpreter Shi Zhe] (Beijing: Renmin Chubanshe, 2005), 237.

50. It was renamed as the Chinese People's Political Consultative Conference (CPPCC).

51. For the draft, see "Guanyu Zhou Enlai Yu Gongtong Gangling Qicao Guocheng De Yizu Wenxian" [Some Documents Concerning Zhou Enlai's Participation to the Drafting of the Common Program], *Dang De Wenxian*, no. 2 (2003): 4-12.

52. Liu Yitao and Xue Peisong, "Mao Zedong Yu Xin Zhengzhi Xieshang Huiyi" [Mao Zedong and the New Political Consultative Conference], in Shi Guangshu (ed.), *Yinlai Shuguang De Shenghui: Xin Zhengzhi Xieshang Huiyi Qinli Ji* [Grand Meeting in the Dawn: Record of Personal Participation to the New Political Consultative Conference] (Beijing: Zhongguo Wenshi Chubanshe, 1987), 227; Huqiaomu Huiyi Maozedong Bianxie Zu (ed.), "Mao Zedong Yu Gongtong Gangling De Zhiding" [Mao Zedong and the Making of the Common Program], *Dangdai Zhongguoshi Yanjiu*, no. 1 (1994): 11; Wang Hongyan, "Sanci Qicao Sanci Mingming De Gongheguo Linshi Xianfa" [The Republic's Provisional Constitution Being Drafted and Named for Three Times], *Zhongheng*, no. 11 (2002): 42.

53. Xu Chongde, *Zhonghua Renmin Gongheguo Xianfashi* [Constitutional History of the People's Republic of China] (Fujian: Fujian Renmin Chubanshe, 2005), vol. 1, 30.

54. Huqiaomu Huiyi Maozedong Bianxie Zu (ed.), "Mao Zedong Yu Gongtong Gangling De Zhiding" [Mao Zedong and the Making of the Common Program], *Dangdai Zhongguoshi*

Yanjiu, no. 1 (1994): 11; Wang Hongyan, "Sanci Qicao Sanci Mingming De Gongheguo Linshi Xianfa" [The Republic's Provisional Constitution Being Drafted and Named for Three Times], *Zhongheng*, no. 11 (2002): 42; Huang Dingchen, "Xin Zhengxie De Fenggong Weiji Jiang Yongzai Shice" [Great Achievements of the New Political Consultative Conference will be Record in History], in Shi Guangshu (ed.), *Yinlai Shuguang De Shenghui: Xin Zhengzhi Xieshang Huiyi Qinli Ji* [Grand Meeting in the Dawn: Record of Personal Participation to the New Political Consultative Conference] (Beijing: Zhongguo Wenshi Chubanshe, 1987), 118. However, it has remained unknown about the details of these repeated revisions within and outside of the CCP on the draft, except that its title was changed to "the common program of China's Political Consultative Conference" on September 5. For this, see Wang Hongyan, "Sanci Qicao Sanci Mingming De Gongheguo Linshi Xianfa" [The Republic's Provisional Constitution Being Drafted and Named for Three Times], *Zhongheng*, no. 11 (2002): 42.

55. Gao Jianzhong (ed.), *Zhongguo Renmin Zhengzhi Xieshang Huiyi Chengli Jishi* [Documentary of the Establishment of the CPPCC] (Beijing: Dangdai Zhongguo Chubanshe, 2002), 221-222; Dongbiwu zhuanxiezu, *Dong Biwu Zhuan 1886-1975* [Biography of Dong Biwu 1886-1975] (Beijing: Zhongyang Wenxian Chubanshe, 2006), vol. 2, [illegible].

56. Dong Biwu, "Guanyu Caoni Zhonghua Renmin Gongheguo Zhongyang Renmin Zhengfu Zuzhifa De Jingguo Jiqi Jiben Neirong De Baogao" [Report on the Making of the Organic Law of the Central People's Government of the People's Republic of China and Its Basic Content], in Yang Jiangxin, Shi Guangshu, and Yuan Tinghua (eds.), *Wuxing Hongqi Cong Zheli Shengqi-Zhonghua Renmin Zhengzhi Xieshanghuiyi Dansheng Jishi Ji Ziliao Xuanbian* [Five-Star Red Flag Rises From Here: The Birth of the Chinese People's Political Consultative Conference and Selection of Relevant Documents] (Beijing: Wenshi Ziliao Chubanshe, 1984), 519-520.

57. Dongbiwu zhuanxiezu, *Dong Biwu Zhuan 1886-1975* [Biography of Dong Biwu 1886-1975] (Beijing: Zhongyang Wenxian Chubanshe, 2006), vol. 2, 647-649; Dong Biwu, "Guanyu Caoni Zhonghua Renmin Gongheguo Zhongyang Renmin Zhengfu Zuzhifa De Jingguo Jiqi Jiben Neirong De Baogao" [Report on the Making of the Organic Law of the Central People's Government of the People's Republic of China and Its Basic Content], in Yang Jiangxin, Shi Guangshu, and Yuan Tinghua (eds.), *Wuxing Hongqi Cong Zheli Shengqi-Zhonghua Renmin Zhengzhi Xieshanghuiyi Dansheng Jishi Ji Ziliao Xuanbian* [Five-Star Red Flag Rises From Here: The Birth of the Chinese People's Political Consultative Conference and Selection of Relevant Documents] (Wenshi Ziliao Chubanshe, 1984), 519-520; Lei Jieqiong, "Wo Canjia Yijie Zhengxie De Huiyi" [My Memory of Participating the First Political Consultative Conference], in Shi Guangshu (ed.), *Yinlai Shuguang De Shenghui: Xin Zhengzhi Xieshang Huiyi Qinli Ji* [Grand Meeting in the Dawn: Record of Personal Participation to the New Political Consultative Conference] (Beijing: Zhongguo Wenshi Chubanshe, 1987), 101.

58. Shidai Shuju (ed.), *Cong Zhongguo Renmin Zhengzhi Xieshang Huiyi Dao Zhongyang Renmin Zhengfu Chengli* [From the Chinese People's Political Consultative Conference to the Establishment of the Central People's Government] (Shanghai: Shidai Shuju, 1949), 42-44.

59. Zhongguo Renmin Zhengzhi Xieshang Huiyi Diyi Jie Quanti Huiyi Xinwen Chu (ed.), *Zhongguo Renmin Zhengzhi Xieshang Huiyi Diyi Jie Quanti Huiyi Huikan* [Bulletin of the First Plenary of the Chinese People's Political Consultative Conference], no. 2 (1949): 2.

60. Shidai Shuju (ed.), *Cong Zhongguo Renmin Zhengzhi Xieshang Huiyi Dao Zhongyang Renmin Zhengfu Chengli* [From the Chinese People's Political Consultative Conference to the Establishment of the Central People's Government] (Shanghai: Shidai Shuju, 1949), 136-137.

61. Zhongguo Renmin Zhengzhi Xieshang Huiyi Diyi Jie Quanti Huiyi Xinwen Chu (ed.), *Zhongguo Renmin Zhengzhi Xieshang Huiyi Diyi Jie Quanti Huiyi Huikan* [Bulletin of the First Plenary of the Chinese People's Political Consultative Conference], no. 8 (1949): 1.

62. The Common Program of the Chinese People's Political Consultative Conference (adopted by the First Plenary Session of the Chinese People's Political Consultative Conference on September 29, 1949), Art. 12.

63. The Common Program of the Chinese People's Political Consultative Conference (adopted by the First Plenary Session of the Chinese People's Political Consultative Conference on September 29, 1949), Art. 13.

64. The Common Program of the Chinese People's Political Consultative Conference (adopted by the First Plenary Session of the Chinese People's Political Consultative Conference on September 29, 1949), Art. 12.

65. The Common Program of the Chinese People's Political Consultative Conference (adopted by the First Plenary Session of the Chinese People's Political Consultative Conference on September 29, 1949), Art. 15.

66. The Organic Law of the Central People's Government of the People's Republic of China (adopted by the First Plenary Session of the Chinese People's Political Consultative Conference on September 29, 1949), Art. 6.

67. The Organic Law of the Central People's Government of the People's Republic of China (adopted by the First Plenary Session of the Chinese People's Political Consultative Conference on September 29, 1949), Art. 4.

68. The Organic Law of the Central People's Government of the People's Republic of China (adopted by the First Plenary Session of the Chinese People's Political Consultative Conference on September 29, 1949), Art. 5.

69. The Organic Law of the Central People's Government of the People's Republic of China (adopted by the First Plenary Session of the Chinese People's Political Consultative Conference on September 29, 1949), Art. 16.

70. The Organic Law of the Central People's Government of the People's Republic of China (adopted by the First Plenary Session of the Chinese People's Political Consultative Conference on September 29, 1949), Art. 13.

71. The Organic Law of the Central People's Government of the People's Republic of China (adopted by the First Plenary Session of the Chinese People's Political Consultative Conference on September 29, 1949), Art. 18.

72. The Organic Law of the Central People's Government of the People's Republic of China (adopted by the First Plenary Session of the Chinese People's Political Consultative Conference on September 29, 1949), Art. 32.

73. The Organic Law of the Central People's Government of the People's Republic of China (adopted by the First Plenary Session of the Chinese People's Political Consultative Conference on September 29, 1949), Art. 3.

74. The Organic Law of the Central People's Government of the People's Republic of China (adopted by the First Plenary Session of the Chinese People's Political Consultative Conference on September 29, 1949), Art. 7.

75. Dong Biwu, "Guanyu Caoni Zhonghua Renmin Gongheguo Zhongyang Renmin Zhengfu Zuzhifa De Jingguo Jiqi Jiben Neirong De Baogao" [Report on the Making of the Organic Law of the Central People's Government of the People's Republic of China and Its Basic Content], in Yang Jiangxin, Shi Guangshu, and Yuan Tinghua (eds.), *Wuxing Hongqi Cong Zheli Shengqi-Zhonghua Renmin Zhengzhi Xieshanghuiyi Dansheng Jishi Ji Ziliao Xuanbian* [Five-Star Red Flag Rises From Here: The Birth of the Chinese People's Political Consultative Conference and Selection of Relevant Documents] (Beijing: Wenshi Ziliao Chubanshe, 1984), 521.

76. The Organic Law of the Central People's Government of the People's Republic of China (adopted by the First Plenary Session of the Chinese People's Political Consultative Conference on September 29, 1949), Art. 4.

77. Zhang Zhiran, "Zhongyang Renmin Zhengfu Zuzhifa Pouxi" [Analysis of the Organic Law of the Central People's Government], in Bai Yan (ed.), *Zhongguo Renmin Zhengzhi Xieshanghuiyi Gongtong Gangling (Xuexi Ziliao)* [The Common Program of the Chinese People's Political Consultative Conference (Study Materials)] (Lianyi Chubanshe, 1950), 109-111.

78. The Organic Law of the Central People's Government of the People's Republic of China (adopted by the First Plenary Session of the Chinese People's Political Consultative Conference on September 29, 1949), Art. 10.

79. The Organic Law of the Central People's Government of the People's Republic of China (adopted by the First Plenary Session of the Chinese People's Political Consultative Conference on September 29, 1949), Art. 14.

80. The Organic Law of the Central People's Government of the People's Republic of China (adopted by the First Plenary Session of the Chinese People's Political Consultative Conference on September 29, 1949), Art. 15, paragraph 3.

81. The Organic Law of the Chinese People's Political Consultative Conference of the People's Republic of China (adopted by the First Plenary Session of the Chinese People's Political Consultative Conference on September 29, 1949), Art. 7, paragraph 3, subparagraph 3.

82. The Organic Law of the Central People's Government of the People's Republic of China (adopted by the First Plenary Session of the Chinese People's Political Consultative Conference on September 29, 1949), Art. 13, paragraph 2.

83. Li Ge, "Guanyu 1949-1954 Nian Zhongyang Renmin Zhengfu De Guoran Wenti" [Several Issues Concerning the Central People's Government during 1949 and 1954], *Dang De Wenxain*, no. 4 (1996): 78; "1949-1954 Nian Zhongyang Renmin Zhengfu Zuzhi Jigou Shezhi Jiqi Bianhua" [Organization of the Central People's Government and Relevant Changes during 1949 and 1954], *Dang De Wenxain*, no. 5.1 (2001): 86-87.

84. The Organic Law of the Central People's Government of the People's Republic of China (adopted by the First Plenary Session of the Chinese People's Political Consultative Conference on September 29, 1949), Art. 7, paragraph 2.

85. The Organic Law of the Central People's Government of the People's Republic of China (adopted by the First Plenary Session of the Chinese People's Political Consultative Conference on September 29, 1949), Art. 5.

86. The Organic Law of the Central People's Government of the People's Republic of China (adopted by the First Plenary Session of the Chinese People's Political Consultative Conference on September 29, 1949), Art. 8.

87. The Organic Law of the Central People's Government of the People's Republic of China (adopted by the First Plenary Session of the Chinese People's Political Consultative Conference on September 29, 1949), Art. 10.

88. The Organic Law of the Central People's Government of the People's Republic of China (adopted by the First Plenary Session of the Chinese People's Political Consultative Conference on September 29, 1949), Art. 8.

89. The Organic Law of the Central People's Government of the People's Republic of China (adopted by the First Plenary Session of the Chinese People's Political Consultative Conference on September 29, 1949), Art. 12.

90. The Organic Law of the Central People's Government of the People's Republic of China (adopted by the First Plenary Session of the Chinese People's Political Consultative Conference on September 29, 1949), Art. 10.

91. The Organic Law of the Central People's Government of the People's Republic of China (adopted by the First Plenary Session of the Chinese People's Political Consultative Conference on September 29, 1949), Art. 15.

92. The Organic Law of the Central People's Government of the People's Republic of China (adopted by the First Plenary Session of the Chinese People's Political Consultative Conference on September 29, 1949), Art. 9.

93. Dong Biwu, "Guanyu Caoni Zhonghua Renmin Gongheguo Zhongyang Renmin Zhengfu Zuzhifa De Jingguo Jiqi Jiben Neirong De Baogao" [Report on the Making of the Organic Law of the Central People's Government of the People's Republic of China and Its Basic Content], in Yang Jiangxin, Shi Guangshu, and Yuan Tinghua (eds.), *Wuxing Hongqi Cong Zheli Shengqi-Zhonghua Renmin Zhengzhi Xieshanghuiyi Dansheng Jishi Ji Ziliao Xuanbian* [Five-Star Red Flag Rises From Here: The Birth of the Chinese People's Political Consultative Conference and Selection of Relevant Documents] (Wenshi Ziliao Chubanshe, 1984), 522.

94. The Organic Law of the Central People's Government of the People's Republic of China (adopted by the First Plenary Session of the Chinese People's Political Consultative Conference on September 29, 1949), Art. 14.

95. Zhang Zhiran, "Zhongyang Renmin Zhengfu Zuzhifa Pouxi" [Analysis of the Organic Law of the Central People's Government], in Bai Yan (ed.), *Zhongguo Renmin Zhengzhi Xieshanghuiyi Gongtong Gangling (Xuexi Ziliao)* [The Common Program of the Chinese People's Political Consultative Conference (Study Materials)] (Lianyi Chubanshe, 1950), 113.

96. The Organic Law of the Central People's Government of the People's Republic of China (adopted by the First Plenary Session of the Chinese People's Political Consultative Conference on September 29, 1949), Art. 5.

97. The Organic Law of the Central People's Government of the People's Republic of China (adopted by the First Plenary Session of the Chinese People's Political Consultative Conference on September 29, 1949), Art. 18.

98. Zhang Zhiran, "Zhongyang Renmin Zhengfu Zuzhifa Pouxi" [Analysis of the Organic Law of the Central People's Government], in Bai Yan (ed.), *Zhongguo Renmin Zhengzhi Xieshanghuiyi Gongtong Gangling (Xuexi Ziliao)* [The Common Program of the Chinese People's Political Consultative Conference (Study Materials)] (Lianyi Chubanshe, 1950), 114.

99. Zhongguo Renmin Zhengzhi Xieshang Huiyi Diyi Jie Quanti Huiyi Xinwen Chu (ed.), *Zhongguo Renmin Zhengzhi Xieshang Huiyi Diyi Jie Quanti Huiyi Huikan* [Bulletin of the First Plenary of the Chinese People's Political Consultative Conference], no. 10 (1949): 2.

100. Zhongguo Renmin Zhengzhi Xieshang Huiyi Diyi Jie Quanti Huiyi Xinwen Chu (ed.), *Zhongguo Renmin Zhengzhi Xieshang Huiyi Diyi Jie Quanti Huiyi Huikan* [Bulletin of the First Plenary of the Chinese People's Political Consultative Conference], no. 11 (1949): 3.

101. *Renmin Ribao*, October 1, 1949.

102. For a brief documentary introduction of the establishment of diplomatic relations between PRC and the USSR, see Lian Zhengbao et al. (ed.), *Jiemi Waijiao Wenxian Zhonghua Renmin Gongheguo Jianjiao Dangan 1949-1955* [Declassifying Diplomatic Documents: Documents of the People's Republic of China Concerning Establishment of Diplomatic Relations 1949-1955] (Beijing: Zhongguo Huabao Chubanshe, 2006), 12-45.

103. See Dieter Heinzig, *The Soviet Union and Commuist China, 1945-1950: The Arduous Road to the Alliance* (Armonk, NY: M.E. Sharpe, 2004), 265; Sergi N. Goncharov, John W. Lewis, and Xue Litai, *Uncertain Partners: Stalin, Mao, and the Korean War* (Stanford: Stanford University Press, 1993), 86; Pang Xianzhi and Jin Chongji (eds.), *Mao Zedong Zhuan 1949-1976* [Biography of Mao Zedong 1949-1976] (Beijing: Zhongyang Wenxian Chubanshe, 2003), vol. 1, 31;

104. See Dieter Heinzig, *The Soviet Union and Commuist China, 1945-1950: The Arduous Road to the Alliance* (Armonk, NY: M.E. Sharpe, 2004), 275.

105. See Dieter Heinzig, *The Soviet Union and Commuist China, 1945-1950: The Arduous Road to the Alliance* (Armonk, NY: M.E. Sharpe, 2004), 293.

106. Zhonggong Zhongyang Wenxian Yanjiushi (ed.), *Jiangguo Yilai Mao Zedong Wengao* [Writings of Mao Zedong since the Founding of the People's Republic of China] (Beijing: Zhongyang Wenxian Chubanshe, 1987), vol. 1, 211-213.

107. Dieter Heinzig, *The Soviet Union and Commuist China, 1945-1950: The Arduous Road to the Alliance* (Armonk, NY: M.E. Sharpe, 2004), 337; Sergi N. Goncharov, John W. Lewis, and Xue Litai, *Uncertain Partners: Stalin, Mao, and the Korean War* (Stanford: Stanford University Press, 1993), 110.

108. Sergi N. Goncharov, John W. Lewis, and Xue Litai, *Uncertain Partners: Stalin, Mao, and the Korean War* (Stanford: Stanford University Press, 1993), 110; Bu Xiuyan and Zhang Ruixuan (trans.), *Liangda Lingxiu Si Dalin Yu Mao Zedong* [Two Great Leaders: Stalin and Mao Zedong] (Sichuang: Sichuang Renmin Chubanshe, 1999), 254.

109. Shi Zhe, *Shi Zhe Koushu Zhongsu Guanxi Jianzhenglu* [Shi Zhe's Oral Documentary about the Sino-Ussr Relations] (Beijing: Dangdai Zhongguo Chubanshe, 2005), 49.

110. Bu Xiuyan and Zhang Ruixuan (trans.), *Liangda Lingxiu Si Dalin Yu Mao Zedong* [Two Great Leaders: Stalin and Mao Zedong] (Sichuang: Sichuang Renmin Chubanshe, 1999), 255-258.

111. Dieter Heinzig, *The Soviet Union and Commuist China, 1945-1950: The Arduous Road to the Alliance* (Armonk, NY: M.E. Sharpe, 2004), 264.

112. Sergi N. Goncharov, John W. Lewis, and Xue Litai, *Uncertain Partners: Stalin, Mao, and the Korean War* (Stanford: Stanford University Press, 1993), 86, 110.

113. Sergi N. Goncharov, John W. Lewis, and Xue Litai, *Uncertain Partners: Stalin, Mao, and the Korean War* (Stanford: Stanford University Press, 1993), 110.

114. Yang Huolin, 1949-1954 Nian De Zhongguo Zhengzhi Tizhi [Political System of China During 1949 and 1954] (unpublished PHD thesis, 2005), at 195.

115. Zhonggong Zhongyang Wenxian Yanjiushi (ed.), *Jiangguo Yilai Mao Zedong Wengao* [Writings of Mao Zedong since the Founding of the People's Republic of China] (Beijing: Zhongyang Wenxian Chubanshe, 1987), vol. 2, 80-81.

116. Xu Dashen (ed.), *Gongheguo Shiji* [Records of the Republic] (Jilin: Jilin Renmin Chubanshe, 1996), 434-435.

117. There are also two different opinions. One held that there were only twenty-nine meetings of the council, see Li Ge, "Guanyu 1949-1954 Nian Zhongyang Renmin Zhengfu De Guoran Wenti" [Several Issues Concerning the Central People's Government during 1949 and 1954], *Dang De Wenxain*, no. 4 (1996): 78. The other one thought there were thirty-five meetings, and the last one was a temporary meeting. See Xu Chongde, *Zhonghua Renmin Gongheguo Xianfashi* [Constitutional History of the People's Republic of China] (Fujian: Fujian Renmin Chubanshe, 2005), vol. 1, 65.

118. Zhonggong Zhongyang Wenxian Yanjiushi (ed.), *Jiangguo Yilai Mao Zedong Wengao* [Writings of Mao Zedong since the Founding of the People's Republic of China] (Beijing: Zhongyang Wenxian Chubanshe, 1987), vol. 1, 242-243.

119. Pang Xianzhi and Jin Chongji (ed.), *Mao Zedong Zhuan 1949-1976* [Biograph of Mao Zedong 1949-1976] (Beijing: Zhongyang Wenxian Chubanshe, 2003), vol. 1, 31.

120. Li Ge, "1949-1954 Nian Zhongyang Renmin Zhengfu Zuzhi Jigou Shezhi Jiqi Bianhua" [Organization of the Central People's Government and Relevant Changes during 1949 and 1954], *Dang De Wenxain*, no. 5.1 (2001): 88.

121. Li Ge, "1949-1954 Nian Zhongyang Renmin Zhengfu Zuzhi Jigou Shezhi Jiqi Bianhua" [Organization of the Central People's Government and Relevant Changes during 1949 and 1954], *Dang De Wenxain*, no. 5.1 (2001): 88.

122. *Renmin Ribao*, January 8, 1950.

123. Li Ge, "1949-1954 Nian Zhongyang Renmin Zhengfu Zuzhi Jigou Shezhi Jiqi Bianhua" [Organization of the Central People's Government and Relevant Changes during 1949 and 1954], *Dang De Wenxain*, no. 5.1 (2001): 88.

124. Xu Dashen (ed.), *Gongheguo Shiji* [Records of the Republic] (Jilin: Jilin Renmin Chubanshe, 1996), 942-943.

125. Zhonggong Zhongyang Wenxian Yanjiushi (ed.), *Jiangguo Yilai Mao Zedong Wengao* [Writings of Mao Zedong since the Founding of the People's Republic of China] (Beijing: Zhongyang Wenxian Chubanshe, 1987), vol. 1, 288-289.

126. Zhonggong Zhongyang Wenxian Yanjiushi (ed.), *Jiangguo Yilai Mao Zedong Wengao* [Writings of Mao Zedong since the Founding of the People's Republic of China] (Beijing: Zhongyang Wenxian Chubanshe, 1987), vol. 1, 288-289.

127. Zhongyang Renmin Zhengfu Fazhi Weiyuanhui (ed.), *Zhongyang Renmin Zhengfu Weiyuanhui Faling Huibian (1951)* [Collection of Decrees Issued by the Central People's Government Councile (1951)] (Beijing: Renmin Chubanshe, 1953), 19.

128. Zhongyang Renmin Zhengfu Fazhi Weiyuanhui (ed.), *Zhongyang Renmin Zhengfu Weiyuanhui Faling Huibian (1951)* [Collection of Decrees Issued by the Central People's Government Councile (1951)] (Beijing: Renmin Chubanshe, 1953), 49.

129. Zhongyang Renmin Zhengfu Fazhi Weiyuanhui (ed.), *Zhongyang Renmin Zhengfu Weiyuanhui Faling Huibian (1952)* [Collection of Decrees Issued by the Central People's Government Councile (1952)] (Beijing: Renmin Chubanshe, 1954), 64.

130. Li Ge, "1949-1954 Nian Zhongyang Renmin Zhengfu Zuzhi Jiegou Shezhi Jiqi Bianhua" [Organization of the Central People's Government and Relevant Changes during 1949 and 1954], *Dang De Wenxian*, no. 6.2 (2001): 58-60; Qin Lihai, "Jaingguo Zhichu Zhengfu Dangzu De Sheli Yu Dangzheng Guanxi De Chuli" [The Establishment of the Party Group in the Government and the Handling of the Relationship between the Party and the Government in Early Time after the Founding Year], *Jinan Daxue Xuebao*, no. 2 (2009): 77-78.

131. Yang Huolin, "1949-1954 Nian De Zhongguo Zhengzhi Tizhi" [Political System of China During 1949 and 1954] (unpublished PHD thesis, Party School of the CCPCC, 2005), 53.

132. See Zhonggong Zhongyang Wenxian Yanjiushi (ed.), *Jiangguo Yilai Mao Zedong Wengao* [Writings of Mao Zedong since the Founding of the People's Republic of China] (Beijing: Zhongyang Wenxian Chubanshe, 1987), vol. 2, 542-543.

133. Li Ge, "Guanyu 1949-1954 Nian Zhongyang Renmin Zhengfu De Guoran Wenti" [Several Issues Concerning the Central People's Government during 1949 and 1954], *Dang De Wenxain*, no. 4 (1996): 81; "1949-1954 Nian Zhongyang Renmin Zhengfu Zuzhi Jiegou Shezhi Jiqi Bianhua" [Organization of the Central People's Government and Relevant Changes during 1949 and 1954], *Dang De Wenxian*, no. 6.2 (2001): 60-62.

134. It is an idea based on Mao Zedong's understanding of Marxist doctrine.

135. Pang Xianzhi and Jin Chongji (eds.), *Mao Zedong Zhuan 1949-1976* [Biograph of Mao Zedong 1949-1976] (Beijing: Zhongyang Wenxian Chubanshe, 2003), vol. 1, 236-240.

136. Pang Xianzhi and Jin Chongji (eds.), *Mao Zedong Zhuan 1949-1976* [Biograph of Mao Zedong 1949-1976] (Beijing: Zhongyang Wenxian Chubanshe, 2003), vol. 1, 240-242.

137. Mu Zhaoyong, *Diyijie Quanguo Renmin Daibiao Dahui Shilu* [The First National People's Congress Session] (Guangdong: Guangdong Renmin Chubanshe, 2006), 32-37; Han Dayuan, *1954 Nian Xianfa Yu Xin Zhongguo Xianzheng* [The 1954 Constitution and New China's Constitutionalism] (Hunan: Hunan Renmin Chubanshe, 2004), 53-56.

138. A different opinion suggested that the government structure had not ensured the direct and regular control over the administration by the CPGC chairman. See Li Ge, "1949-1954 Nian Zhongyang Renmin Zhengfu Zuzhi Jiegou Shezhi Jiqi Bianhua" [Organization of the Central People's Government and Relevant Changes during 1949 and 1954], *Dang De Wenxian*, no. 6.2 (2001): 60.

139. Qin Lihai, "Jaingguo Zhichu Zhengfu Dangzu De Sheli Yu Dangzheng Guanxi De Chuli" [The Establishment of the Party Group in the Government and the Handling of the Relationship between the Party and the Government in Early Time after the Founding Year], *Jinan Daxue Xuebao*, no. 2 (2009): 79-80.

140. Li Ge, "1953 Nian Fan Fensan Zhuyi Wenti Chutan" [Study on the Issue of Anti-Seperationism in 1953], Shixue Jikan, no. 4 (2001): 52-53.

141. Zhonggong Zhongyang Wenxian Yanjiushi (ed.), *Jiangguo Yilai Mao Zedong Wengao* [Writings of Mao Zedong since the Founding of the People's Republic of China] (Beijing: Zhongyang Wenxian Chubanshe, 1987), vol. 3, 682.

142. Zhonggong Zhongyang Wenxian Yanjiushi (ed.), *Jiangguo Yilai Mao Zedong Wengao* [Writings of Mao Zedong since the Founding of the People's Republic of China] (Beijing: Zhongyang Wenxian Chubanshe, 1987), vol. 1, 535.

143. Li Ge, "1953 Nian Fan Fensan Zhuyi Wenti Chutan" [Study on the Issue of Anti-Seperationism in 1953], *Shixue Jikan*, no. 4 (2001): 48-56.

144. Zhonggong Zhongyang Wenxian Yanjiushi (ed.), *Jianguo Yilai Zhongyao Wenxian Xuanbian* [Colletion of Selected Important Documents since the Founding of the PRC] (Beijing: Zhongyang Wenxian Chubanshe, 1993), 67-71.

145. Wu Ganqun, "Zai Xihuating Zhou Zongli Shenbian Gongzuo" [Working beside Premier Zhou in Xihuating], in Han Taihua (ed.), *Zhongguo Gongchandang Ruogan Lishi Wenti Xiezhen* [Portrait of Some Historicial Issues of the CCP] (Beijing: Zhongguo Yanshi Chubanshe, 1998), 480-481. The author had worked in the office the Premier of the GAC since June 1950. See Han Taihua (ed.), 476.

146. http://cpc.people.com.cn/GB/69112/73583/73600/5039894.html.

147. Qin Lihai, "Jaingguo Zhichu Zhengfu Dangzu De Sheli Yu Dangzheng Guanxi De Chuli" [The Establishment of the Party Group in the Government and the Handling of the Relationship between the Party and the Government in Early Time after the Founding Year], *Jinan Daxue Xuebao*, no. 2 (2009): 80; Li Ge, "1949-1954 Nian Zhongyang Renmin Zhengfu Zuzhi Jiegou Shezhi Jiqi Bianhua" [Organization of the Central People's Government and Relevant Changes during 1949 and 1954], *Dang De Wenxian*, no. 6.2 (2001): 63; "1953 Nian Fan Fensan Zhuyi Wenti Chutan" [Study on the Issue of Anti-Seperationism in 1953], *Shixue Jikan*, no. 4 (2001): 55.

Chapter Five

Constitutional Making of the Chairmanship in 1954

STALIN'S SUGGESTION AND PROBLEM TO THE CCP

Stalin's Suggestion of Constitutional Making

During his visit in 1952, Liu Shaoqi wrote a letter to Stalin, not only introducing Mao Zedong's new idea, but also raising the issue of constitutional-making in China:

> The issue of constitutional-making has been raised within the CCP in China . . . we think we do not have to make a constitution in the transitional period at present, and use the Common Program as a constitution. The Common Program can be revised by the Plenum of the CPPCC or NPC. After the class relationship in China achieves substantial change later, i.e., China achieves socialism basically, we can make a constitution then, when we can basically make a socialist constitution.[1]

The letter suggested that the CCP still preferred basing its governance on political negotiations among major participants. Although preoccupied with the issue of succession to him, Stalin still met Liu Shaoqi and answered his letter. He not only endorsed Mao Zedong's new idea to transition to socialism,[2] but also suggested making a constitution for such a transitional period for almost the same reasons he had given about three years ago:

> If you do not make a constitution and conduct election, your enemies will disseminate two accusations against you. Firstly, they can say that your government was not elected by the people; secondly, your country had no constitution. Since the CPPCC is not elected by the people, they can accuse

> you of establishing your government on the basis of force and your own will. Besides, the Common Program is not adopted by a congress elected by the people. Instead, it was submitted by the CCP and agreed upon by other parties. Therefore they also can accuse you of having no law. You should take these accusations from enemies both at home and abroad and give them no excuse. I agree your idea in your letter to transform the Common Program into a constitution, i.e., the basic law. Of course such a constitution is a raw product, but it is better to have one than without a constitution . . . there is one more problem in China. At present your government is a united one, hence the government cannot be responsible only to one party, and instead, it should be responsible to all parties. If so, it will be hard to protect the state secrecy. I think foreigners have known some of your important confidential information. For example, your government delegation will come to us, and then the United States and Britain know we are going to discuss the issue of Lushunkou. Since you have other political parties, the government has to account to them and have to discuss with them the important state affairs, in turn the United States and Britain will also know about these state affairs as many of them maintain relationship with the United States and Britain. If your plans are known by enemies, it will be harmful to you. If you win the majority in the election, you can form a one-party government.[3]

This had been the third time that Stalin made a similar suggestion to the CCP. The first was made in July 1949 when Liu Shaoqi paid his secret visit to Moscow, and the second was in 1950 when Mao Zedong paid his state visit to Moscow.

Stalin's suggestion had merits, because modern government had been founded on election and the constitution. If China could have to go without a constitution for quite a long time, problems concerning legitimacy and security could arise, as suggested by Stalin. On the other hand, this also indicated that Stalin was still suspicious about the CCP's so-called new democratic practices. For Stalin, the CCP would not be a true Marxist party and China would not be a true socialist country, if without a government of his style, which had been followed by the Eastern European countries during 1949 and 1950.

Mao Zedong's Idea of "Two Fronts"

Soon the CCP changed its mind and accepted Stalin's suggestion of constitutional making.[4] On December 24, 1952, Zhou Enlai advised on behalf of the CCP that the CPPCC National Committee should propose the Central People's Government to convene the National People's Congress and make a constitution in 1953.[5] Then, on January 13, 1953, the twentieth meeting of the CPGC accepted this proposal and decided accordingly.[6] A Constitutional Drafting Committee of thirty-two members headed by Mao Zedong was also set up[7] based on the nomination of Mao Zedong.[8]

What kind of government organization should be codified by this new constitution? Since the middle of 1952, the CCP had taken actions to restructure the government, moving toward the Stalinist model. As a result, by the middle of 1953, the government system stipulated by the Common Program and the Organic Law had been substantially modified, in which Mao Zedong had been in tight command of government affairs and he must have been satisfied with this new government structure, as indicated by Liu Shaoqi in his letter to Stalin.

But it would not be feasible any more since Stalin questioned and the CCP decided to move closer to Moscow. The Stalinist government could be a better choice. After all, Moscow had become the only example for China to follow in its pursuit of becoming a socialist country. In fact, after the CCP decided to make the constitution, the CCP had considered seriously following Stalin's example and fully adopting the Russian model. It had been suggested within the CCP that the Council of Ministers of the former Soviet Union could be adopted for China's highest administrative body of the government,[9] and the organization of the CCP had also been suggested to reform by adding new positions of vice-chairman or secretary general.[10] It seemed that the CCP had intended the CCP's chairman and vice-chairman to form a presidium, but had been uncertain about the choice between the secretary general and the presidium.[11]

Seemingly, Mao Zedong did not want a complete embrace of the Soviet model. While it was a heavy burden to lead such a big and under-developed country like China, his health had been deteriorating, for which he had to take sick leave three times since 1949. He was also affected greatly by the death of his eldest son in the Korean War.[12] It would be better for him if he could be relieved from such a heavy workload, even to a certain degree. It was said that on hearing the death of Stalin, Mao Zedong was in such a low mood as to give up his government chairmanship.[13] If the Russian form of government was fully adopted for the new Chinese government, the center of government power would be changed from the post of the chairman of the Central People's Government to the new chairman of the Council of Ministers. If Mao Zedong continued to take the lead in the country, he would surely have to follow the example of Stalin and take the new post of the chairman of the Council of Ministers in the new Chinese government, which had already been suggested by Zhou Enlai as early as January 1949 in their talk with "Stalin's ear" Mikoyan during his secret visit to China. This meant no difference to Mao Zedong from his CPG chairmanship, in both of which he served as the final decision maker and took direct responsibility for government affairs. Therefore, for the sake of his health, Mao Zedong could not have preferred the Soviet model.

More importantly, while inviting advice from Stalin, Liu Shaoqi and his Chinese delegation also noticed that Stalin's health had been deteriorating and the struggle to succeed him after his death had already begun in Moscow. This struggle reminded Chinese leaders of the succession to Mao Zedong and made them, including Mao Zedong himself, think more about it when designing the constitution. If the Russian model was followed, Moscow's experience of power struggles for succession could be repeated in China after Mao Zedong died. Having witnessed it, Mao Zedong suggested at around the latter half of 1953 that the CCP Central Secretariat, which became the PSC later in 1956 by the CCP Eighth National Congress, could be divided into "two fronts," that is, Mao Zedong would retire to the second front, while other CCP leaders who were younger than him remained in the first front.[14]

Years later, he explained this idea as follows:

> Why was the Central Committee divided into two fronts? It was because of my bad health and the lessons of the Soviet Union. Malenkov was chosen by Stalin, but he was not so experienced. He had not been in power before the death of Stalin, and lost power soon after Stalin's death. I wanted to help to establish the authorities of Liu Shaoqi and Deng Xiaoping before I died . . .[15]

> Considering Malenkov could not take control, the Russian government met problems, and the revisionist line emerged there, I suggested the division of the first and second front to make the country more secure. Before the eleventh Plenum of the eighth Central Committee, I had been in the second front and not involved with daily business, letting many works done by others. By this way, I thought they could establish their own reputation among the people so that the country would not suffer much turbulence when I died.[16]

These explanations indicated that Mao Zedong had thought Moscow's experience as a failure, which could be lessons for China to learn from. If Stalin had put his chosen successor in power earlier, the chosen successor would not have been so easily ousted, and Stalin's policy could be not be revised. In other words, Mao Zedong had thought that his successors should be those who were not only younger than him in age, but also capable of governance, and more importantly, would stick to his policies.

To choose the right successors, Mao Zedong decided to put his candidates on stage before instead of after his death. This meant that Mao Zedong had to give up his powers, at least part if not all, and share with his successors. By dividing the CCP Central Secretariat into two fronts, other CCP leaders could manage the regular working of the party-state as the first front, among which his successor would gradually take the lead, whereas Mao Zedong retreated to the second front, maintained supervision on the first front, and enjoyed the final say on major policies to ensure the first front is on the right track set by him. To be concise, the first front leaders were on the stage as apprentices, while Mao Zedong played behind scenes to ensure policies were on his track.

This could be beneficial for both sides. On one hand, by retiring to the second front, Mao Zedong could extract himself from daily state affairs, thus being saved from the tiresome chores and able to more focus on major policy issues. As implied by Mao Zedong, if those first front leaders were proved to be faithful executors of his policies in the course of apprenticeship, they could succeed him after his death; if their performance was not satisfactory and they were found to be revisionist like Khrushchev, he still had the time to change his successors. On the other hand, other younger CCP leaders would take care of the daily operation, accumulating experience in running the country.

Such an idea is not new to the Chinese. In ancient China, many emperors had adopted this method to decide their successors, in which they play behind their candidate successors to choose those who could faithfully perform their policies. The timely idea of "two fronts" suggested that Mao Zedong could have intended to use this traditional way of succession to solve Stalin's problem.

Then what about the government? No solid evidence has been found that Mao Zedong had also divided the government into "two fronts" and an independent office of chairmanship had been on his mind as early as then. To the contrary, it seemed that he had only intended to apply his idea of two fronts to the CCP, without referring to the government side of the party-state. It was said that Mao Zedong had intended not to serve as the state chairman and only serve as the CCP chairman, whereas Liu Shaoqi, his apparent successor, would take the post of the government chairmanship or the speaker of the congress.[17] In this case, taking into consideration that Mao Zedong could have not wanted to be the chairman of the Council of Ministers, it could mean that Mao Zedong could have truly intended to retreat completely from the new government. As the second front, he could only hold the CCP chairmanship and maintain a control on the first front leaders, who also concurrently held positions in the government, such as Liu Shaoqi.

Mao Zedong might have preferred such an arrangement, but it was interrupted by Gao Gang's challenge to Liu Shaoqi,[18] Mao Zedong's apparent successor. Although Gao Gang failed in the end, his attempts suggested that Liu Shaoqi's candidacy as Mao Zedong's successor had not been so firmly established within the CCP, not only being opposed by some other CCP senior members, like Gao Gang,[19] but also possibly Mao Zedong's suspicions because of their differences about policies that China should adopt.[20]

For all these reasons, Mao Zedong had to change his idea and continue to work in the government. To strike a balance between Mao Zedong's wish to be relieved from the heavy workload and political needs for him, a new position different from the previous chairmanship could be necessary for this new situation in which Mao Zedong could be relived from the burden to a certain degree, while maintaining his control over the governance on the whole. In other words, after the interruption of Gao Gang, the government also had to be divided into "two fronts" and a government position similar to Mao Zedong's status as the "second front" leader was demanded.

CONSTITUTIONAL MAKING OF THE CHAIRMANSHIP

Chairmanship Suggested by Mao Zedong

Since December 27, 1953, Mao Zedong led a team of CCP members and started to draft the constitution in Hang Zhou,[21] the Chinese city famed as "heaven on earth." His draft then would be submitted to the Constitutional Drafting Committee as a basis for further discussion. Mao Zedong personally made a working schedule for this team, in which some constitutions were listed by Mao Zedong as references, including the constitutions of the Soviet Union, the People's Republic of Romania, the Polish People's Republic, German Democratic Republic, Czechoslovakia Republic, and France as well as China's constitutional documents made before 1949. In particular, among these different constitutional documents, he commented that the German and Czech constitutions were quite detailed and had their own uniqueness, whereas the French constitution was a good example of a capitalist cabinet system.[22]

What made the German and Czech constitutions unique? While following the basic structure of the Soviet Union, both constitutions had a presidency, thus being different from those of Romania and Poland. The Czechoslovak Republic had a constitution adopted on February 29, 1920, which was "mainly shaped in accordance with the constitutional patterns of the Western European democracies and adhered to the doctrine of separation of powers."[23] After the communists took full control of the government, it adopted a second constitution on May 9, 1948, which was the one referred to by Mao Zedong. Although the people's democracy and socialism were claimed as goals by this constitution, it still retained elements of the old constitution, including the principle of separation of powers and the presidency.[24] According to this constitution, the Czech president was elected by the National Assembly as the head of state[25] and could exercise a dozen of "powers and functions" ("Zhiquan" in Chinese),[26] including proposing, convening, postponing, and dissolving the Assembly,[27] and commanding the armed forces. Most distinctively, he would take no responsibility for any of his "duties" ("Zhiwu" in Chinese), which was to be borne by the administration.[28] His documents could only be effective when co-signed by corresponding administrative officials. Similar to its predecessor, this presidency was regarded as "the greatest single institutional departure from Soviet constitutionalism."[29]

On the contrary, the German president was a quite weak one. Elected and removed by both chambers,[30] he represented the country in international relations,[31] performed several functions,[32] excluding commanding the armed forces, to be effective either with co-signature of the premier or relevant government ministers,[33] or based on proposals of certain committee of the chambers.[34] Besides, the French constitution adopted in 1946 also provided a presidency.

Mao Zedong must have noticed these different presidencies and could have been inspired by them. In the original drafts that he made and discussed with his CCP colleagues, an office of chairmanship had been designed independent from the NPC and the State Council.[35] Such an independent chairmanship finally took its shape in the "Constitutional Draft of the People's Republic of China (First Draft)" (the first draft) submitted by Mao Zedong on behalf of the CCP to the Constitutional Drafting Committee in its first meeting held on March 23, 1954.

According to the first draft, the chairman was to be elected among PRC citizens who had reached the age of thirty-five and had the right to vote and to stand for election,[36] and removed from office by the NPC[37] with a term of office of five years[38] until the new chairman was elected by the succeeding NPC.[39] He was provided by article 41 with six items of "powers and functions," which could be divided into two categories, depending on whether the chairman had to obtain the prior decisions of the NPC and its Standing Committee (NPCSC). The first category was those provided by the first paragraph of article 41:

> 1, in pursuance of the decisions of the NPC and NPCSC, the chairman shall exercise powers and functions including: I. to promulgate laws, other ordinances with legal effect and other orders. II. to appoint or remove the premier, vice-premiers, ministers and deputy ministers in charge of ministries or commissions, and members of the Council of National Defense. III. to confer state medals and titles of honor. IV. to proclaim general amnesties and grant pardons. V. to proclaim martial law, a state of war, order of mobilization.

The second category was those "powers and functions" provided by the other five paragraphs of article 41 that the chairman could perform without the decisions of the NPC and NPCSC, including:

> 2, propose the NPC and its Standing Committee. 3, appoint or remove chairman and vice-chairman of governments of those provinces, municipalities directly under the Central Government, autonomous regions, autonomous provinces. 4, represent the PRC, appoint or remove plenipotentiary representatives abroad, receive foreign diplomatic representatives and ratify treaties concluded with foreign states. 5, command the armed forces and server as the chairman of the Council of National Defense. 6, convene the vice-chairman, premier and other persons concerned for a Supreme State Conference whenever necessary.

Apart from the chairmanship, based on Mao Zedong's suggestion,[40] an office of vice-chairman was also provided to exercise those functions and powers on behalf of the chairman that the chairman may entrust to him[41]; when the chairman was recalled, dead, or incapacitated for a prolonged period, the vice-chairman should exercise the full functions and powers of the chairman before the NPCSC should convene to elect a new chairman.[42]

Compared with the Common Program, this was an improvement. During that period, the vice-chairman of the CPGC could only assist the chairman and no details were provided regarding such assistance. In 1949, when Mao Zedong paid his first state visit to the former Soviet Union, Liu Shaoqi, who had been the vice-chairman of the CPGC, had been designated by the CCP Politburo to act as the deputy chairman on his behalf.[43] It was unconstitutional for the CCP Politburo to make such a decision, and the new provision could be a remedy to it.

The Chairman in a Soviet Government

At first glance, such a personal office of chairman resembles a Western presidency very much. But Mao Zedong thought otherwise. In the first meeting of the Constitutional Drafting Committee, he compared the proposed Chinese government with that of the USSR:

> What is called in the Soviet Union as the Supreme Soviet is the NPC in China, the Presidium of the Soviet Union is China's the NPCSC, and the Council of Ministers is China's State Council. Compared with the Soviet Union, we have one more chairman.[44]

According to him, the chairman was similar to Kliment Yefremovich Voroshilov:

> The chairman is an equivalent of less than half of Kliment Yefremovich Voroshilov. The chairman is less than, not up to, the half of Voroshilov, because the Standing Committee deliberates on everything, and turn its decisions to the chairman to promulgate.[45]

Voroshilov was the chairman of the Presidium of the Supreme Soviet of the former Soviet Union. So Mao Zedong suggested that the chairman was originated from the Supreme Soviet Presidium; the chairman and the NPCSC would be equal to the Supreme Soviet Presidium. In other words, the Supreme Soviet Presidium of the former Soviet Union, or the Central People's Government Council was split into two organs in China, that is, the chairman and the NPCSC.

The role of the chairman was neither decision making nor execution:

> Those decisions made by the Congress should be promulgated by the chairman, but he cannot promulgate those that the Congress does not decide. Also the chairman could not execute, which belongs to the State Council.[46]

Such a new division of the chairman would not change the Soviet nature of Chinese government because it was subordinate to the NPC and enjoyed no independence:

> He (the chairman) cannot act on his own. He is not opposed to the NPC and its Standing Committee. Instead, he follows them.[47]

Especially, the chairman could be recalled by the NPC and not dissolve the NPC.[48] Therefore, Mao Zedong claimed that the chairman was not a Western-style president who could oppose and dissolve the congress.[49] In a word:

> In substance we are the same as the Soviet Union, because our chairman is not personal president and cannot dissolve the NPC. Our country is collective leadership, represented by an individual.[50]

The Chairman as the "Buffer"

However, when it came to those functions of the chairman provided by article 41 of the draft, Mao Zedong became contradictory. On one hand, he insisted on the supremacy of the NPC by claiming:

> What is provided in the first fourth paragraphs (of article 41) is nothing but mere formality. Especially, whereas the second paragraph provides that the chairman can propose, his proposal is not decisive, subject to the will of the NPC. If the NPC has no intention to accept, he cannot do anything.[51]

But he also had to admit that the chairman would be more than formal:

> In the sixth paragraph, the chairman convenes the Supreme State Conference if necessary. Although it is not clearly stipulated what can be discussed in the conference, he cannot transgress the NPC. 'If necessary' means that few conferences will be convened unless in emergencies when big things occur.[52]

As no provision was made regarding what the emergencies would be, this suggested that the chairman had discretion on the time to convene the Supreme State Conference by defining the emergency and could have freedom in conducting the conference. Thus the chairman had a share in policy making and could become another "Standing Committee" on special occasions.

On the other hand, the execution of the State Council was also shared by the chairman:

> In the fifth paragraph, the chairman is the chairman of the Council of National Defense, whereas the State Council has a defense department. So we make another layer by dividing some work from the State Council to the Council of National Defense.[53]

As a result, "these two paragraphs mean that the chairman has some something to do, not just routines like eating."[54] In other words, the chairman's functions are both formal and substantial, sharing powers with the other two organs.

Why had he introduced such a division of power into the Stalinist government? He explained as following:

> It is for the security of the country to establish the chairman. China is a big country, the purpose of adding a chairman is to make it safer. We have the speaker, the premier, and now we have the chairman, it becomes safer because it will be impossible for all of them to be out of order at the same time . . . the chairman can play a role of buffer between the State Council and NPCSC.[55]

In his mind, national security and the need of a buffer in the government were his major purposes to establish the chairmanship. Why would the country be more secure with a chairman? When making this constitution, China had been established amid the Cold War, just fighting against "its enemy" in Korea. It had been rumored that the United States could use nuclear weapons against mainland China. There was no wonder that national security was the top priority in such a critical situation:

> The reason to establish a chairman is the same as to divide the CCP's leadership into the first front and second front, and consider devising the vice-chairman and secretary general within the CCP. These are Mao Zedong's important proposal regarding the system of leadership to ensure security of the Party and State.[56]

In other words, by adding a new "layer" of the chairmanship, the government was further divided and would have multiple "fronts," among which destroying the chairman could not paralyze the others.

Secondly, he thought there was a need to install a buffer between the NPCSC and the State Council. Why? Mao Zedong must have realized from experiences both at home and the former Soviet Union that two different types of concentration of power would occur in the Soviet model of government. The power could be concentrated either into the hands of the head of the deliberative branch, as in his own case as the chairman of the China Soviet Republic during the period of the First Soviet Congress and the chairman of the Central People's Government of PRC during the Common Program period, or into the hands of the head of the executive organ, whereas the deliberative organ became a figure, as in the case of Zhang Wentian as the chairman of the Council of People's Commissars during the period of the Second Soviet Congress of the CSR and Stalin as the chairman of the Council of Ministers in the former Soviet Union. Now with an individual chairmanship taking shares in policy making and administration, such extremes could be avoided and the power structure of the government could be better balanced.

Needless to say, this was also what Mao Zedong wanted. As he chose to be succeeded step by step, he would have to release his power part by part. By so doing, the government power previously concentrated into his hands was divided and shared among the CCP leaders. As the first step, his chosen successors would take different government positions, run the state on the stage, and act as the first front, whereas he took the "buffer," maintained control on major policies and the armed forces, and supervised their performances as a standby second front.

Therefore, considering international situations and domestic political needs, Mao Zedong delicately designed such a chairmanship incorporating certain elements of separation of power, thus creating an office with a Western appearance for the Stalinist government. As confessed by Mao Zedong:

> Among those people's democratic countries, the Czech and Germany have similar institutions. They call them as presidents, whereas we call it as 'chairman.'[57]

REVISIONS TO THE CHAIRMANSHIP

After deliberation, the Constitutional Drafting Committee decided to submit the first draft for discussion to the CPPCC National Committee, leading organs of main administrative regions, provinces and cities, democratic parties, peoples' organizations as well as the military organs. Amid these discussions,[58] the organization of the state organs provided in the first draft, including the chairman, was revised by the CCP in a notice[59] issued before May 6, 1954, possibly a response to the results of the CPPCC's discussions.[60] Thus another constitutional draft was produced by the CCP (the revised draft).

Is the Chairman the Head of State?

The first major revision made to the first draft was a new article stipulating the chairman was the head of state of the PRC. The CCP seemed to have different opinions about whether the chairman was the head of state. Mao Zedong opposed such an idea, and the original draft prepared by his team in Hangzhou made no express provision in this regard. When his draft was discussed within the CCP, a new clause was added to provide so, but it was later deleted because of objection from Mao Zedong. Therefore, when the first draft turned out, it did not have such an article.

However, in discussions organized by the CPPCC National Committee, it was repeatedly suggested by participants that the chairman should be provided as the head of state.[61] In response, that article was added in the revised draft, which also was supported by the CPPCC in its proposed constitutional draft.[62]

Later, when all these discussions were completed, all drafts and suggestions turned to the Constitutional Drafting Committee for consideration.[63] In its sixth meeting, some committee members held that the chairman should not be provided as the head of state. For example, those CCP members changed their attitudes toward this issue once again and were against this article for the following reasons:

> We are the people's congress, the chairman exercises his functions and powers based on the decision of the NPC and its Standing Committee. Therefore, at most, the chairman could be thought as much as a 'head of state with partial functions and powers,' but not of 'the head of state.' Otherwise it would be unscientific. Therefore, we think it will not hurt the status of the chairman without such a clear provision. Instead, it will be hard for us to explain if we adopt this provision.[64]

But some other committee members, who did not belong to the CCP, were in favor of it and held that it should be made clear that the chairman was the head of state, or at least "the representative of the State," "the leader of the State," "the leader of the people," "the supreme leader of the country," "the State's representative in foreign affairs," and so on. Otherwise, "it would go against the idea and wishes of the people," as they argued.[65]

This controversy was finally decided by Mao Zedong in the next meeting of the Constitutional Drafting Committee. When a non-CCP committee member continued to ask about it, Mao Zedong replied, "The chairman is not the head of state. I think we had better not to stipulate him as the head of state."[66] He explained why it should be deleted as following:

> It was said that the abolishment of a certain clause[67] was because some people (Mao Zedong) was very modest. This is not true. It is not because that I am modest. Rather it is inappropriate, unreasonable and unscientific if we keep that clause. In a country of people's democracy like ours, that kind of inappropriate stipulation should not be made.[68]

As a result, when the constitutional draft was published for national discussion,[69] that article was removed from the draft. Again, despite it not being widely supported by the Chinese populace,[70] the national discussion did not change the status quo.

But some non-CCP people thought that "this issue still exists in many people's minds," and suggested making some explanations when submitting the constitutional draft to the first NPC. In response, Liu Shaoqi made a special remark in his "Report on the Draft Constitution of the People's Republic of China" delivered to the first NPC as follows:

> The functions and powers of the head of state in our country are jointly exercised by the Standing Committee of the National People's Congress, which is elected by the National People's Congress, and by the Chairman of the People's Republic of China. This conforms to the actual situation of our country and is based on our experience in the building up of the highest bodies exercising state power since the founding of the People's Republic of China. Ours is a collective head of state. Neither the Standing Committee nor the Chairman of the People's Republic of China has powers exceeding those of the National People's Congress.[71]

His explanation was accepted by the NPC together with the constitutional draft. Thus, the chairman was finally construed as a "partial" head of state of the PRC.

The Chairman's "Power" or "Duty"?

The second major revision that the CCP made to the first draft concerned the chairman's jobs stipulated in article 41 of the first draft, which had been provided as his "powers and functions" and could be divided into two categories, as discussed previously. The phrase "power and function" could have originated from Mao Zedong because he had used it in his initial drafts to refer to jobs that the chairman could fulfill.[72] Seemingly he thought those jobs were the chairman's "powers and functions." This phrase was accepted by the CCP in the first draft, not only in its article 41, but also in other places of the first draft whenever the chairman's jobs were generally mentioned. For example, the first draft also provided that the chairman exercise his "power and function" until the new chairman was elected by the NPC[73]; the vice-chairman could perform some or all "power and function" of the chairman on his behalf.[74]

In the revised draft, the first category of the chairman's jobs, that is, the first paragraph of article 41 referring to those "powers and functions" that the chairman had to perform in pursuance with the decision of the NPC and NPCSC, became a new article and the phrase "powers and functions" in it was rewritten as "duties" ("Zhiwu" in Chinese).[75]

Among the second category of the chairman's jobs, that is, those five "powers and functions" provided in the remaining five paragraphs of article 41 that the chairman could do without the decisions of the NPC and NPCSC, the fourth paragraph, stipulating the chairman to represent the PRC, appoint or remove the Chinese diplomats, receive foreign diplomats, and approve treaties concluded with other countries, was further revised and became an independent clause. The revision to it was the insertion of the condition of "the decision of the NPC and NPCSC" before the chairman could "appoint or remove the Chinese diplomats and approve treaties concluded with other countries." Thus, these two items that used to be the chairman's "powers and functions" were regrouped to the first category. Taking into consideration of the revision to the first paragraph, it could be understood that "to appoint and remove Chinese diplomats and approve international treaties" now also were the chairman's "duty."

As for the remaining four paragraphs of the second category, two were abolished, that is, the second paragraph authorizing the chairman to propose the NPC and NPCSC and the third paragraph to appoint or remove local government heads, and the fifth and sixth paragraph also became individual articles. Although none of these new articles mentioned the phrase "power and function" in their wordings any longer, they could still be understood as the chairman's "powers and functions" because the phrases "powers and functions" that were generally mentioned in other articles of the first draft remained unchanged in the revised draft,[76] from which it could be inferred that those jobs that the chairman could do without conditions, that is, "to convene the supreme state conference, command the military forces, represent the country and receive foreign diplomats," could still be regarded as his "powers and functions."

After all of these revisions, those jobs included in the first paragraph of article 41 of the first draft and "to appoint and remove Chinese diplomats and approve international treaties" were the chairman's duties, whereas the rest of the jobs remained as his "powers and functions." Such a division was in accordance with Mao Zedong's explanations because it not only helped to strengthen the supremacy of the NPC as the highest state organ, but it also agreed with his definition of both the first and the fourth paragraphs of article 41 as formalities and the fifth and sixth paragraph as a "buffer" between the NPCSC and the State Council with some independence.

However, these revisions would be contradictory. Since there were other "powers and functions" that were generally mentioned in the first draft and they remained unchanged,[77] what kind of works could be regarded as these "powers and functions"? For example, the chairman was provided to perform his "powers and functions" until the new chairman was elected; could this be understood that the chairman's "power and function" excluded the first groups of his constitutional works as these were revised as his "duties"? Obviously it could not and should be understood as to include both groups. The same contradiction could occur when it came to terms of the other two stipulations requiring the vice-chairman to exercise "powers and functions" of the chairman on his behalf under certain circumstances.

More specifically, the choice of "duty" could also contradict with the chairman's role in the Supreme State Conference. As revised, now the chairman became the chairman of the Supreme State Conference. Apart from the vice-chairman, premier, and the vice-premier, he could convene the chairman and vice-chairman of the NPCSC, the vice-chairman of the Council of National Defense, the chairman of the Supreme People's Court and the procurator-general of the Supreme People's Procuratorate for such a Conference. If necessary, he could also specify other persons concerned to attend. The views resulted from the Supreme State Conference can also be submitted by the chairman, according to the nature of the views, respectively to the NPC and NPCSC, the Central People's Government, or other government bodies for their consideration and decision. Hence, compared with the sixth paragraph of article 41 in the first draft, the chairman had been accorded with a leading role in the Supreme State Conference, by which he could override the decisions of the NPC and NPCSC "when necessary."

Therefore, in the following discussions of the Constitutional Drafting Committee, the choice between the phrases "power and function" and "duty" became an issue that was subject to change time and again.

Then what is the difference between "duty" ("Zhiwu" in Chinese) and "power and function" ("Zhiquan" in Chinese)? According to the explanation made by one member of the Constitutional Drafting Committee, in Chinese, "quan" had an additional element of independent decision than "wu" because "wu" means "affair," whereas "quan" means power to make a decision on something.[78] Accordingly, those works that the chairman had to perform based on decisions of the NPC and NPCSC were not the chairman's "powers and functions"; instead, they were his "duties." Liu Shaoqi supported this opinion and thought that "duty" should be adopted. According to his idea, the chairman must promulgate the law made by the NPC and NPCSC and he could not do otherwise. If those were "powers and functionsm," it would mean that he could decide to promulgate or not.[79] To the contrary, possibly to avoid that contradiction analyzed in the above, a third opinion suggested that the word "duties" be deleted from the revised draft, thus giving no answer as to whether those works of the chairman in the original first paragraph were "powers and functions" or "duties."[80] This suggestion could help to avoid the controversy and hence was a compromise.

At first, the Constitutional Drafting Committee accepted the revision and adopted "duties" in its revisions.[81] But somehow in its seventh meeting, it was changed back again from "duties" to "powers and functions," which was further adopted by the CPGC in its thirtieth meeting.[82] But this was not the end. When the constitutional draft was published for national discussion on June 15, the third opinion was adopted in the published text, with the phrase of "powers and functions" being deleted,[83] and this option was maintained in the constitution when it was passed by the NPC and promulgated.[84]

The Chairman's Relationship with the State Council

According to Mao Zedong's explanation, the chairman had no interference with the administration of the State Council because:

> . . . The chairman also cannot execute, because it is the responsibility of the State Council . . . the chairman is also not the government, the State Council does not have to report to the chairman. It is the State Council, not the chairman, which should take any responsibility that may arise.[85]

He also pointed out that the chairman shared the military power with the State Council:

> With regard to the chairman's functions and powers, according to the fifth paragraph of article 41 (of the first draft), the chairman is also the chairman of the Council of National Defense, whereas the State Council has a defense department. So we make another layer by dividing some work from the State Council to Council of National Defense.[86]

Therefore, in the first draft, the chairman was the commander of the armed forces[87] and could appoint or remove members of the Council of National Defense[88] based on the decisions of the NPCSC,[89] whereas the State Council had the power to "guide the construction of the defence forces."[90]

Besides, the chairman was also involved with the civil administration of the State Council in terms of government personnel affairs. In accordance with the decision of the NPC and NPCSC, he could appoint and remove key officials of the State Council, including the premier and vice-premier[91]; independently, he also could appoint or remove certain local government heads based on legal provisions.[92]

In the revised draft, the chairman's involvement with government personnel appointments was restricted. At the central level, the chairman was newly provided with the power to nominate the premier, the vice-chairman, and other members of the Council of National Defense, thus adding an element of "checks and balances" into the "division of military power" between the chairman and the State Council. At the local level, his power to appoint and remove local government heads was deleted, thus he could not exert influence on local governments any longer. As a result, the chairman's influence on the administration was limited to the central level.

Although these revisions were all accepted by subsequent discussions and deliberations, if taking into consideration the chairman's involvement with the administration, including the personal nomination, the Supreme State Conference, and division of military work, it would be contradictory to Mao Zedong's explanation that the chairman take no responsibility for the administration. Based on the constitution, the chairman had two powers that had to do with the civil administration, that is, the power to nominate the premier[93] and convene the Supreme State Conference. Both powers enabled the chairman to exert direct and indirect influence on the State Council. First of all, the chairman could set national policy for the State Council to carry out by convening the Supreme State Conference, thus having direct impact on the administration. As the constitution made no definition on what time was necessary, what types of affairs of state were important, it was all up to the chairman to decide when to convene such a conference and what kind of issue could be raised in the conference. If the chairman thought his policies were important, he could convene the premier for such a conference and submitted his views to the State Council for implementation. Undoubtedly, the premier should have to take some responding actions to the chairman even if no further procedural or substantive requirements had been made by the constitution in this regard. Besides, by the power to nominate the premier, the chairman could exert an indirect influence on the state administration through the premier as he could choose the person who was in favor of his policies to take charge of the State Council.

The Vice-Chairman

Apart from these major revisions, provisions concerning the vice-chairman were also improved by the revised draft. With the same terms of office and election as the chairman,[94] the vice-chairman was not only provided to assist the chairman in his work,[95] but also could exercise parts of powers and functions of the chairman on his behalf with his authorization[96] or when he was incapacitated for a prolonged period by reason of health.[97] He could even succeed the chairman if the chairmanship fell vacant until the term of the chairman ended and a new chairman was elected into office.[98] Besides, the term of the office of chairman was reduced from five years to four years.[99] All of these revisions went through various discussions and deliberations and finally became a part of the constitution.[100]

On September 15, 1954, the First National People's Congress held its first session in Beijing, in which the final version of the constitutional draft was submitted and Liu Shaoqi, representing the Constitutional Drafting Committee, made a speech titled "Report on the Draft Constitution of the People's Republic of China."[101] Five days later, it was put for vote.[102] The 1,197 deputies in attendance all voted in favor of it. Then the constitution was passed and promulgated on the next day by the NPC.[103]

In a word, by taking lessons from home and abroad and aiming to solve the succession to him, Mao Zedong proposed an individual chairmanship in the constitution, thus adding elements of Western ideas of separation of powers to the Stalinist structure of government. Such a chairmanship was weakened and centralized in the constitutional-making process after various rounds of revisions, with contradictions remaining. Being different from the almighty CPG chairman during the period of the Common Program, the new chairmanship was better defined and far more limited in its scope of jurisdiction, with "necessary" policy-making power, allegedly no administrative responsibility, shared power in military affairs, and complete irrelevance to the judicial bodies.

In comparison, the 1954 constitution made substantial changes to the chairmanship, which not only separated the chairman from the NPC and provided it as an independent office taken by an individual, but also curtailed its powers and functions to a certain degree. The new chairman no long directed all policy making; instead, he could only make major policies in necessary circumstances. In terms of the administration, he could nominate the candidate for the premiership, continue to command military forces, and perform certain allegedly nominal functions. Besides, he had no connection with the judiciary. Externally, he was provided to represent the PRC in its foreign relations and receive foreign diplomats; upon the decision of the NPCSC, he could appoint or recall Chinese diplomats and ratify treaties. Officially, such a weakened chairmanship was construed as a partial head of state.

Among all chairmanships and presidencies that the PRC has ever had, this chairmanship is the one most close to Western presidency. The separation of the chairman from the presidium is a clear departure from the Stalinist model of government. It was as late as in 1990 that the former Soviet Union had revised its constitution and installed an independent presidency separated from the Presidium of the Supreme Soviet. More importantly, the Chinese chairmanship had incorporated certain elements of separation of powers characterized by Western constitutions. By sharing policy-formulating power and commanding the armed forces, he could put "checks and balances" on the NPCSC and State Council, thus serving as a "buffer" as so-called by its designer Mao Zedong. In a certain way, the Chinese chairmanship is much similar to the French presidency provided by the French constitution adopted in 1958, which also can nominate the premier, promulgate legislations, appoint government officials, deploy and receive diplomats, command the army, and make policy statement.

NOTES

1. "Liu Shaoqi Yijiu Wuer Fangsu Wenxian Xuanzai" (Yijiu Wuer Nian Jiuyue –Shi'er yue) [Selected Documents Concerning Liu Shaoqi's Visit to the Former Soviet Union in 1952 (September to December of 1952)], *Dang De Wenxian*, no. 1 (2005): 9.

2. "Liu Shaoqi Yijiu Wuer Fangsu Wenxian Xuanzai" (Yijiu Wuer Nian Jiuyue –Shi'er yue) [Selected Documents Concerning Liu Shaoqi's Visit to the Former Soviet Union in 1952 (September to December of 1952)], *Dang De Wenxian*, no. 1 (2005): 10.

3. "Liu Shaoqi Yijiu Wuer Fangsu Wenxian Xuanzai" (Yijiu Wuer Nian Jiuyue –Shi'er yue) [Selected Documents Concerning Liu Shaoqi's Visit to the Former Soviet Union in 1952 (September to December of 1952)], *Dang De Wenxian*, no. 1 (2005): 11-12. Shi Zhe, *Wo De Yisheng* [My Life] (Beijing: Renmin Chubanshe, 2001), 407-408.

4. Weng Youwei, "Zhonghua Renmin Gongheguo Diyibu Xianfa Zhiding Kanlun" [Study on the Making of the First Constitution of the People's Republic of China], *Shixue Yuekan*, no. 11 (2007): 65.

5. Xu Chongde, *Zhonghua Renmin Gongheguo Xianfashi* [Constitutional History of the People's Republic of China] (Fujian: Fujian Renmin Chubanshe, 2005), vol. 1, 107. Han Dayuan, *1954 Nian Xianfa Yu Xin Zhongguo Xianzheng* [The 1954 Constitution and New China's Constitutionalism] (Hunan: Hunan Renmin Chubanshe, 2004), 60.

6. *Renmin Ribao*, January 15, 1953.

7. *Renmin Ribao*, January 15, 1953.

8. Xu Chongde, *Zhonghua Renmin Gongheguo Xianfashi* [Constitutional History of the People's Republic of China] (Fujian: Fujian Renmin Chubanshe, 2005), vol. 1, 110.

9. Pang Xianzhi and Jin Chongji (eds.), *Mao Zedong Zhuan 1949-1976* [Biography of Mao Zedong 1949-1976] (Beijing: Zhongyang Wenxian Chubanshe, 2003), vol. 1, 278; Pang Song, *Mao Zedong Shidai De Zhongguo (1949-1976)* [China in the Era of Mao Zedong (1949-1976)] (Beijing: Zhongyang Wenxian Chubanshe, 2003), vol. 1, 433-434; Zhao Jialiang and Zhan Xiaoji, *Banjie Mubei Xia De Wangshi* [Stories behind the Half Tombstone] (Hong Kong: Dafeng Chubanshe, 2008), 17.

10. Pang Xianzhi and Jin Chongji (ed.), *Mao Zedong Zhuan 1949-1976* [Biography of Mao Zedong 1949-1976] (Beijing: Zhongyang Wenxian Chubanshe, 2003), vol. 1, 278; Pang Song, *Mao Zedong Shidai De Zhongguo (1949-1976)* [China in the Era of Mao Zedong (1949-1976)] (Beijing: Zhongyang Wenxian Chubanshe, 2003), vol. 1, 433-434.

11. According to a record made by a senior CCP cadre on February 25, 1954, Zhou Enlai said it had been suggested whether the secretary general or presidium could be adopted for the CCPCC. See Zhao Jialiang and Zhan Xiaoji, *Banjie Mubei Xia De Wangshi* [Stories behind the Half Tombstone] (Hong Kong: Dafeng Chubanshe, 2008), 17.

12. Li Yinqiao and Han Guixin, *Mao Zedong He Ta De Weishizhang* [Mao Zedong and His Chief Bodyguard] (Beijing: Jiefangjun Chubanshe, 2002), 234; *Zai Mao Zedong Shenbian Shiwu Nian* [Fifteen Years alongside Mao Zedong] (Hebei: Hebei Renmin Chubanshe, 2006), 2nd ed., 237-238.

13. Li Yinqiao and Han Guixin, *Mao Zedong He Ta De Weishizhang* [Mao Zedong and His Chief Bodyguard] (Beijing: Jiefangjun Chubanshe, 2002), 234; *Zai Mao Zedong Shenbian Shiwu Nian* [Fifteen Years alongside Mao Zedong] (Hebei: Hebei Renmin Chubanshe, 2006), 2nd ed., 237-238.

14. Pang Xianzhi and Jin Chongji (eds.), *Mao Zedong Zhuan 1949-1976* [Biography of Mao Zedong 1949-1976] (Beijing: Zhongyang Wenxian Chubanshe, 2003), vol. 1, 278; Jin Chongji (ed.), *Liu Shaoqi Zhuan* [Biography of Liu Shaoqi] (Beijing: Zhongyang Wenxian Chubanshe 1998), vol. 2, 743; Deng Xiaoping, *Deng Xiaoping Wenxuan (1975-1982)* [Selection of Deng Xiaoping (1975-1982)] (Beijing: Renmin Chubanshe 1983), 257; Liu Ying, *Liu Ying Zishu* [Narrative History of Liu Ying] (Beijing: Renmin Chubanshe, 2005), 226.

15. Mao Zedong, *Zai Zhongyang Zhengzhi Gongzuo Huibao Huiyi Shang De Jianghua* [Speech at the Meeting of Reporting Central Political Work] (October 24, 25, 1966).

16. Pang Xianzhi and Jin Chongji (eds.), *Mao Zedong Zhuan 1949-1976* [Biography of Mao Zedong 1949-1976] (Beijing: Zhongyang Wenxian Chubanshe, 2003), vol. 2, 1449-1450.

17. Zhao Jialiang and Zhan Xiaoji, *Banjie Mubei Xia De Wangshi* [Stories behind the Half Tombstone] (Hong Kong: Dafeng Chubanshe, 2008), 45-46, 113.

18. Although different opinions existed concerning the reasons behind Gao Gang's challenge to Liu Shaoqi, the fact that Gao Gang challenged Liu Shaoqi's succession to Mao Zedong has been commonly agreed. See Pang Xianzhi and Jin Chongji (eds.), *Mao Zedong Zhuan 1949-1976* [Biography of Mao Zedong 1949-1976] (Beijing: Zhongyang Wenxian Chubanshe, 2003), vol. 1, 278; Pang Song, *Mao Zedong Shidai De Zhongguo (1949-1976)* [China in the Era of Mao Zedong (1949-1976)] (Beijing: Zhongyang Wenxian Chubanshe, 2003), vol. 1, 433-434; Zhao Jialiang and Zhan Xiaoji, *Banjie Mubei Xia De Wangshi* [Stories behind the Half

Tombstone] (Hong Kong: Dafeng Chubanshe, 2008), 23. For the English study on the case of Gao Gang, see F. C. Teiwes, *Politics at Mao's Court: Gao Gang and Party Factionalism in the Early 1950s* (New York: M.E. Sharpe, 1990).

19. Gao Gang had once won support from several senior CCP leaders before Mao Zedong took actions.

20. For a brief discussion about disagreements and controvercies between Liu Shaoqi and Mao Zedong; see, for example, Cong Jin, *Quzhe Fazhan De Suiyue* [Years of Tortous Development] (Zhengzhou: Henan Renminchubanshe, 1989), 599-606; Jin Chunming, *Wenhua Dageming Lunxi* [Study on the Cultural Revolution] (Shanghai: Shanghai Renmin Chubanshe, 1985), 57-85.

21. For introduction to Mao Zedong's work in Hang Zhou, see Xu Chongde, *Zhonghua Renmin Gongheguo Xianfashi* [Constitutional History of the People's Republic of China] (Fujian: Fujian Renmin Chubanshe, 2005), vol. 1, 110-112; Xu Wendong, "Xin Zhongguo Diyibu Xianfa De Zong Shejishi: Mao Zedong Liuzhuang Caoxian Yiwen" [The General Designer of the First Constitution of New China: Stories about Mao Zedong's Constitutional Making in Liuzhuang], *Dangshi Zhongheng*, no. 5 (1994), 25-26; Wang Qiu, "Wusi Xianfa Dansheng Ji" [The Birth of the May 4th Constitution], *Dangshi Bocai*, no. 2 (2005): 47-48.

22. Mao Zedong, "Guanyu Xianfa Qicao Xiaozu De Gongzuo Jihua Gei Liu Shaoqi Bing Zhongyang De Dianbao" [Telegram from Mao Zedong to Liu Shaoqi and Tthe CCPCC about the Working Plan of the Constitutional Drafting Small Group], in Zhonggong Zhongyang Wenxian Yanjiushi (ed.), *Jianguo Yilai Zhongyang Wenxian Xuanbian* [Selection of Important Documents Since the Founding of the People's Republic of China] (Beijing: Zhongyang Wenxian Chubanshe, 1993), 437-438; Zhonggong Zhongyang Wenxian Yanjiushi (ed.), *Mao Zedong Wenji* [Collection of Mao Zedong's Writings] (Beijing: Renmin Chubanshe, 1996), vol. 5, 320.

23. William B. Simons (ed.), *The Constitutions of the Communist World* (The Hague: Martinus Nijhoff Publishers, 1984), 136.

24. Barbara Jancar-Webster, *Czechoslovakia and the Absolute Monopoly of Power: A Study of Political Power in a Communist System* (New York: Praeger Publishers, 1971), 55.

25. Jieke Siluo Fake Gongheguo Xianfa [Constitution of the Czechoslovakia Republic] (adopted on May 9, 1948), Art. 6, in Zhongyang Renmin Zhengfu Fazhi Weiyuanhui Bianyishi (ed.), *Renmin Minzhu Guojia Xianfa Huibian* [Collection of Constitutions of People's Democratic Countries] (Beijing: Renmin Chubanshe, 1953), 62.

26. Jieke Siluo Fake Gongheguo Xianfa [Constitution of the Czechoslovakia Republic] (adopted on May 9, 1948), Art. 74, in Zhongyang Renmin Zhengfu Fazhi Weiyuanhui Bianyishi (ed.), *Renmin Minzhu Guojia Xianfa Huibian* [Collection of Constitutions of People's Democratic Countries] (Beijing: Renmin Chubanshe, 1953), 79.

27. Jieke Siluo Fake Gongheguo Xianfa [Constitution of the Czechoslovakia Republic] (adopted on May 9, 1948), Art. 74, paragraph 3, in Zhongyang Renmin Zhengfu Fazhi Weiyuanhui Bianyishi (ed.), *Renmin Minzhu Guojia Xianfa Huibian* [Collection of Constitutions of People's Democratic Countries] (Beijing: Renmin Chubanshe, 1953), 80.

28. Jieke Siluo Fake Gongheguo Xianfa [Constitution of the Czechoslovakia Republic] (adopted on May 9, 1948), Art. 76, in Zhongyang Renmin Zhengfu Fazhi Weiyuanhui Bianyishi (ed.), *Renmin Minzhu Guojia Xianfa Huibian* [Collection of Constitutions of People's Democratic Countries] (Beijing: Renmin Chubanshe, 1953), 81.

29. Barbara Jancar-Webster, *Czechoslovakia and the Absolute Monopoly of Power: A Study of Political Power in a Communist System* (New York: Praeger Publishers, 1971), 55.

30. Deyizhi Minzhu Gongheguo Xianfa [Constitution of the German Democractic Republic] (adopted May 30, 1949, effective on October 7, 1949), Art. 101, paragraph 1 and Art. 103, in Zhongyang Renmin Zhengfu Fazhi Weiyuanhui Bianyishi (ed.), *Renmin Minzhu Guojia Xianfa Huibian* [Collection of Constitutions of People's Democratic Countries] (Beijing: Renmin Chubanshe, 1953), 161, 162.

31. Deyizhi Minzhu Gongheguo Xianfa [Constitution of the German Democractic Repūblic] (adopted May 30, 1949, effective on October 7, 1949), Art. 105, paragraph 1, in Zhongyang Renmin Zhengfu Fazhi Weiyuanhui Bianyishi (ed.), *Renmin Minzhu Guojia Xianfa Huibian* [Collection of Constitutions of People's Democratic Countries] (Beijing: Renmin Chubanshe, 1953), 162.

32. Deyizhi Minzhu Gongheguo Xianfa [Constitution of the German Democractic Republic] (adopted May 30, 1949, effective on October 7, 1949), Art. 104, and 105, in Zhongyang Renmin Zhengfu Fazhi Weiyuanhui Bianyishi (ed.), *Renmin Minzhu Guojia Xianfa Huibian* [Collection of Constitutions of People's Democratic Countries] (Beijing: Renmin Chubanshe, 1953), 162.

33. Deyizhi Minzhu Gongheguo Xianfa [Constitution of the German Democractic Republic] (adopted May 30, 1949, effective on October 7, 1949), Art. 106, in Zhongyang Renmin Zhengfu Fazhi Weiyuanhui Bianyishi (ed.), *Renmin Minzhu Guojia Xianfa Huibian* [Collection of Constitutions of People's Democratic Countries] (Beijing: Renmin Chubanshe, 1953), 162.

34. Deyizhi Minzhu Gongheguo Xianfa [Constitution of the German Democractic Republic] (adopted May 30, 1949, effective on October 7, 1949), Art. 107, in Zhongyang Renmin Zhengfu Fazhi Weiyuanhui Bianyishi (ed.), *Renmin Minzhu Guojia Xianfa Huibian* [Collection of Constitutions of People's Democratic Countries] (Beijing: Renmin Chubanshe, 1953), 162.

35. Xu Chongde, *Zhonghua Renmin Gongheguo Xianfashi* [Constitutional History of the People's Republic of China] (Fujian: Fujian Renmin Chubanshe, 2005), vol. 1, 113-116.

36. Xianfa Chugao [The first draft of the Constitution] (1954) (PRC), Art. 38

37. Xianfa Chugao [The first draft of the Constitution] (1954) (PRC), Art. 26, 29.

38. Xianfa Chugao [The first draft of the Constitution] (1954) (PRC), Art. 39.

39. Xianfa Chugao [The first draft of the Constitution] (1954) (PRC), Art. 42.

40. Xu Chongde, Zhonghua Renmin Gongheguo Xianfashi [Constitutional History of the People's Republic of China] (Fujian: Fujian Renmin Chubanshe, 2005), vol. 1, at 114.

41. Xianfa Chugao [The first draft of the Constitution] (1954) (PRC), Art. 43.

42. Xianfa Chugao [The first draft of the Constitution] (1954) (PRC), Art. 44.

43. About Liu Shaoqi's performance on behalf of Mao Zedong during this period of time; see Zhonggong Zhongyang Wenxian Yanjiushi (ed.), *Jianguo Yilai Liu Shaoqi Wengao* [Writings of Liu Shaoqi since the Founding of the People's Republic of China] (Beijing: Zhongyang Wenxian Chubanshe, 1998), vol. 1. Liu Shaoqi had acted on as Mao Zedong's deputy for three terms; see Ma Yunfei, "Liu Shaoqi Dangxuan Guojia Zhuxi Qianhou" [How was Liu Shaoqi Elected as the State Chairman], *Bainian Chao*, no. 3 (2001): 30-31.

44. Mao Zedong, "Zai Xianfa Qicao Weiyuanhui Diyici Huiyi Shang De Chahua" [Mao Zedong's Speech in the First Meeting of the Constitutional Drafting Committee], *Dang De Wenxian*, no. 1 (1997): 10.

45. Xu Chongde, *Zhonghua Renmin Gongheguo Xianfashi* [Constitutional History of the People's Republic of China] (Fujian: Fujian Renmin Chubanshe, 2005), 2nd ed., vol. 1, 121.

46. Mao Zedong, "Zai Xianfa Qicao Weiyuanhui Diyici Huiyi Shang De Chahua" [Mao Zedong's Speech in the First Meeting of the Constitutional Drafting Committee], *Dang De Wenxian*, no. 1 (1997): 10.

47. Xu Chongde, *Zhonghua Renmin Gongheguo Xianfashi* [Constitutional History of the People's Republic of China] (Fujian: Fujian Renmin Chubanshe, 2005), vol. 1, 118-119.

48. Mao Zedong, "Zai Xianfa Qicao Weiyuanhui Diyici Huiyi Shang De Chahua" [Mao Zedong's Speech in the First Meeting of the Constitutional Drafting Committee], *Dang De Wenxian*, no. 1 (1997): 11.

49. Xu Chongde, *Zhonghua Renmin Gongheguo Xianfashi* [Constitutional History of the People's Republic of China] (Fujian: Fujian Renmin Chubanshe, 2005), vol. 1, 118.

50. Xu Chongde, *Zhonghua Renmin Gongheguo Xianfashi* [Constitutional History of the People's Republic of China] (Fujian: Fujian Renmin Chubanshe, 2005), vol. 1, 119.

51. Mao Zedong, "Zai Xianfa Qicao Weiyuanhui Diyici Huiyi Shang De Chahua" [Mao Zedong's Speech in the First Meeting of the Constitutional Drafting Committee], *Dang De Wenxian*, no. 1 (1997): 11.

52. Mao Zedong, "Zai Xianfa Qicao Weiyuanhui Diyici Huiyi Shang De Chahua" [Mao Zedong's Speech in the First Meeting of the Constitutional Drafting Committee], *Dang De Wenxian*, no. 1 (1997): 11.

53. Mao Zedong, "Zai Xianfa Qicao Weiyuanhui Diyici Huiyi Shang De Chahua" [Mao Zedong's Speech in the First Meeting of the Constitutional Drafting Committee], *Dang De Wenxian*, no. 1 (1997): 11.

54. Mao Zedong, "Zai Xianfa Qicao Weiyuanhui Diyici Huiyi Shang De Chahua" [Mao Zedong's Speech in the First Meeting of the Constitutional Drafting Committee], *Dang De Wenxian*, no. 1 (1997): 11.

55. Mao Zedong, "Zai Xianfa Qicao Weiyuanhui Diyici Huiyi Shang De Chahua" [Mao Zedong's Speech in the First Meeting of the Constitutional Drafting Committee], *Dang De Wenxian*, no. 1 (1997): 11.

56. Pang Xianzhi and Jin Chongji (ed.), Mao Zedong Zhuan 1949-1976 [Biography of Mao Zedong 1949-1976], vol. 1, (Beijing: Zhongyang Wenxian Chubanshe, 2003), at 324.

57. Mao Zedong, "Zai Xianfa Qicao Weiyuanhui Diyici Huiyi Shang De Chahua" [Mao Zedong's Speech in the First Meeting of the Constitutional Drafting Committee], *Dang De Wenxian*, no. 1 (1997): 10.

58. In these discussions, about 8,000 people participated and about 5,900 suggestions were produced, all of which have been documented into a twenty-five-volume book titled "Xianfa Caoan Chugao Taolun Yijian Huiji" [Compilation of Suggestions in Discussions of the First Draft of the Constitution]. See Zhonghua Renmin Gongheguo Xianfa Qicao Weiyuanhui Banggongshi (ed.), *Xianfa Caoan Chugao Taolun Yijian Huiji* [Compilation of Suggestions in Discussions of the First Draft of the Constitution], vol. 1-25.

59. The CCP's notice was titled as "Duiyu Zhonghua Renmin Gongheguo Xianfa Caoan (Chugao) Dier Zhang Diyi, Er, San, Si Jie De Xiugai Yijian" [Opinions on the Revisions of the First, Second, Third and Fourth Section of the Second Chapter of the Constitutional Draft (the First Draft) of the People's Republic of China]. See Zhonghua Renmin Gongheguo Xianfa Qicao Weiyuanhui Bangongshi, Quanguo Zhengxie Xianfa Qicao Zuotanhui Gezu Zhaojiren Lianxi Huiyi Guanyu "Zhonghua Renmin Gongheguo Xianfa Caoan (Chugao) De Zhengshi Xiugai Yijian" ["Formal Revising Opinions of the Draft Constitution of the People's Republic of China (First Draft)" Submitted by the Joint Meeting of Group Conveners of Talks on Constitutional Draft Organized by the CCPCC], 43.

60. The first 17 volumes of "Xianfa Caoan Chugao Taolun Yijian Huiji" [Compilation of Suggestions in Discussions of the First Draft of the Constitution] recorded those suggestions and opinions resulted from discussions taking place before May 6, 1954, mainly organized by the National Committee of the CPPCC. Therefore, the CCP's revision possibly was made based on those results of the first seventeen volumes.

61. Zhonghua Renmin Gongheguo Xianfa Qicao Weiyuanhui Banggongshi (ed.), *Xianfa Caoan Chugao Taolun Yijian Huiji* [Compilation of Suggestions in Discussions of the First Draft of the Constitution], vol. 1, 15; vol. 6, 1, 2, 5-6, 8, 9.

62. Zhonghua Renmin Gongheguo Xianfa Qicao Weiyuanhui Bangongshi, Quanguo Zhengxie Xianfa Qicao Zuotanhui Gezu Zhaojiren Lianxi Huiyi Guanyu "Zhonghua Renmin Gongheguo Xianfa Caoan (Chugao) De Zhengshi Xiugai Yijian" ["Formal Revising Opinions of the Draft Constitution of the People's Republic of China (First Draft)" Submitted by the Joint Meeting of Group Conveners of Talks on Constitutional Draft Organized by the CCPCC], Art. 40. It was made on May 22, 1954.

63. The committee had held nine meetings altogether to discuss the constitutional draft.

64. Xu Chongde, *Zhonghua Renmin Gongheguo Xianfashi* [Constitutional History of the People's Republic of China] (Fujian: Fujian Renmin Chubanshe, 2005), 2nd ed., vol. 1, 135-136.

65. Xu Chongde, *Zhonghua Renmin Gongheguo Xianfashi* [Constitutional History of the People's Republic of China] (Fujian: Fujian Renmin Chubanshe, 2005), 2nd ed., vol. 1, 136.

66. "Xianfa Qicao Weiyuanhui Diqici Huiyi Taolun Tongguo Xianfa Caoan Jilu" [Record of the Seventh Meeting of the Constitutional Drafting Committee to Discuss and Adopt the Constitutional Draft], *Dang De Wenxian*, no. 1 (1997): 16.

67. It is the clause of head of state. See Pang Xianzhi and Jin Chongji (eds.), *Mao Zedong Zhuan 1949-1976* [Biography of Mao Zedong 1949-1976] (Beijing: Zhongyang Wenxian Chubanshe, 2003), vol. 1, 336; Gong Yuzhi, *Dangshi Zaji Erji* [The Second Volume of Notes about the CCP's History] (Zhejiang: Zhejiang Renmin Chubanshe, 2004), 312, 327-329.

68. Mao Zedong, *Guanyu Zhonghua Renmin Gongheguo Xianfa Caoan* [About the Draft Constitutional of the Pople's Republic of China], in Zhonggong Zhongyang Wenxian Yanjiushi

(ed.), *Jiangguo Yilai Mao Zedong Wengao* [Writings of Mao Zedong since the Founding of the People's Republic of China] (Beijing: Zhongyang Wenxian Chubanshe, 1987), vol. 1, 506.

69. The whole country spent almost three months on discussion, in which about 150 million people participated. See Xiao Xinli (ed.), *Mao Zedong Yu Gongheguo Zhongda Lishi Shijian* [Mao Zedong and Important Historical Event of the Republic] (Beijing: Renmin Chubanshe, 2001), 133. All those suggestions made during this public discussion have been compiled into a fourteen-volume book titled "Quanguo Renmin Taolun Xiancao Yijian Huibian" [Compilation of Suggestions from the National Discussion about the Constitutional Draft].

70. See *Quanguo Renmin Taolun Xiancao Yijian Huibian* [Compilation of Suggestions from the National Discussion about the Constitutional Draft], vol. 3, 61; vol. 6, 52; vol. 10, 87; vol. 12, 45, 46, 49; vol. 13, 134.

71. Liu Shaoqi, *Collected works of Liu Shao Ch'I 1945-1957* (Kowloon, Hong Kong: Union Research Institute, 1969), 297.

72. Mao Zedong, "Dui Zhonghua Renmin Gongheguo Xianfa Caoan De Piyu" [Notes about the Constitutional Draft of the People's Republic of China], in Zhonggong Zhongyang Wenxain Yanjiushi (ed.), *Jiangguo Yilai Mao Zedong Wengao* [Writings of Mao Zedong since the Founding of the People's Republic of China] (Beijing: Zhongyang Wenxian Chubanshe, 1987), vol. 1, 455.

73. Xianfa Chugao [The first draft of the Constitution] (1954) (P.R.C.), Art. 42.

74. Xianfa Chugao [The first draft of the Constitution] (1954) (PRC), Art. 43, 44.

75. Zhonghua Renmin Gongheguo Xianfa Qicao Weiyuanhui Bangongshi, Quanguo Zhengxie Xianfa Qicao Zuotanhui Gezu Zhaojiren Lianxi Huiyi Guanyu "Zhonghua Renmin Gongheguo Xianfa Caoan (Chugao) De Zhengshi Xiugai Yijian" ["Formal Revising Opinions of the Draft Constitution of the People's Republic of China (First Draft)" Submitted by the Joint Meeting of Group Conveners of Talks on Constitutional Draft Organized by the CCPCC], Art. 42.

76. Zhonghua Renmin Gongheguo Xianfa Qicao Weiyuanhui Bangongshi, Quanguo Zhengxie Xianfa Qicao Zuotanhui Gezu Zhaojiren Lianxi Huiyi Guanyu "Zhonghua Renmin Gongheguo Xianfa Caoan (Chugao) De Zhengshi Xiugai Yijian" ["Formal Revising Opinions of the Draft Constitution of the People's Republic of China (First Draft)" Submitted by the Joint Meeting of Group Conveners of Talks on Constitutional Draft Organized by the CCPCC], Art. 46, 47, 48.

77. Zhonghua Renmin Gongheguo Xianfa Qicao Weiyuanhui Bangongshi, Quanguo Zhengxie Xianfa Qicao Zuotanhui Gezu Zhaojiren Lianxi Huiyi Guanyu "Zhonghua Renmin Gongheguo Xianfa Caoan (Chugao) De Zhengshi Xiugai Yijian" ["Formal Revising Opinions of the Draft Constitution of the People's Republic of China (First Draft)" Submitted by the Joint Meeting of Group Conveners of Talks on Constitutional Draft Organized by the CCPCC], Art. 46, 47, 48.

78. Xu Chongde, *Zhonghua Renmin Gongheguo Xianfashi* [Constitutional History of the People's Republic of China] (Fujian: Fujian Renmin Chubanshe, 2005), vol. 1, 127.

79. Cai Dingjian, *Xianfa Jingjie* [Explanation on the Constitution] (Beijing: Falv Chubanshe, 2004), 366.

80. Xu Chongde, *Zhonghua Renmin Gongheguo Xianfashi* [Constitutional History of the People's Republic of China] (Fujian: Fujian Renmin Chubanshe, 2005), vol. 1, 133.

81. Zhonghua Renmin Gongheguo Xianfa Qicao Weiyuanhui Duiyu Zhonghua Renmin Gongheguo Xianfa Caoan (Chugao) De Xiugai Yijian [Revising Opinions of the Constitutional Drafting Committee of the People's Republic of China to the Constitutional Draft of the People's Republic of China (The First Draft)], Art. 42. It is shown on the cover page of this document that it was printed in June, 1954 by "Zhonggong Zhongyang Huadong Ju Bangongting" [The Office of the Eastern-China Bureau of the CCPCC]. Therefore, it could be a result of the first six meetings of the Constitutional Draft Committee, all of which were convened by Liu Shaoqi.

82. Zhonghua Renmin *Gongheguo Xainfa Caoan* [Constitutional Draft of the People's Republic of China] (adopted by the 30th Meeting of the Central People's Government Council on June 14, 1954), Art. 40. Both the seventh meeting of the Constitutional Draft Committee and the 30th conference of the Central People's Government Council were presided by Mao Ze-

dong. Besides, the Central People's Government Council had held three conferences to discuss the constitutional draft, that is, the 30th, 34th, and a temporary conference.

83. Zhonghua Renmin Gongheguo Xainfa Caoan [Constitutional Draft of the People's Republic of China], *Renmin Ribao*, June 15, 1954, Art. 40.

84. Zhonghua Renmin Gongheguo Xianfa [Constitution] (1954) (P.R.C.), *Renmin Ribao*, September 21, 1954, Art. 40.

85. Mao Zedong, "Zai Xianfa Qicao Weiyuanhui Diyici Huiyi Shang De Chahua" [Mao Zedong's Speech in the First Meeting of the Constitutional Drafting Committee], *Dang De Wenxian*, no. 1 (1997): 10-11.

86. Mao Zedong, "Zai Xianfa Qicao Weiyuanhui Diyici Huiyi Shang De Chahua" [Mao Zedong's Speech in the First Meeting of the Constitutional Drafting Committee], *Dang De Wenxian*, no. 1 (1997): 11.

87. Xianfa Caoan Chugao [The Constitutional Draft (the First Draft)], Art. 41, paragraph 5.

88. Xianfa Caoan Chugao [The Constitutional Draft (the First Draft)], Art. 41, paragraph 1.

89. Xianfa Caoan Chugao [The Constitutional Draft (the First Draft)], Art. 36, paragraph 10.

90. Xianfa Caoan Chugao [The Constitutional Draft (the First Draft)], Art. 16, paragraph 11.

91. Xianfa Caoan Chugao [The Constitutional Draft (the First Draft)], Art. 41, paragraph 1.

92. Xianfa Caoan Chugao [The Constitutional Draft (the First Draft)], Art. 41, paragraph 2.

93. Zhonghua Renmin Gongheguo Xainfa [Constitution] (1954) (PRC), Art. 27, paragraph 5.

94. The second paragraph of article 46 of the Revised Draft; Zhonghua Renmin Gongheguo Xianfa Qicao Weiyuanhui Bangongshi, Quanguo Zhengxie Xianfa Qicao Zuotanhui Gezu Zhaojiren Lianxi Huiyi Guanyu "Zhonghua Renmin Gongheguo Xianfa Caoan (Chugao) De Zhengshi Xiugai Yijian" ["Formal Revising Opinions of the Draft Constitution of the People's Republic of China (First Draft)" Submitted by the Joint Meeting of Group Conveners of Talks on Constitutional Draft Organized by the CPPCC], 83.

95. The first paragraph of article 46 of the Revised Draft; Zhonghua Renmin Gongheguo Xianfa Qicao Weiyuanhui Bangongshi, Quanguo Zhengxie Xianfa Qicao Zuotanhui Gezu Zhaojiren Lianxi Huiyi Guanyu "Zhonghua Renmin Gongheguo Xianfa Caoan (Chugao) De Zhengshi Xiugai Yijian" ["Formal Revising Opinions of the Draft Constitution of the People's Republic of China (First Draft)" Submitted by the Joint Meeting of Group Conveners of Talks on Constitutional Draft Organized by the CPPCC], 83.

96. The first paragraph of article 46 of the Revised Draft; Zhonghua Renmin Gongheguo Xianfa Qicao Weiyuanhui Bangongshi, Quanguo Zhengxie Xianfa Qicao Zuotanhui Gezu Zhaojiren Lianxi Huiyi Guanyu "Zhonghua Renmin Gongheguo Xianfa Caoan (Chugao) De Zhengshi Xiugai Yijian" ["Formal Revising Opinions of the Draft Constitution of the People's Republic of China (First Draft)" Submitted by the Joint Meeting of Group Conveners of Talks on Constitutional Draft Organized by the CPPCC], at 83.

97. The first paragraph of article 48 of the Revised Draft; Zhonghua Renmin Gongheguo Xianfa Qicao Weiyuanhui Bangongshi, Quanguo Zhengxie Xianfa Qicao Zuotanhui Gezu Zhaojiren Lianxi Huiyi Guanyu "Zhonghua Renmin Gongheguo Xianfa Caoan (Chugao) De Zhengshi Xiugai Yijian" ["Formal Revising Opinions of the Draft Constitution of the People's Republic of China (First Draft)" Submitted by the Joint Meeting of Group Conveners of Talks on Constitutional Draft Organized by the CPPCC], at 85.

98. The second paragraph of article 48 of the Revised Draft; Zhonghua Renmin Gongheguo Xianfa Qicao Weiyuanhui Bangongshi, Quanguo Zhengxie Xianfa Qicao Zuotanhui Gezu Zhaojiren Lianxi Huiyi Guanyu "Zhonghua Renmin Gongheguo Xianfa Caoan (Chugao) De Zhengshi Xiugai Yijian" ["Formal Revising Opinions of the Draft Constitution of the People's Republic of China (First Draft)" Submitted by the Joint Meeting of Group Conveners of Talks on Constitutional Draft Organized by the CPPCC], at 85.

99. The first paragraph of article 41 of the Revised Draft; Zhonghua Renmin Gongheguo Xianfa Qicao Weiyuanhui Bangongshi, Quanguo Zhengxie Xianfa Qicao Zuotanhui Gezu Zhaojiren Lianxi Huiyi Guanyu "Zhonghua Renmin Gongheguo Xianfa Caoan (Chugao) De Zhengshi Xiugai Yijian" ["Formal Revising Opinions of the Draft Constitution of the People's Republic of China (First Draft)" Submitted by the Joint Meeting of Group Conveners of Talks on Constitutional Draft Organized by the CPPCC], 85.

100. Zhonghua Renmin Gongheguo Xianfa [Constitution] (1954) (PRC), Art. 44, 45, 46.
101. Liu Shaoqi, *Collected works of Liu Shao Ch'I 1945-1957* (Kowloon, Hong Kong: Union Research Institute, 1969), 297.
102. Before voting, the constitutional draft had been further revised by the Central People's Government Council based on the opinions from the PNPC deputies, but not concerned with the chairmanship. See Xu Chongde, *Zhonghua Renmin Gongheguo Xianfashi* [Constitutional History of the People's Republic of China] (Fujian: Fujian Renmin Chubanshe, 2005), vol. 1, 30.
103. *Renmin Ribao*, September 21, 1954.

Chapter Six

Chairman Mao Zedong from 1954 to 1959

CHAIRMAN MAO'S PERFORMANCE IN OFFICE

Mao Zedong Elected as the Chairman

On September 27, 1954, the first NPC started to elect the governmental officials. As a result of the election, the CCP's control over the new government was increased greatly. During the Common Program period, many leaders of democratic parties and prominent non-CCP figures had been elected as senior government officials, such as the vice-chairman of the CPGC and vice-premier of the GAC, taking up about one-third of the leading positions in the GAC.[1] But after the first NPC, none of them was elected as vice-chairman and vice-premier. Instead, they were all elected into the NPCSC, taking up thirty-nine positions out of its seventy-nine members and eight out of its thirteen vice-chairmen. Even though thirteen non-CCP people were elected into the ministerial offices of the State Council, they counted for just about one-third of all ministerial offices and one-fourth of all members of the State Council.[2] Therefore, with the changes of non-CCP people's positions, the CCP occupied half of the NPCSC and a majority in the State Council, apart from the chairmanship. Hence, the one-party government suggested by Stalin was basically established in China.

Before the election, a list of candidates for top governmental positions had been produced from several rounds of consultations between the CCP and other political parties, which was then submitted to the NPC jointly by 109 deputies from the thirty-three delegations to the NPC.[3] As the only candidate for the chairmanship, Mao Zedong was elected into office by 1,210 deputies without opposition, whereas Zhu De became the vice-chairman.[4]

After the election, the chairman's office was established, with a head being appointed by the chairman.[5]

The Supreme State Conference

According to the constitution, overseeing the Supreme State Conference was an important function for the chairman to perform. As the constitution provided few details about its working, the Supreme State Conference had been very flexible in practice in terms of its frequency, duration, and participants. Throughout his five years in office, Mao Zedong convened sixteen Supreme State Conferences all together. The frequency of conference had been in decline. It is estimated that five such conferences could have convened by the end of 1955,[6] four each in 1956 and 1957 when the "Great Leap-Forward" took place, two in 1958, and only one in 1959 before he was succeeded by Liu Shaoqi. Participants to these conferences had also been fluctuating from thirty-seven persons in the tenth conference to about 1,800 at the eleventh conference, expanding to include people not clearly provided by the constitution, such as distinguished figures in different social circles, local government officials, university principles, scholars, and so on.[7] Generally, the duration of these conferences was days,[8] varying from a half day, like the sixth conference, to several days, such as the eleventh, which was enlarged and held from February 27 to March 1, 1957.[9]

In spite of irregularities in these respects, the Supreme State Conference had become an important way for Mao Zedong to be involved with the state affairs by raising and discussing various issues that were all significant to the development of the country at that time. First of all, government works were discussed in the conferences, which set important government policies, and produced specific proposals for legislation and administrative action. For example, in a Supreme State Conference held on May 12, 1955, Mao Zedong suggested that the policy for the elimination of counterrevolutionaries should be "be alert to eliminate every counterrevolutionary; avoid any bias to accuse any innocent one," which became a guiding line for that movement.[10] The "Double-Hundred" policy was officially announced at another conference held on May 2, 1956,[11] which was the seventh conference.[12]

In particular, agriculture was an issue repeatedly discussed in the Supreme State Conference. It was first raised in a Supreme State Conference held from October 19-21, 1955, by discussing a standard charter for agricultural cooperatives.[13] Then in the sixth conference, held on January 25, 1956,[14] a draft outline for China's agricultural development from 1956 to 1969 was discussed,[15] which was raised again in the thirteenth conference[16] convened on October 14, 1957.[17] The draft was finally submitted to and adopted by the NPC. Other important government works were also brought to discussion before being submitted for deliberation by the NPC. In the fourteenth conference undertaken on January 28, 1958, the state budget and economic plan was discussed.[18] The next one, held in September 1958, discussed overall domestic and international situations.[19] Specific administrative decisions were also made as a result of the conferences.

Second, political consultation was also conducted in the Supreme State Conference between the CCP and democratic parties as well as other social sectors. One of these consultations was Mao Zedong's call to the democratic parties to help the CCP's "Rectification Movement," which was made in the twelfth[20] and thirteenth conferences[21] all convened in 1957. Then in his last Supreme State Conference held on April 15, 1959, to make preparation for the second NPC,[22] Mao Zedong explained to his participants why Liu Shaoqi was decided by the CCP as the candidate for the next chairman.

More specifically, ideological issues were also raised and discussed in some of these conferences, such as those concerning Mao Zedong's idea about "contradictions within people," by which he first suggested on February 7, 1957, that properly handling contradictions within the people should be the main theme of Chinese political life. He took two conferences to illustrate his idea and solicit opinions from participants. On February 26, 1957, he held the tenth conference with thirty-seven participants, discussing the contradictions among the people and the contradictions between the people and its enemy.[23] From the next day until March 1, he invited more people to convene an enlarged Supreme State Conference, that is, the eleventh, to discuss the issue of how to properly handle the contradiction within the people. First, Mao Zedong illustrated his ideas in the afternoon of February 27. Then, for the next day and a half, those 1,800 participants were divided into groups to discuss his ideas. In the afternoon of March 1, all participants joined together again and some of them gave individual speeches.[24] By such an arrangement, this sizable conference can only be comparable to a plenary session of the NPC.

In a word, during Mao Zedong's term, the Supreme State Conference became a forum where Mao Zedong could coordinate the workings of the government, intervene in state affairs, conduct political consultations, and illustrate his ideological ideas.[25] However, with these multiple functions, he had already trespassed the constitutional provisions and could contravene with other state organs, such as the NPC and CPPCC.[26]

Dispute Over the "Grand Marshal"

The dominance of Mao Zedong in the CCP's collective leadership as its chairman not only made prominent the Supreme State Conference above other state establishments, but also could add substance to those formalities required by the constitution that the government chairman had to fulfill according to the decision of the NPC and its Standing Committee. In February

1955, the NPCSC adopted an ordinance on military ranking and awarding of medals. In this new law, a rank of Grand Marshal was provided. As an initial plan, it was suggested that Mao Zedong be ranked as Grand Marshal and awarded a medal, but he refused. Later, this suggestion was raised again in an NPCSC meeting and gained wide support from attending NPCSC members, including those non-CCP members. A non-CCP member even asked, "if the NPCSC made the decision, what could Mao Zedong do except to accept?"[27] He implied that constitutionally Mao Zedong had to follow if the NPCSC made such a decision.

However, knowing Mao Zedong's opposition, the NPCSC chairman Liu Shaoqi, who presided over the meeting, insisted on not doing so. In reply to that question, he responded that, although the NPCSC could make a decision it still had to be promulgated by the chairman by issuing an order; what if the chairman did not issue such an order? Instead, Liu Shaoqi proposed not making a decision in that meeting unless they could persuade Mao Zedong to accept this suggestion when they met him in person. Afterwards, when this suggestion was put forward to Mao Zedong for his approval, he expressly rejected it once again. Hence, the Grand Marshal was left vacant.[28]

Delegation of Power to the NPCSC

While Mao Zedong chaired the Republic, he had also concurrently held the position of the CCP chairman. It must have been a burdensome job to lead such a great country and an escalating party.[29] Chairman Mao Zedong needed to rest and took a period of leave in the latter half of 1955. According to the constitution, the vice-chairman, Zhu De, should have to fill in the absence of the chairman. However, it had been a practice within the CCP that Liu Shaoqi, then the chairman of the NPCSC, acted on behalf of Chairman Mao Zedong when the latter took leave. It may be because of this that on December 28, 1955, a resolution was passed by the first NPCSC in its thirtieth meeting, providing that "the chairman of the NPCSC should receive foreign diplomats when the chairman and vice-chairman of PRC take leave or are away."[30]

MAO ZEDONG'S RESUMPTION OF TWO FRONTS

Mao Zedong's Failed Attempt to Resign

After learning Khrushchev's report about Stalin, Mao Zedong thought more about state affairs and decided to resume his old idea of two fronts,[31] which had previously been interrupted by the incident of Gao Gang and Rao Sushi. As early as in the middle of 1956 when preparing for the CCP's forthcoming Eighth National Congress, Mao Zedong suggested resigning from the office of the chairman, then the party's chairmanship later, indicating a two-step plan of succession. He told his senior party colleagues that he did not want to take a second term. Although his partners had discussed and held that "it is feasible in the future when time is ripe," his request had been rejected because they thought "it is not for now."[32]

However, partly because it was so burdensome to be chairman, and partly in view of the succession of the CCP's leadership, Mao Zedong soon repeatedly demanded he not be elected for a second term.[33] He made his idea public in the Twelfth Supreme State Conference on April 30, 1957, when he told the participating members of democratic parties that:

> I must resign the state chairman in the second National People's Congress next year to reduce my workload so that I can focus on some major issues. Switzerland has a seven-member committee, with the president rotating among them. We can also rotate in several years and adopt the policy of getting out gradually.[34]

It is very interesting that he mentioned the Swiss presidency as an example. Based on the principle of separation of powers, the Swiss administration was executed by its Federal Council, which included seven members nominated by several political parties and elected by its congress, that is, the Federal Assembly, without term of office. Election of the Swiss president was made by the assembly from these seven members with a one-year term of office, which became a formality according to the system of seniority.[35] One of the two main functions of the Swiss president was the formal duty of representing the country at home and abroad,[36] and the other one was the chairmanship of the Federal Council meeting held twice a week, in which he was not dominant in the meeting,[37] because each member had equal voting and all seven members made decisions collectively. Therefore, although the Swiss president is similar to the Chinese chairman by working in a collective decision-making group without term of office, it is different from the latter in that the Chinese chairman functioned on a different principle in theory, and as a dominating figure in that group in practice. However, compared to the Swiss president, Mao Zedong could suggest that the Chinese chairman would be reduced to a figurehead of state if taken by other people rather than himself.

Proposal of Constitutional Revision

The next day, on hearing about this news, two non-CCP members wrote a letter to Liu Shaoqi and Zhou Enlai, proposing that:

> We think that, considering the reality of our country, now we are under a great transformation in the transition from democratic revolution to socialist revolution. We have gone through rather well during the past seven years. But we should admit that development far exceeds consolidation, in other words, we

> cannot say that the country has been well consolidated. Even further, Taiwan has not been liberated and the two international camps are in severe struggle. Therefore, in such a period, we had better not change our supreme leaders. Although the collective leadership should be stressed, our people have not got used to it in such a short period of time, and personal authority in the collective leadership remains essential to hold our people tight together. It seems to us that the chairman had better take one more term and one more provision can be added as "no more than two terms should be consecutively held" after the second paragraph of the thirty-ninth constitutional article stating "the term of office is four years". After this, we can act according to law . . . as for the delegation of power and function, two or three vice-chairmen should also be provided by the constitution. Two years ago, the NPC Standing Committee chairman was entrusted to receive foreign diplomats, for which the constitution should be revised . . . also we need pay much attention to the heavy workload of our leaders and should easy their burden when arranging domestic and foreign affairs.[38]

Four days later, Mao Zedong commented on this letter that:

> I agree with the suggestion to revise constitution. The state chairman and vice-chairman can take a second term when they are elected again after their first term. Comrade Deng Xiaoping please makes relevant preparation so that the constitution can be revised by the National People's Congress this year. Two reasons should be clarified for why I will not take a second term: (1) it has been eight years since I take the position as the chairman of Central People's Government and the chairman of the People's Republic of China consecutively, I may not take a second term; (2) since the constitution is made, I will have one more term to go if I can pursue a second term and do not take it consecutively. If I leave this position temporarily from 1958, I can concentrate on some important issues (for example I can give report on main themes in the Supreme State Conference in the capacity of the CCP chairman or its Politburo member when it is necessary). This would be more beneficial to the nation comparatively. At present, I have too much work, which extremely obstructs my study. Now more and more senior leaders within the CCP agree with me, while many non-CCP people disagree due to litter exchange of ideas. Therefore, it is necessary to put this idea forward and exchange views and opinions calmly.[39]

By leaving the chairmanship temporarily and giving necessary reports, Mao Zedong showed his intention for a prolonged influence of his policies. Then that proposal would not be preferable because he had to retire upon the completion of two terms and would not be able to control the policy afterwards. To win more support for his idea, Mao Zedong required wider discussion. In a CCP document, he directed:

> Before this September, the issue of my resignation should be considered. It should be debated among cadres in various levels, in factories and cooperative

> societies to seek opinions from our cadres and people so that most of them agree. This is because by getting rid of the state chairman and focusing on the CCP chairman, I can save more time to do more work as required by the party. It will also be beneficial to my health. If there is any disagreement during debate among the people, it should made clear to them that I can take some position as this if any emergency occurs in our country and the party decides. Now we are in a time of peace, it is better to get rid of one of the chairman positions. The CCP Politburo and many comrades at central and local level have agreed with my request and thought it was a good idea. Please explain all of these to all cadres and people to prevent any misunderstanding.[40]

He even asked the Chinese diplomat to Britain to make his attempt public.[41] Finally, his request was endorsed by the CCP in the sixth plenum of the eighth CCPCC held on December 10, 1958,[42] whereas the proposal to revise the constitution was not put into action.

A Step-by-Step Plan of Succession

Apart from Mao Zedong's withdrawal from the state chairmanship, the CCP's organization of its supreme leadership was also changed for the purpose of succession. A new office of the vice-chairmen of the CCP was installed, which was taken by Liu Shaoqi, Zhou Enlai, Zhu De, and Chen Yun, all of whom formed the PSC together with Chairman Mao Zedong to perform the function of the Central Secretariat. In other words, the PSC replaced the Central Secretariat.

According to Mao Zedong, such a measure was suggested by Liu Shaoqi and made as a lesson from the Soviet Union:

> It was comrade Liu Shaoqi who suggested the adoption of four vice-chairmen. With several vice-chairmen and a GS, there are several windbreaks around me. If an atomic bomb falls upon us who happens to stay together, another election could have to be held. But if there is only some of us who are injured or sick, or dead by accident, others can always hold on and the country would not suffer as much as the former Soviet Union, which was devastated by the death of Stalin. We should take caution against that situation. In the meantime, it is good to have a few more people to handle works.[43]

For the new PSC, Mao Zedong also divided them into two groups by age:

> I think some of us, including Zhu De and me, and Liu Shaoqi in between, excluding Zhou Enlai, Chen Yuan and Deng Xiaoping who were younger generation, are those who run errands. We cannot play leading roles now as we are not qualified. What we can do is to maintain the situation and assist the young generations.[44]

In his eyes, Zhu De and he were the older generation, who were then still on the stage and could have to retire sooner or later to let the younger people, like Liu Shaoqi, Zhou Enlai, Chen Yun, and Deng Xiaoping, take charge. In other words, he implied that in the new PSC, he and Zhu De belonged to the second front, whereas the other three younger vice-chairmen were the first front.

While the PSC was re-established, the Central Secretariat was reduced to an executive organ of the new PSC and given a new head: the General Secretary, which was an old title taken by Chen Duxiu previously and now also a member of the new PSC. Recommended by Mao Zedong, Deng Xiaoping became the new GS. By including the GS as one of the "wind-breaks," Mao Zedong could have considered Deng Xiaoping the successor to Liu Shaoqi. In that case, the PSC would be divided into "three fronts," among which Mao Zedong was well in the center surrounded by two fronts.

As a result of this organizational adjustment, the principle of deliberation and execution was applied to the CCP's decision-making process, with the PSC making decisions and the Central Secretariat specialized on execution. In other words, the Central Secretariat was the CCP's "State Council," whereas the PSC was the mini "NPCSC" of the CCP. By then, so far as the central level was concerned, the Stalinist party-state was finally established in China, in which both state apparatus were virtually controlled by the CCP with paralleled and corresponding organs[45] by way of overlapping membership,[46] and further ultimately controlled by one decision maker, that is, Mao Zedong.

But the Chinese had its own innovations. In Moscow, Stalin maintained his control over the party-state either from the party as the General Secretary before 1940, or by taking the governmental post of the chairman of the Council of Ministers since 1940 till his death. Stalin personally had not commanded the armed forces. Mao Zedong maintained his control by both chairmanships, that is, the CCP's chairmanship and the state chairmanship, both of which were new to the Russians, especially the state chairman. Besides, in China, as the military was a separate force, both Chinese chairmanships were further supplemented by a military chairmanship.

Yet Mao Zedong's innovation was more than this. The state chairmanship was only a part of his idea of two fronts, the end of which was an honorary chairmanship he suggested for the CCP:

> I am ready not to take the party's chairmanship at a proper time and ask you to give me a title of honorary chairman. Will the honorary chairman do anything? Surely he will do anything as much as he can.[47]

Thus taking Moscow's experience as a lesson, Mao Zedong conceived a multiple-step plan of succession using the idea of two fronts. As the first step, he would retire from the government by evacuating the state chairmanship, but he would keep the CCP's chairmanship; then the PSC would be divided into two fronts by the age of the members and he would further retreat to the second front as the chairman. Later on, as conditions were met, he would further retire from the CCP's chairmanship and only take an honorary title. He could even envision a consultative committee in the far future, formed by those retired senior party cadres, like himself.[48] Therefore, the state chairmanship was an interim post corresponding to the party's chairman in the second front.

In practice, Mao Zedong had just started his plan. After resigning the state chairmanship, he was going to take the next step, that is, to retreat to the second front within the PSC. As matter of fact, in the CCP's Eighth National Congress, the CCP's report was delivered by Liu Shaoqi instead of Mao Zedong. This could be seen as a sign that Mao Zedong was taking steps to retire, similar to Stalin's move in the nineteenth congress of the CPSU in which Malenkov gave the report instead of Stalin.

This is a delicate plan, but it is in contradiction with the CCP's organizing principle of democratic centralism. According to democratic centralism, the PSC members were equal to each other in terms of decision making. But the division of two fronts would make the first front leaders subject to the final control of the second front leader with respect to the choice of policy, because the former had to follow the latter if to have a successful succession. As a result, these two fronts were no more on equal footing, whereas the line between them in their decision-making power would have to be drawn by practice along the progress of succession.

More problematic is the division of responsibility among the CCP chairman and his successors in such a plan. As the collective leader of the party-state, the PSC was supposed to take responsibility for the governance as a whole. Now with the division of two fronts, which front would take final responsibility, hence be accountable to the constitution and people, when controversies occurred concerning the policy making and execution, which had been proved common by the earlier history of the CCP? Even for the honorary chairman, would he not intervene in the operation of the party-state? Eventually the succession could be faulted for this dilemma of responsibility. Beside, so far in his plan, Mao Zedong had not mentioned the succession to the CCP's CMC chairman, which had been the stepping-stone in his own way to the peak of power.

CONCENTRATION OF POWER BY MAO ZEDONG

However, one thing is clear. In Mao Zedong's mind, the focus of power was on the side of the party, not the state. As suggested by the principle of the combination of deliberation and execution, the party made the decision and the state executed it. And more importantly, he could not give up his power completely. When he said that he would do anything he could even if he assumed the honorary chairmanship, it could be suspected that he would keep the power in his hands and remain as the real decision maker of the party-state.

In the same meeting in which Liu Shaoqi was nominated as the candidate of the state chairmanship, Mao Zedong made a concluding speech to the whole participants. He said:

> The decision-making power should be concentrated to the Politburo Standing Committee and Central Secretariat. I am the commander-in-chief, and Deng Xiaoping is the deputy commander, plus several correspondents.[49]

This indicated that while he resigned the state chairmanship, he was not going to relieve any power to Liu Shaoqi and retire to the second front immediately.

On the contrary, he became further prominent within the PSC. As early as January 1958, it was discovered by the CCP senior cadres that Liu Shaoqi, the only CCP member who could previously discuss with Mao Zedong on an equal footing, had gradually lost such equality. Instead, Mao Zedong was developing superiority within the CCP, including his PSC colleagues.[50] Several months later, in the second session of the CCP's Eighth National Congress, the applause for Mao Zedong by his CCP colleagues reached its peak since the founding of the PRC, being considered as the prescursor of the personality cult in 1960s.[51] Just after the session, Premier Zhou Enlai asked to resign from the premiership to take responsibility for taking measures to offset Mao Zedong's Great Leap Forward policy.[52] Although the request was denied, his authority as the premier was further undermined by the PSC's decision to set up special party groups to direct the government works, such as finance and economy, political and legal affairs, the foreign affairs, scientific works, culture and education, and so on. Accordingly, Mao Zedong's grip on the government was further expanded to the economic issues.[53]

In particular, it was further decided in July 1958 that the CMC chairman of the CCP was the commander of the armed forces.[54] As required by the constitution, the Council of National Defense had been established in 1954, with Mao Zedong as the chairman and including twenty-nine non-CCP people in its ninety-seven members. But the CND was actually considered as a consultative organ, and the true leader of the armed forces remained to be the CCP. Just a few days after the first NPC election, a Central Military Commission was set up by the CCP, under direct control of its Politburo and the Central Secretariat, to take full responsibility for the military affairs, with Mao Zedong as the chairman of this new commission.[55] Now with the new decision, the double leadership over the armed forces was replaced by the sole command of the CMC chairman of the CCP, that is, Mao Zedong.

In the end, before Liu Shaoqi took the office of chairmanship from Mao Zedong, Mao Zedong had also virtually distinguished himself from the rest of his PSC peers and established his absolute authority firmly above his CCP colleagues.

NOTES

1. Li Molong, "Guanyu Xieshang Jianguo Shoujie Zhongyang Renmin Zhengfu Danren Lingdao Zhiwu Dangwai Minzhu Renshi Suozhan Bili Xinshi" [New Idea about the Percentage of Non-CCP Democratic Persons Taking Leading Position in the first Central People's Government after the Consulation on the Founding of the PRC], in *Lianhe Shibao* [United Newspaper], October, 26, 2010.

2. Mu Zhaoyong, *Diyijie Quanguo Renmin Daibiao Dahui Shilu* [The First National People's Congress Session] (Guangdong: Guangdong Renmin Chubanshe, 2006), 204-205.

3. Mu Zhaoyong, *Diyijie Quanguo Renmin Daibiao Dahui Shilu* [The First National People's Congress Session] (Guangdong: Guangdong Renmin Chubanshe, 2006), 191.

4. Mu Zhaoyong, *Diyijie Quanguo Renmin Daibiao Dahui Shilu* [The First National People's Congress Session] (Guangdong: Guangdong Renmin Chubanshe, 2006), 196-197.

5. Zhou Fang, *Woguo Guojia Jigou* [The Structure of the State of Our Country] (Beijing: Zhongguo Qingnian Chubanshe, 1955), 66.

6. It is reported that the Sixth Supreme State Conference was held on January 25, 1956. See *Renmin Ribao*, January 26, 1956.

7. Li Lin, "Zuigao Guowu Huiyi Zuzhi Jiegou Jiqi Gongneng Fenxi" [Analysis on the Organization and Function of the Supreme State Conference], *Zhonggong Dangshi Yanjiu*, no. 1 (2005): 64.

8. Li Lin, "Zuigao Guowu Huiyi Zuzhi Jiegou Jiqi Gongneng Fenxi" [Analysis on the Organization and Function of the Supreme State Conference], *Zhonggong Dangshi Yanjiu*, no. 1 (2005): 64-65.

9. *Renmin Ribao*, March 3, 1957.

10. Xu Chongde, Zhonghua Renmin Gongheguo Xianfashi [Constitutional History of the People's Republic of China] (Fujian: Fujian Renmin Chubanshe, 2005), vol. 1, at 207.

11. Pang Xianzhi and Jin Chongji (ed.), *Mao Zedong Zhuan 1949-1976* [Biography of Mao Zedong 1949-1976], vol. 1, (Beijing: Zhongyang Wenxian Chubanshe, 2003), at 491.

12. Mao Zedong, "Mao Zedong Zai Zuigao Guowu Huiyi Diqici Huiyi Shang De Jianghua Jilu" [Record of Mao Zedong's Speech in the Seventh Supreme State Conference], in Pang Xianzhi and Jin Chongji (ed.), *Mao Zedong Zhuan 1949-1976* [Biography of Mao Zedong 1949-1976], vol. 1, (Beijing: Zhongyang Wenxian Chubanshe, 2003), at 492, footnote 1.

13. Li Lin, "Zuigao Guowu Huiyi Zuzhi Jiegou Jiqi Gongneng Fenxi" [Analysis on the Organization and Function of the Supreme State Conference], *Zhonggong Dangshi Yanjiu*, no. 1 (2005): 64.

14. Yang Jiandang, "Zuigao Guowu Huiyi Zhidu Tanlue" [Study on the System of the Supreme State Conference], *Yunnan Xingzheng Xueyuan Xuebao*, no. 4 (2006); Li Lin, "Zuigao Guowu Huiyi Zuzhi Jiegou Jiqi Gongneng Fenxi" [Analysis on the Organization and Function of the Supreme State Conference], *Zhonggong Dangshi Yanjiu*, no. 1 (2005): 64.

15. *Renmin Ribao*, January 26, 1956.

16. Li Lin, "Zuigao Guowu Huiyi Zuzhi Jiegou Jiqi Gongneng Fenxi" [Analysis on the Organization and Function of the Supreme State Conference], *Zhonggong Dangshi Yanjiu*, no. 1 (2005): 64.

17. *Renmin Ribao*, October 14, 1957.

18. Pang Xianzhi and Jin Chongji (eds.), *Mao Zedong Zhuan 1949-1976* [Biography of Mao Zedong 1949-1976] (Beijing: Zhongyang Wenxian Chubanshe, 2003), vol. 1, 781.

19. Pang Xianzhi and Jin Chongji (eds.), *Mao Zedong Zhuan 1949-1976* [Biography of Mao Zedong 1949-1976] (Beijing: Zhongyang Wenxian Chubanshe, 2003), vol. 1, 862; Remin Ribao, September 6 and 9, 1958.

20. Pang Xianzhi and Jin Chongji (eds.), *Mao Zedong Zhuan 1949-1976* [Biography of Mao Zedong 1949-1976] (Beijing: Zhongyang Wenxian Chubanshe, 2003), vol. 1, 619-620.

21. *Renmin Ribao*, October 13, 1957.

22. *Renmin Ribao*, September 16, 1959.

23. Pang Xianzhi and Jin Chongji (eds.), *Mao Zedong Zhuan 1949-1976* [Biography of Mao Zedong 1949-1976] (Beijing: Zhongyang Wenxian Chubanshe, 2003), vol. 1, 620.

24. *Renmin Ribao*, March 3, 1957.

25. Li Lin, "Zuigao Guowu Huiyi Zuzhi Jiegou Jiqi Gongneng Fenxi" [Analysis on the Organization and Function of the Supreme State Conference], *Zhonggong Dangshi Yanjiu*, no. 1 (2005): 66; Yang Jiandang, "Zuigao Guowu Huiyi Zhidu Tanlue" [Study on the System of the Supreme State Conference], *Yunnan Xingzheng Xueyuan Xuebao*, no. 4 (2006): 46-47.

26. Yang Jiandang, "Zuigao Guowu Huiyi Zhidu Tanlue" [Study on the System of the Supreme State Conference], *Yunnan Xingzheng Xueyuan Xuebao*, no. 4 (2006): 48.

27. Song Renqiong, *Song Renqiong Huiyilu* [Memoirs of Song Renqiong] (Beijing: Jiefangjun Chubanshe, 2007), 273-275. The author was a general of the People's Liberation Army.

28. Song Renqiong, *Song Renqiong Huiyilu* [Memoirs of Song Renqiong] (Beijing: Jiefangjun Chubanshe, 2007), 273-275. It is said that the uniform of the Grand Marshal is still kept in the National Military Museum in Beijing.

29. In 1949 when the PRC was founded, the CCP had about 4.5 million members; by 1951, its members increased to 5.8 million; and by the end of June 1953, the figure reached about 6.4 millions. See Pang Song, *Mao Zedong Shidai De Zhongguo (1949-1976)* [China in the Era of Mao Zedong (1949-1976)] (Beijing: Zhongyang Wenxian Chubanshe, 2003), vol. 1, 262, 268.

30. Quanguo Renmin Daibiao Dahui Changwu Weiyuanhui Bangongting Yanjiushi (ed.), *Zhonghua Renmin Gongheguo Renmin Daibiao Dahui Wenxian Ziliao Huibian (1949-1990)* [Compilation of Documents of the National People's Congress of the People's Republic of China] (Beijing: Zhongguo Minzhu Fazhi Chubanshe, 1991), 309.

31. Pang Xianzhi and Jin Chongji (eds.), *Mao Zedong Zhuan 1949-1976* [Biography of Mao Zedong 1949-1976] (Beijing: Zhongyang Wenxian Chubanshe, 2003), vol. 1, 510.

32. Zhonggong Zhongyang Wenxian Yanjiushi (ed.), *Jiangguo Yilai Mao Zedong Wengao* [Writings of Mao Zedong since the Founding of the People's Republic of China] (Beijing: Zhongyang Wenxian Chubanshe, 1987), vol. 1, 457.

33. He may be tired of those ceremonial routines required by the job; see Ma Yunfei, "Liu Shaoqi Dangxuan Guojia Zhuxi Qianhou" [How was Liu Shaoqi Elected as the State Chairman], *Bainian Chao*, no. 3 (2001): 26. Also, he may take lessons from Stalin because he once commented to his close guard that stalin had been very tired and he did not want to be the chairman either; see Ye Zilong, *Ye Zilong Huiyilu* [Memoirs of Ye Zilong] (Beijing: Zhongyang Wenxian Chubanshe, 2000), 255-256. Besides, Mao Zedong also suffered a lot from the loss of his son in the Korean War in 1953.

34. Pang Xianzhi and Jin Chongji (eds.), *Mao Zedong Zhuan 1949-1976* [Biography of Mao Zedong 1949-1976] (Beijing: Zhongyang Wenxian Chubanshe, 2003), vol. 1, 672-673; Li Feng, "Woguo Guojia Zhuxi Zhidu De Bianqian" [Evolution of the State Chairmanship], *Fujian Dangshi Yuekan*, no. 3 (2004): 41.

35. Christopher Hughes, *The Federal Constitution of Switzerland* (Oxford: Clarendon Press, 1954), 109-110.

36. Christopher Hughes, *The Federal Constitution of Switzerland* (Oxford: Clarendon Press, 1954), 109.

37. Nicholas Gillett, *The Swiss Constitution: Can It be Exported?* (Bristol: Youth Eduction Service, 1989), 23.

38. See Ma Yunfei, "Liu Shaoqi Dangxuan Guojia Zhuxi Qianhou" [How was Liu Shaoqi Elected as the State Chairman], *Bainian Chao*, no. 3 (2001): 26-27.

39. Gao Jimin, "Mao Zedong Qingci Guojia Zhuxi Fengbo" [The Storm of Mao Zedong's Request to Resign the State Chairman], *Dangshi Wenyuan*, no. 4 (2005); Ma Yunfei, "Liu

Shaoqi Dangxuan Guojia Zhuxi Qianhou" [How was Liu Shaoqi Elected as the State Chairman], *Bainian Chao*, no. 3 (2001): 27.

40. Zhonggong Zhongyang Wenxian Yanjiushi (ed.), *Jiangguo Yilai Mao Zedong Wengao* [Writings of Mao Zedong since the Founding of the People's Republic of China] (Beijing: Zhongyang Wenxian Chubanshe, 1987), vol. 7, 64.

41. Ma Yunfei, "Liu Shaoqi Dangxuan Guojia Zhuxi Qianhou" [How was Liu Shaoqi Elected as the State Chairman], *Bainian Chao*, no. 3 (2001): 26-27; Gao Jimin, "Mao Zedong Qingci Guojia Zhuxi Fengbo" [The Storm of Mao Zedong's Request to Resign the State Chairman], *Dangshi Wenyuan*, no. 4 (2005).

42. *Renmin Ribao*, December 18, 1958.

43. Pang Xianzhi and Jin Chongji (eds.), *Mao Zedong Zhuan 1949-1976* [Biography of Mao Zedong 1949-1976] (Beijing: Zhongyang Wenxian Chubanshe, 2003), vol. 1, 519-520.

44. Pang Xianzhi and Jin Chongji (eds.), *Mao Zedong Zhuan 1949-1976* [Biography of Mao Zedong 1949-1976] (Beijing: Zhongyang Wenxian Chubanshe, 2003), vol. 1, 520.

45. L. G. Churchward, *Contemporary Soviet Government* (Revised 2nd Edition) (London: Routledge & Kegan Paul, 1975), 224-225.

46. L. G. Churchward, *Contemporary Soviet Government* (Revised 2nd Edition) (London: Routledge & Kegan Paul, 1975), 227.

47. Pang Xianzhi and Jin Chongji (eds.), *Mao Zedong Zhuan 1949-1976* [Biography of Mao Zedong 1949-1976] (Beijing: Zhongyang Wenxian Chubanshe, 2003), vol. 1, 520.

48. Pang Xianzhi and Jin Chongji (eds.), *Mao Zedong Zhuan 1949-1976* [Biography of Mao Zedong 1949-1976] (Beijing: Zhongyang Wenxian Chubanshe, 2003), vol. 2, 1,666.

49. Lin Yunhui, *Wutuobang Yundong: Cong Da Yuejin Dao Da Jihuang (1958-1961)* [The Utopian Movement: From the Great Leapforward to Great Famine (1958-1961)] (Hong Kong: The Chinese University Press, 2008), 419-422.

50. Lin Yunhui, *Wutuobang Yundong: Cong Da Yuejin Dao Da Jihuang (1958-1961)* [The Utopian Movement: From the Great Leapforward to Great Famine (1958-1961)] (Hong Kong: The Chinese University Press, 2008), 33.

51. Lin Yunhui, *Wutuobang Yundong: Cong Da Yuejin Dao Da Jihuang (1958-1961)* [The Utopian Movement: From the Great Leapforward to Great Famine (1958-1961)] (Hong Kong: The Chinese University Press, 2008), 60.

52. Lin Yunhui, *Wutuobang Yundong: Cong Da Yuejin Dao Da Jihuang (1958-1961)* [The Utopian Movement: From the Great Leapforward to Great Famine (1958-1961)] (Hong Kong: The Chinese University Press, 2008), 71.

53. Lin Yunhui, *Wutuobang Yundong: Cong Da Yuejin Dao Da Jihuang (1958-1961)* [The Utopian Movement: From the Great Leapforward to Great Famine (1958-1961)] (Hong Kong: The Chinese University Press, 2008), 72. The decision was issued within the CCP on June 16th, 1958.

54. Zhou Jian, Zhongguo Junshi Fashi [History of Military Law of China] (Beijing: Falv Chubanshe, 2008), at 453-454.

55. Zhou Jian, *Zhongguo Junshi Fashi* [History of Military Law of China] (Beijing: Falv Chubanshe, 2008), 453-454; Pang Song, *Mao Zedong Shidai De Zhongguo (1949-1976)* [China in the Era of Mao Zedong (1949-1976)] (Beijing: Zhongyang Wenxian Chubanshe, 2003), vol. 1, 450.

Chapter Seven

Chairman Liu Shaoqi from 1959 to 1966

LIU SHAOQI ELECTED AS THE SECOND CHAIRMAN

As it became clear that Mao Zedong did not pursue a second term, two other CCP leaders, Zhu De and Liu Shaoqi, had been considered as the candidates to be the next chairman.[1] Zhu De did not want to take this job and recommended Liu Shaoqi instead.[2] In reply to a letter written by Dong Biwu, Mao Zedong confirmed that Liu Shaoqi had been agreed to be the candidate of the chairmanship and his nomination would be sent to the CCP's Central Committee for final confirmation.[3] On April 5, 1959, the seventh plenum of the eighth CCPCC meeting entered its third day, discussing candidates for government positions.[4] The GS Deng Xiaoping proposed Liu Shaoqi as the candidate for the next state chairman. His proposal was accepted and Liu Shaoqi's candidature was thus endorsed.[5]

On behalf of the CCP Politburo, Deng Xiaoping explained his proposal as follows:

> Several comrades are suitable for this position, for example, comrade Zhu De and a few other old comrades in our party. However, after our consideration, it is better for comrade Liu Shaoqi to take this position because the state chairman is not only an honorable position, but also has to fulfill considerable specific and troublesome work, like overseas visits, talks and receptions, etc. Therefore, it is a better choice for him to take the position of state chairman concurrently for his ability, experience, prestige and his responsibility in our party.[6]

On April 15, 1959, Mao Zedong also explained the CCP's nomination of Liu Shaoqi to non-CCP people in the Sixteenth Supreme State Conference. He said:

> Why was comrade Liu Shaoqi nominated for the state chairman, not comrade Zhu De? Comrade Zhu De is highly prestigious, and comrade Liu Shaoqi is also so. Then why did we choose the latter instead of the former? Because in our party, I am one of those who are in charge, but I do not take care of daily business. Sometimes I do, sometimes I do not. Who is often in charge? It is comrade Liu Shaoqi. Whenever I left Beijing, Liu Shaoqi took charge on my behalf. It has been this for years ever since Yan'an period. Ten years have gone since we come to Beijing. Therefore he is more suitable for the position. In the meantime, comrade Zhu De recommended him strongly.[7]

Liu Shaoqi was duly elected as the second chairman of the PRC by the second NPC on April 27, 1959, and reelected to a second term on January 4, 1965.[8]

HIS PERFORMANCE OF CONSTITUTIONAL FUNCTIONS

Chairman Liu's Active Diplomacy

Compared to Chairman Mao, Liu Shaoqi seems far more active in China's foreign affairs amid China's "second high tide of diplomacy."[9] Notably, he signed about a dozen international documents that China concluded with other countries. Those documents not only included four joint communiqués[10] and five joint statements,[11] but also two bilateral treaties, respectively, concerning friendship relations and border issue.[12] Besides, he issued a declaration in the capacity of Chinese chairman in July 1966.[13]

He paid more overseas visits, starting in November 1960 when he was invited by the former Soviet Union to pay a state visit, which had been his first overseas visit since succession.[14] He further visited Indonesia, Burma, Cambodia, Vietnam, and North Korea in 1963.[15] Without knowing the coming storm of the Cultural Revolution, he went on his last state visits to Pakistan, Afghanistan, and Myanmar in March and April 1966.[16]

He also received foreign diplomats and visiting guests. His last appearance before foreign guests as the state chairman was on August 5, 1966, when he received a delegation from Zambia.[17] On the same day, he was informed by Zhou Enlai not to continue to appear in public and meet foreign visitors officially.[18] On December 11 of that year, he cosigned a message of greeting to Kenya, which was his last official act with respect to the diplomacy.[19]

Chairman Liu's Home Services

Chairman Liu Shaoqi was also active at home, but less substantial as provided by the constitution. On one hand, he issued four decrees of special pardons,[20] which was new to his predecessor. On the other hand, his two major constitutional functions had been substantially reduced. According to the constitution, he should concurrently hold the office of the chairman of the Council of National Defense and command the armed forces. In practice, he was only recorded to convene the CND twice,[21] but actually could not exercise real command throughout his term of office because Mao Zedong remained in control of the armed forces as the chairman of the CCP's CMC.[22] On September 26 of the year, the Politburo decided that the CMC of the CCP would be chaired by Mao Zedong, assisted by three chairmen, that is, Lin Biao, He Long, and Nie Rongzhen, among whom Lin Biao was the vice-chairman handling the daily affairs.[23] Liu Shaoqi was excluded from the military leadership.

He could convene the Supreme State Conference, but it had been minimized greatly in terms of its frequency, duration, participants, and scope of issues. In total, he was reported to convene far fewer Supreme State Conferences, only five times, all of which lasted only one or two days and the attendance was also reduced sharply from the maximum 1,600 persons to about sixty persons.[24] Issues discussed in these conferences were also limited to the general discussion on the national situation and preparations for the NPC. For example, on August 24, 1959, he convened his first Supreme State Conference after being elected, discussing overall situation and national economy.[25] Then the Supreme State Conference was interrupted for more than two years and was not held again until March 1962 for the second one and November 1963 for the third one, both of which were also discussing domestic and international affairs.[26] His last two conferences were held in December 1964, discussing preparations for the forthcoming third NPC, including the CCP's suggestions about candidates for government posts.[27]

Therefore, to a large extent, the Supreme State Conference was reduced to a formality during Liu Shaoqi's terms of office. This is understandable. As he was only one member of the CCP collective decision making and subject to Mao Zedong's ideological supremacy, he could only declare policies and conduct political consultations with the approval of Mao Zedong, but not act like Mao Zedong, using the SSC as a forum where he could independently solicit ideas for policies from participants and give ideological orientations to them. Besides, after the Anti-Rightist movement, the CCP's relationship with those democratic people reached its lowest; as the national economy worsened since 1959, disagreements were also arising within the CCP.[28] All of these could have made impossible to convene the SSC as usual.

RISE AND FALL OF CHAIRMAN LIU IN THE "FIRST FRONT"

Chairman Liu's Succession Endorsed

It could appear that Liu Shaoqi mainly served as a figurehead of state in the office of chairmanship. However, this can only be applied to the government side of the party-state and should not be taken for granted. The other side of the party-state was Liu Shaoqi's rise and fall within the CCP's collective leadership as the first front leader and Mao Zedong's successor.

While Liu Shaoqi was elected as the second state chairman, the CCP chairman Mao Zedong was pushing forward with his radical Great Leap Forward policies, against which opposition from his CCP colleagues continued to develop in the meantime. To settle their disagreement about the agricultural work, Mao Zedong proposed convening two meetings successively in Southern and Northern China. On March 10, 1961, Mao Zedong personally presided the first meeting in Guangzhou, attended by Zhou Enlai, Zhu De, Deng Xiaoping, and so on, whereas Liu Shaoqi held the second meeting in Beijing on the next day. Upon the completion of the Guangzhou meeting, Mao Zedong was going to send a participant whom he called as the correspondent to inform Beijing the results, Zhou Enlai and Deng Xiaoping suggested that it could be better to combine these two meetings together to avoid any misinformation. Hence, the four PSC members in Beijing, that is, Liu Shaoqi, Zhou Enlai, Chen Yun, and Deng Xiaoping, flew to Guangzhou to join Mao Zedong, who set the topics for the new meeting.[29] By that time, Mao Zedong was still out in the first front, whereas Liu Shaoqi was in the second front.

Seemingly, the Guangzhou meeting did not solve their disputes. So all the PSC members, except Lin Biao, went to the countryside to investigate the true situation. Based on their findings, they met again in Beijing on May 21. During this new meeting, Liu Shaoqi made severe critiques on Mao Zedong's radical policies.[30] Since then, modification to Mao Zedong's Great Leap Forward policies expanded from agriculture to other areas,[31] during which time Mao Zedong retreated to the second front, whereas the younger PSC members who used to work in the second front went to the first front.

Accordingly, Liu Shaoqi's influence began to ascend, with Mao Zedong's silence. For example, Mao Zedong did not attend the Politburo meeting held in July, which changed his policy concerning scientific work, but he gave his permission to this change.[32] Also, he did not preside over the meeting held in August in Lu Shan, Jiangxi province, modifying the industrial policies; instead, it was presided over by Liu Shaoqi, Zhou Enlai, and Deng Xiaoping.[33] War criminals were also pardoned.[34]

On September 24, 1961, during the talk with British General Bernard Law Montgomery, Mao Zedong confirmed that Liu Shaoqi was his successor.[35] This suggests that Liu Shaoqi moved a step forward in his succession to Mao Zedong. According to Mao Zedong's plan, the next step for Chairman Liu Shaoqi would be the CCP's chairman.

Worsening Policy Disputes Between Two Chairmen

As adjustments to Mao Zedong's radical policies continued, the disagreements between Mao Zedong and Liu Shaoqi turned into disputes, which first appeared in the "Meeting of Seven Thousand People" held from January 11 to February 7 of 1962.[36] After the meeting, Mao Zedong started to question whether Liu Shaoqi could pursue the "capitalist road" with the widening of their differences.[37] On July 6, 1962, Mao Zedong returned to Beijing from his "Northern Expedition." A debate was said to break out between these two chairmen:

> Mao Zedong questioned Liu Shaoqi: 'what are you anxious for? Can't you hold on more? Why did you not resist?' Liu Shaoqi replied that: 'so many people died, both of us will be recorded in the history; people have started to eat each other, and this will be written in books!' But Mao Zedong did not back down and still stick to the political issues: 'now three red-flags have been denied and land been distributed, if you do not resist to them, what will happen after I die?' In the end, Liu Shaoqi gave up debate and offered his suggestion: three red-flags will not be given up, the People's Commune will not be dissolved, whereas the high quotas will not be pursued and the public canteen will be closed.[38]

Facing Mao Zedong's fighting back, Liu Shaoqi and other CCP leaders had to be self-critical.[39]

But this did not work anymore. By the end of 1964, their disputes gradually turned into open conflict.[40] When Liu Shaoqi was elected for a second term on January 3, 1965,[41] an enlarged PSC meeting was held on the same day. In this meeting, the two chairmen finally had an open conflict, which led Mao Zedong to pull the state chairman Liu Shaoqi down, directly resulting in the breakout of the Cultural Revolution.[42]

Chairman Liu Removed from Office

In the storm of the Cultural Revolution, Liu Shaoqi was caught in the dilemma of accountability for his policies, from which the CCP first GS Chen Duxiu had also suffered. On one hand, he had to be accountable to the party chairman Mao Zedong, who had been endorsed by the party constitution as the one correctly applying Marxism and Leninism to the Chinese situation. On the other hand, he personally felt accountable to the constitution as the state chairman,[43] even if the constitution had not expressly demanded his responsibility. He once remarked in a senior CCP meeting well after the

"Meeting of Seven Thousand People" that "presidents in foreign countries should have announced to abolish certain constitutional rights if they had been in such an acute situation of national economy."[44]

Therefore, Liu Shaoqi tried to solve it by constitutional ways. He made several attempts to resign from the office of the state chairman,[45] but the constitution did not provide for such a presidential resignation. He requested to convene the NPC to remove him.[46] The NPC did have the power to remove him from office, but he might not have known at that time that the highest state organ had been ordered to stop function by Kang Sheng.[47] As a result, the NPC had been unable to convene to consider any of his requests to resign or be removed. Even if the NPC could convene, the constitution did not provide how such a removal could be proceeded. When he was deprived of personal freedom, he tried to protest by the constitution, which had provided that no deputy to the NPC could be arrested or placed on trial without the consent of the NPC or, when the NPC was not in session, of its Standing Committee, but he failed. By then, law and order had been destroyed by politics. It was the CCP's enlarged twelfth plenum of the eighth CCPCC held in 1968 that removed his chairmanship,[48] of which he could have been unaware till his death.

THE ABOLISHMENT OF THE CHAIRMANSHIP

Deputy Chairman Dong Biwu

With Liu Shaoqi's downfall, the office of chairman was left vacant. This became an issue when the new Pakistan ambassador started his term of office in China and had to deliver his letter of credence to the Chinese head of state. With the permission of Mao Zedong, the vice-chairman, Dong Biwu, was recommended by Zhou Enlai to fulfill these formalities of receiving foreign ambassadors and sending out Chinese diplomats.[49]

This could do for a while when China's diplomacy reached its lowest level as the Cultural Revolution continued. The honeymoon between China and the former Soviet Union ended and a border war broke out in 1969. China's relations with other countries also dropped severely. During the period from May 1966 to April 1969, only one overseas visit was made by Premier Zhou Enlai, whereas foreign guests reduced sharply with only six foreign heads of state and government visiting China.[50] This saved the need for a formal head of state for the time being.

However, in the 1970s, the vice-chairman could not suffice as China's diplomacy reversed its decline and made a third high tide. From 1970 to 1971, twenty-five countries newly established diplomatic relations with China, eighteen of which were in the third world.[51] In November 1971, the PRC finally replaced the ROC in the United Nations.

In view of all these new diplomatic developments, Dong Biwu was further decided by the CCP in the capacity of deputy chairman to invite heads of state of Somalia, Sri Lanka, Zambia, Mexico, Mali, Cambodia, France, Tanzania, and Mauritania to pay state visits to China.[52] Surely this decision could not have been made without Mao Zedong's permission. By far it has been unknown when such a decision was made. But it could be in February 1972,[53] because according to a Chinese official report, Dong Biwu's first appearance with this new title was on February 24, sending a telegram to Kuwait in celebration of Kuwait's sixteenth National Holiday,[54] whereas on the third of that month, he was still the vice-chairman, making a phone call to Nepal together with Premier Zhou Enlai. Coincidently, in the same month, United States President Nixon paid the historical pioneering visit to China from the February 21-28. Understandably, Nixon would feel better received by his Chinese host titled as the deputy chairman rather than the vice-chairman.

From then on, Dong Biwu served in this new capacity until his death three years later[55] when the constitution was revised and the office of the chairman was abolished by Mao Zedong. His last official appearance as the deputy chairman was on January 16, 1975, when he received the first Malaysian ambassador to China.[56]

Chairman Abolished from the Constitution

In 1970, Mao Zedong sent a letter to Zhou Enlai requesting to "revise the constitution but do not set up the chairmanship." On August 23, 1970, the CCP's Ninth National Congress convened its second session. When it came to the constitutional revision, most participants, including Mao Zedong's designated successor, Lin Biao, and Premier Zhou Enlai, all suggested that the office of chairmanship be kept in the new constitution and Mao Zedong take this position. However, Mao Zedong repeatedly rejected.[57]

Why did Mao Zedong insist on removing the chairmanship from the constitution against the opinion of others? He might have personally disliked it,[58] he might not have wanted Lin Biao to take this position,[59] he might not have wanted to take the ceremonial burden[60] he might not have wanted to be thought of by the people that he had pulled down Liu Shaoqi for this position,[61] or he might not have wanted to repeat the disastrous history.[62]

The 1954 constitution was not meant to be everlasting; instead, it was just transitory. As introduced in previous parts, the 1954 constitution had been regarded not a socialist one. When China achieved its socialist transformation in 1956, as remarked by Mao Zedong, this constitution became obsolete. In time, a new constitution would surely have to be adopted when Mao Zedong finally had his socialist utopia in place. Then the chairmanship provided by the 1954 constitution had to be reconsidered.

On one hand, such a constitutional chairmanship was both theoretically controversial and practically problematic. It was controversial in constitutional theory. Although the NPC was the highest state organ with the power to elect and recall the state chairman, the state chairman could convene the Supreme State Conference, to which the chairman of the NPCSC should be a participant. What if these two chairmen were in conflict? Such an uncertainty had been exposed by the debate during the constitutional making on the issue whether the chairman was the head of state. The 1954 constitution had provided a half-way answer that the chairman only represented the PRC in foreign affairs, but not domestically. For this constitutional ambiguity, no solutions had been provided.

Politically, the authority of the chairmanship was highly personal. The constitutional provisions of this office had never been a true description of China's political reality under increasing impact of the changing international climate: for Mao Zedong, the paramount leader of the party and state, the chairmanship was incomparable to his ultimate decision-making power; for Liu Shaoqi, Mao Zedong's heir, the office did not agree with his tortuous political ups and downs. In a word, the fate of the state chairman had been decided by the CCP, and ultimately by the CCP's chairman, Mao Zedong.

In particular, more than this uncertainty, the chairmanship was potentially risky to the party-state. As a precaution against Moscow's failure to solve the succession problem, Mao Zedong conceived the "two-front" arrangement, in which the chairmanship was a starting step of the overall succession plan. However, such a way of succession had ambiguities in responsibility between the holder and his successor in each step of this plan. As Mao Zedong tried to maintain the final decision-making power, there would always be tensions between him and his successors, as proved by the case of Liu Shaoqi and Lin Biao. In absence of some adjudication system with final authority, all these ambiguities and disputes, even conflicts, had to be resolved by politics. Since the idea of two fronts had been proved to fail, the succession plan had to be reconsidered and the chairmanship could also be useless.

Mao Zedong must have been fully aware of the great political potential provided by the flexible constitutional office of the chairmanship. On one hand, Mao Zedong had proved by his own experience what the chairman could bring about if fully equipped. During his conflict with Liu Shaoqi, it had also been proved that the chairmanship could be a true threat to his leadership. On the other hand, as a master of Chinese traditional culture, he must have been alert by the earlier Gao-Rao incident about the tragic bloodshed facts that had happened repeatedly among the warlords for the supreme emperorship in various dynasties after the founding emperor died throughout China's ancient history. Therefore it would be better to abolish this office and put the state under direct control of the collective leadership of the CCP.

Virtually, such an uncertain chairmanship was personal, made for no one other than Mao Zedong. When commenting on Gao Gang's failed challenge to Liu Shaoqi, Mao Zedong once said that, "Gao Gang wanted to be the state chairman, but he was not suitable because the chairman has to bear great responsibility and should be taken by a more authoritative person."[63] In the CCP, there could be no other person more authoritative than Mao Zedong himself. If Mao Zedong could not manage such a chairmanship, who else could be expected to do with it?

Ideologically, there might be no place for a chairmanship in Mao Zedong's concept of socialism to be endorsed by the new constitution. Mao Zedong had always put the party before the state; while the chairmanship had so much uncertain potential, it would be better to have none than one, even a figurehead of state. Besides, the chairman was abnormal to the Stalinist government, and the new Chinese socialist constitution could be at least close to the Stalinist constitution that had no chairman, if not surpassing it.

CONCLUSION

During the constitutional making, Mao Zedong had made it clear that powers and functions of the chairman were intended to be more nominal than substantive, and the chairman enjoy little administrative responsibility.[64] However, as the first chairman, Chairman Mao Zedong not only had the power to veto the PSC's collective decisions, but he continued to hold power even after he evacuated the state chairmanship till his death, and designated his successors time and again. One can conclude that the chairman's seemingly nominal powers to convene the Supreme State Conference, to nominate the premier, and intervene in military and in foreign affairs had turned out to be substantive in practice in China's domestic politics; on the whole, powers and functions of the chairmanship provided by the 1954 constitution were characterized by a combination of nominal and real powers ("Xu Zhong You Shi," "Xu Xu Shi Shi," in Chinese).[65]

But this conclusion seemingly cannot be applied to the second chairman, Liu Shaoqi. To solve the succession problem suggested by the case of the Soviet "big brother," Mao Zedong conceived the "two fronts" arrangement, by which he was in "the second front," whereas other CS members headed by his designated successor Liu Shaoqi were in "the first front." As the first step to succeed Mao Zedong, Liu Shaoqi took the chairmanship from him in 1959. Liu Shaoqi had been supposed to take the CCP's chairmanship and even the proposed CCP's honorary chairmanship step by step after Mao Zedong retired from them at future times as determined by Mao Zedong, if without the "dilemma of accountability" undermined such a way of step-by-step succession. With the worsening of policy controversies, constitutional conflicts between the overshadowed state Chairman Liu Shaoqi and the dominant CCP chairman, Mao Zedong became critical and ended with the downfall of the former personally and institutionally in the storm of the Cultural Revolution. Being displaced from the office, Liu Shaoqi had been unable to exercise whatever constitutional power and function ever since he started his second term. Therefore, during the 1954 constitution period, the written constitutional provisions did not reflect the true power of the chairman in practice.

Mao Zedong not only established the PRC, but he also left two constitutions with and without the office of chairman, respectively. Intentionally designed in the 1954 constitution, the chairmanship had become a transitory point along the way of succession from the CCP to the constitutional state with its great political potential provided by its constitutional uncertainty and political ambiguities. As Mao Zedong split with his CCP partners over how to build a so-called socialist state along their utopian march, the chairmanship was first destroyed personally, and then abolished officially from the 1975 constitution decisively. Yet mysteriously, the chairmanship could serve in China's diplomacy as a figurehead of state, thus leaving an unfinished legacy about how to make a chairmanship to serve the party-state, if to have one for China.

NOTES

1. Gao Jimin, "Mao Zedong Qingci Guojia Zhuxi Fengbo" [The Storm of Mao Zedong's Request to Resign the State Chairman], *Dangshi Wenyuan*, no. 4 (2005).

2. Jin Chongji (ed.), *Liu Shaoqi Zhuan* [Biography of Liu Shaoqi] (Beijing: Zhongyang Wenxian Chubanshe 1998), vol. 2, 837; Gao Jimin, "Mao Zedong Qingci Guojia Zhuxi Fengbo" [The Storm of Mao Zedong's Request to Resign the State Chairman], *Dangshi Wenyuan*, no. 4 (2005); Ma Yunfei, "Liu Shaoqi Dangxuan Guojia Zhuxi Qianhou" [How was Liu Shaoqi Elected as the State Chairman], *Bainian Chao*, no. 3 (2001): 29.

3. Zhuanxie Zu, *Dong Biwu Zhuan* [Biography of Dong Biwu] (Beijing: Zhongyang Wenxian Chubanshe 2006), vol. 2, 997.

4. Zhonggong Zhongyang Wenxian Yanjiu Shi (ed.), *Liu Shaoqi Nianpu* [Chronicle of Liu Shaoqi] (Beijing: Zhongyang Wenxian Chubanshe, 1996), vol. 2, 453.

5. Gao Jimin, "Mao Zedong Qingci Guojia Zhuxi Fengbo" [The Storm of Mao Zedong's Request to Resign the State Chairman], *Dangshi Wenyuan*, no. 4 (2005); Feng Zhijun, *Mao Zedong yu Lin Biao* [Mao Zedong and Lin Biao] (Xianggang: Huangcheng Tushu Youxian Gongsi, 1998), 4th ed., 540.

6. Jin Chongji (ed.), *Liu Shaoqi Zhuan* [Biography of Liu Shaoqi] (Beijing: Zhongyang Wenxian Chubanshe 1998), vol. 2, 837; Gao Jimin, "Mao Zedong Qingci Guojia Zhuxi Fengbo" [The Storm of Mao Zedong's Request to Resign the State Chairman], *Dangshi Wenyuan*, no. 4 (2005); Ma Yunfei, "Liu Shaoqi Dangxuan Guojia Zhuxi Qianhou" [How was Liu Shaoqi Elected as the State Chairman], *Bainian Chao*, no. 3 (2001): 29.

7. Jin Chongji (ed.), *Liu Shaoqi Zhuan* [Biography of Liu Shaoqi] (Beijing: Zhongyang Wenxian Chubanshe 1998), vol. 2, 837-838; Gao Jimin, "Mao Zedong Qingci Guojia Zhuxi Fengbo" [The Storm of Mao Zedong's Request to Resign the State Chairman], *Dangshi Wenyuan*, no. 4 (2005); Ma Yunfei, "Liu Shaoqi Dangxuan Guojia Zhuxi Qianhou" [How Was Liu Shaoqi Elected as the State Chairman], *Bainian Chao*, no. 3 (2001): 30.

8. *Renmin Ribao*, April 28, 1959, and January 4, 1965.

9. Shi Zhifu (ed.), *Zhonghua Renmin Gongheguo Duiwai Guanxi Shi* [History of Foreign Relationship of the PRC between 1940 and October 1989] (Beijing: Beijing Daxue Chubanshe, 1994), 182.

10. Liu Chongwen, Zhonggong Zhongyang Wenxian Yanjiu Shi, and Chen Shaochou (eds.), *Liu Shaoqi Nianpu 1898-1969* [The Chronicle of Liu Shaoqi 1898-1969] (Beijing: Zhongyang Wenxian Chubanshe, 1996), 493, 538, 542, 593.

11. Liu Chongwen, Zhonggong Zhongyang Wenxian Yanjiu Shi, and Chen Shaochou (eds.), *Liu Shaoqi Nianpu 1898-1969* [The Chronicle of Liu Shaoqi 1898-1969] (Beijing: Zhongyang Wenxian Chubanshe, 1996), at 499, 574, 576, 577, 579.

12. Liu Chongwen, Zhonggong Zhongyang Wenxian Yanjiu Shi, and Chen Shaochou (eds.), *Liu Shaoqi Nianpu 1898-1969* [The Chronicle of Liu Shaoqi 1898-1969] (Beijing: Zhongyang Wenxian Chubanshe, 1996), 542, 615.

13. Liu Chongwen, Zhonggong Zhongyang Wenxian Yanjiu Shi, and Chen Shaochou (eds.), *Liu Shaoqi Nianpu 1898-1969* [The Chronicle of Liu Shaoqi 1898-1969] (Beijing: Zhongyang Wenxian Chubanshe, 1996), 645.

14. Jin Chongji (ed.), *Liu Shaoqi Zhuan* [Biography of Liu Shaoqi] (Beijing: Zhongyang Wenxian Chubanshe 1998), vol. 2, 921.

15. Liu Chongwen, Zhonggong Zhongyang Wenxian Yanjiu Shi, and Chen Shaochou (eds.), *Liu Shaoqi Nianpu 1898-1969* [The Chronicle of Liu Shaoqi 1898-1969] (Beijing: Zhongyang Wenxian Chubanshe, 1996), at 496, 499, 573, 574, 575, 577, 580.

16. Gu Baozi, "Shangyu Yu Lai Shi Jiedao Chufang Renwu: Liu Shaoqi Zuihou Yici Chufang" [Receiving the Task of Foreign Visit When the Storm is Coming: The Last Foreign Visit of Liu Shaoqi], *Xiang Chao*, no. 1 (2008).

17. Liu Chongwen, Zhonggong Zhongyang Wenxian Yanjiu Shi, and Chen Shaochou (ed.), Liu Shaoqi Nianpu 1898-1969 [the Chronicle of Liu Shaoqi 1898-1969] (Beijing: Zhongyang Wenxian Chubanshe, 1996), at 648.

18. Zhonggong Zhongyang Wenxian Yanjiushi Erbu (ed.), *Liu Shaoqi Zishu* (Beijing: Jiefangjun Wenyi Chubanshe, 2003), 220; Roderick MacFarquhar and Michael Schoenhals, *Mao's Last Revolution*, (Cambridge, MA: The Belknap Press of Harvard University Press, 2006), 91.

19. Lowell Dittmer, *Liu Shaoqi and the Chinese Cultural Revolution* (New York: M.E. Sharpe, 1998), rev. ed., 83.

20. Liu Chongwen, Zhonggong Zhongyang Wenxian Yanjiu Shi, and Chen Shaochou (eds.), *Liu Shaoqi Nianpu 1898-1969* [The Chronicle of Liu Shaoqi 1898-1969] (Beijing: Zhongyang Wenxian Chubanshe, 1996), 461, 496, 543, 573. For a brief discussion on China's seven special pardons, see Wang Xiangping, "Xin Zhongguo Lishi Shang De Qici Tese De Juece Guocheng Jiqi Jingyan Qishi" [Decision-making of and Lesson from Seven Special Pardons in the History of New China], at http://dangshi.people.com.cn/GB/144956/10093144.html.

21. Liu Chongwen, Zhonggong Zhongyang Wenxian Yanjiu Shi, and Chen Shaochou (eds.), *Liu Shaoqi Nianpu 1898-1969* [The Chronicle of Liu Shaoqi 1898-1969] (Beijing: Zhongyang Wenxian Chubanshe, 1996), 456, 613.

22. Xu Chongde, *Zhonghua Renmin Gongheguo Xianfashi* [Constitutional History of the People's Republic of China] (Fujian: Fujian Renmin Chubanshe, 2005), 2nd ed., vol. 1, 206.

23. Hu Angang, *Zhongguo Jiti Lingdao Tizhi* [Collective Leadership of China] (Beijing: Zhongguo Renmin Chubanshe, 2013), 28, fn2.

24. *Renmin Ribao*, August 25, 1959; March 22, 1962; November 17, 1963; December 19, 1964; January 1, 1965.

25. *Renmin Ribao*, August 25, 1959.

26. *Renmin Ribao*, March 22, 1962; November 17, 1963.

27. *Renmin Ribao*, December 19, 1964; January 1, 1965. Yang Shangkun, *Yangshangkun Riji* [Diary of Yang Shangkun] (Beijing: Zhongyang Wenxian Chubanshe, 2001), vol. 2, 483.

28. Qian Yangli, *Lishi De Bianju: Cong Wanjiu Weiji Dao Fanxiu Fangxiu* [Historical Change: From Saving the Crisis to the Anti-Revisionism and Prevent Revisionism] (Hong Kong: the Chinese University Press, 2008), 213.

29. Lin Yunhui, *Wutuobang Yundong: Cong Da Yuejin Dao Da Jihuang (1958-1961)* [The Utopian Movement: From the Great Leap Forward to Great Famine (1958-1961)] (Hong Kong: The Chinese University Press, 2008), 658-661.

30. Lin Yunhui, *Wutuobang Yundong: Cong Da Yuejin Dao Da Jihuang (1958-1961)* [The Utopian Movement: From the Great Leap Forward to Great Famine (1958-1961)] (Hong Kong: The Chinese University Press, 2008), 684-687.

31. Lin Yunhui, *Wutuobang Yundong: Cong Da Yuejin Dao Da Jihuang (1958-1961)* [The Utopian Movement: From the Great Leap Forward to Great Famine (1958-1961)] (Hong Kong: The Chinese University Press, 2008), 730.

32. Lin Yunhui, *Wutuobang Yundong: Cong Da Yuejin Dao Da Jihuang (1958-1961)* [The Utopian Movement: From the Great Leap Forward to Great Famine (1958-1961)] (Hong Kong: The Chinese University Press, 2008), 745-746.

33. Lin Yunhui, *Wutuobang Yundong: Cong Da Yuejin Dao Da Jihuang (1958-1961)* [The Utopian Movement: From the Great Leap Forward to Great Famine (1958-1961)] (Hong Kong: The Chinese University Press, 2008), 726-727.

34. Lin Yunhui, *Wutuobang Yundong: Cong Da Yuejin Dao Da Jihuang (1958-1961)* [The Utopian Movement: From the Great Leap Forward to Great Famine (1958-1961)] (Hong Kong: The Chinese University Press, 2008), 758-760.

35. Ma Yunfei, "Liu Shaoqi Dangxuan Guojia Zhuxi Qianhou" [How was Liu Shaoqi Elected as the State Chairman], *Bainian Chao*, no. 3 (2001): 31-33, 42.

36. Qian Yangli, *Lishi De Bianju: Cong Wanjiu Weiji Dao Fanxiu Fangxiu* [Historical Change: From Saving the Crisis to the Anti-Revisionism and Prevent Revisionism] (Hong Kong: the Chinese University Press, 2008), 124.

37. *Zhang Suhua: Bianju Qiqianren Dahui Shimo* [The Change: The Whole Story of "Seven-Thousand-People Meeting"] (Beijing: Zhongguo Qingnian Chubanshe, 2006), 287-288.

38. Qian Yangli, *Lishi De Bianju: Cong Wanjiu Weiji Dao Fanxiu Fangxiu* [Historical Change: From Saving the Crisis to the Anti-Revisionism and Prevent Revisionism] (Hong Kong: the Chinese University Press, 2008), 110-111.

39. Qian Yangli, *Lishi De Bianju: Cong Wanjiu Weiji Dao Fanxiu Fangxiu* [Historical Change: From Saving the Crisis to the Anti-Revisionism and Prevent Revisionism] (Hong Kong: the Chinese University Press, 2008), 284.

40. Qian Yangli, Lishi De Bianju: Cong Wanjiu Weiji Dao Fanxiu Fangxiu [Historical Change: from Saving the Crisis to the Anti-Revisionism and Prevent Revisionism] (Hong Kong: the Chinese University Press, 2008), at 399-406.

41. *Renmin Ribao*, January 4, 1965.

42. Jin Chongji (ed.), *Liu Shaoqi Zhuan* [Biography of Liu Shaoqi] (Beijing: Zhongyang Wenxian Chubanshe 1998), vol. 2, 971-974.

43. *Zhang Suhua: Bianju Qiqianren Dahui Shimo* [The Change: The Whole Story of "Seven-Thousand-People Meeting"] (Beijing: Zhongguo Qingnian Chubanshe, 2006), 285.

44. Yuan Baohua, "Dui Guomin Jingji De Jianku Tiaozheng" [Difficult Adjustment to National Economy], in *Dangdai Zhongguoshi Yanjiu* [Study on Contemporary History of China], no. 1 (2002): 14.

45. Jin Chongji (ed.), *Liu Shaoqi Zhuan* [Biography of Liu Shaoqi] (Beijing: Zhongyang Wenxian Chubanshe 1998), vol. 2, 1049, 1055, 1068-1069; Pang Xianzhi and Jin Chongji (eds.), *Mao Zedong Zhuan 1949-1976* [Biography of Mao Zedong 1949-1976] (Beijing: Zhongyang Wenxian Chubanshe, 2003), vol. 2, 1534; Li Pingping, et al., *Xiangei Nin Huannian Women Baba Liu Shaoqi* [To You: In Memory of Our Father Liu Shaoqi], *Worker's Daily*, December 5, 6, 8, 1980; Jin Chongji (ed.), *Liu Shaoqi Zhuan* [Biography of Liu Shaoqi] (Beijing: Zhongyang Wenxian Chubanshe 1998), vol. 2, 1049, 1055, 1068-1069.

46. Jin Chongji (ed.), *Liu Shaoqi Zhuan* [Biography of Liu Shaoqi] (Beijing: Zhongyang Wenxian Chubanshe 1998), vol. 2, 1049, 1055, 1068.

47. Mu Zhaoyong, *Diyijie Quanguo Renmin Daibiao Dahui Shilu* [The First National People's Congress Session] (Guangdong: Guangdong Renmin Chubanshe, 2006), 226-227. It was said that a military group had been sent by Mao Zedong to the NPC and NPCSC to stop their work. See John Wilson Lewis and Xue Litai, *Zhongguo Junshi Juece Jizhi Ji Taiwan Chongtu*

[China's Military Decision-Making Mechanism and Taiwan Conflict] (Carle Place, NY: Mingjing Chubanshe, 2007), 145.

48. Jin Chongji (ed.), *Liu Shaoqi Zhuan* [Biography of Liu Shaoqi] (Beijing: Zhongyang Wenxian Chubanshe 1998), vol. 2, 1072.

49. Ma Jiseng, *Waijiaobu Wenge Jishi* [Documentary of the Ministry of Foreign Affairs in the Cultural Revolution] (Hong Kong: the Chinese University Press, 2003), 289; Zhonggong Zhongyang Wenxian Yanjiushi (ed.), *Zhou Enlai Nianpu (1949-1976)* [Chronicle of Zhou Enlai (1949-1976)] (Beijing: Zhongyang Wenxian Chubanshe, 1997), 265; Dongbiwu Zhuanxiezu, *Dong Biwu Zhuan 1886-1975* [Biography of Dong Biwu 1886-1975] (Beijing: Zhongyang Wenxian Chubanshe, 2006), vol. 2, 1054.

50. Shi Zhifu (ed.), *Zhonghua Renmin Gongheguo Duiwai Guanxi Shi (1949.10-1989.10)* [History of Foreign Relations of the People's Republic of China (1949.10-1989.10)] (Beijing: Beijing Daxue Chubanshe, 1994), 193-194.

51. Wang Taiping (ed.), *Zhonghua Renmin Gongheguo Waijiaoshi* [History of Diplomacy of the People's Republic of China] (Beijing: Shijie Zhishi Chubanshe 1999), vol. 3, 8.

52. Dongbiwu Zhuanxiezu, *Dong Biwu Zhuan 1886-1975* [Biography of Dong Biwu 1886-1975] (Beijing: Zhongyang Wenxian Chubanshe, 2006), vol. 2, 1071.

53. Another source suggests that it could be possibly in the latter half of 1971 when Dong Biwu started to act as the deputy chairman in foreign exchanges because "on November 11th, the Pakistan President paid a state visit to China 'on the invitation of the Deputy Chairman Dong Biwu.'" See Dongbiwu Zhuanxiezu, *Dong Biwu Zhuan 1886-1975* [Biography of Dong Biwu 1886-1975] (Beijing: Zhongyang Wenxian Chubanshe, 2006), vol. 2, 1066-1067. But this could be a mistake, because such a state visit is not found in the *Renmin Ribao*, which also reports Bong Biwu, in the capacity of the vice-chairman, sending telegram to Cambodia on November 7 and receiving credentials from foreign ambassadors to China on November 25. See *Renmin Ribao*, November 8 and 26, 1971.

54. *Renmin Ribao*, February 25, 1972.

55. *Renmin Ribao*, April 4, 1975.

56. Dongbiwu Zhuanxiezu, *Dong Biwu Zhuan 1886-1975* [Biography of Dong Biwu 1886-1975] (Beijing: Zhongyang Wenxian Chubanshe, 2006), vol. 2, 1072.

57. Pang Xianzhi and Jin Chongji (eds.), *Mao Zedong Zhuan 1949-1976* [Biography of Mao Zedong 1949-1976] (Beijing: Zhongyang Wenxian Chubanshe, 2003), vol. 2, 1565-1576.

58. Wang Nianyi and He Shu, "She Guojia Zhuxi Wenti Lunxi" [Study on the Issue of Establishing the State Chairmanship] in Ding Kaiwen (ed.), *Chongsheng Lin Biao Zuian* [Restatement of Lin Biao Case] (Hong Kong: Mirror Press, 2004), 159.

59. Feng Zhijun, *Mao Zedong Yu Lin Biao* [Mao Zedong and Lin Biao] (Hong Kong: Huangfu Tushu Youxian Gongsi, 1998), 542.

60. Ding Kaiwen, "She Guojia Zhuxi He Mao Zedong De Kunjing" [Establishment of the State Chairmanship and the Dilemma of Mao Zedong], in Ding Kaiwen (ed.), *Chongsheng Lin Biao Zuian* [Restatement of Lin Biao Case] (Hong Kong: Mirror Press, 2004), 176.

61. Ding Kaiwen, "She Guojia Zhuxi He Mao Zedong De Kunjing" [Establishment of the State Chairmanship and the Dilemma of Mao Zedong], in Ding Kaiwen (ed.), *Chongsheng Lin Biao Zuian* [Restatement of Lin Biao Case] (Hong Kong: Mirror Press, 2004), 176.

62. Ding Kaiwen, "She Guojia Zhuxi He Mao Zedong De Kunjing" [Establishment of the State Chairmanship and the Dilemma of Mao Zedong], in Ding Kaiwen (ed.), *Chongsheng Lin Biao Zuian* [Restatement of Lin Biao Case] (Hong Kong: Mirror Press, 2004), 176.

63. Ye Zilong, *Ye Zilong Huiyilu* [Memoirs of Ye Zilong] (Beijing: Zhongyang Wenxian Chubanshe, 2000), 255. Besides, it should be noted that Mao Zedong only made this comment afterward and it should not be regarded as evidence that the chairmanship had been envisioned by Mao Zedong before the constitutional making.

64. Xu Chongde, *Zhonghua Renmin Gongheguo Xianfa Shi* [Constitutional History of the People's Republic of China] (Fujian: Fujian Renmin Chubanshe, 2003), 191, 325.

65. Xu Chongde, *Zhonghua Renmin Gongheguo Xianfa Shi* [Constitutional History of the People's Republic of China] (Fujian: Fujian Renmin Chubanshe, 2003), 324-330; Han Dayuan, *1954 Nian Xianfa Yu Xin Zhongguo Xianzheng* [The 1954 Constitution and New China's Constitutionalism] (Hunan: Hunan Renmin Chubanshe, 2004), 423-424.

Chapter Eight

Constitutional Making of the Presidency in 1982

CONTROVERSIES OVER THE RESTORATION OF THE CHAIRMANSHIP

On August 8, 1980, Deng Xiaoping delivered a speech on the system of the party and the state in an enlarged Politburo meeting, in which he suggested that the CCP would advise the NPC to revise the constitution and the new one should provide that the state power not be concentrated excessively.[1] Then a proposal was sent by the CCP to the Presidium of the third session of the fifth NPC, claiming that the constitution adopted in 1978 had not been compatible with the new situation in China, and a comprehensive revision had to be made; therefore, it was advised that a revising committee, whose members were also suggested by the CCP in the meantime, be established to take charge of the constitutional revision, and a draft constitution be published for national discussion in the first half of 1981, which would then be passed by the fourth session of this Congress so that the new NPC could be elected to function based on this new constitution.[2] This proposal was accepted by the NPC accordingly.[3]

No sooner than the revising committee started to work, people became divided over the issue of reestablishing the office of chairman. Some people opposing the office held that the chairmanship had been abolished for quite a long time and people got used to the new situation without a chairman[4]; the chairmanship in the 1954 constitution had been made for no one other than Mao Zedong and had exerted little function in reality.[5] Furthermore, it had been vacant for many years and Mao Zedong had been against such an idea; the abolishment of it could help to prevent a personal cult and tyranny, and promote democracy in state affairs; if this office were to be set up, it would require extra administrative staff for this new institution and go against the task of downsizing government manpower, which was being undertaken then.[6] Therefore, those functions fulfilled by the chairman could be performed by the chairman of the NPCSC or by the premier.[7]

However, more people supported the chairmanship and argued that it could not necessarily lead to personal tyranny,[8] Stalin's theory of collective head of state had not been well reasoned,[9] the chairmanship had been an institution with Chinese characteristics and in agreement with the custom and wishes of Chinese people,[10] and since it had been abolished in an abnormal situation, its reestablishment could be helpful to normalize the state political life.[11] More importantly, the chairman could be useful for both internal and external purposes. Internally, he could help to separate the ruling party from the government,[12] prevent the concentration of power into one hand,[13] achieve a reasonable division of functions among different state organs,[14] act as a buffer between the NPCSC and the State Council,[15] fulfill certain functions that other organ could not do, such as the nomination of the premier,[16] promulgate legislations and orders,[17] and command the armed forces.[18] Especially, as China was a big country and had conducted frequent international exchanges, the chairman could also play a role in this regard. He could serve as the head of state, without which some foreign heads of state could think negatively when being invited by other Chinese officials, like the chairman of the NPCSC[19]; by sharing some duties in foreign affairs, the chairman could help to relieve the workload of the premier and the chairman of the NPCSC so that they could focus more on their own business.[20]

During this process, five different drafts were produced.[21] Although these drafts have not been disclosed, it seemed that the first three of them had proposed a chairmanship,[22] which could be similar to that of 1954 constitution because it was provided with the power to convene the Supreme State Conference.[23] But certain new elements seemed to be added to it, because it could return the NPCSC's decisions for reconsideration,[24] transforming that uncertain political practice of checks and balances into a constitutional requirement. This could be a reflection of the fact that in these discussions, some people suggested that the new constitution should be made based on the principle of separation of powers, instead of the previous people's congress system.[25]

DENG XIAOPING'S SUPPORT FOR THE CHAIRMANSHIP

The CCP had overseen the constitutional revision throughout the whole process,[26] but its senior leaders were also divided over the chairmanship. In the PSC, Deng Xiaoping had repeatedly spoken in favor of the chairmanship. As early as March 18, 1981, he showed his support for the chairmanship: "we had better to restore the chairmanship. China is a great country and it will be beneficial for the country to have a chairman."[27]

He was right. China is a great country, but it was weak after the Cultural Revolution and had lagged behind the rest of the world. To narrow the gap, Deng Xiaoping, after taking power from Hua Guofeng, Mao Zedong's chosen successor who insisted on the "two whatevers," demanded a new policy of "reform and open-door," in which it would be Western countries, such as the United States and European countries, rather than the former Soviet Union, that China would open its door to. An official similar to the president would surely help to facilitate his policy, at least in matters of international formality, which had been proved by Deputy Chairman Dong Biwu before.

So he also took action. In July, he personally put Peng Zhen in charge of the constitutional making, who had been familiar with the legal affairs and chosen as the vice director of the revising committee, but had not been available for this new task previously because he had been occupied with the trial of "the Gang of Four."[28] More importantly, Peng Zhen was politically close to Deng Xiaoping,[29] who explained to Peng Zhen why the chairmanship should be reestablished:

> The title of 'Chairman Mao' started in the period of Jiangxi Revolutionary Base, when he (Mao Zedong) was the chairman of the Provisional Central People's Government of the China Soviet Republic. Since then, such a title has been used by the people to show their respect and love for him.[30]

In response to the controversies arising in the constitution-making process, Deng Xiaoping also instructed that the new chairmanship should be less substantive, not taking charge of or interfering with any government affairs and making no specific decisions,[31] possibly because Deng Xiaoping personally did not want to take this new office. On July 18, Deng Xiaoping told Jing Yong, the famous Hong Kong writer, that

> Your Mingpao proposed that I take the post of the state chairman. Certainly I am qualified for it. However, I do want to live longer and serve more for the country and people. If I take the chairmanship, I am afraid that my life would be shortened. With respect to the state chairmanship, we are still considering and no decision has been made as yet.[32]

Besides, Deng Xiaoping specifically stressed to Peng Zhen that the four cardinal principles, people's democratic dictatorship, and democratic centralism should also be written into the constitution.[33]

Taking Deng Xiaoping's directions, Peng Zhen suggested that the 1954 constitution should be the model for the new constitution, and this was accepted.[34] Then another draft was made out in about December 1981.[35] According to Peng Zhen's report about this draft filed in December, Deng

Xiaoping's ideas were mostly incorporated. In particular, the new chairmanship could be a combination of the 1954 model and Deng Xiaoping's requirement. On one hand, it was provided to represent the country at home and abroad, and command the armed forces; on the other hand, it could not interfere with the government work and take any administrative responsibility.[36] As a result, the power to convene the Supreme State Conference seemed to be deleted in this draft.

However, the constitutional making was postponed, "as some major issues are still in search for solution amid the reform on government system and it could not be completed as scheduled."[37] The chairmanship can be among those "major issues," because the controversy over it had not been settled as then. Deng Xiaoping's speech in July indicated the uncertainty about the chairmanship, which was manifested once again in September when he told the Japanese visitors that: "establishment of the chairmanship is an important issue in our current constitutional revision, together with others, which are all easy to deal with,"[38] suggesting the controversy was not over. Several months later, it was also reported that the controversy was the cause for the postponement of constitutional making.[39]

Deng Xiaoping personally reviewed Peng Zhen's report twice and gave more instructions on related issues concerning the constitutional draft, including the chairmanship.[40] Although no details had been disclosed about his instructions in these circumstances, his support for the chairmanship could still be discerned. By February 1982, a revised draft was completed and provided a Council of National Defense headed by a chairman, intended to strengthen the collective leadership in the military affairs and promote democracy by including some non-CCP people.[41]

When this draft was submitted to the CCP for approval, a Politburo member claimed that Deng Xiaoping was the only one who would be fit for the new office of chairman if to have one, but this could increase his workload and damage his health[42]; if Deng Xiaoping was unwilling to take this role, then there would be no one else and the office should not be established.[43] Deng defended by replying that: "someone else can also take the office, except me" and "it should be set up as long as the country demands, we should not decide the state system for sake of one particular person."[44]

In the end, Deng Xiaoping won.[45] The CCP approved the draft with some further revisions, and then turned it to the revising committee for deliberation. In the committee's second meeting, the chairman in the CCP's final draft was written as to represent the state at home and abroad, not interfering with the government affairs and taking administrative responsibility.[46] Both the Council of National Defense and the Supreme State Conference were abolished,[47] but the chairman could also command the armed forces.[48]

"A TITULAR HEAD OF STATE"

The Chairmanship Not Commanding the Military

Why was the Council of National Defense abolished by the CCP at the last minute? In the early stages of the constitutional-making process, opposition had argued that it had never had a meeting ever since its establishment in 1954.[49] Their argument told the truth. As a matter of fact, the real commander of the armed forces had been the CCP's Central Military Commission. Possibly this opinion was accepted by the CCP. Besides, as China was claimed to have achieved the socialism and the CCP's control over the state apparatus was supposedly as tight as possible, as in the case of the former Soviet Union, it would be understandable that those non-CCP members in the Council of National Defense be further cleared out of the armed forces.

However, the arrangement in the CCP's final draft was questioned by the revising committee in the second meeting. As Cheng Siyuan, a non-CCP member of the revising committee, questioned:

> How will the chairman command the military? In the 1954 constitution, he concurrently chaired the Council of National Defense. But the Council of National Defense had no substance, and the CCP's Central Military Commission was in real command. I suggest making the CCP's Central Military Commission a state organ and the chairman also chairs it, thus commanding the military through this organ. We should decide this issue when the old revolutionaries are still alive to lay the foundation for the nation's long term safety and good governance. The relationship between the National Defense Ministry and Military Commission is that of military administration and military order, which should be divided, i.e., National Defense Ministry manages military administration, including budget, constructions, ranking, appointment and removal of officials, awards, punishment and exercises, etc, whereas the Military Commission should issue military orders, exercise the power to command and direct wars, etc.[50]

And he was not alone. Similar ideas had already been raised during the constitutional-making process before,[51] and a group of Chinese legal scholars was also reported to support the reestablishment of the chairman to command the armed forces.[52] They were far-sighted. As Deng and other senior cadres were still alive, they could take things under control and have the capacity to put the armed forces into the law's jurisdiction. But after they died, younger leaders would lack their authority and have to seek more legitimacy from the law to remedy, when the military is so crucial to leave to the absence of law.

However, while Deng Xiaoping had already insisted not taking the state chairmanship and decided to retire to the second front, there also had been demand within the CCP for him to command the army.[53] Therefore, the state chairmanship had to be separated from the army, and another chairmanship of military affairs had to be established. In other words, the state chairman and the chairman of the Central Military Commission had to be taken by different persons.[54] Once again, the constitution had to be tailored for a specific person.[55]

After taking all these opinions and suggestions into consideration, possibly on April 5, 1982,[56] Deng Xiaoping decided that the constitution should provide the chairmanship of the CMC; both the state chairman and the CMC chairman would be elected by the NPC. In other words, a new chairmanship and a separate state organ, that is, the CMC would be set up.

Hence, the constitutional draft was further revised. In the draft submitted to the third meeting of the revising committee for discussion, a new section was included, creating a new state organ, that is, the CMC, whereas the state chairman no longer commanded the armed forces.[57] According to the constitutional draft published for national discussion afterwards, this new section had four articles, providing that the CMC direct the armed forces, its chairman assume overall responsibility for its work, the term of office of its chairman be five years and he serve no more than two consecutive terms, and it be accountable to the NPC and NPCSC.[58] Besides, the State Council was also provided to "direct the building of national defence,"[59] thus sharing responsibility for the military affairs with the CMC.

Being published, various concerns were raised to the relationship among the CCP, the CMC, and the State Council.[60] Particularly, people in the military were worried that it could change the CCP's leadership over the military. To clarify, a notice, drafted by Peng Zhen, was issued by the CCP to the armed forces, declaring that the CMC would not only be a state organ, but also belong to the party; it was the same organ with two official titles and would not jeopardize the CCP's leading role in the army; the Defense Department of the State Council would be under the direct supervision of the CCP's Central Military Commission; the State Council would take charge of the national defense construction, including defense budget, expenses, staffing, equipment, supply, exercises, institutional building, and so on.[61]

More suggestions were put forward to improve relevant stipulations. For example, some advised that the constitution should make clearer stipulation on the CCP's leadership over the army, in particular, the chairman of the CCP's CMC should take the post of the chairman of the state CMC; the organization of the state CMC should be defined by the constitution or specific law; the state CMC should be under the supervision of the NPC and report to it.[62] Some others held that the division of powers and functions between the CMC and the Defense Department should be made clear in the constitution so that the Defense Department could take charge of military administration, including the budget and building, whereas the state CMC could command and lead the army in war.[63]

After considering these suggestions, the revising committee made further amendments to relevant stipulations. Taking into consideration of attentions from home and abroad, the section titled as the Central Military Commission was still maintained in the constitutional text, to avoid any negative ideas about China by foreign governments. As a response to the concern with the organization of the CMC, two provisions were made, one of which provided that the commission be composed of the chairman, vice-chairman, general-secretary, and ordinary members, and the other of which said that the organization of the NPC, NPCSC, and other state organs was prescribed by laws. On the other side, the limitation of two consecutive terms on the chairman was abolished on the grounds that the military was different from other state affairs and it would be better for the constitution not make a specific limitation on his terms. The idea that the CCP's leadership over the army should be provided in the text was rejected, as the CCP's leading role in the state, including in the army, was stipulated in the foreword of the constitution; since the military operation was concerned with state secrets, it would better not report its work to the NPC and NPCSC.[64] Besides, no division was provided for the CMC and Defense Department.[65]

Then a new draft was produced and presented to Deng Xiaoping, who took two days to consider it. After consulting some of his CCP colleagues, including Peng Zhen and Yang Shangkun, the future president, he personally rewrote the section of the Central Military Commission, which provided that the commission directed the armed forces and its chairman took overall responsibility for the work; the chairman was responsible to the NPC and NPCSC.[66] As a result, this section was reduced from four articles to two,[67] which was later adopted by the NPC.[68]

Abolishment of the Supreme State Conference

The second change made in the CCP's final draft concerning the state chairmanship was the abolishment of the Supreme State Conference. Why was it abolished? In the era of the 1954 constitution, the Supreme State Conference had not only been a way by which Mao Zedong directed the administration, but also a forum where Mao Zedong consulted his new policies with other people, especially with non-CCP people. It was explained by some Chinese scholars that such an arrangement had put the government under multiple leaderships, divided the supreme state power, and involved the chairman with the administrative affairs[69]; by abolishing it, the chairman could get rid of administrative affairs completely and concentrate on his own business; the distinction between the power and function of the chairmanship and the State Council could be better distinguished.[70] Besides, since there were more channels of political consultation with non-CCP people, there was no need to maintain the Supreme State Conference.[71]

Term of Office

The third difference between the new state chairmanship and its predecessor was about terms of office. Whereas the 1954 constitution had only provided the four-year term of office, the new constitution not only extended it one more year to reach five years, the same as that of the NPC, for both the chairman and vice-chairman, but also provided both of them to serve no more than two consecutive terms.[72] The age requirement for the state chairmanship was also increased from the previous thirty-five years old to forty-five years old.[73]

The idea of restricting the chairmanship to two terms had been suggested in 1953 and 1956, and the 1954 constitution had been intended to revise, but ended mysteriously without any result. The first state chairman, Mao Zedong, had only taken this office for one term, but had been holding the office of the CCP's chairmanship and the chairmanship of the CCP's Central Military Commission to the end of his life, which became the power base for him to launch the disastrous Cultural Revolution from the second front. Now by adopting this new constitutional device, it was expected to help to curtail personality cult and individual tyranny, select new and younger leaders, rejuvenate the national leadership, improve working efficiency, and better solve the issue of leadership's succession and maintain the stability of governmental policies.[74]

Undoubtedly, this was a great progress to limit the term of office. With such a limitation, no one can take the position for more than ten years, thus putting an end to Chinese thousands-years tradition of life-long public service. However, as commented, in spite of such an improvement, if those leaders would take major government posts in turn, the life-long service could possibly not be ended.[75] Besides, the failure to put this limitation on the military chairmanship also indicated that the CCP leaders had not been ready to accept this new constitutional idea unreservedly.

The Succession to the Chairmanship

The fourth improvement made to the chairmanship was the new provisions regarding its succession. According to the 1954 constitution, the vice-chairman should succeed the chairmanship when it fell vacant. In 1955, a decision had been made by the NPCSC that its chairman could receive foreign ambassadors when the chairman and vice-chairman were on vacation or out of office.[76] When making the new constitution in 1982, such a way of succession was accepted by the drafters[77] and adopted by the NPC, as follows:

> In case the office of the Vice-President of the People's Republic of China falls vacant, the National People's Congress shall elect a new Vice-President to fill the vacancy. In the event that the offices of both the President and the Vice-

> President of the People's Republic of China fall vacant, the National People's Congress shall elect a new President and a new Vice-President. Prior to such election, the Chairman of the Standing Committee of the National People's Congress shall temporarily act as the President of the People's Republic of China.[78]

Hence the succession to the chairmanship was further improved constitutionally, by which the vice-chairman was the first successor to the chairmanship, and the chairman of the NPCSC was the second one.

Is the Chairman the Head of State?

In spite of these improvements to the chairmanship, there were still issues that remained unsettled, one of which was the constitutional status of the new chairmanship. Whether the chairman was the head of the state had been a major controversy during the constitutional making in 1954. It had been confirmed, but overruled by Mao Zedong in the last minute before the constitutional draft was published. Finally, the chairman was provided by the constitution to "represents the People's Republic of China externally."[79]

When the constitution was revised in 1982, this issue was raised again amid the deliberation on the chairman to be installed in the new constitution. It seemed that the constitutional drafters reached new consensus over this issue, and the new chairmanship was provided as one who "represents the People's Republic of China internally and externally" by the CCP's drafts[80] and the draft that was published for national discussion.[81] This could virtually accord the chairman the status of the head of state.

On hearing of this, Peng Zhen, who was in charge of the constitutional-revising work, rejected it by quoting Mao Zedong's words,[82] which had been spoken out by Liu Shaoqi in his report on the making of 1954 constitution, that not only the chairman acted as the head of state jointly with NPCSC, but also other state organs, such as the NPCSC and the State Council, could represent the state in different situations when dealing with different state affairs.[83] In other words, the chairman was just a member of the leading collective that represents the country.

Again, Mao Zedong's idea about the relationship between the chairmanship and the NPC, and the collective leadership emphasized by the new leaders, seemed to prevail again. When the constitution was ratified, the published provision was revised as to "receive foreign diplomatic representatives on behalf of the People's Republic of China."[84] Compared with the 1954 constitution, the new chairman's role was further limited to diplomatic receipts when representing PRC.

Undefined Responsibility of the Chairmanship

Another undefined issue was the responsibility of the chairman. Back in 1954, drafters had disputed whether those constitution functions of the chairman were his "power" or "duty." Impliedly, the chairman should follow the example of the State Council and take responsibility to the NPC and NPCSC if they were his powers, or he should not be held accountable for these acts if they would be no more than procedural and ceremonial duties. As the chairman's function was mixed with substance, the 1954 constitution had not made clear a stipulation in this regard. On the other hand, as Mao Zedong suggested that the president be recalled,[85] the 1954 constitution also provided in its article 28 that the NPC has power to remove the chairman from office.

In this new round of constitutional making, Deng Xiaoping could think likewise and preferred the new chairman being a nominal figure bearing no responsibility in administration. Based on Deng Xiaoping's instruction, the CCP's early drafts had provided that the chairman not to interfere with the administration of the government and share any administrative responsibility.[86] Considering the new chairman no longer commanded the military and could not convene the SSC, it was almost true.

But this provision was still questioned by the revising committee. It was argued that when receiving foreign guests and making visits to foreign countries, the chairman could not avoid talking about state affairs[87]; the chairman's power to nominate the premier was also in contradiction with this.[88] More importantly,

> Since our country has adopted the collective leadership and the chairman is one representative of this collective body, how can we say that the chairman not interfere with the government and take administrative responsibility?[89]

As a result, such stipulations were deleted from the published draft,[90] which was then accepted by the NPC. Hence, the new constitution inherited the practice of its 1954 model, only providing that the NPC could remove the chairman from office in article 63. Such an arrangement has raised academic doubt. Why have both constitutions made such provisions if the president bears no responsibility? In other words, the chairman has been implied to be accountable in certain situations.[91]

NOMINATION, VOTING, AND REMOVAL OF THE CHAIRMANSHIP

Similar to the 1954 one, the 1982 constitution only provides that the chairman be elected and removed by the NPC, it does not articulate about how the election and removal should be conducted. However, a new Organic Law of the NPC had also been ratified by the same session of the fifth NPC, which not only outlines the nomination and voting methods of the chairman, but also provides a way to remove the chairman.

In this law, three steps are provided for the nomination of a chairman candidate. Firstly, a preliminary list of candidates for top government posts, including that for chairman, and chairman and vice-chairman of the state CMC, will be submitted by the NPC Presidium to the delegations; then consultations are conducted among these delegations regarding these candidates, after which a formal list should be produced in the end by the Presidium "based on the opinion of the majority of deputies."[92] When the NPC is convened to vote on this formal list, the secret ballot, show of hands, or other method of voting can be decided by the Presidium to use in the election.[93] If considering to remove the chairman from office, three or more delegations or at least one-tenth of the number of the deputies can submit a proposal of removal to the NPC. The Presidium then should turn it to the congress for deliberation.[94]

On December 4, 1982, the constitution was adopted by the NPC by 3,040 deputies, with only three abstentions.[95] It not only declared the establishment of socialism, but also reinstalled the controversial chairmanship with new appearance. Officially, the new chairman was translated in English as "president" instead of "chairman" as it had used to, thus giving it a Western appearance and also distinguishing it from the other "chairmen" provided by the constitution, such as the chairman of the NPCSC and the chairman of the CMC.

To conclude, the 1982 constitution, the fourth constitution of the PRC, restored the chairmanship as a presidency, which continues to enjoy the independence and be an office taken by an individual, but is weakened greatly in terms of its powers and functions. Internally, he lost his policy forum of SSC and can no longer command the armed forces, in spite that he continued to nominate the candidate for the premiership and perform those nominal functions. Externally, even though he continues to appoint or recall Chinese diplomats, and ratify or abrogate treaties and important agreements, upon decision of the NPCSC, he can only act "on behalf of the PRC" when receiving foreign diplomats.

Compared with the 1954 constitution, the presidency has been much more institutionalized by adopting certain Western practices. Not only he is limited by two terms of office, the Western practice that had long been suggested to adopt, and has one more successor standing by, that is, the chairman of the NPCSC, plus the vice-president, but also is provided with mechanisms of election, removal, and resignation decided by the NPC and NPCSC. As a result, the presidency is no more than a well-institutionalized executive body performing a few constitutional functions.

However, when it comes to the relationship of the presidency to other governmental organs, it is further away from its Western counterpart and more close to the Stalinist model. By abolishing the Supreme State Conference and separating the presidency from military command, elements of checks and balances characterized the Western constitutions in Mao Zedong's model have been eliminated, thus making the presidency no long the "buffer" in the government and more orthodox, which was based on the Marxist principles of democratic centralism. It was a mere component of the executive branch serving certain ceremonial functions in China's external affairs. In a sense, the presidency became more professional and less democratic than its predecessor.

Such a presidency was generally regarded as a figurehead of state, suggesting there is no need to place checks on it. However, the president could nominate the premier and have his say in foreign affairs. Without clear constitutional endorsement, there is no guarantee that the president would not interfere with the premier's administration, at least on diplomacy. Scholars also suggest that the president could turn into someone with substantive power when he holds other offices concurrently, which includes the CMC chairman of the PRC, the General Secretary (GS) of the CCP, and the CMC chairman of the CCP.[96] More importantly, the new Chinese president would belong to the CCP's collective leadership. Therefore, the real political substance of such a presidency could have to be decided in practice by the holder's relative strength in this collective, rather than the constitutional definitions.

NOTES

1. Deng Xiaoping, "Dang He Guojia Lingdao Zhidu De Gaige" [Reform of the Party and State's Leadership] in *Selection of Deng Xiaoping* (Beijing, Renmin Chubanshe, 1994), 2nd ed., 339.
2. Wang Peiying (ed.), *Zhongguo Xianfa Wenxian Tongbian* [Selection of Constitutional Documents of China] (Beijing: Zhongguo Minzhu Fazhi Chubanshe, 2007), rev. ed., 75.
3. Standing Comm. Nat'l People's Cong. Gaz., no. 5 (1980).
4. Xu Chongde, *Zhonghua Renmin Gongheguo Xianfashi* [Constitutional History of the People's Republic of China] (Fujian: Fujian Renmin Chubanshe, 2005), 2nd ed., vol. 2, 367.
5. Xu Chongde, *Zhonghua Renmin Gongheguo Xianfashi* [Constitutional History of the People's Republic of China] (Fujian: Fujian Renmin Chubanshe, 2005), 2nd ed., vol. 2, 373.
6. Cai Dingjian, *Xianfa Jingjie* [Explanation on the Constitution] (Beijing: Falv Chubanshe, 2004), 96.
7. Xu Chongde, *Zhonghua Renmin Gongheguo Xianfashi* [Constitutional History of the People's Republic of China] (Fujian: Fujian Renmin Chubanshe, 2005), 2nd ed., vol. 2, 367, 369, 371, 373, 378.
8. Xu Chongde, *Zhonghua Renmin Gongheguo Xianfashi* [Constitutional History of the People's Republic of China] (Fujian: Fujian Renmin Chubanshe, 2005), 2nd ed., vol. 2, 366.
9. Xu Chongde, *Zhonghua Renmin Gongheguo Xianfashi* [Constitutional History of the People's Republic of China] (Fujian: Fujian Renmin Chubanshe, 2005), 2nd ed., vol. 2, 371.

10. Cai Dingjian, *Xianfa Jingjie* [Explanation on the Constitution] (Beijing: Falv Chubanshe, 2004), 96.

11. Cai Dingjian, *Xianfa Jingjie* [Explanation on the Constitution] (Beijing: Falv Chubanshe, 2004), 96.

12. Xu Chongde, *Zhonghua Renmin Gongheguo Xianfashi* [Constitutional History of the People's Republic of China] (Fujian: Fujian Renmin Chubanshe, 2005), 2nd ed., vol. 2, 369, 373, 378.

13. Xu Chongde, *Zhonghua Renmin Gongheguo Xianfashi* [Constitutional History of the People's Republic of China] (Fujian: Fujian Renmin Chubanshe, 2005), 2nd ed., vol. 2, 373.

14. Cai Dingjian, *Xianfa Jingjie* [Explanation on the Constitution] (Beijing: Falv Chubanshe, 2004), 96.

15. Xu Chongde, *Zhonghua Renmin Gongheguo Xianfashi* [Constitutional History of the People's Republic of China] (Fujian: Fujian Renmin Chubanshe, 2005), 2nd ed., vol. 2, 367, 373.

16. Xiao Weiyun, "Woguo Guojia Zhuxi Zhidu De Huifu He Fazhan" [Reestablishment and Development of Our Country's State Chairmanship], *Renmin Ribao*, December 28, 1982.

17. Zhang Youyu and Xu Chongde, "Xin Xianfa Caoan De Jiben Jingshen" [Basic Spirits of the New Draft Constitution], *Renmin Ribao*, May 17, 1982; Xu Chongde, *Zhonghua Renmin Gongheguo Xianfashi* [Constitutional History of the People's Republic of China] (Fujian: Fujian Renmin Chubanshe, 2005), 2nd ed., vol. 2, 378.

18. Xiao Weiyun, "Woguo Guojia Zhuxi Zhidu De Huifu He Fazhan" [Reestablishment and Development of Our Country's State Chairmanship], *Renmin Ribao*, December 28, 1982.

19. Wang Hanbin, "Deng Xiaoping Qinzi Zhidao Qicao Yijiu Baer Nian Xianfa" [Deng Xiaoping Personally Instructed the Drafting of the Constitution in 1982], *Fazhi Ribao*, August 19, 2004; Xu Chongde, *Zhonghua Renmin Gongheguo Xianfashi* [Constitutional History of the People's Republic of China] (Fujian: Fujian Renmin Chubanshe, 2005), 2nd ed., vol. 2, 405, 408.

20. Zhang Youyu and Xu Chongde, "Xin Xianfa Caoan De Jiben Jingshen" [Basic Spirits of the New Draft Constitution], *Renmin Ribao*, May 17, 1982; Xu Chongde, *Zhonghua Renmin Gongheguo Xianfashi* [Constitutional History of the People's Republic of China] (Fujian: Fujian Renmin Chubanshe, 2005), 2nd ed., vol. 2, 367, 405, 408; Cai Dingjian, *Xianfa Jingjie* [Explanation on the Constitution] (Beijing: Falv Chubanshe, 2004), 96.

21. Xu Chongde, *Zhonghua Renmin Gongheguo Xianfashi* [Constitutional History of the People's Republic of China] (Fujian: Fujian Renmin Chubanshe, 2005), 2nd ed., vol. 2, 381-384. But there is a different opinion concerning these drafts. See Chao Ying and Guo Hong, "Zhonghua Renmin Gongheguo De Sibu Xianfa: Fang Quanguo Renda Falv Weiyuanhui Zhuren Weiyuan Yang Jingyu" [Four Constitutions of the People's Republic of China: An Interview with the Directing Member of the Legal Committee of the National People's Congress Yang Jingyu], *Bainian Chao*, no. 7 (2004): 7-8.

22. Xu Chongde, *Zhonghua Renmin Gongheguo Xianfashi* [Constitutional History of the People's Republic of China] (Fujian: Fujian Renmin Chubanshe, 2005), 2nd ed., vol. 2, 382-384.

23. Xu Chongde, *Zhonghua Renmin Gongheguo Xianfashi* [Constitutional History of the People's Republic of China] (Fujian: Fujian Renmin Chubanshe, 2005), 2nd ed., vol. 2, 383.

24. Xu Chongde, *Zhonghua Renmin Gongheguo Xianfashi* [Constitutional History of the People's Republic of China] (Fujian: Fujian Renmin Chubanshe, 2005), 2nd ed., vol. 2, 384.

25. Peng Zhen, *Lun Xin Zhongguo De Zhengfa Gongzuo* [Discussion on the Political and Legal Work of the New China] (Beijing: Zhongyang Wenxian Chubanshe, 1992), 271; Chao Ying and Guo Hong, "Zhonghua Renmin Gongheguo De Sibu Xianfa: Fang Quanguo Renda Falv Weiyuanhui Zhuren Weiyuan Yang Jingyu" [Four Constitutions of the People's Republic of China: An Interview with the Directing Member of the Legal Committee of the National People's Congress Yang Jingyu], *Bainian Chao*, no. 7 (2004): 7-8.

26. "The constitutional draft has been deliberated by the Central Secretariat of the CCPCC for eight times, and the Politburo three times"; see Li Haiwen and Wang Yanling, "Pengzhen Dui Xianxing Xianfa De Gongxian: Fang Renmin Daxue Jaoshou Xu Chongde" [Peng Zhen's Contribution to the Current Constitution: An Interview with Professor Xu Chongde in Renmin

University], in Li Haiwen and Wang Yanling (eds.), *Shiji Duihua-Yi Xin Zhongguo Fazhi Dianji Ren Pengzhen* [Century Dialogue: Memory of the Founder of the Legal System of the New China Peng Zhen] (Beijing: Qunzhong Chubanshe, 2002), 138. Another opinion holds that "the CCPCC Politburo deliberated the revised constitutional draft for eight times"; see Peng Zhen Zhuan Bianxie Zu and Tian Youru, *Peng Zhen Zhuanlue* [A Brief Biography of Peng Zhen] (Beijing: Renmin Chubanshe, 2007), 322. The third opinion is that "the CCPCC Politburo and Secretariat held eight meetings specially to deliberate (the draft)"; see Wang Hanbin, "Deng Xiaoping Qinzi Zhidao Qicao Yijiu Baer Nian Xianfa" [Deng Xiaoping Personally Instructed the Drafting of the Constitution in 1982], *Fazhi Ribao*, August 19, 2004.

27. Len Rong and Wang Zouling (eds.), *Deng Xiaoping Nianpu (1975-1979)* [Chronicle of Deng Xiaoping (1975-1979)] (Beijing: Zhongyang Wenxian Chubanshe, 2004), vol. 2, 721.

28. Cai Dingjian, *Xianfa Jingjie* [Explanation on the Constitution] (Beijing: Falv Chubanshe, 2004), 81.

29. Cai Dingjian, *Xianfa Jingjie* [Explanation on the Constitution] (Beijing: Falv Chubanshe, 2004), 81, fn2.

30. Len Rong and Wang Zouling (ed.), *Deng Xiaoping Nianpu (1975-1979)* [Chronicle of Deng Xiaoping (1975-1979)] (Beijing: Zhongyang Wenxian Chubanshe, 2004), vol. 2, at 760-761.

31. Wang Hanbin, "Deng Xiaoping Qinzi Zhidao Qicao Yijiu Baer Nian Xianfa" [Deng Xiaoping Personally Instructed the Drafting of the Constitution in 1982], *Fazhi Ribao*, August 19, 2004.

32. "Zhonggong Zhongyang Fu Zhuxi Deng Xiaoping De Tanhua Jilu" [Record of Talk with the CCPCC Vice Chairman Deng Xiaoping], Mingbao Yuekan, no. 9 (1981): 4.

33. Peng Zhen, *Lun Xin Zhongguo De Zhengfa Gongzuo* [Discussion on the Political and Legal Work of the New China] (Beijing: Zhongyang Wenxian Chubanshe, 1992), 271.

34. Xu Chongde, "Peng Zhen Yu 1982 Nian Xianfa De Xiugai Gongzuo" [Peng Zhen and the Constitutional Making in 1982], in *Zhonggong Dangshi Ziliao* (Beijing: Zhonggong Dangshi Chubanshe, 2001), vol. 80, 59; Peng Zhen Zhuan Bianxie Zu and Tian Youru, *Peng Zhen Zhuanlue* [A Brief Biography of Peng Zhen] (Beijing: Renmin Chubanshe, 2007), 371; Wang Hanbin, "Deng Xiaoping Qinzi Zhidao Qicao Yijiu Baer Nian Xianfa" [Deng Xiaoping Personally Instructed the Drafting of the Constitution in 1982], *Fazhi Ribao*, August 19, 2004.

35. Liu Ronggang, "1982 Nian Xianfa De Zhiding Guocheng Jiqi Lishi Jingyan" [Process and Historical Experience of the Constitutional Making in 1982], in *Dangdai Zhongguo Shi Yanjiu*, no. 1 (2005): 44; Cai Dingjian, *Xianfa Jingjie* [Explanation on the Constitution] (Beijing: Falv Chubanshe, 2004), 82.

36. See Quanguo Renda Changweihui Bangongting 1982 Xianfa Xiugai Dangan Di 32 Juan [Record of Revisions to the 1982 Constitution of the Office of the Standing Committee of the National People's Congress, Volume 32], in Liu Ronggang, "1982 Nian Xianfa De Zhiding Guocheng Jiqi Lishi Jingyan" [Process and Historical Experience of the Constitutional Making in 1982], *Dangdai Zhongguo Shi Yanjiu*, no. 1 (2005): 44-45. It is suggested that the introduction about the chairmanship was newly added to his report written on December 19, 1982, because Peng Zhen did not mention it in his speech to his draft team made on December 16. See Peng Zhen Zhuan Bianxie Zu and Tian Youru, *Peng Zhen Zhuanlue* [A Brief Biography of Peng Zhen] (Beijing: Renmin Chubanshe, 2007), 318.

37. *Renmin Ribao*, December 14, 1982.

38. Len Rong and Wang Zouling (eds.), *Deng Xiaoping Nianpu (1975-1979)* [Chronicle of Deng Xiaoping (1975-1979)] (Beijing: Zhongyang Wenxian Chubanshe, 2004), vol. 2, 768.

39. Mou Runsun, "Lun Zhonggong Yanci Xiuxian Yu Jianli Xingxian Jichu" [The Postponement of the Constitutional Making by the CCP and Establishment of the Basis for Implementation of the Constitution], *Mingbao Yuekan*, no. 1 (1982): 19; Zhao Cong, "Yuan Wei Sheli Guojia Zhuxi Wenti Jin Yi Yan" [A Piece of Advice for the Issue of the Establishment of the State Chairman], *Mingbao Yuekan*, no. 1 (1982): 22; Wang Dezhao, "Yuanze Yu Renshi" ["Principal" and "Personnel"], *Mingbao Yuekan*, no. 1 (1982): 24.

40. Len Rong and Wang Zouling (eds.), *Deng Xiaoping Nianpu (1975-1979)* [Chronicle of Deng Xiaoping (1975-1979)] (Beijing: Zhongyang Wenxian Chubanshe, 2004), vol. 2, 792-793.

41. Chen Sixi and Liu Songshan, "Xianfa Queli Guojia Zhongyang Junshi Weiyuanhui De Jingguo" [The Process of Establishing the Central Military Commission in the Constitution], *Renda Yanjiu*, no. 3 (2001): 12-13.

42. Len Rong and Wang Zouling (eds.), *Deng Xiaoping Nianpu (1975-1979)* [Chronicle of Deng Xiaoping (1975-1979)] (Beijing: Zhongyang Wenxian Chubanshe, 2004), vol. 2, 801.

43. Wang Hanbin, "Deng Xiaoping Qinzi Zhidao Qicao Yijiu Baer Nian Xianfa" [Deng Xiaoping Personally Instructed the Drafting of the Constitution in 1982], *Fazhi Ribao*, August 19, 2004.

44. Len Rong and Wang Zouling (eds.), *Deng Xiaoping Nianpu (1975-1979)* [Chronicle of Deng Xiaoping (1975-1979)] (Beijing: Zhongyang Wenxian Chubanshe, 2004), vol. 2, 801.

45. On April 15, 1982, when receiving Romania president, Hu Yaobang, then chairman of the CCP, confirmed the establishment of the Chinese president. See Jiang Benliang, *Gei Gongheguo Lingdao Ren Zuo Fanyi* [Interpreting for the National Leaders] (Shanghai: Shanghai Cishu Chubanshe, 2007), 201-207, 262.

46. Xu Chongde, *Zhonghua Renmin Gongheguo Xianfashi* [Constitutional History of the People's Republic of China] (Fujian: Fujian Renmin Chubanshe, 2005), 2nd ed., vol. 2, 392-393.

47. Xu Chongde, *Zhonghua Renmin Gongheguo Xianfashi* [Constitutional History of the People's Republic of China] (Fujian: Fujian Renmin Chubanshe, 2005), 2nd ed., vol. 2, 392.

48. Xu Chongde, *Zhonghua Renmin Gongheguo Xianfashi* [Constitutional History of the People's Republic of China] (Fujian: Fujian Renmin Chubanshe, 2005), 2nd ed., vol. 2, 405.

49. Xu Chongde, *Zhonghua Renmin Gongheguo Xianfashi* [Constitutional History of the People's Republic of China] (Fujian: Fujian Renmin Chubanshe, 2005), 2nd ed, vol. 2, 381.

50. Xu Chongde, *Zhonghua Renmin Gongheguo Xianfashi* [Constitutional History of the People's Republic of China] (Fujian: Fujian Renmin Chubanshe, 2005), 2nd ed., vol. 2, 405.

51. Xu Chongde, *Zhonghua Renmin Gongheguo Xianfashi* [Constitutional History of the People's Republic of China] (Fujian: Fujian Renmin Chubanshe, 2005), 2nd ed., vol. 2, 381.

52. "Zhongogng Jueding She Guojia Zhuxi, Tongshuai Quanguo Wuzhuang Budui" [The CCP Decided to Establish the Chairman to Command the Armed Forces], *Pai Shing*, no. 20 (1982): 5.

53. Cai Dingjian, *Xianfa Jingjie* [Explanation on the Constitution] (Beijing: Falv Chubanshe, 2004), 314, fn1.

54. Chen Sixi and Liu Songshan, "Xianfa Queli Guojia Zhongyang Junshi Weiyuanhui De Jingguo" [The Process of Establishing the Central Military Commission in the Constitution], *Renda Yanjiu*, no. 3 (2001): 14; Wang Hanbin, "Deng Xiaoping Qinzi Zhidao Qicao Yijiu Baer Nian Xianfa" [Deng Xiaoping Personally Instructed the Drafting of the Constitution in 1982], *Fazhi Ribao*, August 19, 2004.

55. Cai Dingjian, *Xianfa Jingjie* [Explanation on the Constitution] (Beijing: Falv Chubanshe, 2004), 314, fn1; 316, fn2.

56. On that day, Deng Xiaoping had a conversation with Peng Zhen about the constitutional making. See Len Rong and Wang Zouling (eds.), *Deng Xiaoping Nianpu (1975-1979)* [Chronicle of Deng Xiaoping (1975-1979)] (Beijing: Zhongyang Wenxian Chubanshe, 2004), vol. 2, 811.

57. Chen Sixi and Liu Songshan, "Xianfa Queli Guojia Zhongyang Junshi Weiyuanhui De Jingguo" [The Process of Establishing the Central Military Commission in the Constitution], *Renda Yanjiu*, no. 3 (2001): 14; Xu Chongde, *Zhonghua Renmin Gongheguo Xianfashi* [Constitutional History of the People's Republic of China] (Fujian: Fujian Renmin Chubanshe, 2005), 2nd ed., vol. 2, 419.

58. Zhonghua Renmin Gongheguo Xianfa Caoan [The Constitutional Draft of the People's Republic of China], *Renmin Ribao*, April 26, 1982, chapter 3, section 4.

59. Zhonghua Renmin Gongheguo Xianfa Caoan [The Constitutional Draft of the People's Republic of China], *Renmin Ribao*, April 26, 1982, chapter 3, section 4, Art. 89, paragraph 11.

60. Xu Chongde, *Zhonghua Renmin Gongheguo Xianfashi* [Constitutional History of the People's Republic of China] (Fujian: Fujian Renmin Chubanshe, 2005), 2nd ed., vol. 2, 455-456, 465.

61. Wang Hanbin, "Deng Xiaoping Qinzi Zhidao Qicao Yijiu Baer Nian Xianfa" [Deng Xiaoping Personally Instructed the Drafting of the Constitution in 1982], *Fazhi Ribao*, August 19, 2004.

62. Chen Sixi and Liu Songshan, "Xianfa Queli Guojia Zhongyang Junshi Weiyuanhui De Jingguo" [the Process of Establishing the Central Military Commission in the Constitution], Renda Yanjiu, no. 3 (2001): 15.

63. Cai Dingjian, *Xianfa Jingjie* [Explanation on the Constitution] (Beijing: Falv Chubanshe, 2004), at 397.

64. Chen Sixi and Liu Songshan, "Xianfa Queli Guojia Zhongyang Junshi Weiyuanhui De Jingguo" [the Process of Establishing the Central Military Commission in the Constitution], *Renda Yanjiu*, no. 3 (2001): 15-16.

65. Cai Dingjian, *Xianfa Jingjie* [Explanation on the Constitution] (Beijing: Falv Chubanshe, 2004), 397.

66. Wang Hanbin, "Deng Xiaoping Qinzi Zhidao Qicao Yijiu Baer Nian Xianfa" [Deng Xiaoping Personally Instructed the Drafting of the Constitution in 1982], *Fazhi Ribao*, August 19, 2004.

67. Cai Dingjian, *Xianfa Jingjie* [Explanation on the Constitution] (Beijing: Falv Chubanshe, 2004), 397.

68. Xianfa [constitution] (1982) (PRC), Art. 93, 94.

69. Wang Dexiang, "Shilun Woguo Guojia Zhuxi Zhidu" [Discussion about Our Country's State Chairmanship], *Renmin Ribao*, June 3, 1982.

70. Wang Dexiang, "Shilun Woguo Guojia Zhuxi Zhidu" [Discussion about Our Country's State Chairmanship], *Renmin Ribao*, June 3, 1982.

71. Xiao Weiyun, "Woguo Guojia Zhuxi Zhidu De Huifu He Fazhan" [Reestablishment and Development of Our Country's State Chairmanship], *Renmin Ribao*, December 28, 1982.

72. Zhonghua Renmin Gongheguo Xianfa Caoan [The Constitutional Draft of the People's Republic of China], *Renmin Ribao*, April 26, 1982, Art. 79, paragraph 2.

73. Zhonghua Renmin Gongheguo Xianfa Caoan [The Constitutional Draft of the People's Republic of China], *Renmin Ribao*, April 26, 1982, Art. 79, paragraph 1.

74. Zhang Qifu and Li Buyun, "Yixiang Yiyi Shengyuan De Gaige" [A Reform with Great Significance], *Renmin Ribao*, July 9, 1982.

75. Xu Chongde, *Zhonghua Renmin Gongheguo Xianfashi* [Constitutional History of the People's Republic of China] (Fujian: Fujian Renmin Chubanshe, 2005), 2nd ed., vol. 2, 467.

76. Cai Dingjian, *Xianfa Jingjie* [Explanation on the Constitution] (Beijing: Falv Chubanshe, 2004), 370-371; Guanyu Zhonghua Renmin Gongheguo Zhuxi He Fu Zhuxi Xiujia Huo Waichu Qijian You Quanguo Renmin Daibiao Dahui Changwu Weiyuanhui Weiyuan Zhang Jieshou Waiguo Shijie De Jueding [Decision Concerning the Receipt of Foreign Diplomatic Representatives by the Chairman of the Standing Committee of the National People's Congress when the Chairman and Vice Chairman of the People's Republic of China is on Vacation or Absent from Office], Standing Comm. Nat'l People's Cong. Gaz. (December 1955).

77. Zhonghua Renmin Gongheguo Xianfa Caoan [The Constitutional Draft of the People's Republic of China], *Renmin Ribao*, April 26, 1982, Art. 79, paragraph 1.

78. Xainfa [constitution] (1982) (PRC), Art. 84.

79. Xianfa [constitution] (1954) (PRC), Art. 41.

80. Xu Chongde, *Zhonghua Renmin Gongheguo Xianfashi* [Constitutional History of the People's Republic of China] (Fujian: Fujian Renmin Chubanshe, 2005), 2nd ed., vol. 2, 392;

81. "Zhonghua Renmin Gongheguo Xianfa Caoan" [The Constitutional Draft of the People's Republic of China], *Renmin Ribao*, April 26, 1982, Art. 78.

82. Xu Chongde, *Zhonghua Renmin Gongheguo Xianfashi* [Constitutional History of the People's Republic of China] (Fujian: Fujian Renmin Chubanshe, 2005), 2nd ed., vol. 2, 825.

83. Xiao Weiyun, "Woguo Guojia Zhuxi Zhidu De Huifu He Fazhan" [Reestablishment and Development of Our Country's State Chairmanship], *Renmin Ribao*, December 28, 1982; Wu Jie, Lian Xisheng, and Wei Dingren (eds.), *Zhonghua Renmin Gongheguo Xianfa Shiyi* [Explanation of the Constitution of the People's Republic of China] (Beijing: Falv Chubanshe, 1984), 131.

84. Xian fa [constitution] (1982) (PRC), Art. 81.

85. Xu Chongde, Zhonghua Renmin Gongheguo Xianfashi [Constitutional History of the People's Republic of China] (Fujian: Fujian Renmin Chubanshe, 2003), 176-177.

86. Xu Chongde, *Zhonghua Renmin Gongheguo Xianfashi* [Constitutional History of the People's Republic of China] (Fujian: Fujian Renmin Chubanshe, 2005), 2nd ed, vol. 2, at 392-393.

87. Xu Chongde, *Zhonghua Renmin Gongheguo Xianfashi* [Constitutional History of the People's Republic of China] (Fujian: Fujian Renmin Chubanshe, 2005), 2nd ed., vol. 2, 397.

88. Xu Chongde, *Zhonghua Renmin Gongheguo Xianfashi* [Constitutional History of the People's Republic of China] (Fujian: Fujian Renmin Chubanshe, 2005), 2nd ed., vol. 2, 408.

89. Xu Chongde, *Zhonghua Renmin Gongheguo Xianfashi* [Constitutional History of the People's Republic of China] (Fujian: Fujian Renmin Chubanshe, 2005), 2nd ed., vol. 2, 408.

90. Zhonghua Renmin Gongheguo Xianfa Caoan [The Constitutional Draft of the People's Republic of China], *Renmin Ribao*, April 26, 1982, Art. 79, paragraph 1.

91. Xu Chongde, *Zhonghua Renmin Gongheguo Xianfashi* [Constitutional History of the People's Republic of China] (Fujian: Fujian Renmin Chubanshe, 2003), 826.

92. Zhonghua Renmin Gongheguo Quangou Renmin Daibiao Dahui Zuzhi Fa [Organic Law of the National People's Congress] (adopted by the fifth NPC on December 10, 1982) (PRC), Art. 9.

93. Zhonghua Renmin Gongheguo Quangou Renmin Daibiao Dahui Zuzhi Fa [Organic Law of the National People's Congress] (adopted by the fifth NPC on December 10, 1982) (PRC), Art. 18.

94. Zhonghua Renmin Gongheguo Quangou Renmin Daibiao Dahui Zuzhi Fa [Organic Law of the National People's Congress] (adopted by the fifth NPC on December 10, 1982) (PRC), Art. 15.

95. Yang Jingyu, "Xianfa De Wending He Yushi Jujin" [the Cosntitution's Stability and Development with the Time], Guangming Ribao, December 17, 2003.

96. Yang Haikun (ed.), *Kuaru Xin Shijie De Zhongguo Xianfa Xue-Zhongguo Xianfaxue Yanjiu Xianzhuang Yu Pingjia* [Study on Chinese Constitutional Law in the New Century: Current Situation and Evaluation of Study on Chinese Constitutional Law] (Beijing: Zhongguo Renshi Chubanshe, 2001), 460.

Chapter Nine

Presidents Li Xiannian and Yang Shangkun from 1983 to 1993

"POLITICIAN" LI XIANNIAN ELECTED TO THE PRESIDENCY

The CCP's Nomination of Li Xiannian as the Candidate

As provided by the Organic Law, the NPC Presidium was crucial to the presidential election because it nominated and determined the candidate for the congress to vote. But no measures had been made with regard to its decision-making process. Then how was Li Xiannian nominated by the Presidium? Practically, he was recommended by the CCP. As a part of its leadership, CCP proposed a list of candidates for top government offices to the Presidium, which was explained by Peng Zhen in its second meeting on June 13.

It was reported that, when the constitution was being drafted, informal consideration had been made with regard to the candidate for the presidency within the CCP. Within the CCP, the establishment of this office had been related to the person who would hold it. If the presidency and chairmanship of the state CMC could be taken by one person, Deng Xiaoping would be the only one choice. If Deng Xiaoping would not take it, then these two offices had to be occupied by two different persons, and a number of CCP leaders had been suggested for the presidential candidate, including Li Xiannian.[1]

Although Deng Xiaoping had received the most support and been the most popular one,[2] he had insisted on not taking the presidency.[3] Instead he recommended Li Xiannian.[4] His recommendation had been accepted by the CCP Politburo, and Li Xiannian had been included on the proposed list of candidates.

Before the convening of the Sixth National People's Congress, the CCP had held a so-called "Democratic Consultative Meeting"[5] on May 31 and June 1 to consult on the proposed list with the NPCSC, the National Committee of the CPPCC, and leaders of democratic parties.[6]

The NPC's Election of President Li Xiannian

On June 4, 1983, the First Session of the Sixth NPC, the first NPC after the new constitution came into force, held a preparatory meeting, presided by Peng Zhen, the vice-chairman of the fifth NPCSC. The meeting elected a Presidium of 164 members. Then the Presidium held its first meeting and decided sixteen members as the standing chairmen, with Peng Zhen being ranked as the first one of them.[7]

Based on the constitution and Organic Law, the First Session of the Sixth NPC passed a "Measure on the Voting and Passage of Bills" on June 7, deciding that the presidential voting should conducted by secret ballot[8]; deputies could agree, disagree on the nominated candidate, or choose any other person, even abstain.[9] To be elected into office, the candidate should win more than half of the votes.[10]

On the morning of June 11, the Presidium held its second meeting. After hearing Peng Zhen's explanation of the proposed list of candidates for major governmental offices, Presidium members discussed and agreed that it was the formal list and submitted it to the delegations for consideration. Resumes of candidates were also dispersed after the meeting.[11] From June 13 to 18, the NPC was divided into 113 groups to deliberate on the formal list of candidates.[12] On June 17, the Presidium held the third meeting, which finalized a list of candidates to submit to the NPC for election.[13]

The election was conducted in the afternoon of June 18. Two rounds of voting were conducted. At the first round of voting, Li Xiannian was elected as the third president of the PRC. After hearing of his election into office, Li Xiannian submitted a letter to the NPC immediately, nominating Zhao Ziyang as the candidate for premiership, who was elected into office at the second round of voting, together with Deng Xiaoping elected as the chairman of the state CMC.[14] On the same day, the Sixth NPC announced Li Xiannian as the president to the public in its first notice.[15]

PRESIDENT LI XIANNIAN'S HOME SERVICE FROM 1983 TO 1988

Issuing Presidential Orders

Constitutionally, President Li Xiannian had to perform several duties relating to China's domestic affairs based on the decisions of the NPC or NPCSC, including to promulgate statutes, to appoint or remove senior officials in the State Council, to make honorary conferment, to issue special pardons and mobilization orders, and to proclaim martial law and a state of war.[16] But he had only fulfilled the first two items while in office.

Since the time of Mao Zedong, the presidential orders has been used as an official document recording the president's performance of his constitutional duties to appoint or remove officials at the ministerial level in the State Council, promulgate statutes, and ratify or abrogate foreign treaties and agreements. During his five-year term in office, President Li Xiannian had issued sixty-five presidential orders altogether,[17] out of which forty-five were about the promulgation of laws and eighteen were about the appointment and removal of governmental officials.

Appointing Deputy Premier

On June 18, 1983, President Li Xiannian issued his first presidential order, appointing Zhao Ziyang as the new premier.[18] Since then, Zhao Ziyang served as the premier until he was elected as the CCP's General Sectary in the first Plenary Session of the thirteenth CCPCC held on November 2, 1987, after Hu Yaobang resigned from that post. As required by Deng Xiaoping's idea of separating the government from the party, Zhao Ziyang could not take both positions at the same time and had to give up one of them.

On November 14, Zhao Ziyang wrote to President Li Xiannian, asking to resign from the premiership and proposing Li Peng, then vice-premier, to act as the deputy premier before the forthcoming Seventh NPC decided a new premier.[19] This was new to the constitution, which made no provision concerning the resignation of the premier and the post of the deputy premier. However, the constitution did stipulate that the premier candidate should be nominated by the president, not the former premier. But this stipulation seemed to be ignored. On the following day, President Li Xiannian referred this issue to the NPCSC for consideration,[20] who accepted Zhao's resignation and his proposal. Hence, Li Peng was decided as the deputy premier,[21] and fulfilled that role until April 1988, when he was elected as the new premier by the new NPC.[22] President Li Xiannian should have issued a presidential order to announce his appointment of Li Peng as the deputy premier based on the decision of the NPCSC, but in fact he did not.

His Expanded Civil Services

In spite of these incomplete fulfillments of his constitutional duties, President Li Xiannian had practically been involved with Chinese internal affairs in the capacity of the president by other ways. For example, he made a nationwide speech through television and radio broadcasting in 1984,[23] he made inspections of local governments and regions, such as Guizhou, a Chinese province, after he returned from state visits to Thailand and Cambodia in 1985.[24] He also met people, took part in different activities, and conducted communications by letters, phone calls, and telegrams, and even offered personal inscriptions, and so on.

PRESIDENT LI XIANNIAN'S EXTERNAL SERVICES

His Three Constitutional Duties

Except for those fulfillments in internal affairs, President Li Xiannian also had to perform three constitutional duties relating to China's diplomacy. First, he had to receive foreign diplomatic representatives on behalf of China. Second, he should also appoint or recall Chinese diplomats to other countries, which were irregular in time and recorded in the gazettes of the NPCSC by relevant announcements. Last, he was required to ratify or abrogate treaties and important agreements. Although the Chinese government had joined or approved twenty-five international treaties or bilateral agreements,[25] only two of them were ratified by President Li Xiannian in his orders, which were the joint declarations on the issues of Hong Kong and Macao between China and the UK in 1984 and Portugal in 1987, respectively.

Serving as the Head of State at Foreign Receptions

In practice, President Li Xiannian had acted far beyond those three constitutional duties and completed those services that were usually performed by the head of state. For instance, at home, foreign visitors he received had outnumbered the constitutional definition, expanding from foreign diplomats to other governmental officials, private organizations, and individual persons. Apart from receiving guests, he also invited other countries' heads of state to visit China, held welcome ceremonies and state banquets for them, talked with visitors, appeared at the signing ceremonies, attended feast given by foreign guests, made phone calls to pay regard to visitors when they were traveling within China, said farewell at the hotel or even the train station when foreign visitors were returning home, and so on.

Appointing Special Envoys

Noticeably, during his term of office, several officials had been dispatched abroad as the president's special envoys to conduct certain diplomatic tasks. The first one was in March 1986, when a governmental minister was sent to Portugal on behalf of President Li Xiannian to attend a new Portuguese president's inauguration ceremony.[26] After that, the same minister acted as the special envoy of the Chinese government and went to Stockholm to attend the funeral of Sweden's prime minister.[27] In 1988, two more special envoys on his behalf were also sent to Suriname in February[28] and Saudi Arabia in April[29] respectively.

Seemingly, the practice of deploying special envoys had been adopted by the PRC long before. As early as 1962, a Chinese vice-minister of foreign affairs was sent to several developing countries on behalf of the Chinese government, a vice-chairman of the NPCSC flew to Egypt as "the special envoy of the PRC" to attend the funeral of the Egyptian president in 1970, and a Chinese vice-premier went to Nepal on behalf of the Chinese government in 1975. But those were very limited occasions.[30] Since President Li Xiannian took office, it had been used more frequently. Apart from those three presidential representatives, a dozen special envoys had also been dispatched, mostly on behalf of the Chinese government, to various foreign countries and regions.[31] Besides, in a few specific cases, several envoys were titled either in the capacity of China,[32] China and the CCP,[33] or Chinese government and the CCP.[34]

Most of all these special envoys had been for ceremonial purposes, such as attending inaugural ceremonies, funerals, National Day celebrations, and so on. But there were also a few special envoys who conducted substantial diplomatic tasks. For example, Qian Qichen, who later became the Chinese foreign minister, had served as the special envoy delegated to negotiate with the former Soviet Union for the normalization of bilateral relations.[35] Another special envoy concerning the Middle East affairs was also sent to the Arabian region amid the war between Iraq and Iran in 1987.[36]

Different from the presidents of the United States who initiated the practice of sending special envoys abroad and had full power in deciding their special envoys,[37] President Li Xiannian's role in dispatching Chinese special envoys had been unknown. On one side, China had no law defining the scope of "plenipotentiary representatives abroad," thus whether the special envoys could be regulated by the constitution was unclear. On the other side, the gazettes of the NPCSC had never reported any relevant appointments of special envoys, including those special envoys acting on behalf of President Li Xiannian. Therefore, whether all of these special envoys should be appointed by the president after being decided by the NPCSC, as in the case of Chinese ambassadors, is still uncertain in law.

Paying State Visits to Other Countries

Literally, the president has no constitutional obligation to visit foreign countries. However, once elected, President Li Xiannian paid state visits to twenty-two countries all together during his five-year term of office. His first state visits were made to Pakistan, Jordan, Turkey, and Nepal in the capacity of

PRC President in 1984, after which he also visited Romania, the former Yugoslavia, Spain, Portugal, and Malta in the same year. Since then, President Li Xiannian visited more countries, including Myanmar (1985), Thailand (1985), Canada (1985), the United States (1985), North Korea, Bangladesh (1986), Sri Lanka (1986), Egypt (1986), Somalia (1986), Madagascar (1986), France (1987), Italy (1987), Luxembourg (1987), Belgium (1987).

Some of his visits were of historical significance because they had been the first time a Chinese head of state paid the host country since the founding of PRC. For example, his visit to Jordan was the first one to Jordan and the Arabian world.[38] His visit to the United States had been the first one paid by the Chinese head of state since the establishment of diplomatic relationships between both countries in 150 years,[39] and also been the first diplomacy by the head of states between these two countries.

Talks with the host had been the major part of the president's visits to other countries. For example, during his visit to Turkey, President Li Xiannian had an individual talk with the Turkish president.[40] Besides, he could give a speech on his arrival or in the state banquet given by the host country, meet and talk with other concerned organizations and people, attend signing ceremonies of agreements concluded between both countries, hold thanks feasts, speak to the press, visit local facilities, send flowers, and enjoy various entertainments, such as concerts, and so on.

Above all these forms of participation in China's foreign affairs, President Li Xiannian had also made communications on behalf of the Chinese government and Chinese people to other governments and officials, by sending message of celebration, sympathy, condolence, tribute, thanks, and so on, via telegram or telephone. On a few occasions, he also received honorary titles and conferment from foreign governments.

HIS REAL POLITICAL INFLUENCE AS AN EXPERIENCED POLITICIAN

His Membership in the CCP's PSC and Domestic Influence

While serving as the Chinese president, Li Xiannian had also been a member of the CCP's PSC, together with Deng Xiaoping, Chen Yun, Hu Yaobang, and Zhao Ziyang. Born in 1909, Li Xiannian was a long-time revolutionary cadre experienced in military, economic, and foreign affairs.[41] During the era of Mao Zedong, Li Xiannian had remained stable in high government positions relating to economic and foreign affairs as a major assistant to Premier Zhou Enlai, when Deng Xiaoping and Chen Yun had fluctuated in politics. However, when elected into the presidency in 1983, his influence had been in decline. By then he had reached the age of seventy-four and was one of those old cadres, who had been intended by Deng Xiaoping to retire soon. In the

PSC, while the younger members, that is, Hu Yaobang and Zhao Ziy. were in the first front directly handling party and state affairs to carry o Deng Xiaoping's reform and open-door policy, Li Xiannian belonged to the second front, together with Deng Xiaoping and Chen Yun, who made decisions collectively on major issues, with Deng Xiaoping as the chief one setting the keynote policy and making major decisions. Hence, his political decision-making power could be rather limited, possibly only to major issues and important personnel appointments or removals, and he could only be able to exert indirect influence on domestic affairs, which had been operated by the younger first front leaders. His adherence to the past planned-economy experience had also prevented him from getting much involvement with Deng Xiaoping's policy making and relevant implementations, for which he was said to be one of the most conservative and opposed person among the oldest CCP cadres.[42]

His Substantial Involvement with China's Diplomacy

As much as the collective decision making was emphasized for the PSC, the division of work was also stressed among its members. Approximately at the same time when Li Xiannian was elected as the president, he was decided to take charge of affairs concerning Hong Kong and Macau and continued to head the Central Leading Group of Foreign Affairs (CLGFA).[43] Thus he had direct influence on China's foreign affairs and could exert certain substantial power in China's diplomacy in those areas that were directly under his control, like affairs concerning Hong Kong and Macau,[44] or those affairs he had been familiar with, such as the relations with the former Soviet Union and some other former socialist countries, possible with Deng Xiaoping's final endorsement.

For example, 1984 was the fortieth anniversary of Romania's National Day and Romania had invited China to send a high-level official delegation to attend its ceremony. Since Romania had been a special friend to China and Li Xiannian had paid two visits to attend its twentieth and thirtieth anniversaries in 1964 and 1974, respectively, he was decided by China to pay a third visit to Romania, a state visit in the capacity of president.

To make the visit successful, President Li Xiannian personally met with officials from the State Council relating to the foreign affairs. In the meeting, he not only set guiding principles for his speech and talk that were going to be made during his visit, but also paid attention to the members of Chinese delegation and other etiquette details.

On August 20, 1984, President Li Xiannian started his state visit to Romania. During his nine-day visit, he had three talks with Romanian leader Ceausescu, in which he took the opportunity to announce China's new foreign policy that was taking shape under the direction of Deng Xiaoping.

Referring to China's relationship between the USSR, he not only asked Ceausescu to pass his message to the USSR that China would not go against the USSR together with the United States, implying China would pursue an independent foreign policy, but also pointed out that the essential obstacle to the normalization of the Sino-USSR relation was the withdrawal of military force from Cambodia by Vietnam and the USSR.[45]

This policy was further endorsed by Deng Xiaoping in the next year when Deng Xiaoping met Ceausescu in Beijing. Deng Xiaoping asked Ceausescu to help to deliver his message that if the USSR could make Vietnam withdraw military force from Cambodia, he or Hu Yaobang, the CCP's GS, would be willing to meet the USSR leader Gorbachev.[46]

"GENERAL" YANG SHANGKUN'S SUCCESSION TO THE PRESIDENCY

The CCP's Nomination of Yang Shangkun

On March 15, 1988, the thirteenth CCPCC convened its second plenary meeting. The Politburo introduced to the meeting a list of people, which previously had been prepared by the Politburo and consulted with non-CCP persons through democratic consultative meetings. After discussion in groups, the meeting confirmed this list and decided to submit it to the NPC.[47]

Aspiration for Democracy within the NPC

On March 24, the First Session of the Seventh NPC convened. It seemed to be undermined by an aspiration for more democracy. According to the Organic Law, a preparatory meeting was held first. As recommended by the Council of the Chairmen of the sixth NPCSC, a Presidium of 162 members was elected by the deputies in the meeting by hand voting.[48] However, when it came to discuss the candidates for the NPC committees, deputies were dissatisfied with the old age of some candidates, and some veto votes and abstentions were cast.[49]

Dissatisfaction continued to develop. When the draft of "Measures for Election" was given to deputies for deliberation after being approved by the Presidium in its second meeting held on March 28, some deputies had different opinions and put forward several suggestions. They suggested that joint nomination by deputies used in the election of local government leaders should also be adopted in the election of top governmental officials, such as the president; the election of officials should be separated from the NPC's decision on government officials at different times and by different procedures; and it should be provided that when the nominated candidates win votes from less than half of all deputies, a new candidate should be nominated. In the Presidium's following meeting, the Presidium accepted the latter two suggestions, but rejected the first one on the grounds that the Organic Law did not provide that way of joint nomination.[50]

On April 5, the Presidium held its fourth meeting, in which a CCP Politburo member introduced the CCP's proposed list of names for top governmental positions to be elected by the NPC on behalf of the CCP. The Presidium accepted and turned it to the delegations for deliberation.[51] Brief resumes of those candidates were also dispersed to deputies for reference. Although deputies could know about the candidates by those few hundred words in their resumes, they had been increasingly complained about the old age of candidates of governmental leaders. To ensure satisfactory results, deputies were persuaded, and even disciplined, to cast their votes according to the majority.[52]

While deputies were striving inside the Great Hall, democracy was also voiced outside. The *People's Daily* published a letter from a Chinese citizen, expressing his dissatisfaction of the simple notification of election results and suggesting the NPC should announce the list of candidates to the public after being decided by the Presidium.[53] However, such an appeal had not been accepted.

The NPC's Election

On August 8, 2,883 deputies gathered together in the morning and started to vote. According to the "Measures for Election," the presidential election was a matching one.[54] Voting was completed about one hour later and the NPC adjourned, waiting for counting. Counting was delayed. Although abstention votes were allowed to be cast in this election, they had to be counted by hand because abstentions had not been programmed in the electronic calculator that was used to count affirmative and veto votes.[55]

When it came time to announce the results, reporters and foreign diplomats were asked to step out,[56] and then the executive chairman of the Presidium declared the results: 2,725 deputies voted for the only candidate, Yang Shangkun, with 124 vetoes and 34 abstentions.[57] Noticeably, the CCP's former GS, Hu Yaobang, who had stepped down for his support for democracy, also received votes from twenty-six deputies as the president.[58]

According to the explanation made by the NPCSC's Committee of Legal Affairs on March 30, 1988, the candidate should win more than half votes from all deputies, if to be elected into office.[59] So Yang Shangkun was declared the winner of the election.[60] He would succeed Li Xiannian as the fourth president. On the following day, President Yang Shangkun was also decided by the NPC as the vice-chairman of the state CMC upon the nomination of Deng Xiaoping, who had been elected as its chairman by the NPC on the previous day.[61]

On the closing day of the NPC, President Yang Shangkun delivered a speech, swearing that he would perform his constitutional power and function properly.[62] This was the first time in PRC history that the Chinese president ever made such an announcement when being elected into office.

His Political Influence as the "House Keeper"

In the CCP's thirteenth National Congress held in 1987, in which Yang Shangkun was elected into the Politburo, Deng Xiaoping's plan to rejuvenate the CCP had been further implemented. In the PSC, Deng Xiaoping, Chen Yun, and Li Xiannian, had all retired, thus leaving the highest decision-making organ full of younger generations headed by the GS Zhao Ziyang, who was intended by Deng Xiaoping as his successor.[63] As a result, President Yang Shangkun was different from his predecessor President Li Xiannian. Only being a Politburo member and not a part of the new highest decision-making organ, President Yang Shangkun could understandably have less involvement with the CCP's decision-making process. In particular, the Central Leading Group of Foreign Affairs was transferred from the hand of Li Xiannian to the new Premier Li Peng. Thus the president lost control of the CCP's foreign policy formulation.

Compared with Li Xiannian, President Yang Shangkun's experience had also been rather limited to the party and military affairs, without taking any position in the government. He joined the CCP as early as 1925 and had studied in the former Soviet Union. After returning to China in 1930, he became a leader in the Red Army. He went through the famous Long March, participated in the "Zunyi meeting" as one of the army leaders, among which others included Lin Biao and Peng Dehuai. Since 1945, Yang Shangkun had been put in charge of the office of CCPCC for twenty years, known as the "General House Keeper" of the CCPCC, until he was purged from office by Mao Zedong in 1965, well on the eve of the Cultural Revolution.[64]

But President Yang Shangkun also had his own uniqueness. Although Deng Xiaoping retired from the PSC, he continued to take command of the military as the chairman of the CMC, whereas Zhao Ziyang, his chosen successor and the CCP's GS, served as the first vice-chairman and President Yang Shangkun as the standing vice-chairman in the state CMC. This was a deliberate arrangement. As Yang Shangkun was loyal to Deng Xiaoping, Deng Xiaoping could be assured with his guardian. On the other hand, Zhao Ziyang had no experience in the military, Yang Shangkun could give him a hand to succeed Deng Xiaoping and take control of the military gradually. Therefore, while performing those ceremonial duties and not interfering with state affairs, President Yang Shangkun was thought to be influential in the military.[65]

Such a role of President Yang Shangkun as "the house keeper" became much more apparent in the decision making of the CCP when Zhao Ziyang was removed from office and Jiang Zeming took his place amid the political turbulence of the June 4 movement. Since Jiang Zeming was decided as a result of the compromise between Deng Xiaoping and other old cadres, Deng Xiaoping could not give his full trust to this new GS. Before being picked up by those old cadres, Jiang Zeming had little working experience in the CCP's highest decision-making level. In view of this new situation, the much more experienced President Yang Shangkun could be given a new task, not only to help, but also to supervise Jiang Zeming on behalf of Deng Xiaoping. It was speculated that a secret consensus had been reached when Jiang Zeming's appointment as the GS was approved by the fourth session of the thirteenth CCPCC, giving Yang Shangkun the privilege to attend all meeting of the new PSC, to which he had not belonged.[66] Such a prominence of President Yang Shangkun could also be sensed from the official reports.[67] Therefore, after Jiang Zeming replaced Zhao Ziyang, President Yang Shangkun earned extra influence in the new PSC.

But such implicit political influence of President Yang Shangkun did not last long, as Jiang Zeming gradually took command. Power conflicts were rumored to break out between them.[68] In the end, President Yang Shangkun lost his position in the Politburo and military in the CCP's fourteenth congress held in 1993, thus being completely retired from politics.

President Yang's Abbreviated Home Services from 1988 to 1993

In office, President Yang Shangkun had generally followed the examples set by his predecessor and performed both his constitutional duties and those expanded services. In five years, he had issued seventy-two presidential orders, seven more than his predecessor, and in which fifty-nine were to promulgate laws and thirteen were about official appointments and removals. He was the first PRC president who made the commitment to the constitution to the NPC upon election. He was also the first to deliver New Year's speeches through China International Broadcasting Station to its overseas audience in 1990 and 1991.[69]

However, he could become less important politically, at least in terms of nominating the deputy premier. On November 15, 1989, Premier Li Peng declared in a press conference that Vice-Premier Yao Yilin would act as his deputy when he went on overseas visits.[70] Seemingly, his arrangement had been accepted without any involvement of the president and even the NPC.[71] This practice abbreviated that of the former case, in which President Li Xiannian submitted to the NPC then Premier Zhao Ziyang's resignation from and his proposal of Li Peng as the deputy premier. As a result, the president was further excluded in the appointment of the deputy premier.

His performance in Chinese foreign affairs also seemed to be reduced. Although he received foreign guests, appointed or recalled Chinese representatives, he had paid state visits to a limited number of foreign countries,[72] all of which belonged to the third world. About a dozen special envoys had also been dispatched around the world,[73] but none of those special envoys had been deployed on his behalf; instead, all of them were either in the capacity of the Chinese government or China. Besides, he did not ratify any treaties during his term, despite the fact that China had joined or approved a number of international or bilateral treaties in the same period of time.[74]

LEGAL DEVELOPMENT CONCERNING THE PRESIDENCY

Presidential Election

However, during his term, an emphasis on law could also be discerned from his presidential orders, which recorded an increase of fourteen pieces of legislations promulgated, among which a few laws were made regarding the presidential election, removal, resignation, ratification of foreign treaties and agreements before 1993, and the division of military power between the state CMC and SC after 1993, since the adoption of the constitution and the Organic Law of the NPC in 1982.

In 1989, the "Rules of Procedure for the National People Congress of the PRC" (Rules of Procedure for the NPC) was adopted, which made several improvements to the presidential election required by the constitution and the Organic Law. First of all, a requirement of information disclosure was newly provided, by which the nominator of candidates, that is, the Presidium in the case of the presidential election, should give the NPC basic information about the candidate and make necessary explanations to questions raised by deputies.[75] Although what was the "basic information" was not defined in the law, understandably, it should at a minimum include his age, nationality, and legal capacity to stand for election, because these were required by the constitution.[76]

Second, the secret ballot was limited as the only voting method in the NPC'S election; as such, the ballot-writing place was required to be installed for deputies. To be elected into office, the presidential candidate had to win a simple majority vote of all deputies; the outcome of an election should be announced on the spot, and the number of votes received by the candidate also had to be announced.[77]

Besides, as the past Sixth and Seventh NPC had made special legislation on the elections by their Presidiums respectively, the law also provided that specific measures for elections could be adopted by the NPC at a plenary meeting of the session,[78] so that the future NPC could follow these examples.

Removal of the President

According to the Organic Law, three or more delegations or at least one-tenth of the deputies of the NPC may submit a proposal to the Presidium to remove the president from office, and the Presidium shall then put it to the NPC for deliberation.[79] Now the new legislation not only gave the Presidium the power to propose such a removal,[80] but also required that such a proposal should give reasons and relevant information. The person being proposed to should be removed from office, for instance, the president, was also provided the right to defend themselves at the meeting of the Presidium or plenary meeting of a NPC session, or submit a written statement, which should be printed by the Presidium for distribution at the session.

When receiving the proposal to remove the president, the Presidium could take two different options. The proposal could be either referred to the delegations for deliberation and then put it to vote at a plenary meeting of the NPC session, or the Presidium could propose to the NPC plenary meeting setting up a "Committee of Inquiry into specific questions" (Committee of Inquiry).[81] Such a Committee of Inquiry had been provided in the constitution,[82] and was also further stipulated in this 1989 law.[83] Once established, this committee should submit an investigatory report to the next session of the NPC who could make a resolution accordingly.[84] When the NPC was not in session, the NPCSC could also make a relevant resolution based on the committee's report, if with prior delegation from the NPC.[85] Such resolutions can be adopted by a simple majority vote of all the NPC deputies.[86]

Resignation of the President

Although the constitution does not mention the resignation of government officials, it did happen in 1987 when Zhao Ziyang resigned from the premiership to succeed Hu Yaobang as the CCP's GS. Possibly to make remedy, the NPC Rules of Procedure newly provided an exit for top government officials, including the president, vice-president, and the chairman of the state CMC. To resign from office, the president should submit his resignation to the Presidium if the NPC was in session, who then should turn it to the delegations and plenary meeting of the NPC for decision. If the NPC is not in session, the president's resignation should be given to the Council of the Chairman of the NPCSC, which then forwards it to the NPCSC for decision. If the NPCSC decides to accept his resignation, such a decision has to be confirmed by the next session of the NPC afterwards.[87]

Compared with the removal stipulations, there is a difference implied by law. While the president can file his resignation anytime, no matter whether the NPC is in session or not, he can only be removed when the NPC was in session. According to the 1989 legislation, the Presidium is crucial to the presidential removal. As it could only be formed in a plenary meeting of the NPC session, it is implied that the president could only be removed from office when the NPC is convened for a plenary meeting.

Presidential Ratification of International Treaties and Agreements

The constitution provides that the president ratifies or abrogates "treaties and important agreements" concluded with foreign states, pursuing to the decisions of the NPCSC,[88] but it does not specify what kind of treaties and agreements are important and have to be decided by the NPCSC and by what procedure the president can ratify them. Since the adoption of the constitution in 1982 and prior to the following legislation, only two ratifications were made by President Li Xiannian on the joint declarations between China, the UK, and Portugal, respectively.

In 1990, the Law on the Procedure of the Conclusion of Treaties was adopted, which clarified uncertainties in these regards on one hand, but created new questions.

According to this law, it was enacted in accordance with the constitution and applicable to bilateral or multilateral treaties and agreements and other instruments of the nature of a treaty or agreement concluded between the PRC and foreign states.[89] "Treaties and important agreements" to be decided by the NPCSC is defined to include mainly five categories, including those of a political nature, relating to territory and boundary lines, to judicial assistance and extradition, containing inconsistent stipulations with Chinese laws, and those subject to ratification, and so on.[90] In particular, the term "treaties" was defined by drafters as any written documents concluded between international law subjects about their rights and obligations based on international law, such as charter, statute, Memo of Understanding, joint statement, exchange of notes, and so on, the nature of which was decided by its content rather than its form or name.[91]

To be ratified by the president, the treaty or important agreement should first be examined and verified by the State Council, after which it should be referred to the NPCSC for decision on ratification, upon which the president gives his ratification to it. Notably, the instrument of ratification signed by the president should be countersigned by the minister of foreign affairs,[92] whereas the presidential order promulgating legislations does not have to be co-signed by anyone else. However, if a multilateral treaty or important agreements falls into the scope of those five categories, the accession to it should be decided by the NPCSC, and the instrument of accession for that treaty or important agreement would be signed only by the minister of foreign affairs, without involving the president.[93] Therefore, all those "treaties and important agreements" decided by the NPCSC and published in its gazette are divided into two groups, that is, those to ratify or to accede,[94] and the president only has to ratify and sign on those bilateral "treaties and important agreements."

It was also intended by the drafter that the treaty and agreement could be concluded in the name of the Chinese president; representatives for negotiating and signing treaties and agreements could be appointed by the president; the president could be dispensed with full power for negotiating and signing treaties and agreements.[95] However, the new roles of the president given in the draft would be in conflict with the constitution, because the constitution mentions nothing else for the president in the conclusion of international treaties and agreements, except to ratify upon decision by the NPCSC. Besides, the constitution used the phrase of "treaties and agreements," instead of the single word "treaties." Therefore, possibly to avoid these violations, relevant stipulations were revised when the law was adopted in 1990. Except for the role to ratify, the law mentions nothing else for the president in the conclusion of treaties and agreements. For example, he could not conclude any treaty or agreement in his own name[96]; neither could he appoint any representative for negotiating and signing treaties and agreements.[97]

However, there is also vagueness in this law. One is concerned with whether the president could negotiate and sign treaties and agreements. Seemingly the law finally followed the model of the constitution and did not include clearly the president in the list of persons who had full powers to conduct negotiation and signing. But it was also provided that "the person, dispatched to an international conference or accredited to an international organization by the People's Republic of China, who is at the same time the representative for negotiating treaties or agreements in that conference or organization, unless it is otherwise agreed by the conference or otherwise provided for in the constitution of the organization" had the full power to negotiate and sign treaties and agreements.[98] As a result, the president could be dispatched or accredited as that person, if to bypass the constitution.

If to avoid the constitutional concern, there is another way for the president to negotiate and sign treaties and agreements. According to that law, for treaties and agreements concluded in the name of the PRC or its government, representatives for negotiating and signing should be decided by the State Council, and their full powers should be assigned by the premier or the minister of foreign affairs. Hence, if the president was to negotiate or sign any treaties or agreements, the president had to obtain full powers from the premier or the foreign minister. In this case, the president should be accompanied by the foreign minister at least, so that the constitution could not be violated.

One more uncertainty in that law is related to documents that were not titled as "treaty" or "agreement," such as a joint declaration, communiqué, manifesto, and so on. Although it is recognized that they could be a treaty or agreement,[99] depending on the nature of their content, whether they should be decided by the NPCSC and ratified by the president still remains unclear. According to that law, if they were not concerned with political issues, such as friendly relations with other countries, peace agreements, or boundaries, judicial assistance, and so on, they could be excluded from the NPCSC decision,[100] but they could have to be included if they belonged to those "subject to ratification."[101]

In practice, only President Yang Shangkun signed a "joint declaration" ("Lianhe Gongbao" in Chinese) together with the visiting Turkmenistan president on November 1992,[102] but there is no evidence available suggesting that he had been given the full delegation from the premier or foreign minister, or indicating that such a joint declaration had ever been decided by the NPCSC.

CONCLUSION

Taking lessons from his predecessors, Deng Xiaoping strived to rejuvenate the party-state with his ideas of "separating the party from the state" and "strengthening laws and democracy," by which the CCP's supreme chairmanship was abolished and political power was further divided and put into different hands. While Deng Xiaoping held the military power personally and his intended successors became the GS as the CCP's nominal paramount leader, the presidency was taken successively by Li Xiannian and Yang Shangkun, who were too old to succeed either the nominal GS or the substantial "core of leadership."

Compared with Chairman Mao Zedong and Liu Shaoqi, Presidents Li Xiannian and Yang Shangkun formed a different type of president. Constitutionally, the office of presidency enjoys a number of specified ceremonial functions in China's domestic and foreign affairs. Practically, both of them participated in the political decision making of the Politburo and PSC, their roles had been much more like executor than decision maker, and both presidents had expanded their activities beyond those constitutional provisions. Most notably, their services as the head of state of China in Chinese diplomacy have become much more distinct with China's growing involvement with globalization, mostly by paying outbound and inviting inbound state visits. But one thing remained: all these ceremonial activities could carry political substance, depending on the holder's political authority basically determined by his rank in the CCP's decision-making organs, which was dominated by Deng Xiaoping and a few old cadres.

With the declaration of the completion of socialism in China, the CCP's control over the state apparatus was further tightened, taking all major government posts provided by the constitution. Accordingly, the succession also extended from the presidency to include other top government positions. As a result, succession to the presidency, which used to be the utmost important thing, became only a part of the overall succession plan. As the presidency is not the focus of the CCP's decision making and succession, which had been the CCP's GS, the presidency had been much more lenient for both occupants, compared with the two GSs, that is, Hu Yaobang and Zhao Ziyang, or the previous tragic chairman, Liu Shaoqi. After they retired from the office, they were far less privileged than their predecessor.

NOTES

1. Ke Ge, "Guojia Zhuxi Renxuan Huzhi Yuchu" [The Presidential Candidate is Ready], *Zhengming*, no. 5 (1982): 15.
2. Luo Bing, "Xinge Yong Deng Dang Guojia Zhuxi" [The New Cabinet Supports Deng Xiaoping to Take the Presidency], *Zhengming*, no. 6 (1982): 10.
3. Zhou Nianhua, "Deng Xiaoping Dang 'Guojia Zhuxi'"? [Will Deng Xiaoping Be the "President"?], *Jingbao Yuekan*, no. 10 (1983): 34.
4. Luo Bing, "Deng Xiaoping Tui Li Xiannian Churen Guojia Zhuxi" [Deng Xiaoping Recommends Li Xiannian as the Presidential Candidate], *Zhengming*, no. 6 (1983): 6.
5. It is a meeting held by the CCP with other prominent national figures to discuss important state issues, such as the major national policy, nomination of main governmental officials, and so on. China's eight other political parties, normally, are major participants in such meetings.
6. *Renmin Ribao*, June 2, 1983; Luo Bing, "Guojia Lingdaoren De Chansheng" [The Selection of National Leaders], *Zhengming*, no. 7 (1983): 12.
7. *Renmin Ribao*, June 5, 1983.
8. Zhonghua Renmin Gongheguo Diliujie Quanguo Renmin Daibiao Dahui Diyici Huiyi Xuanju Biaojue He Tongguo Yi'an Banfa [Measures for Election, Voting and Adoption of Bills for the Sixth National People's Congress] (adopted by the First Session of the Sixth NPC on June 7, 1982) (PRC), Art. 3.
9. Zhonghua Renmin Gongheguo Diliujie Quanguo Renmin Daibiao Dahui Diyici Huiyi Xuanju Biaojue He Tongguo Yi'an Banfa [Measures for Election, Voting and Adoption of Bills for the Sixth National People's Congress] (adopted by the First Session of the Sixth NPC on June 7, 1982) (PRC), Art. 6.
10. Zhonghua Renmin Gongheguo Diliujie Quanguo Renmin Daibiao Dahui Diyici Huiyi Xuanju Biaojue He Tongguo Yi'an Banfa [Measures for Election, Voting and Adoption of Bills for the Sixth National People's Congress] (adopted by the First Session of the Sixth NPC on June 7, 1982) (PRC), Art. 6.
11. *Renmin Ribao*, June 12, 1983.
12. *Renmin Ribao*, June 14, 15, 1983.
13. *Renmin Ribao*, June 18, 1983.
14. *Renmin Ribao*, June 19, 1983.
15. *Renmin Ribao*, June 19, 1983.
16. Xianfa [constitution] (1982) (PRC), Art. 80.
17. His last Presidential order was numbered as the 65th. See Standing Comm. Nat'l People's Cong. Gaz, No. 2 (1988), 44.
18. Standing Comm. Nat'l People's Cong. Gaz, No. 3 (1983), 90.
19. *Renmin Ribao*, November 25, 1987.
20. *Renmin Ribao*, November 18, 1987. See also, Li Xiannian Zhuxi Gei Quanguo Renda Daibiao Changwu Weiyuanhui De Laiwen [Letter from President Li Xiannian to the Standing

Committee of the National People's Congress], Standing Comm. Nat'l People's Cong. Gaz, No. 6 (1987), 3.

21. *Renmin Ribao*, November 25, 1987.

22. See http://www.gov.cn/test/2007-11/21/content_811863.htm. This is in the official website of the Chinese government, last visited on July 22, 2008.

23. *Renmin Riba*, 1984.

24. *Renmin Ribao*, March 16, 1985.

25. The number is calculated based on the Standing Comm. Nat'l People's Cong. Gaz.

26. *Renmin Ribao*, March 7, 9, 10, 11, 13, 16, 20, 1986.

27. *Renmin Ribao*, March 13, 16, 20, 1986.

28. *Renmin Ribao*, February 1, 1988.

29. *Renmin Ribao*, April 4, 11, 1988.

30. *Renmin Ribao*, February 7, 1993; May 30, 1996; Li Bin, *Guoji Yiyi Yu Jiaoji Lijie* [International Etiquette and Social Courtesy] (Beijing: Shijie Zhishi Chubanshe, 1985), 2nd ed., 139.

31. *Renmin Ribao*, November 13, 14, 18, 1983; March 1, 12, 24, 27, 28, November 4, December 5, 7, 1984; February 14, 28, March 10, 16, 17, April 8, 14, 23, 24, June 7, July 18, 23, 27, 30, 31, August 26, September 26, 1985; April 7, 15, 16, September 25, October 6, 16, 1986; Janurary 8, 13, 24, March 7, April 14, 24, 27, July 29, 30, August 26, 28, September 3, 24, 1987.

32. *Renmin Ribao*, November 3, 4, 5, 6, 1984; August 6, 8, 10, November 21, 27, 1985.

33. *Renmin Ribao*, March 29, 30, 31, April 1, 2, 3, 7, 1984.

34. *Renmin Ribao*, October 28, 29, 30, 1986.

35. *Renmin Ribao*, March 1, 12, 24, 27, 28, November 4, 1984; April 8, 23, 24, September 26, 1985; April 7, 15, 16, September 25, October 6, 16, 1986; April 14, 24, 24, September 24, 1987.

36. *Renmin Ribao*, July 29, 30, Auguster 26, 28, September 3, 1987.

37. Martin L. Fausold and Alan Shank, *The Constitution and the American Presidency* (Albany: State University of New York Press, 1991), 180.

38. *Renmin Ribao*, March 9, 1984.

39. Sun Muna, "Liangwei Gaoling Yuanshou Zhi Lishixing Huiwu: Zhongguo Guojia Zhuxi Lixiannian Fangmei Jiyao" [Historical Meeting of Two Old Heads of State: A Brief Account of Chinese President Li Xiannian's Visit to the United States], *Jingbao*, no. 8 (1985): 36-37.

40. *Renmin Ribao*, March 15, 1984.

41. For Li Xiannian's experience as a CCP cadre and senior governmental official, see "Huainian Li Xiannian Tongzhi," Bianji Zu (ed.), *Weida De Renmin Gongpu: Huainian Li Xiannian Tongzhi* [A Great People's Servant: In Memory of Comarade Li Xiannian] (Beijing: Zhongyang Wenxian Chubanshe, 1993); Zhu Yu, Cheng Zhensheng, and He Guangyao, *Li Xiannian De Feichang Zhilu* [Extraodinary Road of Li Xiannian] (Beijing: Renmin Chubanshe, 2001); Li Xiannian Zhuan Bianxie Zu (ed.), *Li Xiannian Zhuan (1909-1949)* [Biography of Li Xiannian (1909-1949)] (Beijing: Zhongyang Wenxian Chubanshe, 1999); Zhao Lingyun, *Li Xiannian Zai 1946* [Li Xiannian in 1946] (Beijing: Jiefangjun Chubanshe, 2004); Li Xiannian Zhuan Bianxie Zu (ed.), *Li Xiannian Zhuan (1949-1992)* [Biography of Li Xiannian (1949-1992)] (Beijing: Zhongyang Wenxian Chubanshe, 2009).

42. Zhao Ziyang, *Gaige Licheng* [The Reform History] (Hong Kong: Xin Shiji Chubanshe, 2009), 261, 267-268.

43. Cheng Zhensheng, "Li Xiannian Yu Xianggang, and Aomen Huigui" [Li Xiannian and the Return of Hong Kong and Macou], *Dang De Wenxian*, no. 6 (1999): 38-39.

44. For his influence on Hong Kong and Macau affairs, see Cheng Zhensheng, "Li Xiannian Yu Xianggang, and Aomen Huigui" [Li Xiannian and the Return of Hong Kong and Macau], *Dang De Wenxian*, no. 6 (1999): 38-39.

45. Jiang Benliang, *Gei Gongheguo Lingdao Ren Zuo Fanyi* [Interpreting for the National Leaders] (Shanghai: Shanghai Cishu Chubanshe, 2007), 175-200.

46. Jiang Benliang, *Gei Gongheguo Lingdao Ren Zuo Fanyi* [Interpreting for the National Leaders] (Shanghai: Shanghai Cishu Chubanshe, 2007), 140-144.

47. *Renmin Ribao*, March 15, 16, 20, 23, 1988.

48. *Renmin Ribao*, March 25, 1988. However, an abstention had been missed during the vote counting; see Wu Kangmin, *Renda Huiyi Lu* [Memory of the People's Congress] (Hong Kong: Mingbao Chubanshe, 1990), 180-181.

49. Wu Kangmin, *Renda Huiyi Lu* [Memory of the People's Congress] (Hong Kong: Mingbao Chubanshe, 1990), 188.

50. *Renmin Ribao*, April 2, 1988.

51. *Renmin Ribao*, April 16, 1988.

52. Wu Kangmin, *Renda Huiyi Lu* [Memory of the People's Congress] (Hong Kong: Mingbao Chubanshe, 1990), 141-142.

53. *Renmin Ribao*, April 6, 1988.

54. Zhonghua Renmin Gongheguo Diqijie Quanguo Renmin Daibiao Dahui Diyici Huiyi Xuanju Banfa [Measures for Election for the First Session of the Seventh National People's Congress] (adopted at the First Session of the Seventh National People's Congress on April 2, 1988), Art. 4.

55. *Renmin Ribao*, April 9, 1988; Wu Kangmin, *Renda Huiyi Lu* [Memory of the People's Congress] (Hong Kong: Mingbao Chubanshe, 1990), 193.

56. Hu Yaobang also won twenty-three votes in the election of vice-president, nine and eighteen votes respectively in the election of the NPC's chairman and vice-chairmen, and one vote in the election of chairman of the Central Military Commission. See Wu Kangmin, *Renda Huiyi Lu* [Memory of the People's Congress] (Hong Kong: Mingbao Chubanshe, 1990), 194.

57. Yiu-Chung Wong, *From Deng Xiaoping to Jiang Zemin: Two Decades of Political Reform in the People's Republic of China* (Lanham, MD: University Press of America, 2005), 102; Kevin J. O'Brien, *Reform without Liberalization: China's National People's Congress and the Politics of Institutional Change* (New York: Cambridge University Press, 1990), 142.

58. Wu Kangmin, *Renda Huiyi Lu* [Memory of the People's Congress] (Hong Kong: Mingbao Chubanshe, 1990), 195.

59. Quanguo Renmin Daibiao Dahui Changwu Weiyuanhui Bangongting Yanjiushi (ed.), *Zhonghua Renmin Gongheguo Renmin Daibiao Dahui Wenxian Ziliao Huibian (1949-1990)* [Compilation of Documents of the National People's Congress of the People's Republic of China] (Beijing: Zhongguo Minzhu Fazhi Chubanshe, 1991), 344-345.

60. *Renmin Ribao*, April 9, 1988.

61. *Renmin Ribao*, April 9, 10, 1988.

62. Yang Shangkun, "Zai Qijie Renda Yici Huiyi Shang Yang Shangkun Zhuxi De Jianghua" [Speech of President Yang Shangkun in the First Session of the Seventh National People's Congress], *Renmin Ribao*, April 14, 1988.

63. Zhao Ziyang, *Gaige Licheng* [The Reform History] (Hong Kong: Xin Shiji Chubanshe, 2009), 74, 265-266.

64. Yang Shangkun Tan Zai Zhongban Ershi Nian: Rang Wo Gan Shenme Jiu Gan Shenme [Yang Shangkun Talks about His Twenty Years Life in the Office of the CCPCC: Do What I am Told to Do], in http://cpc.people.com.cn/GB/85037/85038/7656817.html.

65. Gao Xin, *Jiang Zemin De Quanli Zhilu* [Jiang Zemin's Road to Power] (Hong Kong: Mingjing Chubanshe, 1997), 181.

66. Gao Xin, *Jiang Zemin De Quanli Zhilu* [Jiang Zemin's Road to Power] (Hong Kong: Mingjing Chubanshe, 1997), 178.

67. Song Lijun, "Yang Shangkun Yu Jinri Zhongguo: Yingxaing San Baiwan Dajun De Guojia Zhuxi" [Yang Shangkun and Today's China: A President Who Influences Three Million Soldiers], *Guangjiaojing Yuekan* (September 1989): 14; Chen Xufei, "Junzhong Qiangren Yang Shangkun" [Strong Man in the Military Yang Shangkun], *Guangjiaojing Yuekan* (September 1989): 21; Liang Dazhi, "Liangdao Paiming De Beihou" [Behind the Ranking of Leaders], *Guangjiaojing Yuekan* (October 1989): 14.

68. See, for example, Gao Xin, *Jiang Zemin De Quanli Zhilu* [Jiang Zemin's Road to Power] (Hong Kong: Mingjing Chubanshe, 1997), 181; Du Liln, *Jiang Zemin Zhuan* [Biography of Jiang Zemin] (Hong Kong: Mingjing Chubanshe, 1993).

69. Zhonghua Renmin Gongheguo Guowuyuan Gongbao [Gazette of the State Council of the People's Republic of China, St. Council Gaz.], no. 1 (1991); no. 1 (1992).

70. *Renmin Ribao*, November 15, 1989.

71. *Renmin Ribao*, November 17, 1989.

72. During his term of office, President Yang Shangkun had visited North Korea (1989 and 1992), Mexico (1989), Brazil (1989), Egypt (1989), Uruguay (1989), Argentina (1989), United Arab Emirates (1989), Kuwait (1989), Oman (1989), Chile (1989), Indonesia (1991), Thailand (1991), Mongolia (1991), Pakistan (1991), Iran (1991), Singapore (1992), Malaysia (1992), Morocco (1992), Tunisia (1992), and Côte d'Ivoire (1992).

73. *Renmin Ribao*, June 14, 22, July 9, September 15, 1988; July 1, 9, 1989; February 16, March 2, 13, 16, 17, 18, 22, 23, April 20, 30, July 20, 30, August 11, 1990; February 12, 15, 16, 17, 18, 19, 20, 23, 25, May 23, 25, 26, 27, August 20, 21, 1991; January 6, 7, 8, April 23, 26, November 27, 28, 29, 1992; May 7, 26, 27, July 30, November 9, 1993.

74. See Standing Comm. Nat'l People's Cong. Gaz during 1988 and 1993.

75. Rules of Procedure for the NPC (adopted at the Second Session of the Seventh National People's Congress on April 4, 1989, promulgated by the Presidential Decree No. 17 on April 4, 1989, and effective as of the same day), Art. 35.

76. Xianfa [constitution] (1982) (PRC), Art. 79, paragraph 2.

77. Rules of Procedure for the NPC (adopted at the Second Session of the Seventh National People's Congress on April 4, 1989, promulgated by the Presidential Decree No. 17 on April 4, 1989, and effective as of the same day), Art. 36.

78. Rules of Procedure for the NPC (adopted at the Second Session of the Seventh National People's Congress on April 4, 1989, promulgated by the Presidential Decree No. 17 on April 4, 1989, and effective as of the same day), Art. 37.

79. Zhonghua Renmin Gongheguo Quangou Renmin Daibiao Dahui Zuzhi Fa [Organic Law of the National People's Congress] (adopted by the Fifth NPC on December 10, 1982) (PRC), Art. 15.

80. Rules of Procedure for the NPC (adopted at the Second Session of the Seventh National People's Congress on April 4, 1989, promulgated by the Presidential Decree No. 17 on April 4, 1989, and effective as of the same day), Art. 39.

81. Rules of Procedure for the NPC (adopted at the Second Session of the Seventh National People's Congress on April 4, 1989, promulgated by the Presidential Decree No. 17 on April 4, 1989, and effective as of the same day), Art. 39.

82. Xianfa [constitution] (1982) (PRC), Art. 71.

83. Rules Of Procedure for the NPC (adopted at the Second Session of the Seventh National People's Congress on April 4, 1989, promulgated by the Presidential Decree No. 17 on April 4, 1989, and effective as of the same day), chapter 6.

84. Rules of Procedure for the NPC (adopted at the Second Session of the Seventh National People's Congress on April 4, 1989, promulgated by the Presidential Decree No. 17 on April 4, 1989, and effective as of the same day), Art. 48, paragraph 1.

85. Rules of Procedure for the NPC (adopted at the Second Session of the Seventh National People's Congress on April 4, 1989, promulgated by the Presidential Decree No. 17 on April 4, 1989, and effective as of the same day), Art. 48, paragraph 2.

86. Xianfa [constitution] (1982) (PRC), Art. 64, paragraph 2.

87. Rules of Procedure for the NPC (adopted at the Second Session of the Seventh National People's Congress on April 4, 1989, promulgated by the Presidential Decrees No. 17 on April 4, 1989, and effective as of the same day), Art. 38.

88. Xianfa [constitution] (1982) (PRC), article 81.

89. Zhonghua Renmin Gongheguo Dijie Tiaoyue Chengxu Fa [Law on the Procedure of the Conclusion of Treaties] (adopted at the 17th Meeting of the Standing Committee of the Seventh National People's Congress on December 28, 1990, promulgated by Order No. 37 of the President of the People's Republic of China on December 28, 1990, and effective as of the same date) (PRC), Art. 1, 2.

90. Zhonghua Renmin Gongheguo Dijie Tiaoyue Chengxu Fa [Law on the Procedure of the Conclusion of Treaties] (adopted at the 17th Meeting of the Standing Committee of the Seventh National People's Congress on December 28, 1990, promulgated by Order No. 37 of the President of the People's Republic of China on December 28, 1990, and effective as of the same date) (PRC), Art. 7, paragraph 2.

91. Qian Qichen, "Guanyu Zhonghua Renmin Gongheguo Dijie Tiaoyue Chengxu Fa (Caoan) De Shuoming" [Explanation to the Law on the Procedure of the Conclusion of Treaties of the People's Republic of China (draft)], Standing Comm. Nat'l People's Cong. Gaz, No. ? (1990).

92. Zhonghua Renmin Gongheguo Dijie Tiaoyue Chengxu Fa [Law on the Procedure of the Conclusion of Treaties] (adopted at the 17th Meeting of the Standing Committee of the Seventh National People's Congress on December 28, 1990, promulgated by Order No. 37 of the President of the People's Republic of China on December 28, 1990, and effective as of the same date) (PRC), Art. 7.

93. Zhonghua Renmin Gongheguo Dijie Tiaoyue Chengxu Fa [Law on the Procedure of the Conclusion of Treaties] (adopted at the 17th Meeting of the Standing Committee of the Seventh National People's Congress on December 28, 1990, promulgated by Order No. 37 of the President of the People's Republic of China on December 28, 1990, and effective as of the same date) (PRC), Art. 11.

94. Zhonghua Renmin Gongheguo Dijie Tiaoyue Chengxu Fa [Law on the Procedure of the Conclusion of Treaties] (adopted at the 17th Meeting of the Standing Committee of the Seventh National People's Congress on December 28, 1990, promulgated by Order No. 37 of the President of the People's Republic of China on December 28, 1990, and effective as of the same date) (PRC), Art. 15.

95. Qian Qichen, "Guanyu Zhonghua Renmin Gongheguo Dijie Tiaoyue Chengxu Fa (Caoan) De Shuoming" [Explanation to the Law on the Procedure of the Conclusion of Treaties of the People's Republic of China (draft)], Standing Comm. Nat'l People's Cong. Gaz, No. 12 (1990).

96. Zhonghua Renmin Gongheguo Dijie Tiaoyue Chengxu Fa [Law on the Procedure of the Conclusion of Treaties] (adopted at the 17th Meeting of the Standing Committee of the Seventh National People's Congress on December 28, 1990, promulgated by Order No. 37 of the President of the People's Republic of China on December 28, 1990, and effective as of the same date) (PRC), Art. 4.

97. Zhonghua Renmin Gongheguo Dijie Tiaoyue Chengxu Fa [Law on the Procedure of the Conclusion of Treaties] (adopted at the 17th Meeting of the Standing Committee of the Seventh National People's Congress on December 28, 1990, promulgated by Order No. 37 of the President of the People's Republic of China on December 28, 1990, and effective as of the same date) (PRC), Art. 6.

98. Zhonghua Renmin Gongheguo Dijie Tiaoyue Chengxu Fa [Law on the Procedure of the Conclusion of Treaties] (adopted at the 17th Meeting of the Standing Committee of the Seventh National People's Congress on December 28, 1990, promulgated by Order No. 37 of the President of the People's Republic of China on December 28, 1990, and effective as of the same date) (PRC), Art. 6, paragraph 2, subparagraph 4.

99. Ling Bing, "Zhongri Donghai Wenti Yuanze Gongshi De Guojifa Xiaoli" [The International Law Effect of Principal Consensus between China and Japan on Issues concerning East China Sea], unpublished working paper.

100. Zhonghua Renmin Gongheguo Dijie Tiaoyue Chengxu Fa [Law on the Procedure of the Conclusion of Treaties] (adopted at the 17th Meeting of the Standing Committee of the Seventh National People's Congress on December 28, 1990, promulgated by Order No. 37 of the President of the People's Republic of China on December 28, 1990, and effective as of the same date) (PRC), Art. 7, paragraph 2, subparagraphs 1, 2, 3, 4, 5.

101. Zhonghua Renmin Gongheguo Dijie Tiaoyue Chengxu Fa [Law on the Procedure of the Conclusion of Treaties] (adopted at the 17th Meeting of the Standing Committee of the Seventh National People's Congress on December 28, 1990, promulgated by Order No. 37 of the President of the People's Republic of China on December 28, 1990, and effective as of the same date) (PRC), Art. 7, paragraph 2, subparagraph 6.

102. *Renmin Ribao*, November 22, 24, 1992.

Chapter Ten

President Jiang Zemin from 1993 to 2003

THE FORMATION OF JIANG ZEMIN AS "THE CORE OF LEADERSHIP"

GS Jiang Zemin Elected as the President and the CMC Chairman

With the old president, Yang Shangkun, retired from the Politburo in the CCP's Fourteenth National Congress, it became clear that he could not take the second term in the office of the president. Then who would be his successor?

According to official reports, this issue had been considered by the CCP well before the congress, and after the congress a preliminary plan was proposed for candidates for the top government posts and other high-level officials after "repeated consideration and consultation by the PSC and discussion by the Politburo meeting"; on March 4, 1993, the CCP's GS Jiang Zemin personally met with some "well respected old comrades who had retired from the leading positions" about the plan, and they "completely agreed with it"; several days' later, the plan was further consulted by the CCP with non-CCP people and endorsed by the CCP's Central Committee.[1]

On March 24, on behalf of the CCP, Hu Jjintao, then a PSC member and the standing chairman of the Presidium of the First Session of the Eighth NPC concurrently, filed this plan to the Presidium, who decided to accept and deliver it to the NPC delegations for consideration.[2] After one day's consideration by delegations, the Presidium adopted this plan as the final one and decided to put it to vote.[3] On March 27, the CCP GS Jiang Zemin was elected by the Eighth NPC as the new president and the chairman of the state

CMC by 2,858 and 2,894 affirmative votes, respectively, out of all 2,921 deputies present.[4] Upon election, President Jiang Zemin followed the example of his predecessor and claimed he would loyally perform those duties and responsibilities delegated by the constitution.[5]

According to the "Measures for Election and Decisions on Appointment" adopted by the Eighth NPC, in the presidential election, the number of the candidates should be equal to the number of people to be elected,[6] which meant that Jiang Zemin was the only candidate for the presidential election. Based on the official report, it seemed that the CCP's PSC proposed Jiang Zeming as the only presidential candidate. The official report did not mention how the Politburo and its Standing Committee made such a decision, but a Hong Kong media outlet said that it was decided by the voting of the nineteen-member Politburo in a meeting held on February 11, 1993, which seventeen members attended and fifteen were in favor of Jiang Zemin.[7]

However, Jiang Zemin was said to be not the only one who had been interested in the presidency. Several other people, including Li Peng,[8] Qiao Shi,[9] and Wang Zhen,[10] had been said to be competing for this post by some political biographers and reporters. Therefore, the "agreement" of those old cadres, especially Deng Xiaoping, must be very crucial. Without their approval, the Politburo's proposal for Jiang Zemin could have met strong opposition.

As a result, Jiang Zemin had held four political offices concurrently, that is, the CCP's GS, and the presidency and the CMC chairman of both the state and the CCP. Such a choice meant a significant change of the CCP's relation to the state apparatus. According to Deng Xiaoping's theory of separating the party from the state,[11] the CCP should not take the place of the state apparatus. Instead, divisions should be drawn between them. As an effort for this end, a series of measures had been taken,[12] including those important political positions had been put into different hands, such as the military chairman taken by Deng Xiaoping, the CCP's GS taken by Hu Yaobang and Zhao Ziyang, the premiership by Zhao Ziyang and Li Peng, and the presidency by Li Xiannian and Yang Shangkun, successively. But all these practices had been terminated by the election of Jiang Zemin into the presidency.[13]

From "Separating the Party from the State" to "the Core of Leadership"

Why would those old cadres, Deng Xiaoping in particular, favor such a new formula? As a matter of fact, there had been signs moving toward this way as early as in the spring of 1989, when Deng Xiaoping had intended to take action to strengthen the power of the GS Zhao Ziyang. Deng Xiaoping had considered resigning the military chairmanship and letting Zhao Ziyang take it. By doing so, Deng Xiaoping wished he could set an example of complete retirement for other old cadres to follow and Zhao Ziyang could have more political authority in the CCP's decision making by commanding the armed forces. But Zhao Ziyang opposed it, so Deng Xiaoping did not take action.[14]

Deng Xiaoping's idea should have been reinforced by the June 4 movement taking place several months later. During the movement, there had been an attempt to convene the NPCSC to overturn Deng Xiaoping's decision to use military force against the students,[15] but it failed as the NPCSC chairman Wan Li, who was then a Politburo member and been in favor of the students,[16] had not returned from his visit to Canada in time to convene the NPCSC meeting. President Yang Shangkun, also a Politburo member, had also originally been against the use of force, and had not changed his position until Deng Xiaoping made up his mind.[17] For Deng Xiaoping and other of CCP's old cadres, these could have suggested a challenge from the state apparatus that had been separated from the party under the idea of separating the state from the party. While the state apparatus obtained certain autonomy from the CCP, it could seek to achieve greater independence from the CCP, which would ultimately evade from the CCP's leadership over the state. Thus in their views, separation of the state from the party had to be ended and both the CCP and state had to be merged together once again, as Mao Zedong did. To concentrate the state power into the hands of the CCP, the CCP had to tighten its hold on the state apparatus, that is, putting the state posts directly into the hands of the PSC members instead of the Politburo members. As Jiang Zemin justified for such a new practice later after the June 4 movement, the CCP's leadership over the state would not be realized without the CCP's political leadership over the state apparatus.[18]

But this could have not been enough for Deng Xiaoping, a strong man who preferred concentration of power into one hand.[19] He could have wanted a leader like himself. Just when Jiang Zemin was designated as the new GS in June 1989, Deng Xiaoping lectured his new PSC members that:

> Our party has to establish the third generation leading group from now on. Any leading group needs to have a *core* ("hexin" in Chinese), without which its leadership would be unreliable. The core of the first generation leading group had been Chairman Mao, and that of the second generation leading group is in fact me. The third generation leading group must also have one, which should be comrade Jiang Zemin who all of you have accepted.[20]

Deng Xiaoping did not only pay lip service. Five months later, after Jiang Zemin took the office of the CCP's GS, Deng Xiaoping also carried out his original plan to resign from the double military chairmanship that he had not had the opportunity to carry out and Jiang Zemin took both of them. In the fourteenth party congress held in 1992, not only was Jiang Zemin decided to continue in the offices of the GS and the CCP's military chairman, but his major political opponents were removed from power, such as Yang Shangkun, but also the Central Consultative Committee, the power base of the retired old cadres, was abolished. As a result, before being elected as the president and the chairman of the state CMC, Jiang Zemin alone had held two of the most critical posts in the party and fairly erected his status within the CCP as Deng Xiaoping's successor.[21]

However, both posts had their own limitations. When the CCP was separated from the state, the GS had been an awkward position for Hu Yaobang and Zhao Ziyang, both of whom had been prevented from involvement with the State Council's decision making on economic affairs.[22] Although the state would no longer be separated from the CCP, the GS would still have difficulties in having his policies implemented by the government, if without a stake in the government. As the authority of the military commander was mainly in the armed forces, it could only facilitate the implementation in the military field of policies promoted by the GS. In other words, the general secretary, who was supposed to be the main speaker of the CCP's ideologies and Deng Xiaoping's reform and open-door policy, still needed other ways to ensure better implementation of his policies in civil administration of the State Council.

The presidency could help with its political potential and constitutional stipulations. By taking this office, the general secretary would have a stake in the government to voice his policies, which surely would have an impact on domestic politics in an increasingly globalizing country so that the GS could have a chance to be involved with the decision making of the civil administration. More importantly, although economic development would be the first priority for Jiang Zemin to strive for, the president had become increasingly active in China's foreign exchanges, as evidenced by performances of Li Xiannian and Yang Shangkun, and would become more and more important as China opens more. In one word, the presidency would grow into some office with greater significance.

Personally, Jiang Zemin surely wanted this post. Before being put into the position of the CCP's GS, Jiang Zemin had little experience in the CCP's highest decision-making level, and he had not commanded any army or won any battles. He was completely different from his predecessors Mao Zedong and Deng Xiaoping. If without the support of those old cadres, he could not have held on in Beijing for long.[23] But absent of those old cadres, how could he manage without enough political authority, which could only be remedied more by those state institutions than his experience as the Shanghai mayor? Therefore, supported by the old cadres and with his own efforts, Jiang Zemin, "the core of leadership," finally became the president.[24]

What Powers Could "the Core" Have?

Wearing four hats, what could "the core of leadership" mean to President Jiang Zemin? Constitutionally, the presidency was considered as a figurehead, whereas the office of the military chairmanship had been substantial. As the military commander, he had full power to direct the armed forces. Within the CCP, he was both the GS and a PSC member. As the GS, he could chair meetings of the Central Committee, Politburo, and its PSC; direct the working of the Central Secretariat; and set schedules for these meetings. As a PSC member, he would make decisions jointly with his colleagues based on the principle of democratic centralism and take charge of those duties that were assigned to him. Except neither the state constitution nor the CCP's constitution had ever mentioned "the core of leadership."

The concept of "the core of leadership" is not an invention of Deng Xiaoping. It could have come from Stalin and had already been used by Mao Zedong in his lectures. Far back in the era of Chairman Mao, he had frequently used it in his works, referring to the leading clique within the CCP's party committees. For example, amid his efforts to unify the party in 1942, Mao Zedong directed that the local CCP party committee should become the core of leadership, comprising three people in charge of affairs respectively concerning the party committee, government, and army, among whom the more capable one should be the secretary and "leading center" ("Lingdao Zhongxin" in Chinese).[25] By this direction, Mao Zedong also suggested that PSC was the core of leadership at the highest level of the CCP and its chairman, or he, was the leading center.

But Deng Xiaoping narrowed the scope to an individual. In Deng Xiaoping's mind, the core of leadership was no longer a small group. Instead, it was the leading center, or the chairman, and Jiang Zemin should be someone similar to Mao Zedong and him. Apart from the lecture of "the core of leadership," Deng Xiaoping was said to make another one to Jiang Zemin as follows:

> When Chairman Mao was alive, his words were the final decision; when I was alive, my words were the final decision. I will feel assured when your words were the final decision.[26]

If this story is true, Deng Xiaoping could have meant the core of leadership to be someone who could make the final decision, and intended Jiang Zemin to be that person. In this sense, Deng Xiaoping's core of the leadership is another form of Mao Zedong's chairmanship.

However, in reality, Deng Xiaoping was different from Mao Zedong in terms of making final decisions. After taking the CCP's chairmanship, Mao Zedong had held the offices of the CCP's chairman and chairman of the CMC for the rest of his life, even if he retired from the state chairmanship.

As the CCP's chairman, Mao Zedong had enjoyed "the power of last say," a privilege to veto all decisions made by his colleagues, including the second state chairman Liu Shaoqi. Since 1958, his chairmanship had gone so far as to become a personal tyranny.

When it came to Deng Xiaoping, his authority had been much discounted. He was not Mao Zedong. Mao Zedong was an ideological master with a dozen volumes of works, whereas Deng Xiaoping was more practical; while Mao Zedong decided on keynote policies, enjoying the power of having last say, Deng Xiaoping had to make compromises with, even concessions to, other old cadres on major issues even though he could have wanted to follow the example of Mao Zedong and had still remained in control on major issues for a certain period of time after he completely retired from all political positions.

According to the official reports on the fourth plenum of the fourteenth CCPCC held in the latter half of September of that year, the CCP's central leadership had completed the transition from the second generation to the third one.[27] This was construed by outsiders that Deng Xiaoping had finally relieved the control to Jiang Zemin.[28] Since then and till his death in February 1997, Deng Xiaoping was said to restrain himself from interfering with the new leaders, except in rare occasions, such as the Sino-US relations.[29] Therefore, Jiang Zemin and his young PSC colleagues had not obtained full autonomy from the control of Deng Xiaoping until he was able to do so physically.

Then which example should Jiang Zemin follow as the core of his leadership? Jiang Zemin could have thought about Mao Zedong. It was said that during the preparation for the CCP's Fifteenth National Congress held in 1997, the CCP's chairmanship, which had been established by Mao Zedong and abolished by Deng Xiaoping, had been suggested to restore by Jiang Zemin.[30] This was a sign that President Jiang Zemin had fairly consolidated his position since he started to work independently as the core of leadership and his influence had developed to the extent that he could be able to follow the example of Mao Zedong if he succeeded.

It is true that President Jiang Zemin is similar to chairman Mao Zedong in several ways. For example, both of them concurrently held four of the most important posts in China, that is, the CCP's leading post, the state presidency, and the double military chairmanships; whereas Mao Zedong dictated throughout his life, Jiang Zemin's political influence had seemingly not ended with his two terms of the presidency.

However, they are different from each other in other aspects. Their source of political power is different. Mao Zedong obtained his political authority from his warring experience, personality, and political tactics, to which Jiang Zemin could not possibly compare. The way by which they held those posts is different. Mao Zedong held the state chairmanship and the military chairmanship concurrently by constitutional provision, while Jiang Zemin did it by political arrangements. Their political decision-making powers were different also. Mao Zedong had been the CCP's chairmanship for all his life and overthrew the state chairmanship from behind the scenes, but Jiang Zemin's status as the core of leadership could be greatly impeded without the presidency and the military chairmanship, and he had to rely on formal arrangements and informal politics to prolong his influence after his retirement from the presidency. Therefore, President Jiang Zemin as the core of leadership was much more limited politically and constitutionally than Chairman Mao Zedong.

But this suggestion did not come true. The chairmanship was not restored and Jiang Zemin was only decided for the second time as the CCP's GS and the military chairman. It was said that it failed mainly due to opposition from some old cadres who were still alive then and feared the chairmanship might put the collective leadership at risk.[31] As a result, President Jiang Zemin had to maintain his status quo. In the next year, he was elected for a second term in the presidency and chairman of the CMC by the new NPC.[32]

As a result, Jiang Zemin had left with one example: Deng Xiaoping. Then it comes down to three fundamental questions: When could Jiang Zemin become independent from the influence of the second front, that is, those old cardres represented by Deng Xiaoping? Could Jiang Zemin have the power to veto decisions made by his PSC colleagues? And could Jiang Zemin still remain in control after he retired from office? Whereas the first question had been answered by Deng Xiaoping with his own self-restraint, answers to the next two questions remains to be investigated.

PRESIDENT JIANG ZEMIN'S PERFORMANCE IN TWO TERMS

His Fulfillment of Constitutional Duties

During his ten years in office President Jiang Zemin issued 181 orders, 94 in the first term and 87 in the second term, all of which either promulgated laws or were official appointments and removals. No other usages had been found in these presidential orders. Therefore, it seemed that the usage of the presidential order had been settled for these two purposes.

As provided by the constitution, the president also had to ratify the conclusion of international treaties and important agreements based on the NPCSC decision. Although China had entered into many treaties and agreements during the time when Li Xiannian and Yang Shangkun took office, no instruments of ratification had ever been published. Jiang Zemin followed their practices and no instruments of ratification had been found in public, except one rare occasion. In 2002, one instrument of ratification ratified by him was published.[33] The instrument, dated on November 1, 2001, was signed by him and countersigned by then Chinese foreign minister to ratify the treaty concerning China's entry into the World Trade Organization that was to be signed by Shi Guangsheng, then Chinese plenary representative and Chinese minister of foreign trade and economic cooperation, on November 11, 2001, in Doha. The NPCSC had made the decision to approve it on August 25, 2000, but it was published on November 9, 2001, a few days later than the president's ratification, which appeared to reverse the constitutional procedure.

His Unprecedented "Diplomacy by the Head of State"

The practice of "diplomacy by the head of state"[34] had not been new to China and is not an invention of 1990s when Jing Zemin had been in office. Since the founding of the PRC, each Chinese chairman and president had conducted diplomacy, such as paying state visits to other countries. Although the constitution made in 1982 does not provide for the president to conduct state visits to other countries, all these four presidents have always paid such overseas visits. Since the 1980s, the presidents have sent the special envoys on their behalf to some countries in certain cases. However, no one could compare with President Jiang Zemin in terms of scale or influence.

Up till now, Jiang Zemin was the Chinese president who visited the most countries. Chairman Mao Zedong had gone abroad twice and both of them were to the former Soviet Union. The second chairman, Liu Shaoqi, had visited more countries than his predecessor, but the visits were limited to third-world countries. Since 1983, the amount of foreign countries visited by Chinese presidents had been in rising steadily. President Li Xiannian visited twenty-two countries and extended his diplomacy to the developed countries, including the United States and some Western European countries. Although China was boycotted by the developed countries as a result of the June 4 Movement, President Yang Shangkun still visited about twenty countries, so the scale of foreign exchange was largely maintained. But even if all the presidential visits were added together, they could not compare with President Jiang Zemin, who visited more than seventy countries, covering all continents on Earth in ten years of office.

Additionally, he also attended some major international meetings held by important regional and international organizations. For example, he attended the UN Summit and initiated the first meeting by the five heads of states of the UN Security Council member states[35]; he was the only head of state who attended those annual meetings of Asian-Pacific Economic Cooperation Organization for ten consecutive years.[36] In particular, during his time, a new regional organization was given birth, that is, the Shanghai Cooperation Organization, whose founding members included China, Russia, and three other countries in Central Asia.

His Substantial Influence in "Diplomacy by the Head of State"

Being different from Li Xiannian and Yang Shangkun, President Jiang Zemin had been the core of the CCP's leadership; he also solely commanded the armed forces constitutionally. Therefore, he was the most politically important person in China, thus making his diplomacy much more decisive than his two predecessors. According to the CCP's principle of democratic centralism, every PSC member would normally take responsibility for certain areas of state affairs, normally by leading the CCP's Central Leading Groups. It was said that after the CCP's Fourteenth National Congress, the CCP's Central Leading Group of Foreign Affairs (CLGFA) had been put under Jiang Zemin's charge.[37] Previously it had been led by Premier Li Peng, suggesting the dominance over Chinese foreign policy had transferred from the State Council to the presidency. In this case, he could exercise direct control over the implementation of Chinese foreign policies.

One example can best illustrate such a dominant influence exerted by President Jiang Zemin in his conduction of diplomacy. From December 12-13, 2001, President Jiang Zemin spent two days visiting Myanmar. On the second day, news came that the United States would soon declare its withdraw from the anti-missile treaty it concluded with the former Soviet Union in 1972, for which both the United States President Bush and the Russian President Putin wanted to hold an emergent talk with President Jiang Zemin through hot lines.[38] Understandably, some other PSC members who would surely stand by in Beijing when Jiang Zemin had been out for visits were regarded to no avail in this emergency, suggesting that President Jiang Zemin was the final one to decide China's major foreign policy.

Another example of President Jiang Zemin's substantial influence on Chinese foreign affairs concerns Chinese special envoys. As discussed previously, since the founding of the PRC, the American practice of deploying special envoys had been adopted by China and they have been constantly sent to the rest of the world either in the capacity of the Chinese government, the Chinese president, or jointly of the Chinese government and the CCP since the 1980s. More than accepting this practice, President Jiang Zemin had made innovations to it by directly bringing about the creation of the new office of Chinese Special Envoy on the Middle East issues.[39] In April 2000, President Jiang Zemin paid a visit to Palestine. During his talk with Arafat, the Palestinian leader advised that China appoint a special envoy especially for issues concerning the Middle East. His advice was accepted by President Jiang Zemin, who continued to press for implementation. As a result, the Office of Special Envoy on the Middle East issues was established in 2002.[40] By now,

China has appointed two Offices of Special Envoys for special purposes, that is, issues concerning the Middle East and North Korean nuclear development.[41]

The third example of president Jiang Zemin's important influence on Chinese diplomacy could be found in China's so-called "partnership diplomacy." As well known, China had established various kinds of partnership relations with different countries. However, few could imagine that the first strategic partnership that China established with a foreign country had developed due to conversation. In November 1993, President Jiang Zemin paid a state visit to Brazil. In the morning of November 23, the first day of his arrival, President Jiang Zemin held a talk with Brazilian President Itamar Franco. During their conversation, President Jiang Zemin suggested that both sides should set their minds to the future, develop friendly cooperation from a strategic perspective, and establish a long-term, stable, and mutually beneficial relationship. In response, President Franco said that relationship between Brazil and China was a strategic partnership. Then in the afternoon, when the Chinese foreign minister, Qian Qichen, met Amorim, the Brazilian foreign minister, his Brazilian counterpart said that since both heads of state had agreed to establish a strategic partner relationship between China and Brazil, such a status should be recognized by the Chinese government. Hearing of this, Qian Qichen immediately gave his confirmation.[42]

Questions Concerning "Diplomacy by the Head of State"

In diplomacy by the head of state, President Jiang Zemin not only had handled international emergencies, but also made innovations to China's diplomatic practices. One of these innovations was his new function of negotiating and signing international treaties and agreements. During his two terms, President Jiang Zemin signed bilateral statements, agreements, treaties and conventions, communiqués, and manifestos with other foreign heads of state, for instance, the Russian presidents. Disregarding the question of how President Jiang Zemin was authorized to sign these documents, his new practice of signing international treaties and agreements could still give rise to constitutional concerns for the role of the NPCSC.

It seems that the NPCSC handled these documents signed by President Jiang Zemin in different ways. The NPCSC made relevant decisions on those documents titled as "treaties," "conventions," and "agreements," which then have been ratified by the president. Up till now, no decisions have been found made by the NPCSC on other documents such as bilateral statements, communiqués, and manifestos. It could be argued that those documents would require no decision from the NPCSC if they had no substance as to be qualified as "treaties" or "agreements," but it is also questionable as to what could constitute substance in international documents, and different opinions have been proposed to some of those documents.[43] Therefore, even when the president was separated from other political positions, he could still act outside the scope of constitutional provisions.

CONCLUSION

Witnessing the sandwiched awkwardness of the GS cornering between the old cadres in the second front and the first front leaders in the state apparatus, and splits and controversies among the PSC members during the June 4 movement, Deng Xiaoping retreated from his early reforms and reversed his earlier practices of separating the CCP from the state. He not only made his successor, the CCP's GS Jiang Zemin, "the core of the third generation leadership" by taking the presidency and the chairmanship of CMC concurrently in 1993, but he also designated Hu Jintao the youngest PSC member together with Jiang Zemin and Jiang Zemin's successor. This is virtually a return to Mao Zedong's example and an expansion of his idea of "two fronts."

As a result of the step-by-step succession arrangement, political life of President Jiang Zemin far exceeded the constitutional limitation of two terms of office and underwent a "life cycle" of gradually increasing and declining with the extension of his two terms of office. Since his elevation into the PSC as the CCP's new GS, he became the key successor and took part in the CCP's political decision making, but his weight was greatly restricted by those CCP leaders who concurrently held government positions. After he took the double military chairmanships, his political authority began to ascend. When he successfully took the presidency, his power was further consolidated with the aid of those constitutional functions, especially the diplomacy of the head of state. His status as the core of leadership was finally erected with Deng Xiaoping's death. His political power reached its peak when he won a second term of the presidency and the military chairmanship, after which he had to gradually relieve those offices one by one to his successor Hu Jintao, who had served as a "second front" ever since they were both chosen by PSC at the same time.

NOTES

1. *Renmin Ribao*, April 1, 1993.
2. *Renmin Ribao*, April 1, 1993.
3. *Renmin Ribao*, March 27, 1993.
4. *Renmin Ribao*, March 28, 1993.
5. *Renmin Ribao*, April 1, 1993.
6. *Renmin Ribao*, March 21, 1993.

7. Luo Bing, "Renda Qianxi De Renshi Dazhan" [Personnel War before the Eve of the People's Congress], *Zhengming* (March 1993): 6-8. However, the CCP's Politburo elected by the 14th Central Committee had twenty members.

8. Yang Bingzhang, *Xiaoping Dazhuan* [Biography of Xiaoping] (Hong Kong: Shidai Guoji Chuban Youxian Gongsi, 2004), 320.

9. Luo Bing, "Shisi Da Dengceng Renxuan Niding" [Candidates for Top Officials of the Cpc's Fourteenth Congress Decided], *Zhengming* (September 1992): 6-8.

10. Du Lin and Yang Mingdi (trans.), *Jiang Zemin Zhuan* [Biography of Jiang Zemin] (Hong Kong: Mingjing Chubanshe, 1999), 279.

11. For study about Deng Xiaoping's theory of separating the state from the party, see Chen Yizi, "The Decision Process behind the 1986-1989 Political Reforms," in Carol Lee Hamrin and Suisheng Zhao (eds.), *Decision-Making in Deng's China: Perspectives from Insiders* (Armonk, NY: M.E. Sharpe, 1995), 135-139; Hsiao Pen, "Separating the Party from the Government," in Carol Lee Hamrin and Suisheng Zhao (eds.), *Decision-Making in Deng's China: Perspectives from Insiders* (Armonk, NY: M.E. Sharpe, 1995), 153-163.

12. Yan Ying, *Zhongguo Gongchandang Lingdao Tizhi De Lishi Yanbian* [Evolution of the CCP's Leadership System] (Beijing: Zhonggong Dangshi Chubanshe, 2007), 252-254.

13. Kou Jianwen, *Zhonggong Jingying Zhengzhi De Yanbian: Zhidu Hua Yu Quanli Zhuanyi 1978-2004* [Evolution of the CCP's Elite Politics: Institutionalization and Transfer of Power 1978-2004] (Taiwan: Wunan Tushu Gufen Youxian Gongsi, 2005), 141.

14. Zhao Ziyang, *Gaige Licheng* [The Reform History] (Hong Kong: Xin Shiji Chubanshe, 2009), 74, 265-266.

15. Zhao Ziyang, *Gaige Licheng* [The Reform History] (Hong Kong: Xin Shiji Chubanshe, 2009), 52-53.

16. Zhao Ziyang, *Gaige Licheng* [The Reform History] (Hong Kong: Xin Shiji Chubanshe, 2009), 41.

17. Zong Fengming (ed.), *Zhao Ziyang Ruanjing Zhong De Tanhua* [Zhao Ziyang: Captive Conversations] (Hong Kong: Kaifang Chubanshe, 2007), 54-55.

18. Jiang Zemin, *Jiang Zemin Wenxuan* [Selected Works of Jiang Zemin] (Beijing: Renmin Chubanshe, 2006), vol. 1, 112.

19. Zhao Ziyang thought Deng Xiaoping preferred the concentration of power so that things could be done effectively. In particular, he indicated that Deng Xiaoping had once told Chen Yun that there should only be one "mother in law" ("Popo" in Chinese) within the CCP leadership, meaning that power should not be shared and Deng Xiaoping should be the one who made the final decisions. See Zong Fengming (ed.), *Zhao Ziyang Ruanjing Zhong De Tanhua* [Zhao Ziyang: Captive Conversations] (Hong Kong: Kaifang Chubanshe, 2007), 74.

20. Zhonggong Zhongyang Wenxian Bianji Weiyuan Hui (ed.), *Deng Xiaoping Wenxuan* [Selected Works of Deng Xiaoping] (Beijing: Renmin Chubanshe, 1993), vol. 3, 309-310.

21. Robert Lawrence Kuhn, Tan Zheng, and Yu Haijiang et al. (trans.), *Ta Gaibian Le Zhongguo Jiang Zemin Zhuan* [The Man Who Changed China: The Life and Legacy of Jiang Zemin] (Shanghai: Shanghai Yiwen Chubanshe, 2005), 184-185.

22. About Deng Xiaoping's settling disputes within the CCP Politburo Standing Committee, see Zong Fengming (ed.), *Zhao Ziyang Ruanjing Zhong De Tanhua* [Zhao Ziyang: Captive Conversations] (Hong Kong: Kaifang Chubanshe, 2007), 139-140; Zhao Ziyang, *Gaige Licheng* [The Reform History] (Hong Kong: Xin Shiji Chubanshe, 2009), 257-258.

23. Jiang Zeming and his family had worried about this before deciding to go to Beijing. See Robert Lawrence Kuhn, Tan Zheng, and Yu Haijiang et al. (trans.), *Ta Gaibian Le Zhongguo Jiang Zemin Zhuan* [The Man Who Changed China: The Life and Legacy of Jiang Zemin] (Shanghai: Shanghai Yiwen Chubanshe, 2005), 143-144.

24. Zong Fengming (ed.), *Zhao Ziyang Ruanjing Zhong De Tanhua* [Zhao Ziyang: Captive Conversations] (Hong Kong: Kaifang Chubanshe, 2007), 241.

25. Arts. 1 and 3, "Zhongyang Guanyu Jiaqiang Tongyi Lingdao Yu Jingbing Jianzheng De Zhishi" [The CCPCC Direction on Strengthening Unified Leadership and Simplifying Army and Government, December 1, 1942].

26. Zong Fengming (ed.), *Zhao Ziyang Ruanjing Zhong De Tanhua* [Zhao Ziyang: Captive Conversations] (Hong Kong: Kaifang Chubanshe, 2007), 75.

27. See http://cpc.people.com.cn/GB/64162/64168/64567/65396/4441762.html.

28. Gao Xin, *Jiang Zemin De Quanli Zhilu* [Jiang Zemin's Road to Power] (Hong Kong: Mingjing Chubanshe, 1997), 215-219; Du Lin and Yang Mingdi (trans.), *Jiang Zemin Zhuan* [Biography of Jiang Zemin] (Hong Kong: Mingjing Chubanshe, 1999), 321-322; Robert Lawrence Kuhn, Tan Zheng, and Yu Haijiang et al. (trans.), *Ta Gaibian Le Zhongguo Jiang Zemin Zhuan* [The Man Who Changed China: The Life and Legacy of Jiang Zemin] (Shanghai: Shanghai Yiwen Chubanshe, 2005), 208-215.

29. Robert Lawrence Kuhn, Tan Zheng, and Yu Haijiang et al. (trans.), *Ta Gaibian Le Zhongguo Jiang Zemin Zhuan* [The Man Who Changed China: The Life and Legacy of Jiang Zemin] (Shanghai: Shanghai Yiwen Chubanshe, 2005), 219.

30. Zong Fengming (ed.), *Zhao Ziyang Ruanjing Zhong De Tanhua* [Zhao Ziyang: Captive Conversations] (Hong Kong: Kaifang Chubanshe, 2007), 227; Du Lin and Yang Mingdi (trans.), *Jiang Zemin Zhuan* [Biography of Jiang Zemin] (Hong Kong: Mingjing Chubanshe, 1999), 421.

31. Du Lin and Yang Mingdi (trans.), *Jiang Zemin Zhuan* [Biography of Jiang Zemin] (Hong Kong: Mingjing Chubanshe, 1999), 422.

32. *Renmin Ribao*, March 17, 1993.

33. Standing Comm. Nat'l People's Cong. Gaz, special edition, 2002.

34. For study on "diplomacy by the head of state," see David H. Dunn (Ed.), *Diplomacy at the Highest Level: The Evolution of International Summitry* (London: Macmillan, 1996), 3-37; G. R. Berridge, *Diplomacy: Theory and Practice* (New York: Prentice Hall, 1995), 78-96; Elmer Plischke, *Diplomat in Chief: The President at the Summit* (New York: Praeger Publishers, 1986), 1-17.

35. Zhong Zhicheng, *Weile Shijie Geng Meihao: Jiang Zemin Chufang Jishi* [For a Better World: Documentary of Jiang Zemin's Foreign Visits] (Beijing: Shijie Zhishi Chubanshe, 2006), 477-478.

36. Zhong Zhicheng, *Weile Shijie Geng Meihao: Jiang Zemin Chufang Jishi* [For a Better World: Documentary of Jiang Zemin's Foreign Visits] (Beijing: Shijie Zhishi Chubanshe, 2006), 652.

37. Robert Lawrence Kuhn, Tan Zheng, and Yu Haijiang et al. (trans.), *Ta Gaibian Le Zhongguo Jiang Zemin Zhuan* [The Man Who Changed China: The Life and Legacy of Jiang Zemin] (Shanghai: Shanghai Yiwen Chubanshe, 2005), 185. According to this author, Jiang Zemin also took charge of two other Central Leading Small Groups on economic affairs and Taiwan issue. However, there is another opinion that it was Li Peng who took charge of the Central Leading Small Group on foreign affairs and Jiang Zemin led other three groups, that is, the Taiwan issue, financial and economic affairs, and judicial affairs. See Du Lin and Yang Mingdi (trans.), Jiang Zemin Zhuan [Biography of Jiang Zemin] (Hong Kong: Mingjing Chubanshe, 1999), at 278. The third opinion held that Jiang Zemin took charge of the Central Leading Small Group on political and judicial affairs, party displinary affairs, and propaganda affairs. See Gao Xin, Jiang Zemin De Quanli Zhilu [Jiang Zemin's Road to Power] (Hong Kong: Mingjing Chubanshe, 1997), at 198.

38. Zhong Zhicheng, *Weile Shijie Geng Meihao: Jiang Zemin Chufang Jishi* [For a Better World: Documentary of Jiang Zemin's Foreign Visits] (Beijing: Shijie Zhishi Chubanshe, 2006), 584.

39. Zhong Zhicheng, *Weile Shijie Geng Meihao: Jiang Zemin Chufang Jishi* [For a Better World: Documentary of Jiang Zemin's Foreign Visits] (Beijing: Shijie Zhishi Chubanshe, 2006), 426.

40. Zhong Zhicheng, *Weile Shijie Geng Meihao: Jiang Zemin Chufang Jishi* [For a Better World: Documentary of Jiang Zemin's Foreign Visits] (Beijing: Shijie Zhishi Chubanshe, 2006), 433.

41. For a relevant dissusion on Chinese special envoys, in particular those two special envoys, see information on the website of the Chinese Ministry of Foreign Affairs.

42. Zhong Zhicheng, *Weile Shijie Geng Meihao: Jiang Zemin Chufang Jishi* [For a Better World: Documentary of Jiang Zemin's Foreign Visits] (Beijing: Shijie Zhishi Chubanshe, 2006), 50.

43. Ling Bing, *Zhongri Donghai Wenti Yuanze Gongshi De Guojifa Xiaoli* [The International Law Effect of Principal Consensus between China and Japan on Issues concerning East China Sea], unpublished working paper.

Chapter Eleven

President Hu Jintao from 2003 to 2013

PRESIDENT HU JINTAO NOT BEING "THE CORE OF LEADERSHIP"

The New GS Not Being "the Core of Leadership"

In 2002, the CCP convened its sixteenth National Congress. As usual, this congress elected a new Central Committee, Politburo, and its PSC. Unsurprisingly, Hu Jintao became the CCP's new GS because he had been designated as the apparent heir to Jiang Zemin by Deng Xiaoping and stood by for this day for more than ten years. As early as in 1992, he entered the CCP's PSC as the youngest member in the fourteenth party congress for the first time. Five years later, he was kept in this highest decision-making body by the fifteenth party congress. According to Zhao Ziyang, his entry into the PSC was due to the recommendation of Deng Liqun,[1] a conservative CCP senior cadre. It has been alleged by political writers that it was Deng Xiaoping who not only accepted this recommendation and promoted Hu Jintao to the PSC, but also designated him as the successor to Jiang Zemin.[2] Hu Jintao's status as the chosen successor became apparent when he was elected into the office of the vice-president and vice-chairman of the CMC, respectively, in 1998 and 2000.

However, when the new PSC was made public, it was surprisingly announced that Hu Jintao was the "General Secretary," not the "core of leadership." This deviated from the way how Jiang Zemin succeeded Deng Xiaoping. Almost at the same time when Jiang Zemin was appointed as the GS, he was designated by Deng Xiaoping as "the core of the third generation leadership." The GS was coupled with the title of "the core of leadership." Since Hu Jintao was also designated by Deng Xiaoping to succeed Jiang

Zemin, it could be presumed that Deng Xiaoping could have intended Hu Jintao as "the core of the fourth generation leadership."

Hence, how Hu Jintao could succeed Jiang Zemin might be different. Although it had been widely believed that Deng Xiaoping had chosen Hu Jintao as Jiang Zemin's successor, no more details had ever been released about what kind of arrangements Deng Xiaoping had made regarding their succession, including the inheritability of the title of the core of leadership. With the death of Deng Xiaoping, their succession became more mysterious. Jiang Zemin's succession to Deng Xiaoping had been set by Deng Xiaoping, by which Jiang Zemin first took the office of the GS together with the title "the core of leadership," and then the military chairmanship of the CCP and state, then finally became the president. Will Hu Jintao follow the same order of succession as Jiang Zemin and inherit all these offices and titles from him as well?

Among the four offices, only the presidency is subject to the constitutional limit of term of office. According to the constitution, the president should not hold more than two consecutive terms. Because Jiang Zemin already had taken two terms in succession, the presidency would definitely have to change hands in due course. Therefore, Hu Jintao might take this office first. In this case, he would follow the example of Liu Shaoqi. After taking the state chairmanship, Liu Shaoqi had been intended by Mao Zedong to take the CCP's chairmanship and possibly the military chairmanship at a future time. But such an old formula was overthrown by the sixteenth party congress, which changed the way by making Hu Jintao as the GS first.

It is said that there was an agreement among the Central Committee elected by the sixteenth party congress that the new leadership headed by Hu Jintao would seek advice from Jiang Zemin, the core of leadership, on major issues, at least in two years from then on.[3] This could be true because there was a precedent previously in Deng Xiaoping's era when Deng Xiaoping had also been acknowledged to continue in command after he had retired from all political positions, in spite that he remained silent on most issues, partly due to his physical disability, and also partial to his self-restraint in his late years. But he still had exerted a decisive influence on major issues in a few critical occasions.

But it was an embarrassing situation because during that period of time, two cores of leadership had been co-existing, that is, Deng Xiaoping as the core of the second generation and Jiang Zemin as the core of the third generation. To avoid further embarrassment it would be better to pass the title of the core of leadership to Hu Jintao at a later time when Jiang Zemin followed the example of Deng Xiaoping to maintain some prolonged control. After all, Hu Jintao just started his way of succession.

His Election into the Presidency by the NPC

Then understandably, the next office that Hu Jintao would succeed from Jiang Zemin would be the presidency. Several months later, the tenth NPC convened its first session in March 2003. As usual, the congress elected its Presidium, made a measure regarding election and decision of government leaders, and decided the candidates for those leading political offices. On March 15, Hu Jintao was elected as the fourth president by 2,937 deputies in favor of him, with four vetoes and three abstentions.[4]

His Succession to the Military Chairmanship

In Deng Xiaoping's model, the military chairmanships should be the next targets for a complete transition of power from Jiang Zemin to Hu Jintao. Jiang Zemin did not want to give up,[5] but he had to let it go. As there is no constitutional limitation on the term of this office, the question would be: How soon would Jiang Zemin evacuate from both positions? Just about six months later after Jiang Zemin became the GS, Deng Xiaoping resigned from this position and Jiang Zemin succeeded him as the military chairmen of both the CCP and state.

However, it took Hu Jintao about two more years after taking the presidency to become the CCP's military commander, much longer than Jiang Zemin, who did not retire from the military chairmanship until the fourth Plenum of the Sixteenth CCPCC held in September 2004, thus paving the way for Hu Jintao's succession to the state military chairmanship. On March 13, 2005, Hu Jintao was elected duly by the NPC as the new chairman of the state CMC, with 2,886 supporting votes, six vetoes, and five abstentions.[6]

POLITICAL IMPLICATION OF "THE CORE OF LEADERSHIP" NOT BEING INHERITED

"The Core of Leadership" Not Inherited

By 2005, Hu Jintao had taken all those four political offices from his predecessor. Surely this was a great achievement, because it had been a peaceful succession of the CCP after the death of Deng Xiaoping. By Jiang Zemin taking those offices, Deng Xiaoping successfully made a new core of leadership for the CCP. Similarly, Hu Jintao should have become the core of the new leadership.

However, as a matter of fact, this did not happen and the title of the core of leadership has not been passed on to Hu Jintao, even when he became the GS and the CCP's military chairman for the second time in the CCP's Seventeenth National Congress, and was elected for a second term into the offices of presidency and state military chairman in March 2008 by 2,956 NPC deputies.[7] Till the end of his two terms of office, President Hu Jintao had not inherited the title "the core of leadership."

On the contrary, it seems that the title of the core of leadership could still be held by the former president Jiang Zemin. On October 1, 2009, when the PRC celebrated its sixtieth anniversary of its founding, Jiang Zemin appeared together on the Tiananmen Square with the nine PSC members, being ranked as the second one only after Hu Jintao. While other CCP former leaders did not enjoy such a preferential treatment, Jiang Zemin's prominent appearance could suggest that he could still maintain a certain influence as the core of the third-generation leadership even after he has been retired for years, like Deng Xiaoping did in the past.

What could the title mean to President Hu Jintao? Obviously, President Hu Jintao was different from Jiang Zemin and had to accept the prolonged influence of the second front, that is, the third generation of leadership, represented by Jiang Zemin.

Second, without being the core of leadership, Hu Jintao's weight in the PSC could not be comparable to that of his predecessor, resulting in a more equal relationship between Hu Jintao and his PSC colleagues. In other words, Hu Jintao could be in an equal relationship with his PSC colleagues, and could not be able to enjoy the advantages that Jiang Zemin could have as the core of leadership. As a result, Hu Jintao could have to follow the rule of "one person, one vote" and vote equally with his colleagues and would only be able to control those areas of works that had been put under his charge and not interfere with other members' areas of works that they were assigned, except by voting collectively on major issues.

More questionable was the concerned with the issue of the succession to Hu Jintao. As the core of the second-generation leadership, Deng Xiaoping not only decided Jiang Zemin as the core of the third-generation leadership, but also determined Jiang Zemin's successor, that is, Hu Jintao. If such a power to appoint the future successor could be regarded as to belong to the core of leadership, Jiang Zemin would be able to decide who could succeed Hu Jintao. In 2008, while the eleventh NPC elected Hu Jintao again as the president, it also elected Xi Jinping as the vice-president. According to the official report, before the election, Xi Jinping went through a process of "inner-party democracy" ("Dangnei Minzhu," in Chinese).[8] However, it has been speculated that his promotion was contributed to Jiang Zemin. His intimacy with Jiang Zemin could also be found in his meeting with German Chancellor Angela Mekel during his visit to Germany in 2009 when the Chinese vice-president not only presented to his German host two books written by Jiang Zemin, but also paid regard to her on behalf of Jiang Zemin,[9] which could give rise to constitutional queries. If his acts were a part of his official business, he could have obtained authorization from President Hu

Jintao because he constitutionally "may exercise such functions and powers of the president as the president may entrust to him." Otherwise, his acts would be unconstitutional, unless his acts were of a private nature, in which case he could seek to develop a personal relationship with his German host by such a presentation and no constitutional concerns would arise, even if he did it on behalf of Jiang Zemin.

Reduced Authority of President Hu Jintao

Without a paramount leader, decision making in the PSC could become more flattened, in which case the decision-making power of the president in the PSC is decided both by collective decision making and the division of work among its members.[10] First, he has to vote together with his PSC colleagues on major issues[11] and rely on collaboration in voting with his PSC colleagues if to prevail. Second, he can have some areas of works under his charge, which are divided to him and he can have more say. In particular, when he takes charge of relevant Central Leading Small Group (CLSG), such as the CLSGFA, the one concerning foreign affairs, he can be the major decision maker of China's foreign affairs. Third, he enjoys certain functions provided by the party constitution to the GS, such as convening the Politburo and PSC, and presiding over the Central Secretariat,[12] the latter of which could also make him more influencial in the CCP's policy execution. It was alleged that in the PSC decision making, no matter that in the Sixteenth CCPCC or the Seventeenth CCPCC, Hu Jintao could not obtain a majority when voting was cast because he and his supporters did amount to that extent. Hence, compared with his predecessor, President Hu Jintao seems to be less authoritative in the CCP's decision making. In conclusion, not being the core of leadership, President Hu Jintao has been reduced to a more equal member within the PSC than his predecessor.

On the other hand, even if Hu Jintao was less authoritative politically than his predecessor, he is still the president with substantial influence on China's diplomacy because the constitutional institutions could give Hu Jintao the legitimate authority to supplement his deficit within the CCP as the GS. As provided by the constitution, the chairman assumes overall responsibility for the work of the CMC.[13] Hu Jintao could claim his personal responsibility to counter against intervention from other PSC members who could insist on the collective leadership over the army, especially when the military diplomacy is concerned. Furthermore, he can also obtain extra authority by asserting his constitutional functions, especially after the constitution was amended in 2004, which could also give him extra potential to obtain substantial influence by way of "diplomacy of the head of state."

AMBIGUOUS CONSTITUTIONAL AMENDMENT IN 2004

New Function of the President

In 2004, the CCP suggested that the constitution once again be revised.[14] Accordingly, the tenth NPC adopted the fourth constitutional amendment in its second session, by which a new function to "engage in activities involving state affairs" was written into article 81 of the constitution.[15] As such, this article now reads:

> The president of the people's republic of China, on behalf of the people's republic of China, engages in activities involving state affairs and receives foreign diplomatic representatives and, in pursuance of the decisions of the Standing Committee of the National People's Congress, appoints or recalls plenipotentiary representatives abroad, and ratifies or abrogates treaties and important agreements concluded with foreign states.

According to the legislative explanation made by the NPCSC, such a revision was made because "diplomacy by the head of state has become an important way of international exchanges in today's world, and the constitution has to provide for it."[16]

It is true that the diplomacy by the president is not an invention of the 1990s, when Jing Zemin had been in office. As a matter of fact, it has been always practiced since the first president, Li Xiannian, took office in 1982. While the constitution does not provide for the president to conduct state visits to other countries, all four of these presidents have done so. Since the 1980s, the presidents have sent special envoys on their behalf to countries in certain cases. Taking into consideration Chairman Mao Zedong and Liu Shaoqi, Chinese presidents have become growingly active "on behalf of the People's Republic of China" in foreign affairs so as to create many political conventions by their practices, such as signing treaties with other countries with the delegation from the NPC,[17] attending important international meetings, interviewing and reaching major international agreements with the head of states of other countries, announcing the reduction of customs, and promising assistance to other countries.[18] The 2004 amendment can be seen as a remedy to those political practices. In other words, those diplomatic practices established by these presidents suggest that the presidents had exercised their powers and functions outside the constitutional provisions before the 2004 constitutional amendment.

Ambiguous "Activities Involving State Affairs"

While endorsing old practices, it also gives rise to new ambiguities. The first one is the term "activities involving state affairs." As matter of fact, the idea is not new. Far back when the constitution was drafted in 1982, a NPCSC member had suggested that the power and function of the president should include to "pay state visit"[19] to foreign countries. In practice, President Jiang Zemin's performances has acted far beyond the scope of paying state visits to much broader "activities involving state affairs," all of which could give rise to questions such as what are "activities involving state affairs," and would they concern foreign affairs, or do they also refer to those relating to domestic affairs?

Furthermore, whether the president's "activities involving state affairs" needs a prior decision of the NPC and NPCSC is also uncertain. According to the constitutional text, it is written before "in pursuance of the decisions of the Standing Committee of the National People's Congress" and followed by the function of "receiving foreign diplomatic representatives." As the latter function has been always regarded as a ceremonial function without any substance and requires no prior decision from the NPC and NPCSC, such a wording can be construed that this new "activities involving state affairs" is no more than alike and the president can carry out independently from the NPC and NPCSC. If so, this could further suggest that the NPCSC does not have to supervise the president's "activities involving state affairs."

But such a literal understanding could not explain all practices. On one hand, it could not be applied to all practices of President Jiang Zemin; on the other hand, even for Presidents Li Xiannian and Yang Shangkun, who were practically considered as figureheads, the NPCSC still had received reports on their foreign visits submitted by those officials from the State Council who had accompanied presidents' overseas trips, such as the foreign minister. Besides, "receiving foreign diplomatic representatives" can be substantial so as to give the president independence in foreign affairs. In the United States, "in practice, the power to receive, or in particular cases, to refuse to receive ambassadors had made the president the sole official recipient of communications from foreign governments and the sole determiner of which governments the United States will recognize diplomatically."[20] In a word, it remains unclear whether the new function is only ceremonial or a substantial power.

Is the President the Head of State?

More problematic concerns the president's status as the head of state of the PRC. As no clear stipulation has been provided by all those constitutional documents, that is, the 1949 Common Program, and the 1954 and 1982 constitutions, two opposing theories have been suggested in this regard over the years. Among various suggestions, Mao Zedong insisted that the chairman was not the head of state because the chairman was subject to the NPC and performed his duty based on the decisions of the NPC and its Standing

Committee; the chairman was just a representative of the NPC. Based on his idea, the "collective theory" has been the mainstay, claiming that the head of state of the PRC was a collective one and the chairman or president was no more than a representative of this collective head of state.[21] As no constitutional interpretation has been made to give a clear answer to this question, those earlier legislative records were undoubtedly the most authoritative in support of this theory.

But this collective theory has been increasingly challenged by some constitutional lawyers.[22] It has been argued that theoretically, a country should not go along without a head of state[23]; the power and function of the presidency falls into the scope of those heads of state in other countries; the president acting on the decisions of the NPC and NPCSC is just a way that the president carries out his constitutional duty. Practically, it is the president, not the NPC and NPCSC, that has been titled as the head of state and treated alike by Chinese and foreign governments in various occasions, especially during international visits, which has become a political and constitutional convention.[24] Besides, while a collective head of state is not necessarily democratic, an individual head of state does not equal to personal tyranny. Whether the head of state is individual or collective has nothing to do with the prevention of personal tyranny, which relies on a democratic system, rule of law, and strengthened supervision.[25] Therefore, the presidency is the head of state of the PRC.[26]

Now by "diplomacy of the head of state," legislators suggest that the president is the head of state of the PRC. Although its legal validity remains arguable as a piece of legislative explanation, it is the first time that such a clear and positive statement has been made by legislators in this regard and directly in conflict with previous official recordings and academic opinions. If the new explanation takes effect in the future, the president would not have to seek delegation from the premier or the foreign minister to sign a treaty because the Vienna Convention on the Law of Treaties has said that "the head of state can perform all acts relating to the conclusion of a treaty without having to produce full powers."[27] Then Mao Zedong's theory would be fundamentally changed.

While both sides acknowledge that the power and function of the chairmanship and presidency generally conforms to the theoretical category of the head of state,[28] and in practice the president has been treated as the head of state, they disagree on the relationship of the chairman and president with the NPC. The traditional views emphasized the theoretical underpinning of this office that the chairman or president was considered as the representative and subordinate to the NPC. On the other hand, the new opinions stress the practical role of the chairmen and presidents and claim their independence from the NPC based on their performance of constitutional power and function.

Can the NPC system accommodate an individual head of state? It seems that the new opinions are hard to prevail. Supported by original documents, the traditional side has legislative authority and theoretical coherence; those performances by the chairmen and presidents are no more than examples of their representative role on behalf of the collective head of state, and do not necessarily require that the chairman and president should be titled as the head of state. After all, in some foreign countries, the president performs as the head of state without being recognized as the head of state by his constitution, like the president of the United States.

However, the argument concerning personal tyranny does have substance. According to the traditional views, the NPC is the supreme organ that combines deliberation with execution; and other governmental organs, including the president, are no more than enforcement arms of the NPC. By putting the president under the NPC and its Standing Committee, the president surely has no excuse to act independently, thus leaving no chance for personal tyranny by the president. Therefore, in such a theory, the NPC and NPCSC are designed to control the president and prevent him from abusing his power. But to what extent such a theory has been effective in practice needs further investigation.

On the other hand, if the president is accorded as the head of state, his power and function will enjoy the guarantee of the constitution, which makes the NPC and NPCSC less able to exert influence on the president. As the sole representative of PRC, the president would be more independent from the NPC and NPCSC when performing his constitutional power and function. In other words, the president has to be more accountable to the constitution than to the NPC and NPCSC. However, if taking the political reality of the PRC into consideration, it could be unlikely that the constitution could play such a role. Without much more precautions, the constitutional head of state could be no more than another imperial crown to a personal tyranny. Then ultimately, the NPC and NPCSC could be first one to strengthen the responsibility as a constitutional guardian against personal tyranny of the head of state. Therefore, a more fundamental question concerns this dispute: can the NPC and NPCSC effectively achieve this goal?

Power Division between the President and Premier Changed

In retrospect, taking the chairmanship provided by the 1949 Common Program into comparison, it was suggested that over the years, the power and function of this office had been in continuous decline and it has become more and more nominal.[29] However, such a declining trend seemed to be reversed by the 2004 constitutional amendment. It can be more substantial than a mere numeric increase of function. Not only has the diplomacy by the president had great impact on China's internal affairs, as suggested by those above mentioned practical conventions, but also if the "state affairs" is not limited within the boundary of diplomacy and construed to include the domestic affairs.[30] After all, in practice, PRC chairmen and presidents have always been intimately associated with home affairs. If so doing, this constitutional provision can become a way for the president to engage in his activities at home.

More questionable, this constitutional amendment does not clearly require the president to engage in activities involving state affairs "in pursuance of the decisions of the NPC and its Standing Committee," as did for most other powers of the president, the president does not have to seek prior permission from the state's supreme organ. Therefore, this amendment may implicitly have much broader effects over time.

With such constitutional ambiguities, this amendment has some significant political implications. First, it changes the constitutional division of power between the president and premier with respect to China's foreign affairs. Constitutionally, the president takes no responsibility for any administration of the government to the NPC and NPCSC, except in the military field if the president concurrently serves as the military commander. In that case, the president has to share certain military powers with the premier in that the president maintains the power to direct the armed forces,[31] whereas the premier and his State Council exercise the power to "direct and administrate the building of national defence."[32] Up till now, such a constitutional division of military power has been further strengthened by more NPC legislations, such as the Martial Law, National Defense Law, Emergency Law, and the most recent Law on the Armed Police. Although the president serves a number of functions in Chinese diplomacy, the constitution gives more authority to the premier and NPC, and mainly relies on the premier to conduct foreign affairs and conclude treaties and agreements with foreign states that do not have to be decided by the NPC. Now with this could-be-independent "activities involving state affairs," the president takes a bite in the administration of China's foreign affairs.

More importantly, this amendment strengthens the president's role in the whole state apparatus and makes such an office more secure and stable in its life cycle of political authority, which begins when the president takes office, starts to rise after he concurrently takes the office of the chairman of the state CMC, reaches his peak of political power when he wins a second term in office, and then decline when he begins to relieve the office of the CCP's GS. In such an up-and-down cycle, the president would be the most vulnerable to any political disturbances during the period between when he became the GS and is elected into the presidency. During this period of time, he is only the CCP's GS, and holds no position in the state apparatus. Although he can set a new orientation and policies for the government in the capacity of the GS, he has to rely on the collective cooperation of his partners in the PSC, especially those who are taking government posts, to implement his new policies. Personally he can only push the government, but he is unable to take any specific action on his own because he has no official authority in the government. Now with this constitutional amendment, such an inability could be remedied. As soon as the president takes office, he can conduct "activities involving state affairs," thus exerting direct influence on Chinese diplomacy and making an impact indirectly on the operation of the government. He could promote his new policies by "diplomacy of the head of the state" to the world. With China's growing globalization, his international activities surely will have impact at home. If it is interpreted widely, his inspections and visits to local governments would also carry more weight of legality to motivate them to stay in line with his policies. It would be more serious if he was the head of state, by which he could conclude on his own international treaties that have an impact back at home. In a word, by "activities involving state affairs," the president has earned a constitutional weapon to carry out policies that are proposed by him as the CCP's GS.

More interestingly, this amendment could also change the relationship between the constitution and the real politics. As laid out in previous chapters, the constitutional provisions of the presidency have never been the true description of the true political power of its holders. In the past, the president loosely fulfilled his certain ceremonial functions provided by the constitution, mainly as the head of state externally. On the other hand, his real political weight in China had been decided mainly by his status in the CCP's hierarchical decision-making structure, with which the constitutional provisions had no fixed relationship. By this amendment, the president enjoys a certain share in foreign affairs. Thus, if the constitution is to be abided by, any future presidents have to be a permanent member of the CCP's decision-making body concerning foreign affairs, for example, the CCP's Central Leading Small Group of Foreign Affairs, and it is much more unlikely that the future president would be someone like. Thus, for the first time, the constitution has established a linkage to the true politics in terms of foreign affairs, which is similar to the Swiss presidents before that rule was changed.

In summary, President Hu Jintao has followed his predecessor's example by taking all four of these positions together, but in a different way. He had been staying in the PSC as "the second front" successor much longer than Jiang Zemin, during which he had also held official positions such as the vice-president and vice-military chairman, which Jiang Zemin had not undertaken. His order of succession was also different from that of Jiang Zemin. Due to the limitation of two terms of office, the state presidency had to become the second step instead of the last stop. As such, he took the GS first, then the state presidency, and third the double military chairmanships. Accordingly, his political decision-making power has been expanding along with the completion of each step, which started to decline in the new round of power transition triggered by the elevation of Xi Jinping into the PSC, who is widely regarded as the apparent heir.

NOTES

1. Zong Fengming (ed.), *Zhao Ziyang Ruanjing Zhong De Tanhua* [Zhao Ziyang: Captive Conversations] (Hong Kong: Kaifang Chubanshe, 2007), 382.

2. See, for example, Ren Zhichu, *Hu Jintao: China's First Man in the 21st Century* (Hong Kong: Mirror Books, 1998), 2nd ed., 222-225; Ma Ling and Li Ming, *Hu Jintao* (Hong Kong: Mingbao Chubanshe Youxian Gongsi, 2002), 238-239; Ren Zhichu and Wen Siyong, *Hu Jintao Zhuan* [Biography of Hu Jintao] (Hong Kong: Mingjing Chubanshe, 2002), 271-273; Yang Zhongmei, *Zhonggong Xin Lingxiu Hu Jintao* [Hu Jintao: The CCP's New Leader] (Taibei: Taiwan Shibao Wenhua Chuban Qiye Gufen Youxian Gongsi, 2002), 174-175; Ting Wang, *The Leader of Beijing in the 21st Century* (Hong Kong: Celebration Press [illegible]), [illegible] enlarged ed., 211-212.

3. Robert Lawrence Kuhn, Tan Zheng, and Yu Haijiang et al. (trans.), *Ta Gaibian Le Zhongguo Jiang Zemin Zhuan* [The Man Who Changed China: The Life and Legacy of Jiang Zemin] (Shanghai: Shanghai Yiwen Chubanshe, 2005), 425-428.

4. Wu Kangmin, *Huinei Huiwai: Shijie Renda Suibi* [Inside and Outside the Session: Notes about the Tenth National People's Congress] (Hong Kong: Tiandi Tushu Youxian Gongsi, 2007), 321. However, another opinion said that there were 2,939 deputies voting in favor of Hu Jintao in the presidential election. See Robert Lawrence Kuhn, Tan Zheng, and Yu Haijiang et al. (trans.), *Ta Gaibian Le Zhongguo Jiang Zemin Zhuan* [The Man Who Changed China: The Life and Legacy of Jiang Zemin] (Shanghai: Shanghai Yiwen Chubanshe, 2005), 435.

5. Robert Lawrence Kuhn, Tan Zheng, and Yu Haijiang et al. (trans.), *Ta Gaibian Le Zhongguo Jiang Zemin Zhuan* [The Man Who Changed China: The Life and Legacy of Jiang Zemin] (Shanghai: Shanghai Yiwen Chubanshe, 2005), 436.

6. Wu Kangmin, *Huinei Huiwai: Shijie Renda Suibi* [Inside and utside the Session: Notes about the Tenth National People's Congress] (Hong Kong: Tiandi Tushu Youxian Gongsi, 2007), 342.

7. Wenhuipo, March 16, 2008.

8. *Renmin Ribao*, October 24, 2007.

9. See http://news.southcn.com/z/2009-10/13/content_5974595.htm. However, his acts can give rise to the question of constitutionality. If his acts were a part of his official business, he could have obtained authorization from President Hu Jintao because the vice-president "may exercise such functions and powers of the president as the president may entrust to him," as provided by the second paragraph of article 82 of the Chinese constitution (1982). Otherwise, his acts would be unconstitutional. But if his acts was only a private affair, then no constitutional concerns would arise as he could seek to develop a personal relationship with his German host by such a presentation, even if his presentation was on behalf of Jiang Zemin.

10. Art. 10, the Constitution of the CCP, revised by the Seventeenth National Congress in 2007.

11. Article 16, the Constitution of the CCP, revised by the Seventeenth National Congress in 2007.

12. Art. 22, the Constitution of the CCP, revised by the Seventeenth National Congress in 2007.

13. Xianfa [constitution] (1982) (PRC), Art. 93, paragraph 3.

14. For the CCP's suggestion to revise the constitution, see Wang Peiying (ed.), *Zhongguo Xianfa Wenxian Tongbian* [Selection of Constitutional Documents of China] (Beijing: Zhongguo Minzhu Fazhi Chubanshe, 2007), revised ed., 124-126.

15. Zhonghua Renmin Gongheguo Xianfa Xiuzheng [An Amendment to the Constitution of the People's Republic of China] (adopted at the Second Session of the Tenth National People's Congress on March 14, 2004, and published for enforcement by the announcement of the National People's Congress of the People's Republic of China on March 14, 2004), Art. 28.

16. "Guanyu Zhonghua Renmin Gongheguo Xianfa Xiuzheng An (Caoan) De Shuoming" [Explanation about the Amendament (Draft) to the Constitution of the People's Republic of China], in Wang Peiying (ed.), *Zhongguo Xianfa Wenxian Tongbian* [Selection of Constitutional Documents of China] (Beijing: Zhongguo Minzhu Fazhi Chubanshe, 2007), revised ed., 137.

17. Yang Haikun (ed.), *Kuaru Xin Shijie De Zhongguo Xianfa Xue-Zhongguo Xianfaxue Yanjiu Xianzhuang Yu Pingjia* [Study on Chinese Constitutional Law in the New Century: Current Situation and Evaluation of Study on Chinese Constitutional Law] (Beijing: Zhongguo Renshi Chubanshe, 2001), 458.

18. Wei Dingren, Gan Chaoying, and Fu Siming, *Xianfa Xue* [Study on Constitutional Law] (Beijing: Beijing Daxue Chubanshe, 2004), 2nd ed., 540.

19. Xu Chongde, *Zhonghua Renmin Gongheguo Xianfashi* [Constitutional History of the People's Republic of China] (Fujian: Fujian Renmin Chubanshe, 2005), 2nd ed., vol. 2, 446.

20. Sidney M. Milkis and Michael Nelson, *The American Presidency: Origins and Developments, 1776-2002* (Washington, DC: CQ Press, 2003), 4th ed., 48.

21. Yang Haikun (ed.), *Kuaru Xin Shijie De Zhongguo Xianfa Xue-Zhongguo Xianfaxue Yanjiu Xianzhuang Yu Pingjia* [Study on Chinese Constitutional Law in the New Century: Current Situation and Evaluation of Study on Chinese Constitutional Law] (Beijing: Zhongguo Renshi Chubanshe, 2001), 452-453; Hu Jinguang and Han Dayuan (eds.), *Zhongguo Xianfa Fazhan Yanjiu Baogao (1982-2002)* [Research Report on Chinese Constitutional Development (1982-2002)] (Beijing: Falv Chubanshe, 2004), 248-249.

22. Hu Jinguan and Han Dayuan, *Zhongguo Xianfa* [Chinese Constitutional Law] (Beijing: Falv Chubanshe, 2007), 392; Cai Dingjian, *Xianfa Jingjie* [Explanation on the Constitution] (Beijing: Falv Chubanshe, 2004), 330-331; Yang Haikun (ed.), *Kuaru Xin Shijie De Zhongguo Xianfa Xue-Zhongguo Xianfaxue Yanjiu Xianzhuang Yu Pingjia* [Study on Chinese Constitutional Law in the New Century: Current Situation and Evaluation of Study on Chinese Constitutional Law] (Beijing: Zhongguo Renshi Chubanshe, 2001), 454-456.

23. Xu Chongde, *Zhonghua Renmin Gongheguo Xianfa shi* [Constitutional History of the People's Republic of China] (Fujian: Fujian Renmin Chubanshe, 2003), 323, 825-826.

24. Xu Chongde, *Zhonghua Renmin Gongheguo Xianfa shi* [Constitutional History of the People's Republic of China] (Fujian: Fujian Renmin Chubanshe, 2003), 323, 825-826.

25. Zou Pingxue and Fei Chun (eds.), *Xianfa Xue* [Study on Constitutional Law] (Beijing: Zhongguo Minzhu Fazhi Chubanshe, 2006), 2nd ed., 388.

26. Zhu Yingping, "Xianxing Guojia Zhuxi Zhidu Chouyi" [Discussion on Current System of Chinese President], *Faxue*, no. 11 (2000).

27. Vienna Convention on the Law of Treaties, Art. 7, section 2a.

28. About PRC's theory of the head of state, see Xu Chongde, *Guojia Yuanshou* [The Head of State] (Beijing: Renmin Chubanshe, 1982); Yan Jiaqi, *Yuanshou Lun* [Study on the Head of State] (Hong Kong: Zhonghua Shuju Xianggang Fenju, 1987); Zhu Weiping, "Guojia Yuanshou Zhidu Yanjiu" [Study on the Head of State] (unpublished PHD thesis); Zhong Yan, "Gongneng Shijiao Xia De Guojia Yuanshou Zhiquan" [Power and Function of the Head of State from the Functional Perspective] (unpublished master diss.).

29. Xu Chongde (ed.), *Xianfa Xue* [Study on Constitutional Law] (Beijing: Gaodeng Jiaoyu Chubanshe, 2005), 455-456.

30. For example, in the author's interview with Professor Cai Dingjian, a PRC constitutional lawyer who had for a long time worked in the NPCSC, he expressed such an idea that the "state affairs" included domestic affairs.

31. Xianfa [constitution] (1982) (PRC), Art. 93.

32. Xianfa [constitution] (1982) (PRC), Art. 89.

Chapter Twelve

Law and Politics Surrounding the Presidency

A NASCENT RULE OF LAW

Constitutionally, the Chinese presidency has evolved from a traditional personal Chinese title, to a Stalinist political office transplanted from the former Soviet Union, and to an independent state executive office. It has the appearance of a Western-style semi-presidency with delicately provided functions and mechanisms for election and succession. Through these decades of evolution, a nascent rule of law can be discerned from the present-day office of president.

First, the division of the executive power into the hands of the president, premier, and military chairman cannot only set the president and premier in check with each other, but also reduce the risk of monopoly and facilitate specialization of these different powers according to their own nature. Especially, the president's constitutional function has been reduced from a dominant player to someone mainly specializing in diplomacy, thus narrowing the difference between legal provisions and the political reality.

Second, certain legal provisions have been able to define and modify the CCP's political practices. For example, the provision regarding the president's two terms in office has become an indispensable part of political practices, not only curtailing the influence of the strong leaders, forcing the CCP to adjust its arrangements of succession, but also speeding the power transition between different generations of the CCP, and considerably reducing the political fluctuation. The establishment of the state Central Military Commission (CMC) in the constitution not only turns over the control of the armed forces to the state from the CCP, at least literally, but also serves a legal basis for further legal control of the military power that has been accelerated since President Hu Jintao took office.[1]

Third, relevant legal stipulations have provided citizens a route to political participation and to exert influence on the president's services. With the development of civil society in China, there is an increasing demand on the presidency from the general populace. Some have suggested further institutionalization of the presidency, such as the constitutional confirmation of the status of the president as the head of state, establishment of the president's office, requiring the president to swear an oath when taking office.[2] The constitution should make more detailed stipulations as to his functions and powers, and procedures should be made more strict concerning his election and recall.[3] Others want presidential candidates,[4] discussions on the delay in the promulgation of law by presidential order,[5] questions on the power division between the president and premier,[6] and recognition of the issue of letter petitions to the president. Several constitutional amendments were even drafted by scholars to improve relevant provisions regarding the election, qualification, power and function, and responsibility of the president and vice-president.[7] All of these will surely help to improve the presidency.

More broadly, the phrase "rule of law" has been inserted into the constitution and further judicial reform has been planned to give more autonomy to judge.[8] Remarkable improvements also have been made in respect to the CCP. Pledges have been made by the CCP in its constitution to abide by the state constitution,[9] suggesting the focus of the relationship between the CCP and the state has shifted from the CCP to the side of the state. Signs toward democracy in terms of the CCP's succession and decision-making mechanism can also be discerned by the fact that former President Hu Jintao has not been titled as the "core of leadership" and Xi Jinping was officially reported for the first time to be elected by the CCP Central Committee. All these indicate that constitutional rules have been taking root in Chinese politics and gone beyond a legitimizing purpose toward the notion of "checks and balances" characterized in Western constitutionalism.

POLITICAL DOMINANCE OF THE CCP

However, by far the most important part of the presidency functions in a Stalinist party-state is based on the principle of democratic centralism heavily influenced by the ancient Chinese tradition of "rule of man." Hence the constitution has only been a part of rules governing the Chinese presidency, most of which have been changing political rules and practices regarding the CCP's mechanisms of nomination, decision making and succession at its highest-level bureaucracy.

Although by law the president is nominated by the NPC Presidium and elected by the NPC deputies, such nomination and election can be a formality when the NPC convenes no more than a half month each year, and all presidential candidates have been accepted by the NPC without exception and competition. The candidates have been produced according to the CCP's step-by-step succession rules designated by the paramount leaders and determined beforehand by the CCP by way of three major political practices, that is, the CCP's initial selection of presidential candidates nominated by its paramount leaders and incumbent central leaders, then the endorsement of the candidate name list for top government positions by the CCP National Congress,[10] and submission of this list to the NPC presidium by its representative. Competition to succession have occurred but been settled by the paramount leaders. Similar to the NPC deputies, the thousands of general CCP members have had little participation in the party's selection process. In short, the presidential candidates have been decided by their incumbent senior colleagues.

Once in office, the reality of political decision-making authority of Chinese presidents has not only been determined by those constitutional yet seemingly ceremonial and procedural provisions, but more by political rules provided by the party constitutions and political practices, first of which is those decision-making mechanisms at the CCP's supreme level, especially in the CCP's Politburo and PSC. According to the party constitution, the CCP should make its decision based on the principle of democratic centralism, which has been coined as the combination of collective leadership and individual responsibility based on the division of labor.

However, the CCP's highest decision making has been dominated most by Mao Zedong and Deng Xiaoping, who in practice could overturn the collective decisions with their power of veto. Since the death of Deng Xiaoping, the dominance of Chinese presidents, starting from Jiang Zemin, has been declining. As such, the rule of "one person, one vote" could come into play more and more as suggested by the collective leadership, which means that each member in those collective organs, including the president, should have equal weight in decision making. In this case, the president's decision-making weight will be decided by the number of members in these collective organs, which has varied from three people to nine people if one takes the PSC as an example.

But such a rule of equal voting has not been applied universally as yet. According to Hu Jintao's report in the CCP's Seventeenth National Congress in 2007, "the voting method should be pursued in local party committees when deciding major issues and appointing important cadres."[11] This can suggest that the voting method has not yet been fully applied in the CCP's Politburo and PSC.

Then when votings are not adopted, the president has to rely on other rules and practices. As a PSC member, the president can be dominant on those matters that have fallen into his jurisdiction based on the division of labor.[12] As general secretary, he serves both as a legislative chairman and the chief executor, thus he could have a bigger say in setting the agenda for the Politburo and PSC, and in the daily running of the Central Secretariat.

The president's political authority will also be further strengthened if the CCP's political practice of "putting four hats on one head," that is, how many posts the president takes among the CCP's GS, continues to apply, when he concurrently takes the CCP's CMC chairman, "the core of leadership" and the state's CMC chairman.

But the president's political authority has exceeded his two terms of office, that is, ten years, as a result of the CCP's step-by-step succession plan. Before taking the presidency, Jiang Zemin, Hu Jintao, and Xi Jinpin served in the PSC as members. While participating in all of the PSC's decision making, including the nomination of their successors, they could be less active in the PSC as constrained by their apprenticeship along the progress of succession. After retiring from the presidency, all presidents have enjoyed extra-tenure political influence, which also changes according to different political arrangements made for different individuals and informal politics.

Therefore, those constitutional provisions have only been a part of rules governing the real politics concerning the presidency and intermingled with those changing formal and informal political practices. Hence, Chinese presidents have always enjoyed certain substantive power when performing constitutional functions, varying from being an implementer to a dominant, even sometimes ultimate decision maker, depending generally on his role, status, and personal capacity of political coalition in the CCP's collective leadership. The president's external services as the head of state have always been fluctuating abroad and incomplete at home. Domestically, the president could turn those allegedly nominal constitutional functions into real checks and balances on other state offices, thus making the presidency the bridge connecting the CCP and the state apparatus, facilitating the CCP's control over the state and maintaining balances among the CCP major leaders and of the party-state. So far the presidency has been governed more by politics than law.

THE EVOLVING PRESIDENCY

Underlying decades of tortuous, yet dynamic evolution of the Chinese presidency has been the focus on changing foreign influences and local demands on China. At home, Chinese traditions and local situations have made their marks on the presidency. On one hand, the traditions of "rule of man," patriarchal authoritarianism and disdain for law can be clearly distinguished, as evidenced by the power of veto, Mao Zedong's favor for the Chinese title "chairman," Deng Xiaoping's idea of "the core of leadership," the step-by-step succession plan, ambiguous legal wording,[13] the application of political power in a secret, romantic and military style, and no responsibility for the paramount leader, and so on. On the other hand, the heavy workload such a big country posed on its leaders, the developing and transitional situation, and the limited rationality and capacity of any individual demand certain division of power, thus gave rise to the possibility for the president to take some share in the governance.

In the meantime, two different foreign influences have also shaped the Chinese presidency. First are Western ideas, including different presidencies, "diplomacy of the head of state," the idea of rule of law, and so on, all of these ideas had once been almost eliminated, but have been revived after China adopted the open-door and reform policy. The development of Chinese president's diplomacy from "ceremonial diplomacy" to "diplomacy by the head of state," and to current "responsible diplomacy," and recent establishment of the Council of State Security[14] suggests that Western influences on China will continue to affect the presidency.

The second major foreign influence is that of the former Soviet Union, which has left China a heritage of the Stalinist party-state. Although the economic basis of the Chinese party-state has been eroded greatly by freeing people from the planned economy to the market economy, its governance and decision making at the party's highest level has remained basically intact so far. As suggested by President Jiang Zemin's "rule of law" (in Chinese "Yifa Zhiguo") and "rule of merits" (in Chinese "De zhi"), President Hu Jintao's "socialist rule of law" (in Chinese "Shehui Zhuyi Fazhi"), all these factors have been intermingled together in the global context, which surely makes the choice of policies as difficult as ever. While the constitution has been pledged as the highest authority, it has not explicitly provided the accountability of the president either in the capacity of state official or as the nominal party chief. Without the final settlement of the dilemma of responsibility to the constitution, the presidency will continue to evolve.

NOTES

1. Su Yongtong, "Zhongguo Junshi Lifa Da Tisu" [China Speeds Up Its Military Legislations], *Nanfang Zhoumo*, October 9, 2009.

2. Jiang Wei, "Lun Jianli Zhongyu Xianfa De Xuanshi Zhidu" [Establishing the Constitutional Swearing System], *Fashang Yanjiu*, no. 5 (2000), 58-62; Dai Jitao, "Dui Woguo Jianli Guojia Yuanshou Xuanshi Zhidu De Sikao" [On the Establishment of Swearing System for Our Country's Head of State], *Shidai Faxue*, no. 2 (2003), 15-18.

3. Zhu Yingping, "Xianxing Guojia Zhuxi Zhidu Chouyi" [Discussion on Current System of Chinese President], *Faxue*, no. 11 (2000).

4. *Xinjing Bao*, March 24, 2009.

5. Su Junque, "Falv Gongbu Wu Xiaoshi" [Promulgation of Law Is Not Trival], *Nanfang Zhoumo*, December 14, 2008.

6. See http://chentieyuan.blshe.com/post/975/24141, last visited on December 9, 2009. It holds that any news relating to the president should be announced by his office, instead of other institutions such as the Ministry of Foreign Affairs.

7. Yang Haikun (ed.), *Kuaru Xin Shijie De Zhongguo Xianfa Xue-Zhongguo Xianfaxue Yanjiu Xianzhuang Yu Pingjia* [Study on Chinese Constitutional Law in the New Century: Current Situation and Evaluation of Study on Chinese Constitutional Law] (Beijing: Zhongguo Renshi Chubanshe, 2001), 461-463.

8. http://news.xinhuanet.com/mrdx/2013-11/16/c_132892941.htm.

9. General Principles, the Constitution of the CCP, revised by the Seventeenth National Congress in 2007.

10. Liu Siyang, "Sun Chenbing, Liu Gang: Weile Dang He Guojia Xingwang Fada Changzhi Jiuan Dang De Xin Yijie Zhongyang Lingdao Jigou Chansheng Jishi" [For the Party and State's Long-Term Prosperity and Stability: Factual Record of the Production of the Party's New Leading Organs], in *Qiushi Magazine*, Issue 21 (2007), 61-62; Zhang Sutang, Qin Jie, Huo Xiaoguang and Li Yanjie, *Kaichuang Zhongguo Teshe Shehui Zhuyi Shiye Xin Jumian De Jianqiang Lingdao Jiti: Dang De Xin Yijie Zhongyang Lingdao Jigou Chansheng Jishi* [A Strong Collective Leadership to Explore New Phase in the Cause of Socialism with Chinese Characteristics: Factual Record of the Production of the Party's New Leading Organs], at http://news.mod.gov.cn/headlines/2012-11/16/content_4412865.htm.

11. http://news.xinhuanet.com/newscenter/2007-10/24/content_6938568_11.htm.

12. For a brief summary of the division of labor within the PSC during the CCP's Twelfth and Fifteenth National Congresses, see Hu Angang, *Zhongguo Jiti Lingdao Tizhi* [Collective Leadership of China] (Beijing: Zhongguo Renmin Chubanshe, 2013), appendix 2.

13. As evidenced by the 2004 constitutional amendment, the words used in the constitution are simple and general, but with great potential. Such an approach had always been preferred by those constitutional makers such as Mao Zedong and Deng Xiaoping. In other words, ambiguity of constitutional provisions has been a repeated practice.

14. http://news.takungpao.com.hk/mainland/focus/2013-11/2033054.html.

Bibliography

Alexander, Larry, ed. *Constitutionalism: Philosophical Foundations*. Cambridge; New York: Cambridge University Press, 1998.

Allan, T. R. S. *Constitutional Justice: A Liberal Theory of the Rule of Law*. Oxford: Oxford University Press, 2003.

Almqvist, Jessica. *Human Rights, Culture, and the Rule of Law*. Oxford; Portland, OR: Hart Pub., 2005.

Ambroz, Oton. *Realignment of World Power: The Russo-Chinese Schism under the Impact of Mao Tse-Tung's Last Revolution*. New York: R. Speller, 1972.

Anita Chan, Stanley Rosen, and Jonathan Unger, eds. *On Socialist Democracy and the Chinese Legal System: the Li Yizhe Debates*. Armonk: M.E. Sharpe, C1985.

Antieau, Chester James. *The Higher Laws: Origins of Modern Constitutional Law*. Buffalo, NY: W.S. Hein & Co., 1994.

Babington, Anthony. *The Rule of Law in Britain from the Roman Occupation to the Present Day*, 3rd ed. Chichester: B. Rose, 1995.

Bachman, David M. *Bureaucracy, Economy, and Leadership in China: The Institutional Origins of the Great Leap Forward*. New York: Cambridge University Press, 1991.

Banting, Keith G., and Richard Simeon, eds. *Redesigning the State: the Politics of Constitutional Change*. Toronto: University of Toronto Press, 1985.

Barnett, A. Doak. *The Making of Foreign Policy in China: Structure and Process*. London: I.B. Tauris & Co. Ltd., 1985.

———. *Cadress, Bureaucracy, and Political Power in Communist China*. New York: Columbia University Press, 1967.

Bau, Mingchien Joshua B. *Modern Democracy in China*. Arlington, VA: University Publications of America, 1977.

Baum, Richard. *Burying Mao: Chinese Politics in the Age of Deng Xiaoping*. Princeton, NJ: Princeton University Press, 1994.

———, ed. *Reform and Reaction in Post-Mao China: The Road to Tiananmen*. New York; London: Routledge, 1991.

Beatty, David M. *The Ultimate Rule of Law*. Oxford; New York: Oxford University Press, 2004.

Beck, Carl, et al. *Comparative Communist Political Leadership*. New York: D. Mckay Co., 1973.

Belden, Jack. *China Shakes the World*. Harmondsworth: Penguin Books, 1973.

Bellamy, Richard, ed. *Constitutionalism and Democracy*. Aldershot, England; Burlington, VT: Ashgate/Dartmouth, 2006.

Bessette, Joseph M., and Jeffrey Tulis, eds. *The Presidency in the Constitutional Order*. Baton Rouge: Louisiana State University Press, 1981.

Billias, George Athan, ed. *American Constitutionalism Abroad: Selected Essays in Comparative Constitutional History*. New York: Greenwood Press, 1990.

Bishop, John Lyman. *Studies of Governmental Institutions in Chinese History*. Cambridge, MA: Harvard University Press, 1968.

Blythe, James M. *Ideal Government and the Mixed Constitution in the Middle Ages*. Princeton, NJ: Princeton University Press, 1992.

Bo, Yibo. *Ruogan Zhongda Juece Yu Shijian De Huigu*. Beijing: Zhonggong Zhongyang Dangxiao Chubanshe, 1991-1993.

Boorman, Howard L. *Moscow-Peking Axis: Strengths and Strains*. New York: Published for the Council on Foreign Relations by Harper, 1957.

Brandt, Conrad. *Stalin's Failure in China, 1924-1927*. Cambridge: Harvard University Press, 1958.

Campbell, Thomas. *Separation of Powers in Practice*. Stanford, CA: Stanford University Press, 2004.

Cass, Ronald A. *The Rule of Law in America*. Baltimore, MD: Johns Hopkins University Press, 2001.

Chang, Gordon G. *The Coming Collapse of China*. London: Arrow, 2002.

Chang, Gordon H. *Friends and Enemies: The United States, China, and the Soviet Union, 1948-1972.* Stanford, CA: Stanford University Press, 1990.

Cheibub, José Antônio. *Presidentialism, Parliamentarism, and Democracy*. New York, NY: Cambridge University Press, 2007.

Ch'ên, Han-Ming. *New Life for Kiangsi*. Shanghai: The China Publishing Co., 1935.

Chen, Hongtai. *Zhongguo Zhengfu Tixi Yu Zhengzhi: Gainian, Zongjie Yu Tansuo*. Zhengzhou: Henan Renmin Chubanshe, 2005.

Chen, Jianfu. *Chinese Law: Towards an Understanding of Chinese Law, Its Nature and Development*. The Hague; Boston: Kluwer Law International, C1999.

Chen, Lifeng. *Zhongguo Gongchandang Lingdao Tizhi De Lishi Kaocha (1921-2006*). Shanghai: Shanghai Renmin Chubanshe, 2008.

Chen, Hung-yee. "Political Confucianism and Democracy," *Law and Social development*, no. 2 (2009): 3-11.

Chen, Hung-yee. "Is the Confucianism Compatible with the Liberal Constitutional Democracy?" *Journal of Chinese Philosophy*, no. 2 (2007): 195-216.

Chen, Hung-yee. "The Constitutional Amendment of 2004 and the Prospect for Chinese Constitutionalism," *Twenty-first Century*, no. 88 (2005): 67-77.

Christy, Erik Emil. *Influence of the Soviet Union on Chinese Higher Educational and Scientific Development: 1920-1950*. Ann Arbor, MI: University Microfilms International, 1989 [1986].

Clarke, Christopher M. *The Politics of Bureaucratic Reorganization in the People's Republic of China: The State Council, 1949-1979*. S.L.: S.N., 1980.

Cline, Ray S., and Hungdah Chiu, eds. *The U.S. Constitution and the Development of Constitutionalism in China*. Washington, DC: U.S. Global Strategy Council, in Cooperation with University of Maryland Law School East Asian Legal Studies Program, and Association of Chinese Social Scientists in North America, 1988.

Clubb, O. Edmund. *China & Russia: The "Great Game."* New York: Columbia University Press, 1971.

Cohen, Jerome Alan, ed. *Contemporary Chinese Law: Research Problems and Perspectives*. Cambridge, MA: Harvard University Press, 1970.

Cong, Dachang. *When Heroes Pass Away: The Invention of a Chinese Communist Pantheon*. Lanham: University Press of America, 1997.

Costa, Pietro, and Danilo Zolo, eds. *The Rule of Law: History, Theory and Criticism*. Dordrecht, the Netherlands: Springer, 2007.

Dahl, Robert A. *How Democratic Is the American Constitution*. New Haven, CT: Yale University Press, 2001.

———. *Dilemmas of Pluralist Democracy: Autonomy vs. Control*. New Haven, CT: Yale University Press, 1982.

Deng, Lilan. *Yuwai Guannian Yu Bentu Zhengzhi Bianqian: 20 Shiji Ersanshi Nian Dai Zhongguo Zhishi Jie De Zhengzhi Sheji Yu Canzheng*. Beijing: Zhongguo Renmin Daxue Chubanshe, 2003.

Ding, Wang. *Beijing Kuashiji Jiebanren* [The Successors to Power in Beijing across the Century]. Xianggang: Dang Dai Ming Jia Chubanshe, 1997.

Ding, Yijiang. *Chinese Democracy after Tiananmen*. Vancouver: UBC Press, 2001.

Dittmer, Lowell. *China under Reform*. Boulder: Westview Press, 1994.

Dunmore, Timothy. *Soviet Politics, 1945-1953*. New York: St. Martin's Press, 1984.

Dyzenhaus, David, ed. *Recrafting the Rule of Law: The Limits of Legal Order*. Oxford; Portland, OR: Hart Pub., 1999.

Elkin, Stephen L., and Karol Edward Sołtan, eds. *A New Constitutionalism: Designing Political Institutions for a Good Society*. Chicago: University of Chicago Press, 1993.

Elleman, Bruce A. *Diplomacy and Deception: The Secret History of Sino-Soviet Diplomatic Relations, 1917-1927*. Armonk, NY: M.E. Sharpe, 1997.

Ellison, Herbert J., ed. *The Sino-Soviet Conflict, a Global Perspective*. Seattle; London: University of Washington Press, 1982.

Falkenheim, Victor C., ed. *Chinese Politics from Mao to Deng*. New York, NY: Professors World Peace Academy: Distributed by Paragon House, 1989.

Faribank, John K. *Trade and Diplomacy on the China Coast: The Opening of the Treaty Ports, 1842-1854*. Stanford: Stanford University Press, 1953.

Fausold, Martin L., and Alan Shank, eds. *The Constitution and the American Presidency*. Albany: State University of New York Press, 1991.

Feng, Chongyi, and Zhu Xueqin, eds. *Xianzheng Yu Zhongguo*. Xianggang: Xianggang Shehui Kexue Chubanshe Youxian Gongsi, 2004.

Feng, Hui. *The Politics of China's Accession to the World Trade Organization: The Dragon Goes Global*. London; New York: Routledge, 2006.

Feng, Qiuting, Ruilan Gao, and Jiaqi Lu, eds. *Zhongguo Gongchandang Zhizheng Fangshi Tanxi*. Beijing: Zhonggong Zhongyang Dangxiao Chubanshe, 2001.

Fernández Esteban, Maria Luisa. *The Rule of Law in the European Constitution*. The Hague; Boston: Kluwer Law International, 1999.

Fewsmith, Joseph. *China since Tiananmen: The Politics of Transition*. Cambridge; New York: Cambridge University Press, 2001.

Fewsmith, Joseph. *Elite Politics in Contemporary China*. Armonk, NY: M.E. Sharpe, 2001.

Finer, S. E. *Comparing Constitutions*. Oxford: Clarendon Press; New York: Oxford University Press, 1995.

Finkelstein, David M., and Maryanne Kivlehan, eds. *China's Leadership in the 21st Century: The Rise of the Fourth Generation*. Armonk, NY: M.E. Sharpe, 2003.

Finkelstein, David M., and Maryanne Kivlehan, eds. *China's Leadership in the 21st Century*. Armonk, NY: M.E. Sharpe, 2003.

Fleiner-Gerster, Thomas. *Swiss Constitutional Law*. The Hague: Kluwer Law International; Berne: Stæmpfli Publishers, 2005.

Floyd, David. *Mao against Khrushchev: A Short History of the Sino-Soviet Conflict*. London: Pall Mall, 1964.

Friedman, Edward, and Barrett L. McCormick, eds. *What If China doesn't Democratize? The Implications for War and Peace*. Armonk, NY: M.E. Sharpe, 2000.

Gang, Lin, and Xiaobo Hu, eds. *China after Jiang*. Washington, DC: Woodrow Wilson Center Press; Stanford, CA: Stanford University Press, 2003.

Garver, John W. *Chinese-Soviet Relations, 1937-1945: The Diplomacy of Chinese Nationalism*. New York: Oxford University Press, 1988.

Genovese, Michael A., and Lori Cox Han, eds. *The Presidency and the Challenge of Democracy*. New York: Palgrave Macmillan, 2006.

Gillespie, John, and Pip Nicholson, eds. *Asian Socialism and Legal Change: The Dynamics of Vietnamese and Chinese Reform*. Canberra ACT: Australian National University Press: Asia Pacific Press, 2005.

Gillett, Nicholas. *The Swiss Constitution: Can It Be Exported?* Bristol: Youth Education Service, 1989.

Gilley, Bruce. *China's Democratic Future: How It Will Happen and Where It Will Lead*. New York: Columbia University Press, 2004.

Goldman, Merle, and Roderick Macfarquhar, eds. *The Paradox of China's Post-Mao Reforms*. Cambridge, MA: Harvard University Press, 1999.

Goodman, David S. G. *Deng Xiaoping and the Chinese Revolution: A Political Biography*. London; New York: Routledge, 1994.

Gordon, Scott. *Controlling the State: Constitutionalism from Ancient Athens to Today*. Cambridge, MA: Harvard University Press, 1999.

Griffith, William E. *Peking, Moscow, and Beyond: The Sino-Soviet-American Triangle*. Washington: Center for Strategic and International Studies, Georgetown University, 1973.

Guo, Xuezhi. *The Ideal Chinese Political Leader: A Historical and Cultural Perspective*. Westport, CT: Praeger, 2002.

Gurtov, Melvin. *China under Threat: The Politics of Strategy and Diplomacy*. Baltimore, MD: Johns Hopkins University Press, 1980.

Haggard, Stephan, and Mathew D. McCubbins, eds. *Presidents, Parliaments, and Policy*. Cambridge, UK New York: Cambridge University Press, 2001.

Hamilton, Alexander, James Madison, and John Jay. *The Federalist*. Oxford; New York: Oxford University Press, 2008.

Han, Suyin. *Wind in the Tower: Mao Tse-tung and the Chinese Revolution, 1949-1975*. Cape: London, 1976.

Hao, Zaijin. *Xieshang Jianguo: 1948-1949 Zhongguo Dangpai Zhengzhi Rizhi*. Beijing: Renmin Wenxue Chubanshe, 2000.

Harden, Ian. *The Noble Lie: The British Constitution and the Rule of Law*. London: Hutchinson, 1988.

Harding, Harry. *Organizating China: The Problem of Bureaucracy, 1949-1976*. Stanford, CA: Stanford University Press, 1981.

Hart, James S. *The Rule of Law: 1603-1660: Crowns, Courts and Judges*. Harlow, England; New York: Pearson/Longman, 2003.

Hazard, John N. *Communists and Their Law: A Search for the Common Core of the Legal Systems of the Marxian Socialist States*. Chicago: University of Chicago Press, 1969.

He, Qinhua, and Li Xiuqing, eds. *Minguo Faxue Lunwen Jingcui, Xianzheng Falv Pian*. Beijing Shi: Falv Chubanshe, 2002.

Hope, Nicholas C., Dennis Tao Yang, and Mu Yang Li, eds. *How Far Across the River? Chinese Policy Reform at the Millennium*. Stanford, CA: Stanford University Press, 2003.

Hu, Jinguang, and Han Dayuan, eds. *Zhongguo Xianfa Fazhan Yanjiu Baogao, 1982-2002* [Research Reports on Constitutional Development of China]. Beijing: Falv Chuanshe, 2004.

Huang, Jing. *Factionalism in Chinese Communist Politics*. Cambridge; New York: Cambridge University Press, 2000.

Hutchinson, Allan C., and Patrick Monahan, eds. *The Rule of Law: Idea or Ideology*. Toronto: Carswell, 1987.

Ilwain, Charles Howard. *Constitutionalism, Ancient and Modern*, rev. ed. Indianapolis, IN: Amagi/Liberty Fund, 2007.

Jensen, Erik G., and Thomas C. Heller, eds. *Beyond Common Knowledge: Empirical Approaches to the Rule of Law*. Stanford, CA: Stanford University Press, 2003.

Jing, Zhiren. *Zhongguo Lixian Shi*. Taibei: Lianjing Chuban Shiye Gongsi, 1984.

Johnson, Hewlett. *China's New Creative Age*. London: Lawrence and Wishart, 1953.

Jowell, Jeffrey L., and Dawn Oliver, eds. *The Changing Constitution*, 6th ed. Oxford; New York: Oxford University Press, 2007.

Kalb, Marvin L. *Dragon in the Kremlin: A Report on the Russian-Chinese Alliance*. London: V. Gollancz, 1961.

Kaple, Deborah A. *Dream of a Red Factory: The Legacy of High Stalinism in China*. New York: Oxford University Press, 1994.

Keith, Ronald C. *China's Struggle for the Rule of Law*. Basingstoke: Macmillan; New York, NY: St. Martin's Press, 1994.

———. *Law and Justice in China's New Marketplace*. Houndmills, Basingstoke, Hampshire; New York: Palgrave, 2001.
Kim, Ilpyong J. *The Politics of Chinese Communism: Kiangsi under the Soviets*. Berkeley: University of California Press, 1973.
Klochko, Mikhail Antonovich (translated by Andrew Macandrew). *Soviet Scientist in Red China*. New York: Praeger, 1964.
Korbel, Josef. *The Communist Subversion of Czechoslovakia, 1938-1948: The Failure of Coexistence*. Princeton, NJ: Princeton University Press, 1959.
Kou, Jianwen. *Zhonggong Jingying Zhengzhi De Yanbian: Zhidugua Yu Quanli Zhuanyi, 1978-2004*. Taibei Shi: Wu Nan Tushu Chuban Gufen Youxian Gongsi, 2005.
Lampton, David M. *Paths to Power: Elite Mobility in Contemporary China*. Ann Arbor: Center for Chinese Studies, University of Michigan, 1986.
Lampton, David M., ed. *The Making of Chinese Foreign and Security Policy in the Era of Reform: 1978-2000*. Stanford, CA: Stanford University Press, 2001.
Lane, Jan-Erik. *Constitutions and Political Theory*. Manchester, UK; New York: Manchester University Press, 1996.
Lee, Shane R. *The Legal System and Political Development in Communist China, 1949-1969*. Ann Arbor, MI: University Microfilms International, 1982.
Leib, Ethan J., and Baogang He, eds. *The Search for Deliberative Democracy in China*. New York: Palgrave Macmillan, 2006.
Lewis, John Wilson. *Chinese Communist Party Leadership and the Succession to Mao Tse-Tung: An Appraisal of Tensions*. Washington, DC: U.S. Dept. of State, Bureau of Intelligence andResearch, External Research Staff, 1964.
———. *Leadership in Communist China*. Ithaca, NY: Cornell University Press, 1963.
———, ed. *Party Leadership and Revolutionary Power in China*. Cambridge: University Press, 1970.
Li, Hua. *Beijing Yu Mosike: Jiemeng, Duikang, Hezuo*. Beijing: Renmin Chubanshe, 2007.
Li, Weihan. *Huiyi Yu Yanjiu*. Beijing: Zhonggong Dangshi Ziliao Chubanshe, 1986.
Li, Cheng. *China's Leaders: the New Generation*. Lanham MD: Rowman & Littlefield Publishers, C2001.
Liang, Yi, and Li Xiangqian, eds. *Guowai Zhonggong Dangshi Yanjiu Shuping* [Introduction and Evaluation on Foreign Studies on the History of the CPC]. Beijing: Zhonggong Dangshi Chubanshe, 2005.
Lieberthal, Kenneth. *Central Documents and Politburo Politics in China*. Ann Arbor: Center for Chinese Studies, University of Michigan, 1978.
———. *Mao vs Liu? The Cultural Revolution on the Evolution of Urban Policy, 1946-1949*. Hong Kong: Centre of Asian Studies, University of Hong Kong, 1970.
Lieberthal, Kenneth, and Michel Oksenberg. *Policy Making in China Leaders, Structures, and Processes*. Princeton, NJ: Princeton University Press, 1988.
Lieberthal, Kenneth, and David M. Lampton, eds. *Bureaucracy, Politics, and Decision Making in Post-Mao China*. Berkeley: University of California Press, 1992.
Lijphart, Arend, ed. *Parliamentary Versus Presidential Government*. Oxford; Hong Kong: Oxford University Press, 1992.
Lin, Shangli. *Dangdai Zhongguo Zhengzhi Xingtai Yanjiu*. Tianjin Shi: Tianjin Renmin Chubanshe, 2000.
———. *Dangnei Minzhu* [Intra-Party Democracy]. Shanghai: Shanghai Shehui Kexue Chubanshe, 2002.
Lin, Tongfa. *Zhanhou Zhongguo De Bianju: Yi Guomindang Wei Zhongxin De Tantao*. Taibei Shi: Taiwan Shangwu Yinshuguan, 2003.
Lindsay, Michael, ed. *The New Constitution of Communist China: Comparative Analyses*. Taipei: Institute of International Relations, 1976.
Linz, Juan J., and Arturo Valenzuela, eds. *The Failure of Presidential Democracy*. Baltimore, MD: Johns Hopkins University Press, 1994.
Liu, Jiecheng. *Mao Zedong Yu Sidalin Huiwu Jishi*. Beijing: Zhonggong Dangshi Chubanshe, 1997.

Liu, Jizeng, and Lei Mao, eds. *Zhongguo Gongchandang Lingdao Gongzuo Shigao*. Zhengzhou: Henan Renmin Chubanshe, 1988.

Lötveit, Trygve. *Chinese Communism 1931-1934: Experience in Civil Government*, 2nd ed. London: Curzon Press, 1979.

Loughlin, Martin. *Sword and Scales: An Examination of the Relationship between Law and Politics*. Oxford; Portland, OR: Hart, 2000.

Low, Alfred D. *The Sino-Soviet Confrontation Since Mao Zedong: Dispute, Detente or Conflict?* Boulder: Social Science Monographs, 1987.

Lu, Ning. *The Dynamics of Foreign-Policy Decision Making in China*, 2nd ed. Boulder, CO: Westview Press, 2000.

Lu, Yonghong. *China's Legal Awakening: Legal Theory and Criminal Justice in Deng's Era*. Hong Kong: Hong Kong University Press, 1995.

Lubman, Stanley B. *Bird in a Cage: Legal Reform after Mao*. Stanford: Stanford University Press, 1999.

———. *Sino-American Relations and China's Struggle for the Rule of Law*. New York: East Asian Institute, Columbia University, 1997.

———, ed. *China's Legal Reforms*. Oxford; New York: Oxford University Press, 1996.

Lutz, Donald S. *Principles of Constitutional Design*. Cambridge; New York: Cambridge University Press, 2006.

MacCormick, Neil. *Rhetoric and the Rule of Law: A Theory of Legal Reasoning*. Oxford; New York: Oxford University Press, 2005.

MacFarquhar, Roderick. *Mao's Last Revolution*. Cambridge, MA: Belknap Press of Harvard University Press, 2006.

———, ed. *The Politics of China: The Years of Mao and Deng*, 2nd ed. New York: Cambridge University Press, 1997.

———. *The Politics of China, 1949-1989*. Cambridge; New York: Cambridge University Press, 1993.

———. *The Origins of the Cultural Revolution*. New York: Published For the Royal Institute of International Affairs, the East Asian Institute of Columbia University, and the Research Institute on Communist Affairs of Columbia University by Columbia University Press, 1974.

Mantri, Om Prakash. *Five Years in Mao's China*. New Delhi: Perspective Publications, 1964.

Maravall, José Mariá, and Adam Przeworski, eds. *Democracy and the Rule of Law*. Cambridge; New York: Cambridge University Press, 2003.

Marshall, Geoffrey. *Constitutional Conventions: The Rules and Forms of Political Accountability*. Oxford: Clarendon Press, 1984.

———. *Constitutional Theory*. Oxford, Clarendon Press, 1971.

Mattei Dogan, ed. *Pathways to Power: Selecting Rulers in Pluralist Democracies*. Boulder: Westview, 1989.

McCormick, Barrett L. *Political Reform in Post-Mao China: Democracy and Bureaucracy in a Leninist State*. Berkeley; Oxford: University of California Press, 1990.

McHugh, James T. *Comparative Constitutional Traditions*. New York: P. Lang, 2002.

Mclane, Charles B. *Soviet Policy and the Chinese Communists, 1931-1946*. New York: Columbia University Press, 1958.

Milkis, Sidney M. *The American Presidency: Origins and Development 1776-2002*, 4th ed. Washington, DC: CQ Press, 2003.

Mitteis, Heinrich (translated by H. F. Orton). *The State in the Middle Age: A Comparative Constitutional History of Feudal Europe*. Amsterdam: North-Holland Pub. Co.; New York: American Elsevier, 1975.

Moore, John Norton. *Treaty Interpretation, the Constitution and the Rule of Law*. Dobbs Ferry, NY: Oceana Publications, 2001.

Munro, Colin R. *Studies in Constitutional Law*, 2nd ed. Oxford: Oxford University Press, 2005.

Murphy, John Francis. *The United States and the Rule of Law in International Affairs*. Cambridge; New York: Cambridge University Press, 2004.

Nathan, Andrew J. *Chinese Democracy*. New York: Knopf: Distributed by Random House, 1985.

Nathan, Andrew J., Zhaohui Hong, and Steven R. Smith, eds. *Dilemmas of Reform in Jiang Zemin's China.* Boulder, CO: Lynne Rienner Publishers, 1999.

Nathan, Andrew J., and Bruce Gilley, eds. *China's New Rulers: The Secret Files*. London: Granta Books, 2003.

Nelsen, Harvey W. *Power and Insecurity: Beijing, Moscow, and Washington, 1949-1988.* Boulder; London: Lynne Rienner Publishers, 1989.

Nelson, Michael, ed. *The Presidency and the Political System*, 4th ed. Washington, DC: CQ Press, 1994.

Neumann, Franz. *The Rule of Law: Political Theory and the Legal System in Modern Society.* Lamington Spa, UK; Dover, NH: Berg, 1986.

North, Robert Carver. *Moscow and Chinese Communists*, 2nd ed. Stanford, CA: Stanford University Press, 1963.

O'Brien, Kevin J. *Reform without Liberalization: China's National People's Congress and the Politics of Institutional Change*. New York: Cambridge University Press, 1990.

Ogden, Suzanne. *Inklings of Democracy in China.* Cambridge, MA: Harvard University Asia Center, Cambridge, MA: Distributed by Harvard University Press, 2002.

———. *China's Unresolved Issues: Politics, Developments, and Culture*, 3rd ed. Englewood Clifts, NJ: Prentice Hall, 1995.

Ouyang, Qing. *1955 Gongheguo Jiangshuai Da ShouXian*. Jinan: HuangHe Chubanshe, 2008.

Palmer, R. R. *The Age of the Democratic Revolution: A Political History of Europe and America, 1760-1800*. Princeton, NJ: Princeton University Press, 1959-64.

Pan, Wei-Tung. *The Chinese Constitution: A Study of Forty Years of Constitution-Making in China*. Westport, CT: Hyperion Press, 1982.

Peerenboom, Randy. *China's Long March toward Rule of Law*. Cambridge: Cambridge University Press, 2002.

———, ed. *Asian Discourses of Rule of Law: Theories and Implementation of Rule of Law in Twelve Asian Countries, France and the U.S.* London; New York: Routledge Curzon, 2004.

Pfiffner, James P. *The Modern Presidency*, 4th ed. Belmont, CA: Thomson Wadsworth, 2005.

Plischke, Elmer. *Diplomat in Chief: the President at the Summit*. New York: Praeger, 1986.

Potter, Pitman B., ed. *Domestic Law Reforms in Post-Mao China*. Monk, NY: M.E. Sharpe, 1994.

Qin, Lihai. *Minzhu Lianhe Zhengfu Yu Zhengzhi Xieshang Huiyi: 1944-1949 De Zhongguo Zhengzhi*. Beijing: Renmin Chubanshe, 2008.

Qiu, Shi, ed. *Gongheguo Zhongda Juece Chutai Qianhou*. Beijing Shi: Jingji Ribao Chubanshe, 1998.

Raz, Joseph. *Ethics in the Public Domain: Essays in the Morality of Law and Politics*. Oxford: Clarendon Press; New York: Oxford University Press, 1994.

Rousseau, Jean-Jacques. *The Social Contract*. New Haven, CT: Yale University Press, 2002.

Rozman, Gilbert. *The Chinese Debate about Soviet Socialism, 1978-1985*. Princeton, NJ: Princeton University Press, 1987.

Salisbury, Harrison E. *The New Emperors: China in the Ear of Mao and Deng*. Boston: Little, Brown, 1992.

Sampford, C. J. G. *Retrospectivity and the Rule of Law*. Oxford; New York: Oxford University Press, 2006.

Sandoz, Ellis, ed. *The Roots of Liberty: Magna Carta, Ancient Constitution, and the Anglo-American Tradition of Rule of Law*. Columbia: University of Missouri Press, 1993.

Schapiro, Leonard Bertram. *The Government and Politics of the Soviet Union*, rev. ed. New York: Vintage Books, 1967.

Shen, Zhihua. *Zhongsu Tongmeng De Jingji Beijing: 1948-1953*. Xianggang: Xianggang Zhongwen Daxue Xianggang Yatai Yanjiusuo, 2000.

———, and Danhui Li. *Zhanhou Zhongsu Guanxi Ruogan Wenti Yanjiu: Laizi Zhong' e Shuangfang De Dangan Wenxian*. Beijing: Renmin Chubanshe, 2006.

Shi, Jiuqing. *Dangdai Zhongguo Zhengzhi Yunxing Jizhi*, 2nd ed. Jinan Shi: Shandong Renmin Chubanshe, 2002.

Shi, Zhiyu. *Collective Democracy: Political and Legal Reform in China*. Hong Kong: Chinese University Press, 1999.

Shirk, Susan L. *The Political Logic of Economic Reform in China*. Berkeley: University of California Press, 1993.

Shugart, Matthew Soberg. *Presidents and Assemblies: Constitutional Design and Electoral Dynamics*. Cambridge; New York: Cambridge University Press, 1992.

Skach, Cindy. *Borrowing Constitutional Designs: Constitutional Law in Weimar Germany and the French Fifth Republic*. Princeton, NJ: Princeton University Press, 2005.

Song, Liansheng. *Zong Luxian, Da Yuejin, Renmin Gongshe Hua Yundong Shimo*. Kunming Shi: Yunnan Renmin Chubanshe, 2002.

Song, Pang, et al. *Mao Zedong Shidai De Zhongguo (1949-1976)*. Beijing Shi: Zhong Gong Dang Shi Chu Ban She, 2003.

Spence, Jonathan. *Emperor of China: Self-Portrait of K'ang His*. New York: Alfred A. Knopf, 1974.

Stone, Julius. *Quest for Survival: the Role of Law and Foreign Policy*. Cambridge: Harvard University Press, 1961.

Sulzberger, C. L. *The Coldest War; Russia's Game in China*. New York: Harcourt Brace Jovanovich, 1974.

Sun, Chunshan. *Zhongguo De Geren Chongbai: Biaoxian, Weihai, Genyuan Ji Kefu De Tujing*. Zhengzhou Shi: Henan Renmin Chubanshe, 1994.

Swaine, Michael D. *China: Domestic Change and Foreign Policy*. Santa Monica, CA: RAND, 1995.

———. *The Military & Political Succession in China: Leadership, Institutions, Beliefs*. Santa Monica, CA: RAND, 1992.

Swarup, Shanti. *A Study of the Chinese Communist Movement*. Oxford: Clarendon Press, 1966.

Tamanaha, Brian Z. *On the Rule of Law: History, Politics and Theory*. Cambridge, UK; New York: Cambridge University Press, 2004.

Tang, Liang. *Jianjin Minzhu: Biange Zhong de Zhongguo Zhengzhi*. Singapore: Bafang Wenhua Qiye Gongsi, 2004.

Tang, Wenfang. *Party Intellectuals' Demands for Reform in Contemporary China*. Stanford, CA: Hoover Institution on War, Revolution and Peace, Stanford University, 1999.

Tang, Yihong. *Guanjian Wenti: Zhongguo Jijiang Jinxing De Zhengzhi Tizhi Gaige*. Xianggang: Mingjing Chubanshe, 1997.

Tanner, Murray Scot. *The Politics of Lawmaking in Post-Mao China: Institutions, Processes and Democratic Prospects*. Oxford: Clarendon Press, 1999.

Tatalovich, Raymond. *The Presidency and Political Science*. Baltimore, MD: Johns Hopkins University Press, 2003.

Teiwes, Frederick C. *Politics & Purges in China: Rectification and the Decline of Party Norms, 1950-1965*, 2nd ed. Armonk, NY: M.E. Sharpe, 1993.

———. *Leadership, Legitimacy, and Conflict in China: From a Charismatic Mao to the Politics of Succession*. Armonk: M.E. Sharpe, 1984.

Thornton, Richard C. *China, the Struggle for Power, 1917-1972*. Bloomington: Indiana University Press, 1973.

Tian, Baoguo. *Minguo Shi Qi Zhong Su Guan Xi (1917-1949)*. Jinan Shi: Jinan Chu Ban She, 1999.

Townsend, Peter. *China Phoenix: The Revolution in China*. London: Cape, 1955.

Treadgold, Donald W., ed. *Soviet and Chinese Communism: Similarities and Differences*. Seattle: University of Washington Press, 1967.

Tribe, Laurence H. *Constitutional Choices*. Cambridge, MA: Harvard University Press, 1985.

Tung, William L. *The Political Institutions of Modern China*. The Hague: M. Nijhoff, 1964.

Turner, Karen G., James V. Feinerman, and R. Kent Guy, eds. *The Limits of the Rule of Law in China*. Seattle: University of Washington Press, 2000.

Tyau, Min-Chlen T. Z. *China's New Constitution and International Problems*. Arlington, VA: University Publications of America, 1976.

Unger, Jonathan, ed. *The Nature of Chinese Politics: From Mao to Jiang*. Armonk, NY: M.E. Sharpe, 2002.

Urbina Tortella, Sebastián. *Legal Method and the Rule of Law*. The Hague; New York: Kluwer Law International, 2002.

Vandamme, Thomas A. J. A., and Jan Herman Reestman, eds. *Ambiguity in the Rule of Law: The Interface between National and International Legal Systems*. Groningen: Europa Law Pub., 2001.

Vanneman, Peter. *The Supreme Soviet: Politics and the Legislative Process in the Soviet Political System*. Durham, NC: Duke University Press, 1977.

Vermeer, Eduard B., and Ingrid d'Hooghe, eds. *China's Legal Reforms and Their Political Limits*. Richmond, Surrey: Curzon, 2002.

Vibert, Frank. *The Rise of the Unelected: Democracy and the New Separation of Powers*. Cambridge: Cambridge University Press, 2007.

Vile, M. J. C. *Constitutionalism and the Separation of Powers*, 2nd ed. Indianapolis: Liberty Fund, 1998.

Von Mettenheim, Kurt, ed. *Presidential Institutions and Democratic Politics: Comparing Regional and National Contexts*. Baltimore, MD: Johns Hopkins University Press, 1997.

Waller, Derek J. *The Kiangsi Soviet Republic: Mao and the National Congresses of 1931 and 1934*. Berkeley: Center for Chinese Studies, University of California, 1973.

Waltz, Kenneth Neal. *Man, the State, and War: A Theoretical Analysis*. New York: Columbia University Press, 1969.

Wang, Binglin, ed. *Dang de Lingxiu Yu Dangshi Yan Jiu*. Beijing: Zhongyang Wenxian Chubanshe, 2004.

Wang, Chang. *Zhongguo Gaoceng Moulüe,Waijiao Juan*. Xi'an Shi: Shanxi Shifan Daxue Chubanshe, 2001.

Wang, Fei-Ling. *Institutions and Institutional Change in China: Premodernity and Modernization*. Basingstoke: Macmillan; New York: St. Martin's Press, 1998.

Wang, Jianying. *Zhonggong Zhongyang Jicuan Lishi Yanbian Kaoshi (1921-1949)*. Beijing Shi: Zhonggong Dangshi Chubanshe, 2005.

Wang, Kaixi. *Gemo, Chongtu Yu Qutong: Qingdai Waijiao Liyi Zhizheng Touxi*. Beijing: Beijing Shifan Daxue Chubanshe, 1999.

Wang, Renbo. *Xianzheng De Zhongguo Zhidao*. Jinan: Shandong Renmin Chubanshe, 2003.

———. *Xianzheng WenHua Yu JinDai Zhongguo* [Modern China AndIts Constitutional Culture]. Beijing Shi: Falv Chubanshe, 1997.

Wang, Renqin, and Chuanmao Ling. *Dangzhang Xue Yanjiu* [Study on the Party Constitution of The CPC]. Beijing: Jiangdang Duwu Chubanshe, 2000.

Wang, Yongxiang. *Zhongguo Xiandai Xianzheng Yundong Shi*. Beijing: Renmin Chubanshe, 1996.

Wang, Youchun. *Zhongsu Waijiao De Xumu; Cong Youlin Dao Yuefei*. Nangang: Zhongyang Yanjiuyuan Jindai Shi YanJiuSuo, 1963.

Wang, Zhen. *Dongdang Zhong De Tongmeng: Kangzhan Shiqi De Zhongsu Guanxi*. Guilin Shi: Guangxi Shifan Daxue Chubanshe, 1993.

Wesserstrom, Jeffrey, and Elizabeth Perry, eds. *Popular Protest and Political Culture in Modern China*. Boulder: Westview Press, 1992.

Westad, Odd Arne. *Cold War and Revolution: Soviet-American Rivalry and the Origins of the Chinese Civil War, 1944-1946*. New York: Columbia University Press, 1993.

———. *Decisive Encounters: The Chinese Civil War, 1946-1950*. Stanford, CA: Stanford University Press, 2003.

Wheare, K. C. *Modern Constitutions*, 2nd ed. London; New York: Oxford University Press, 1966.

White, Gordon. *Riding The Tiger: the Politics of Economic Reform in Post-Mao China*. Basingstoke: Macmillan, 1993.

Whiting, Allen Suess. *Chinese Domestic Politics and Foreign Policy in the 1970's*. Ann Arbor: Center for Chinese Studies, University of Michigan, 1979.

———. *Soviet Policies in China, 1917-1924*. Stanford, CA: Stanford University Press, 1968.

———. *Contradictions in the Moscow-Peking Axis*. Santa Monica, CA: RandCorp., 1957.

Wilson, Bradford P., and Peter W. Schramm, eds. *Separation of Powers and Good Government*. Lanham, MD: Rowman & Littlefield, 1994.

Wong, John, and Lai Hongyi, eds. *China into the Hu-Wen Era*. Singapore; Hackensack, NJ: World Scientific Pub., 2006.

Wong, John, and Yongnian Zheng, eds. *The Nanxun Legacy and China's Development in the Post-Deng Era*. Singapore: Singapore University Press: World Scientific, 2001.
———. *China's Post-Jiang Leadership Succession: Problems and Perspectives*. Singapore: Singapore University Press, 2002.
Wong, Yiu-Chung. *From Deng Xiaoping To Jiang Zemin: Two Decades of Political Reform in the People's Republic of China*. Lanham, MD: University Press of America, 2005.
Wu, Xiuquan. *Zai Waijiaobu Banian De Jingli, 1950.1-1958.10*. Beijing: Shijie Zhishi Chubanshe, 1983.
Xiang, Qing, Zhifu Shi, and Dexi Liu, eds. *Sulian Yu Zhongguo Geming: 1917-1949*. Beijing: Zhongyang Bianyi Chubanshe, 1994.
Xie, Xinyao. *Guofu Lian'e Ronggong Zhengce Yanjiu*. Taibei Xian Zhonghe Shi: Pami'er Shudian, 1981.
Xing, Heming. *Zhonggong Yanli De Sulian Moshi*. Fuzhou Shi: Fujian Renmin Chubanshe, 2006.
Yang, Guangbin. *Zhongguo Zhengfu Yu Zhengzhi Daolun*. Beijing Zhongguo Renmin Daxue Chubanshe, 2003.
, et al. *Zhongguo Guonei Zhengzhi Jingji Yu Duiwai Guanxi*. Beijing: Zhongguo Renmin Daxue Chubanshe, 2007.
Yang, Haikun, ed. *Kuaru Xin ShiJi De Zhongguo Xianfa Xue: Zhongguo Xianfa Xue Yanjiu Xianzhuang Yu Pingjia*. Beijing: Zhongguo Renshi Chubanshe, 2001.
Yang, Hongshan. *Dangdai Zhongguo Zhengzhi Guanxi*. Beijing: Jingji Ribao Chubanshe, 2002.
Yang, Jinzhi. *Xianzheng Yu Guofang*. Shanghai: Zhengzhong Shuju, 1946.
Yang, Kuisong. *Mao Zedong Yu Mosike De En En Yuan Yuan*. Nanchang Shi: Jiangxi Renmin Chubanshe, 1999.
Yang, Qi. *Fengyu Tongzhou: Jiesong Minzhu Qunying Mimi Ligang Beishang Canjia Zhengxie Shimo Ji*. Xianggang: Xianggang Gejie Wenhua Cujinhui, 2004.
Yang, Shengqun, and Songnian Tian, eds. *Gong heguo Zhongda Juece De Lailong Qumai: 1949-1965*. Nanjing: Jiangsu Renmin Chubanshe, 1995.
Yen, Hawkling Lugine. *A Survey of Constitutional Development in China*. New York: AMS Press, 1968.
Yin, Xiaohu. *Xin Zhongguo Xianzheng Zhilu: 1949-1999*. Shanghai: Shanghai Jiaotong Daxue Chubanshe, 2000.
Yin, Zhengyi, Jiao Yuli, and Peng Jian, eds. *Zhongguo Lingdao Ren Chufang Jishi*. Changsha: Hunan Renmin Chubanshe, 2001.
Young, Earnest. *The Presidency of Yuan Shih-Kai*. Ann Arbor: University of Michigan Press, 1977.
Zang, Xiaowei. *Elite Dualism and Leadership Selection in China*. New York: Routledge Curzon, 2004.
Zeng, Xianghua. *Da Jiaojie: Mao Zedong he Ta de Jichengzhe Men*. Wulumuqi Shi: Xinjiang Renmin Chubanshe, 2001
Zhang, Jinfan, ed. *Zhongguo Fazhi Tongshi*. Beijing Shi: Falv Chubanshe, 1999.
Zhang, Qiyun. *Minzhu Xianzheng Yu Zhongguo Wenhua*. Taibei Shi: Zhonghua Dadian Bianyinghui, 1966.
Zhang, Xipo, and Yanlong Han, eds. *Zhongguo Geming Fazhi Shi*. Beijing: Zhongguo Shehui Kexue Chubanshe, 2007.
Zhang, Zhenjiang. *Lengzhan Yu Neizhan: Meisu Zhengba Yu Guogong Chongtu De Qiyuan, 1944-1946* [Cold War and Civil War]. Tianjin Shi: Tianjin Guji Chubanshe, 2005.
Zhao, Suisheng, ed. *Debating Political Reform in China: Rule of Law vs. Democratization*. Armonk, NY: M.E. Sharpe, 2006.
———. *China and Democracy: The Prospect for a Democratic China*. New York: Routledge, 2000.
Zheng, Yongnian. *Will China Become Democratic? : Elite, Class and Regime Transition*. Singapore: Eastern Universities Press, 2004.
———. *Discovering Chinese Nationalism in China: Modernization, Identity, and International Relations*. Cambridge; New York: Cambridge University Press, 1999.

Zheng, Yushuo, and Binged Kong, eds. *The Outlook for U.S.-China Relations Following the 1997-1998 Summits: Chinese and Cultural Exchange*. Hong Kong: the Chinese University Press, 1999.

Zhong Gong Beijing Shi Haidian Qu Wei, Dang Shi Yan Jiu Shi. *Zhong Gong Zhong Yang Zai Xiangshan*. Beijing: Zhonggong Dangshi Chubanshe, 1994.

Zhonggong Zhongyang Dangshi Yanjiu Shi Diyi Yanjiubu, ed. *Gongchan Guoji, Sulian Yu Zhongguo Geming Guanxi Yanjiu Shuping*. Beijing: Zhonggong Dangshi Chubanshe, 1996.

Zhu, Guobin. *Zhongguo Xianfa Yu Zhengzhi Zhidu* [China's Constitutional Law and Political System]. Beijing Shi: Falv Chubanshe, 2006.

Zhuge, Muqun. *Xianzheng Zhongguo: Wei Zhongguo De Weilai Sheji Kexing, Wending He Gongkaihua De Zhengzhi Zhidu*. Brampton: Mingjing Chubanshe, 1998.

Zhuo, Fan. *Zhonghua Suwei'ai Fazhi Shi*. Nanchang Shi: Jiangxi Gaoxiao Chubanshe, 1992.

Zifcak, Spencer, ed. *Globalisation and the Rule of Law*. London; New York: Routledge, 2005.

Zong, Hairen. *Aimei de Quanli Jiaojie*, 2nd ed. Carle Place, NY: Ming Jing Chu Ban She, 2003.

"'Zongheng' Jingpin Congshu" Bianweihui, ed. *Gongheguo Waijiao Shilu*. Beijing: Zhongguo Wenshi Chubanshe, 2002.

Zou, Dang. *Twentieth Century Chinese Politics: From the Perspectives of Macro-History and Micro-Mechanism Analysis*. Oxford: Oxford University Press, 1994.

Zou, Keyuan. *China's Legal Reform: toward the Rule of Law*. Leiden; Boston: Martinus Nijhoff Publishers, C2006.

Zou, Ximing, ed. *Zhong Gong Zhong Yang Ji Gou Yan Ge Shi Lu 1921.7-1997.9*. Beijing: Zhongguo Dangan Chubanshe, 1998.

Index

About the Author

Zhang Runhua was born in Chongyang County, Hubei province of China. He obtained his BA majoring in economics from Hubei University, master of laws from East China University of Political Science and Law, and a PhD in laws from the Chinese University of Hong Kong. He visited the University of Manchester and Tsinghua University. He is now lecturer at Shanghai Finance University.

CPSIA information can be obtained at www.ICGtesting.com
Printed in the USA
BVOW04*0331291014

372730BV00003B/5/P

9 780739 189894